Music, Mathematics and Language

Keiji Hirata · Satoshi Tojo · Masatoshi Hamanaka

Music, Mathematics and Language

The New Horizon of Computational Musicology Opened by Information Science

Springer

Keiji Hirata
Department of Complex and Intelligent Systems
Future University Hakodate
Hakodate, Hokkaido, Japan

Satoshi Tojo
Graduate School of Information Science
Japan Advanced Institute of Science and Technology
Ishikawa, Japan

Masatoshi Hamanaka
Music Information Intelligence Team
RIKEN Center for Advanced Intelligence Project
Chuo, Tokyo, Japan

https://doi.org/10.1007/978-981-19-5166-4

This Springer imprint is published by the registered company Springer Nature Singapore Pte Ltd.
The registered company address is: 152 Beach Road, #21-01/04 Gateway East, Singapore 189721, Singapore

Preface

We are living in a very rich culture of music. Nowadays, such genre distinctions as jazz, rock, pop, and classical are meaningless. *Fusion* has occurred in 1970s; Miles Davis introduced electric instruments, as well as church modes used in medieval times, and has tried to open a new horizon for the future jazz. Even a professional musician trained in one genre look enjoying other genres. Toru Takemitsu, one of the best-known composers in experimental music, is said to have had a strong compassion with *Sergeant Pepper's Lonely Hearts Club Band* of the Beatles. Such a tendency of mixture would proceed further in future.

At the same time, the authentic classical music seems losing its popularity. Those faithful guardians of tradition may still think that the classical music is a branch of liberal arts for the educated class, and thus they may consider that the faithful replication of written scores is significant. However, archiving the classics and enjoying music are two different things. Classical music was written when there were no recording technology. From the current viewpoint, the reprise of the same phrases is no more needed, and thus we could shorten their playing time to avoid being bored.

In the beginning of twentieth century, many composers tried to break an old style and to innovate music. One such representative is Arnold Schoenberg who tried to destroy the tonality which had governed the traditional music, introducing *dodecaphony*. However, this trial was not successful at acquiring the popularity. On the contrary, so-called popular music seems the most faithful successor of the rather old style of tonal music, consisting of a melody accompanied by harmonic chords, and the style has functioned to evoke our emotions.

Still, we want new music pieces. There appear new pieces on the web every day, and we try to catch them by digital methods like Apple Music, Amazon Prime, YouTube, and so on. We say a new hit song is *new*; surely, there may be a new constituent in a chord, or may be a new progression of chords which has not been heard before, and such an invention would appear furthermore as long as there are an explosive number of their combinations. However, please do not forget that they are still written in *do-re-mi-fa-sol-la-ti-do*, with chords of *do-mi-sol* or *sol-ti-re*. What are alternatives? The temperament of scales has a long history in selecting a diatonic set of notes and in fixing the pitches of these notes in an octave. We feel harmonized when the ratio of two frequencies is a simple rational number, but any two notes are not rigidly harmonic in the currently prevalent 12-tone equal temperament, which is a product of many compromises. Yet, we appear sufficiently adapted to this temperament.

Do we need to abandon the temperament for exploring the new possibilities in music? Then, where is music headed? Who wants the change? Or, will songs are created continuously in the same formalism? Will music forever progress and evolve, or will it saturate at some point? If music is going to saturate somewhere, is there a limit to human creativity? What is music in the first place? Composers, performers, and musicologists of the past must have been raising the same questions and investigating music. They must have taken different approaches and set different goals, wondering what techniques, skills, and knowledge they would need to acquire in order to create new music. The results include actual musical masterpieces, performances, and music theories.

In the last half-century, we obtained an apparatus to mirror our cognitive processes and intelligent functions—a computer. Nowadays, we are able to simulate to some extent our brain functions and intelligent activities inside the computers in isolated environments from the real world, and to even conduct as many experiments that would not be allowed in reality as required. We call a virtual person who owns its independent and subjective cognition an *agent*. The notion of cognition may be different among various psychologists; some requires a perfect *ego*, that is, being conscious of 'self,' and others are rather tolerant of the definition and may call a robot with a simple inference mechanism with independent knowledge base an agent. Naturally, implementing a cognitive and emotional ego agent in computer with a rigorous description in formal language is difficult. In the early days of an electronic computer, such an optimistic prediction that human intelligence could be realized in a computer within 10 or 20 years was prevalent. It was in 1948 when the precursor of the idea for the Turing test was published. Since then, there have been several cycles of enthusiasm and disappointment along with excessive expectations and tireless trials and errors. We are now in the midst of another AI boom, in effect a deep learning boom; these ebbs and flows can be also regarded as the history of development to describe the intelligent activities and functions.

If music is one of the intellectual activities of human beings, we believe that tackling the seemingly unanswered question "what is intelligence in music?" or "what is beauty in music?" using the powerful tool of a computer can provide us with some useful novel insights. It would be meaningful to construct a *computational music theory* based on traditional music theory, just as computational linguistics has been constructed and has produced valuable results based on traditional linguistics. One of the purposes of writing this book was to demonstrate an approach to realizing this computational music theory.

Now, to find the key to realizing computational music theory, let us go back and think about the claim that the origin of music and language is one and the same. As we cannot obtain fossils of old languages, we cannot prove this in the evolutionary linguistics. However, observing various facts, we can convince ourselves that the claim seems somewhat plausible. Apart from such linguistic aspect, the language is the most useful method to externalize the notion of beauty. To express the beauty in language means that we symbolize and find structure of music as language. Jean-Jacques Nattiez, following his master Jean Molino, considered that music could be structured and analyzed with regard to semiology, and thus the meaning of music could be externalized. However, in Nattiez's book, he confessed his own remark included a contradiction[1]. In his interview with virtual himself, he honestly admitted that it was impossible to fully express the music beauty in symbols. As Nattiez finally claimed that there should be an adequate theory of linguistics to construct a meaning of music, we believe that clarifying the *grammar structure* of music is an essential and most steady way to a computational music theory.

In this book, we first consider the meaning of music, regarding *cognitive reality*. To this purpose, we introduce the theory of Heinrich Schenker[2], where he claimed that there was a fundamental skeleton common in every music piece, and we can obtain this via the procedure called *reduction* and how these skeleton worked on our cognition. Next, we consider why the 12-tone equal temperament came to be prevalent in Chap. 2 titled 'The mathematics of ebony and ivory keys.' The equal temperament, as we have told, is a result of compromises; however, we can easily get accustomed to it and can enjoy music with it. This chapter functions as an introduction to mathematical definition of harmony that concerns the ratios of frequency in tonic waves. Chapter 3 'Music and language' explains the fundamentals of grammar theory as well as the compositionality principle, that is, the semantics of a sentence can be composed in parallel to syntactic structure. We will contend that music also possesses the same context-free grammar as natural language though somewhat in a weak sense. In Chap. 4, we explain the most prevalent score notation called Berklee method, which was initiated from Berklee School of Music in New York. Nowadays, we mostly employ chord names according to the method in popular music and consider how efficient this method is. In Chaps. 5 and 6, we give two theories on computational musicology. We first introduce Implication-Realization model (IR model), that is a theory to reflect our human intuition on melody progression. Next, we explain the Generative Theory of Tonal Music (GTTM) with its complementary theory of Tonal Pitch Space (TPS). Chapters 7, 8, and 9 are devoted to the applications of GTTM. In Chap. 7, we discuss algebraic operations on trees. In Chap. 8, we report our efforts to implement GTTM analyzer which retrieves a tree from a given piece. In Chap. 9, we illustrate our work on music *morph*-ing, to generate a new music piece from given two other pieces. Finally, Epilogue, we discuss the future of music with regard to computation and AI, posing Hilbert-style questions.

This book aims at a general reader of music, in addition to professional scientists of music information processing. Therefore, we try to make each chapter be as

---

[1] Jean-Jacques Nattiez. "Je vous prends en flagrant délit de contradiction!" in La Musique, La Recherche, et La Vie, Leméac Editeur Inc., Montréal, (1999/2004).

[2] Heinrich Schenker, Der Freie Satz. Neue musikalische Theorien und Phantasien, Margada, Liège, Belgium (1935).

independent of other chapters as possible. Thus, we would like to share a common interest in discussing 'musicology in computer age' in broader community.

Hakodate, Japan — Keiji Hirata
Ishikawa, Japan — Satoshi Tojo
Tokyo, Japan — Masatoshi Hamanaka
March 2022

Acknowledgements

As authors, we would like to thank everyone who has been involved in our research; research collaborations, discussions and chats at conferences, laboratory visits, hosting residencies, email exchanges, events, and so on have all contributed to the results of our research.

We would like to thank Tory Honor for English rewriting, corrections, and translation.

We would like to thank Mio Sugino of Springer. In fact, we would not have been able to publish this book without the patient but kind encouragement and careful support of Mio Sugino throughout this project.

Much of the work presented in this book was supported by JSPS KAKENHI Grant Numbers 20300035, 23500145, 25330434, 26280089, 16H01744, and 21H03572.

Contents

Chapter 1
Machine that Computes the Meaning of Music

1.1 Music Theory that Enjoys the Benefits of Computers

Until the medieval period, the composers of Western tonal music, when creating new pieces, first analyzed and understood the structures and styles of already existing pieces by themselves. Moving on to the eighteenth century, the public and critics appeared, and then the composers and the researchers of music theory were split. Since then, the theory for composition has been developed as a set of practical rules (compositional methodology), while on the other hand, the analysis and interpretation methods for music have been systematized as music theory in musicology.

Jean-Philippe Rameau, a contemporary of J. S. Bach, a is often referred to as the musical theorist who first formalized the notion of harmony. Ultimately, music theory can be considered as originally being an analysis method for composition, from a historical point of view.

Both musicology and music theory are regarded as one type of knowledge and art that is transmitted from person to person through books and the imitation of body motion. Thus, such knowledge and art have been verbalized and then expressed and accumulated in a format suitable for humans to read and see. As for music, in the books written in natural languages, humans have been discussing and describing what musical notations are best, what performances are most excellent, and what is the meaning of music.

Since the 1940s, the benefits that the advent of computers has brought to humanity include understanding the real world with greater mathematical rigorousness and, as a result, enabling us to precisely simulate and predict phenomena in the world. Here, let us call it mathematical modeling to express on a computer using a computer language the mechanism of understanding and the process of thinking as a human does. This model can be described in a language with a strong grammatical system, unlike the natural languages humans use in daily life. Therefore, such a model allows a computer to realize control and prediction with no ambiguity in comparison to computation realized in natural language, yet, on the other hand, it may cause us to lose something, like the meaning humans share. Hereafter, in this book, we call the

K. Hirata et al., *Music, Mathematics and Language*,
https://doi.org/10.1007/978-981-19-5166-4_1

construction of a mathematical model a formal description or just formalization, in the sense of a working internal representation on a computer.

Thus far, the development of music theory has not benefitted from computers. Then, from now on, what could the development of computers yield to music theory? We assume that one benefit would be allowing us to conduct scientific experiments relating to the human cognitive model of music. What we mean here by scientific is (i) generalized beyond human subjectivity, (ii) supported by facts and evidence to elucidate the phenomena, (iii) having guaranteed reproducibility, and, therefore, (iv) able to refute any generalization inconsistent to the facts.[1] Hence, we think the scientific approach to music could be realized in a procedure as follows; presenting the behavior and mechanism of human musical cognition as a hypothesis, conducting a simulation based on the hypothesis (executing the hypothesis as a computer program), examining how well the hypothesis fits the reality, and assessing the validity of the hypothesis. Although we can also conduct an experiment with human subjects, instead of computer simulation, to assess the hypothesis validity, the experiment would inevitably be adversely influenced by factors such as the experience of musical education that subjects have been receiving the music that subjects have been exposed to, musical preference, and the physiological and/or mental condition of each subject [3].

Along this line, for the past 500 years or more, Western tonal music itself and the composition methodologies have coevolved, as, of course, have performance techniques. Musical knowledge and skills have been inherited and propagated from masters and teachers to apprentices and students by physical training and oral tradition using musical scores, vocals, and musical instruments; here score is not a natural language, but a representation method for music that is sufficiently intuitive. Music theories that have compiled up the musical knowledge and skills are rich in implicit knowledge. We believe that we can approach an answer to what music is if we can express this implicit knowledge as a computer program and execute it.

If we would stand on the findings of such conventional music theories and revisit and rebuild them in light of information technology and AI technology, we might get closer to a certain style of 'computational musicology'. However, the development of computational musicology is far more difficult than it may seem. There is a well-known discovery in the field of artificial intelligence, called Moravec's paradox. Moravec's paradox is a paradoxical observation that a computer has difficulty doing certain things that an infant can easily do, yet a computer can easily do things that an adult has difficulty doing. A similar paradox occurs in music. Let us think of what even an infant can do in music and what happens to an infant. Such things may include distinguishing happy songs from sad ones, remembering similar songs, and associating songs heard with situations such as cleaning the house and going home. Moreover, although infants cannot remember the details of music, they can ruminate on music and enjoy it. An infant can imagine a musical piece from a possibly

[1] Karl Popper, Austrian-British philosopher. Being scientific means that there is a declaration, proposition, and theory (i.e., hypothesis) which have been believed to be true until now, and the hypothesis is refutable by a new experiment and/or observation.

meaningless phrase, say, "delicious song", while it is hard to build a robot that can do such things.

Furthermore, things that are difficult for humans yet easy for computers include accurately tapping beats, correctly recognizing pitch height (absolute pitch), and segregating simultaneous multiple voice lines. Moravec's paradox tells us the fact that the messages exchanged among humans and the contents mutually understood contain much tacit knowledge, for instance, value, connotation, intuition, impression, preference, feeling, association, metaphor, and so on. Also music theory contains much tacit knowledge, and that is what makes it difficult for music theory to be benefitted by computers standing on the findings of music theory.[2]

1.2 A Short History of Program Music

The late nineteenth-century composer Richard Strauss boasted that "There is nothing that cannot be expressed by music." We believe many people would cite Strauss's magnum opus, the opera 'Der Rosenkavalier', in support of this. The opera opens with a sex scene between a Field Marshal's wife and her young lover, and the moment approximately one minute from the beginning is said to be the moment of ecstasy. We can understand what kind of scene this is, because opera has a set and a verbal text, but supposing we were to listen only to the music, would some people understand what it is trying to describe?

The composer Liszt introduced the word *program music* and defined it as a certain type of music that aims to evoke for its listeners specific sights or scenery and mental images. This concept breaks away from the school of classical music, conforming strongly to the attitudes of the romantic composers. Music is loved as something which arouses specific emotions in a listener, thus pieces were created to accompany titles or programs. Berlioz's 'Symphonie Fantastique' is a typical example of this. Specific visual images, such as an evening party waltz or the procession to the guillotine, are conferred on the piece of music, requiring listeners to interpret the piece in accordance with the program intended by the composer. As the title given by a composer and the corresponding literary style are closely connected, early romantic composers have been likened to writers or artists. For example, Mendelssohn is called 'a landscape painter in sounds', and Chopin 'the poet of the piano'.

The term program music was created around this time, however, this way of thinking itself had existed since before Liszt, such as in the Baroque composer Vivaldi's Four Seasons, which expresses the scenery of each season with specific

---

[2] There is a research field of music composition by using computers, that is almost totally unhindered by these difficulties. This field is called algorithmic composition [19]. In algorithmic composition, many employ the approach in which the mathematical concepts and information technologies that have been developed independently from music are applied to composition by computer. The musical genres in question include contemporary music, avant-garde music, experimental music, and media art. Hence, in general, there are few relationships between traditional Western tonal music and composition methodologies for classical music.

instruments. Furthermore, even beyond the classical period, Beethoven's 'Pastoral Symphony' (symphony no. 6, opus number 68) is famous. A short title is assigned to each movement and in the 4th movement the sound of thunder is specifically imitated by instruments. Nevertheless, there is an argument that this piece is purely a mental image and is not program music.

In the second half of the nineteenth century, in reaction to the prosperity of program music, the term *absolute music* was used as an opposing concept. Absolute music is defined as something that is not related to specific mental images or scenes and as a kind of music which makes one feel the abstract beauty of the music itself. The contemporary critic Edualdo Hanslick cast doubt on the program-music orientation of the Romantic composers and severely criticized Wagner and Liszt's exaggeration of emotion, in particular. Hanslick also continued to write harshly negative dissertations on Bruckner, who was a devotee of Wagner. In contrast, Brahms, who, in the same era, is associated with a return to the classical movement, was vindicated by Hanslick and extolled as the principle figure of absolute music.

Nevertheless, this opposition between program music and absolute music is a hazardous argument that is difficult to handle. Firstly, if the aim of program music is to be connected to certain scenes or mental images, can it be said that a work stands up as music when it is simply, for example, imitating the call of a bird with a woodwind instrument? Or if the sound of thunder can be imitated by a series of beats on the timpani, is that a success as program music? Secondly, the evaluation of program music must be based not on the degree of success with which it imitates, but its worth as a piece of music. In other words, this means that "even program music cannot avoid being evaluated as absolute music." If a piece is a well-crafted and beautiful work, it is a success, even as program music. In which case, does program music exist within absolute music and become music of which the listener's interpretation is limited by the program?

One viewpoint within Hanslick's criticism of program music is the assertion that "the reversal of the order of the relative importance of the music and the verbally assigned program is inexcusable." In other words, Hanslick thought that, even if a work that is essentially musical is simply accompanied by a text, it is unorthodox for music to be in the service of a text, as music should only be evaluated within the confines of an aesthetic view of music alone.

We consider that, in later years, this method of evaluation confined to within music has been confuted in various ways. One example is how, at the end of the nineteenth century, when atonal music began to be researched following the collapse of harmonious music, Schoenberg actively attached text to musical pieces. Due to the fact that music by atonality does not substantially relate to people's emotions, to prevent music from degenerating into an insubstantial state and expressing nothing, an effort to connect it to something in this world was needed separately. Thus, above all, the majority of the commercial music mass produced today is accompanied by a text, i.e., 'lyrics.' Furthermore, since the twentieth century, performing arts, i.e., opera or ballet, have lost their place to the overwhelmingly visual media of film. Accordingly, the role of music will change into one of furthering visual effects and creating excitement. Music becomes something that is accompanied by film. Seen from Hanslick's point of view, the genre 'film music' that was to emerge in future years would surely come under criticism.

The aim of this section is not to criticize Hanslick's criticism once more. If Hanslick considered the program school's view that "music must express something" to be too narrow, that is an opinion that undoubtedly hits the mark. As Hanslick says, music has an abstract beauty that does not need to be connected to a specific thing. Accordingly, it is not appropriate to consider that music always "has an inherent meaning" or "contains a message that seeks to convey something." Of course, music is still connected to images and scenery of the real world and can be tinged with a special message, even without an accompanying text. However, it is not always necessarily so. Abstract paintings from the early modern times and after can be thought of in the same way. Abstract paintings do not specifically depict things in this world, yet people can obtain a firm sense of beauty from the moderate balance of colors, lines, and shapes. Thus when 'the meaning of music as absolute music' has been laid out, there is significance in considering aspects such as 'stable structure', rather than the linguistic message.

1.3 Understanding Music from a Gestalt Point of View

From here on in, we move the discussion on, taking the meaning of music as a scientific subject. As mentioned previously, scientific here means writing a computer program based on a model related to musical cognition, running a simulation, then being able to propose a refutable hypothesis. Therefore, let us forget program music for a moment and assume a scientific approach that seeks reproducibility and ubiquity from the standpoint of self-contained and autotelic absolute music. To do this, we take *gestalt* or *intersubjectivity* in human musical cognition as our foundation.

Gestalt is the psychological/perceptual phenomenon recognized when individual components (in terms of music this would be, for example, single pitch events[3]) do not reveal meaning, but a separate meaning first appears when these are integrated. You could also describe it as a kind of psychological/perceptual phenomenon that has a meaning greater than the sum of its parts. For example, in the past, in most Japanese elementary schools, at the beginning and end of a music lesson the music teacher would play three chords while saying "Stand up, bow, sit down" (Fig. 1.1). If these three chords were each played in isolation, that could only be perceived as the three sounds simply being played one by one, yet when the three chords are played in sequence it can be perceived that the progression of the music finishes exactly on the third chord—a kind of perception that absolutely cannot be obtained from the individual chords.

Next, let us introduce the way of thinking known as intersubjectivity. It is considered that each individual's perception, comprehension, thoughts etc. (subjectivity)

[3] An independent sound with attributes of pitch and duration. The individual sounds and chords, etc. that make up music.

Fig. 1.1 Chord progression of 'Stand up, bow, sit down'

regarding the world and the things within it naturally differ, but often people belonging to the same community or place nevertheless tend to share the same subjectivity in certain regards (it can also be said that they belong to the same community or are in the same place because people share the same subjectivity). This disposition that can, regardless of being subjective, agree with others as if being objective is what we call intersubjectivity. For example, the gestalt created by the three chords a music teacher played while saying "Stand up, bow, sit down" must have given the students attending that elementary school a perception of the beginning and end of the lesson. In actuality, the chaining of these three chords is extremely commonplace and can be seen in nursery rhymes, traditional Japanese popular ballads, and even in the ending of Beethoven's 'Ode to Joy'.[4] Nevertheless, there would have been almost no students who had any perception besides that of the beginning and end of the class. Although it is not strange for the perception of chords played in a row to be different for each person, there are such cases in which almost everybody arrives at the same perception in this way. It is said that intersubjectivity applies in this sort of case.

In this gestalt or intersubjectivity, a way of thinking in *layers* becomes involved. That is to say, a subject that has a certain meaning, which is expressed as gestalt, is considered as a higher level, while the individual parts that do not have meaning are considered as the lower levels. However, when one of the parts from a lower level is looked at from an even lower level, as that combination it may carry meaning. Accordingly, there are cases in which these upper/lower levels often yield multistaged hierarchy.

Separation into hierarchy can be thought about in two ways. One is a viewpoint based on the working of gestalt, as described above. The other is the *reductionism* approach, which is a representative way of thinking for comprehending complex systems. The reductionism approach assumes that even if the current target system cannot be understood as a whole, if the operation of appropriately dividing and

[4] Symphony No. 9, Movement IV, bars 247–248 '... Himmlische, dein Heiligtum!', provided all the chords in Fig. 1.1 are transposed to D major.

decomposing the system into small components is carried out in stages (reduction), at some point you will arrive at components simple enough to comprehend, and if you conversely recompose the entire system from there, you can then understand the entire system. In a sense, reductionism is the essence of modern science. When investigating the structure or properties of a material, by a scientific process that material can be broken down into smaller structures and understood from their composition. It is possible to decompose the small structures into even smaller units, i.e., molecules, and even further, until you trace right back to the atomic composition. It could be said that after many years of trial and error were spent on alchemy in the middle ages, materials science was established in the process of explaining the impossibility of that practice.

In music also, hierarchical separation produces the benefit of not confusing the argument. In this section, we are attempting to formalize the meaning of music from which the factors of sensitivity, preference, and artistic quality have been eliminated. Sensitivity and preference are substantially subjective things, so having several people listen to the same music would achieve differing effects. In contrast, the music written on a score is objective and impartial to all people. As we see, there is no direct description on a score about the aforementioned sensitivity, preference and artistic quality, which are things that a listener conceives and perceives. Hence, we would assume that the fundamental layer obtained from a score based on gestalt and intersubjectivity could be dealt with separately from the higher-level subjective concepts such as sensitivity, preference, and artistic quality, which are associated with structures represented in the fundamental layer afterward.[5] Rather, if we attempt to formalize the perception and creation of music without this kind of hierarchical separation, the theory we obtain (which it is actually thought cannot even be called a theory) may have a very narrow range of application (i.e. limited adaptability), is highly context-dependent (i.e. unstable), and has a low degree of conformity with observation (i.e. inaccurate) [6, 7]. Many of the existing music application systems that do not perform the hierarchical separation compensate for the disadvantages described above by limiting to a specific application area, restricting functions, introducing heuristics, and so on, but, unfortunately, it is generally difficult for these systems to function satisfactorily.

There is also evidence which indirectly demonstrates that this kind of thinking that separates layers is general. That is the principle, relating to system usage, known as flexibility-usability tradeoff. This principle states that, when a certain system is being used, a tradeoff will always exist between the system user being able precisely to control the system in the way they intend, and the realization of an easy-to-use system. In other words, when you try to control the system subtly, it becomes necessary to make delicate alterations to various parameters, an operation which is complex and difficult to learn. In contrast, when given a system that is simple and

[5] Originally, in the field of study relating to listening to, composing and performing music, the fact that a scientific approach such as musical cognition exists simultaneously with a philosophical approach such as musical aesthetics implies that in different hierarchies different methodologies which are appropriate to the relevant hierarchies are being employed.

easy to understand and learn, it is difficult to control the system subtly, in the desired way. In actual system usage, the evaluation criteria for dealing with this tradeoff are the gauges and limitations of aspects other than technology, such as preference, habit and legality. The reason we mention the principle of the flexibility-usability tradeoff is that it has a structure in which the lower level comprises layers that people must conform to like the laws of physics, while the upper level comprises layers that are subjective and empirical. What makes this principle so persuasive is that it implicitly supposes the separation of the lower layers that deal with common substantial matters and the upper layers that deal with subjective matters.

1.4 Attribution of Meaning to Melody by Semiotics

What does the word ‘symbol’ make you think of? For example, various symbols appear on maps, representing things such as a police station, town hall or cropland. A weather map shows symbols representing weather fronts such as high air pressure and low air pressure. In scientific study you encounter the symbols corresponding to each of the elements; H, C, O, etc. In astrology, there is a symbol for each constellation of the twelve signs of the zodiac. In electric circuitry, we see the symbols for an AND circuit and an OR circuit. Units of currency like pounds (£) or euros (€) are also written with symbols. Family crests are symbols too. Toilet signs are also symbols. Many companies have chosen company logos, which again are symbols. Above all, mathematics is a treasure trove of symbols. ‘+’, ‘÷’ and integrals are all symbols. Then there are musical scores, a veritable list of symbols. Note ♩, rest 𝄽, and G clef 𝄞 are all symbols. What we would like to focus on is the fact that most of these symbols can be inserted into everyday sentences, as letters. Then of course, letters themselves are symbols too. The hieroglyphs of ancient Egypt are imitations of animals and plants that actually exist, such as vultures and papyrus leaves, taken as letters. There are multiple theories behind the creation of Chinese characters, but the oracle bone scripts discovered from ancient divining bones are hieroglyphs. It is common knowledge that Chinese characters were born from hieroglyphs; Fig. 1.2 shows the process of creating the Chinese characters from hieroglyphs meaning the sun and the moon.

If we elaborate further on symbols and expand our field of thought to include *representation* in general, we see that not only shapes or pictorial symbols such as ‘+’ and ‘★’, but also letters like ‘a’ and ‘ϕ’, and even the geometric patterns on this very paper, are all connected to some sort of meaning. Thus, symbols truly function as signs (representations). For example, by connecting the mark ‘✓’ with the concept of ‘correct’, the mark ‘✓’ becomes a sign and comes to mean ‘correct’. In the Semiotics of the American philosopher and logician Peirce,[6] the meaning of a sign is thought to be born from three elements: 1. a sign or representation, 2.

[6] Charles Sanders Peirce, 1839–1914.

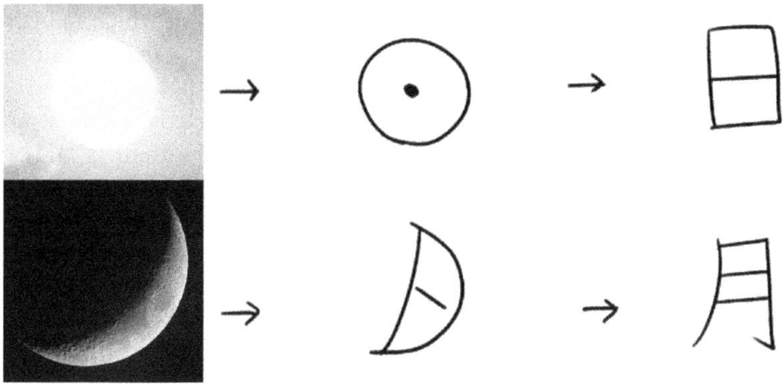

Fig. 1.2 Birth of Chinese characters from hieroglyphs

the thing indicated by the representation (object or result of representation), and 3. an observer or interpreter who is conscious of the result of the representation. For example, '✓' is a sign (representation), 'correct' is the thing the representation indicates and it is the observer who connects '✓' with 'correct'. When an observer becomes involved in assigning meaning to a sign, three types of meaning arise: iconic expression, physical denotation, and abstract symbology. These are called *icon*, *index* and *symbol*, respectively. An icon is, as the name states, a picture or portrait and is similar to the object it indicates, or contains some imitation thereof. Examples of icons are hieroglyphs or the male/female pictures on toilet doors. An index is something that abstracts similarity using the physical relationship or causal relationship to the target. The arbitrariness between the sign and the object is stronger than in the case of an icon. For instance, a typical index is a sign that is quantified and displayed, therefore, a thermometer, barometer, clock and speedometer all come under the category of index. The term 'ex' (used to mean a former boyfriend or girlfriend) which indicates a target that leaves the chronological information and abstracts all other factors can be considered as an index. A symbol is decided by custom and does not display a direct connection to a target that indicates something common to society. That is to say, the connection of the sign to the target is arbitrary. For example, the symbol for a crotchet ♩ does not contain the information that this is a sound which lasts for one fourth of a bar. Morse code and alphabet letters such as ABC are symbols.

The signification of signs changes constantly with time. As an example, try to recall the time machine in the American science-fiction film 'Back to the Future' (1985). That time machine incorporates a vehicle called the DMC-12, produced in 1981 by the American motor company DeLorean. When the DMC-12 was released, the sign 'DMC-12' had the signification of being that car sold by DeLorean. Through 'Back to the Future', the meaning of DMC-12 changed to mean a time machine. Furthermore, in the year 2015, which is both when the future scenes in 'Back to the Future Part II' were set, and the 30-year anniversary of the release of the first film, promotional events were held all around the world, at most of which the DMC-12 appeared. By that time, the DMC-12 had come to signify not only a time machine, but also the film 'Back to the Future' itself.

Using signs, let us consider what is a sign in relation to melody, and how meaning is attributed. For example, say there is a phrase 'do-re-mi-fa do-re-mi-fa'. If you were to listen to this kind of repetition of do-re-mi-fa, as the result of gestalt you would come to recognize do-re-mi-fa as a unit and expect to hear it appear again next. At the same time, you would doubtless recognize it as being exactly the same as the do-re-mi-fa that you had heard so far. Internally, a listener is constantly searching the memory to see whether the phrase they are currently listening to has a connection (same pattern, similarity, etc.) to any part of the phrases they have heard so far. When the listener finds a connection, they recognize a referential relationship between the phrases. Simultaneously, the listener is also constantly predicting, from the phrases heard so far, what the next phrase will be like. Again, a referential relationship is recognized when the phrase heard is as predicted, or not as predicted.[7] In short, reference in music is born from the listener's memory and prediction. Both conjecture of phrases that will appear in the future and recognition of phrases heard in the past are seen as reference, both to future phrases and past phrases, from the phrase currently being listened to. At this time, the phrase currently being listened to (the do-re-mi-fa phrase articulated by gestalt) corresponds to a sign (representation), the conjecture of future phrases, and the phrases heard in the past, correspond to the object or result of representation, and the listener is the observer. This referential relationship models the form of the assignment of meaning to melody.

In a melody, a group of pitch events articulated by gestalt simultaneously works as a sign and the object or result of representation. For example, within the repetition of the phrase do-re-mi-fa, a certain single repetition of do-re-mi-fa is referring to other do-re-mi-fas while at the same time being referred to by other do-re-mi-fas. As one object may be referred to by multiple symbols simultaneously, so one sign may also refer to multiple objects simultaneously.[8] Furthermore, in the reference between signs and objects, there are strong connections and weak connections. For instance, when notes appear repeated in direct succession, such as in do-re-mi-fa do-re-mi-fa, there is a strong connection between the preceding do-re-mi-fa and the succeeding do-re-mi-fa. However, when there is a temporal distance between the appearance of a pitch event sequence as sign and that of a pitch event sequence as object, the connection is weak. In this way, pitch event groups articulated by gestalt construct a referential network of signs and objects and parts of the network that are comparatively strongly connected are recognized as groups. Moreover, groups among which there is a comparatively weak connection form the super group and are recognized as the hierarchical structure of the melody. So far, we have written

[7] This kind of recognition of referential relationships is a way of thinking which is fundamentally connected to the receptivity in Molino's trichotomy, mentioned hereafter, and Sperber (Dan Sperber, 1942–) and Wilson's (Deirdre Wilson, 1941–) relevance theory [23].

[8] This is a characteristic relationship that exists due to the non-existence of demonstrative pronouns in music.

that pitch event sequences articulated by gestalt work as the objects of a sign or representation, but in actual pieces of music, chords and rhythm also work as objects of a sign or representation.

When a listener understands music according to gestalt, it is known that two types of cognitive mechanism are at work: hierarchical grouping of pitch events[9] and networking (creation of graph structure) by reference between pitch events. This being so, it is natural that musical analysis should be carried out based on these two mechanisms. The approach that analyzes music from the position of the former, that is, the hierarchical grouping of pitch events, is Generative Theory of Tonal Music (GTTM).[10] The approach from the position of the latter, that is, the creation of a network by referencing between pitch events, is the Implication-Realization model.[11]

1.5 Categorization of Musical Meaning

We now want to consider the meaning of music, basing our consideration on the semiotics of melody. Before that, however, in this section we determine the concept of emotion in music in the following way. Humans infer whether the musical phenomena to which we are currently listening are the same as, or differ from, what we were expecting based on previous experience, and the resulting psychological changes, such as surprise, uncertainty, stability, nervousness, relaxation etc., we call emotion. Emotion is an intersubjective psychological phenomenon that is temporary and fleeting and does not contain any aesthetic aspects.[12] In the previous section, we discussed the referential relationship between melodies or phrases. The American music scholar and philosopher Meyer[13] insisted that emotion is born out of that referential relationship. A listener, on hearing a certain phrase, predicts, either consciously or subconsciously, what kind of phrase will be heard in the future. If the listener hears a phrase that accords with the prediction, this does not influence the listener's emotion, but when the phrase does not accord with prediction, the listener's emotion is influenced. Prediction can also be called implication or expectation.

Now, what are the elements of music that correspond to the three elements of semiotics? First of all, it is the musical score or musical performance that corresponds to symbolic representation. Next, regarding the thing indicated by a symbolic representation, Meyer classified this from two points of view: The first is the point of view that asks whether the object indicated by the representation is intrinsic or extrinsic; the second is the point of view that asks whether the aim of representation is emotion or form [16]:

---

[9] *cf.* Sect. 1.3.

[10] *cf.* Chap. 6.

[11] *cf.* Sect. 5.1.

[12] A relatively continual and stable personal phenomenon is called mood.

[13] Leonard B. Meyer, 1918–2007.

Thing indicated by representation:

Intrinsic	Meaning of music exists within that music
Extrinsic	Exists within an indicated world outside of music

Aim of representation:

Emotion	Something which grants emotional experience
Form	Abstract form created by the representation itself

Intrinsic and extrinsic can be applied to a substantial reference (indicating the music itself) and an indicative reference (indicating things, concepts, phenomena, and experiences outside music), respectively. Another point of view is that, for a conscious observer, the thing indicated by representation can be divided according to whether the aim is emotional experience born out of reference between representation and result, or whether the aim is the form of symbolic representation itself.

The term intrinsic emotion corresponds to the way, as mentioned above, in which the referential relationship between pitch event sequences articulated by gestalt causes the listener to have expectations or conjectures, and meaning is attached to melody when emotions are roused by whether the expectations are to be realized or not. This is the position of thinking that the meaning of music exists exclusively in the process of listening to music, and that, even when listening to music as absolute music, emotional meaning appears. As we will discuss in a later section, this accords strongly with the meaning of music in the computational view. Extrinsic emotion denotes the position of thinking that, as in program music, a listener connects music to phenomena and concepts apart from music, and whether or not the referenced content can be understood influences emotional expression. This is known as the 'Darling, they are playing our tune phenomenon' [4].[14] When considered in terms of the investigation of the computational meaning of music, this phenomenon is not very important, as it is unstable and vague. Intrinsic form denotes the standpoint of thinking that meaning appears by relating the melodies, harmonies, and rhythms in a piece of music to other melodies, harmonies, and rhythms within the same piece and/or across pieces of music (e.g. a repetition of the same or a slightly altered thing). For example, this means listening to minimalist music,[15] R&B music, which has only one chord,[16] or similar, and recognizing that, for example, 'this form has

[14] The phenomenon in which people frequently seek to connect a certain piece of music to personal matters, circumstances, episodes, etc. from their own lives.

[15] An expressive style or genre which alters melody, harmony, rhythm, etc. little by little while repeating figures, rhythm patterns, and sounds that are largely the same. The fact of feeling, when listening to minimalist music, curiosity as to why one does not get bored even when listening to the same phrase repeatedly for a long time, or why one did not notice that the rhythm pattern had changed, is an example of listening to music and gaining a cognitive-scientific interest, and as such could be classified as extrinsic emotion.

[16] Rhythm and Blues. African-American music born from the intermingling of jazz, blues and gospel in the 1940s. Characterized by rhythmical beats and shouts, it is the original source of the genres that would come to be called soul music, funk, black contemporary, and so on.

Fig. 1.3 Example of extrinsic form: opening of Debussy's Arabesque

value because it is simple'. In particular, the song 'Sex Machine' by James Brown,[17] released in 1970, is mostly composed only of the chord E♭$_7$ and is a monumental work which demonstrated how popular music can be formed just by repeating a specific rhythm pattern.

Regarding examples of the extrinsic form standpoint, a certain kind of work by the contemporary composer Xenakis[18] should be applicable. In 'Pithoprakta', the score of this work was created according to a scientific numerical formula that defines probabilistic behavior. It is (only) the fact that the output conforms to the formula which is important, thus what the listener recognizes as a result of actually listening to the audio sound is not so important. Accordingly, under the categorization of musical meaning described in this book, it is possible to consider that this piece does not aim to produce emotion in people.

Although it cannot easily be placed alongside the previous pieces, there is the arabesque, a form of music so called because the general form of the melody resembles the arabesque patterns that can be seen on the walls of mosques.[19] These pieces were not composed with the aim that the outline of the melody should become an arabesque pattern, rather they aim to rouse intrinsic emotion in the listener, but perhaps we ought to consider that, as a result, they 'happen to' simultaneously be accompanied by the extrinsic form of arabesque pattern (Fig. 1.3).

The field of study which deals with the same discussions and concerns described in this section is called music semiology.

1.6 Reduction Hypothesis and Schenkerian Analysis

The Austrian music scholar Heinrich Schenker[20] proposed his Reduction Hypothesis, which states that musical meaning appears by distinguishing important notes from

[17] James Brown, 1933–2006.

[18] Iannis Xenakis, 1922–2001.

[19] Well-known arabesques include No. 2 of the '25 Etudes' by Burgmüller (Johann Burgmüller, 1806–1874), 'Op. 18 Arabeske in C major' by Schumann (Robert Schumann, 1810–1856), and 'The Two Arabesques' by Debussy (Claude Debussy, 1862–1918).

[20] Heinrich Schenker, 1868–1935.

less important ones due to gestalt (gestalt meaning) and that musical compositions can be reduced to a simpler structure. *Reduction* is the operation of leaving important notes (pitch events) and removing less important notes, in a step-by-step process, to extract a structure equivalent to the outline of a composition [12, 13].[21,22] Then, assuming that it is the fundamental structure (Ursatz) obtained by applying this reduction hypothesis that holds the musical meaning of a composition, Schenker realized the application of the reduction hypothesis as a method of analysis.

Schenker introduced the term prolongation, as a musical concept corresponding to the appearance of gestalt meaning in musical compositions. For example, when a certain pitch event occurs, the pitch event continues to psychologically sound for a while after that, which effects the succeeding musical figures and progressions. Those succeeding figures and progressions are thought to be in a relationship in which they are in harmony dominated by the prolongation of the preceding pitch events. It possibly follows that gestalt meaning appears from this relationship.

According to Schenker, the music written on a musical score is composed of multiple pitch events on the surface, called the foreground (Vordergrund), then, by thinning out the notes contained in the foreground to focus interest on the important notes, one passes through the midground (Mittelgrund) and reaches the background (Hindgrund), i.e., the fundamental structure (Ursatz) of the composition (Fig. 1.4). The foreground and background are the beginning and end, so there is only one of each, but the midground comprises multiple layers. It is the operation of thinning out the midground notes that is reduction. In the upper part of a musical composition's fundamental structure, the fundamental line (Urlinie) governed by the principle of voice leading appears, while in the lower part the bass appears, which is governed by the principle of counterpoint. These upper/lower voices decide the direction in which the music progresses. The fundamental line descends from the thirds, fifths, or octaves in the given key to the tonic. The lower part is the component within the fundamental structure that creates harmony. After ascending a fifth from the tonic to the dominant (I–V), it descends a fifth from the dominant to the tonic (V–I). Schenker explained this composition of a piece of music by comparing it to the way in which living things are composed from every combination of organic binding, saying that the progression of a musical composition is behavior driven by biological urges. The operation working in the opposite direction to reduction and increasing notes, moving from the background toward the foreground, is called elaboration. Elaboration in Schenkerian analysis particularly means linearization and involves making the combined chords of the background conform to the movement of the I–V–I bass part, then distributing them in time direction. Linearization leads to the generation of an arpeggio or linear progression. That is to say, linearization from the background to the foreground is not the operations of generating arbitrary chords and harmonies into the tonal spaces between I–V–I, but those of inserting effective

[21] The latent structure that supports the music, also called underlying structure.

[22] In music theory, reduction is largely used synonymously with hierarchy. Reduction in information science or mathematical logic means the operation of rewriting an expression or a term into a simpler form.

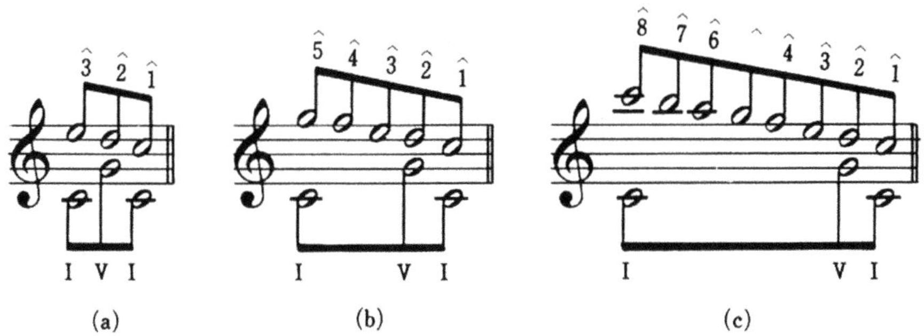

Fig. 1.4 Fundamental structures of a musical composition in Schenkerian theory

chords and harmonies into the spaces in order to preserve the progression of I–V–I. If heading toward the foreground is regarded as the horizontalization (linearization) of the chords, traveling toward the background can be seen as the verticalization (reduction) of the melody.

Although the process of Schenkerian analysis can be explained with intuitive words such as reduction, elaboration, prolongation, and linearization, accurately describing this as an algorithm is difficult. This is also a reason why computer processing of Schenkerian analysis is difficult.

1.7 Analysis of Retrograde

Two things deeply connected to the meaning of music are the act of creation of music and the act of reception of music. Here creation means constructing a musical score or performance from the musical structure or intention when the musician has composed or arranged a piece of music. Reception means extracting the emotions, thoughts and feelings that the listener[23] has recognized. What we call music analysis is regarded as the operation of extracting meaning in the two acts of creation and reception. In this section, based on the trichotomy proposed by the Swiss-born semioticist Jean Molino [17], let us consider music analysis in relation to retrogression of melody (Fig. 1.5).

In his trichotomy, Molino considers three components, which are a sign (in the form of a representation), a sender, and a receiver, then he considers that the meaning of a sign is born from the relationship between these components. A sign is the product of a complex creation process relating to the form or content of a work. A sign is also

[23] The word *listener*, used in music theory works, denotes a person who is sufficiently knowledgeable and well acquainted with the music from the eighteenth to nineteenth centuries, and who can appreciate music analytically. The word does not include inexpert people who have received no musical training. In [11] the term used is *experienced listener*. Such a listener is thought to have greater receptibility and distinction regarding melody than we whose ears are used to the musical culture of the late twentieth century onward.

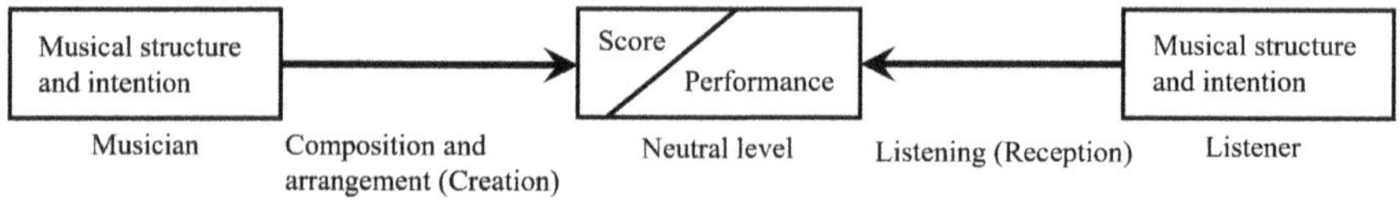

Fig. 1.5 Relationship between musician, score and listener

the starting point of the complex reception process of reconstructing the message that someone is attempting to send. In short, signs are physical traces yielded by the creation process and can be seen as expressing the structure contained within a work. Accordingly, Molino asserts that to analyze the meaning of a sign, we must deal with creation process, reception process, and traces. The creation process and reception process will not necessarily always agree, meaning there is no guarantee that the message will be conveyed accurately from the sender to the receiver, thus Molino considers that the aim of a sign is not communication.[24] In Fig. 1.5, the fact that the score or performance is a physical trace related to the work and can be taken as a target for subjective analysis is important. Therefore, Molino called the physical trace relating to a work the medium level. In Molino's trichotomy an arrow is oriented from the listener to the medium level, which represents how the meaning obtained from what is being heard is constructed by an active sensory process.

Here let us take retrograde of melody as an example and look at how the meaning of music appears in the two acts of creation and reception. As the name implies, retrograde of melody is the technique of following in (time-wise) reverse order a melody which has previously appeared, within the same piece of music. Use of the technique began with its application to plainsong (cantus firmus) in the middle ages and renaissance period (Fig. 1.6).

Retrograde was one esoteric means of expanding musical structure, but in a long melody it cannot be comprehended, just by listening, that the melody is in retrograde, besides which the listener may not be able to withstand listening to such music. Thus, if using this as a technique, the melodies involved inevitably become short and simple. Nevertheless, there is an exceptional masterpiece by J. S. Bach which uses this technique. That masterpiece is 'The Musical Offering'.[25] In the two-part retrograde canon, known as a 'crab canon', the eighteen bar-long piece has a symmetrical structure like a palindrome: the upper and lower parts are reversed after nine bars, and so the retrograde agrees with the original musical composition. Two hundred years after 'The Musical Offering', Schoenberg advocated twelve-tone music (dodecaphony) [10], planning to thoroughly eradicate any sense of tonality by making the twelves notes in an octave appear uniformly. In that technique, the basic melody makes all of the twelve notes each appear once, then the musical composition is composed of melodies that apply transposition, inversion, retrograde or

[24] However, the Swiss mathematician and music scholar Guerino Mazzola (1947–) and his associates use Molino's trichotomy to explain communication in music between a musician and listener [15, p. 13, Fig. 2.1].

[25] German: Musikalisches Opfer.

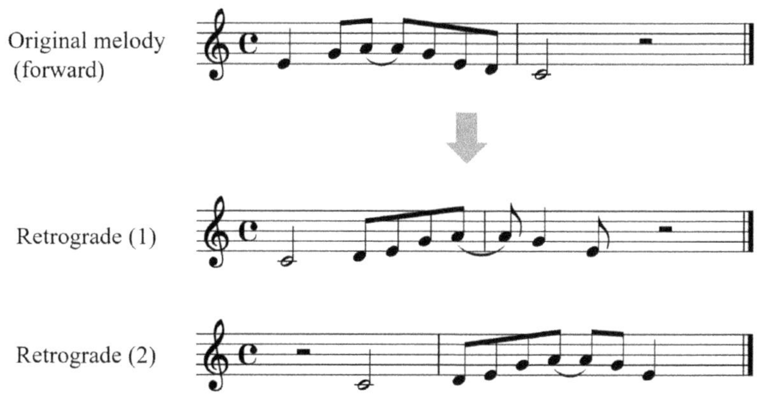

Fig. 1.6 Example of retrograde of melody

retrograde-inversion to the basic melody. By this composition method it is guaranteed that the twelve notes will all appear the same number of times, creating a new standard of music that replaces tonality.[26] When creating a retrograde, there are two ways to handle rests: preserving the positions of the rests in the original melody, as in (1) in Fig. 1.6, or creating a retrograde that includes the rests, as in (2).

In the fourth movement of Beethoven's Piano Sonata No. 29 in B flat major,[27] a fugue produced by the retrograde of the theme can be heard (Fig. 1.7). In the retrograde of the theme that was in B flat major, the rhythm is preserved while the melody is transposed to B flat minor. Beethoven intentionally inserted a retrograde, but, listening to this part without that kind of prior knowledge, it is not easy to understand that it is a retrograde (at least not for anyone who has had no training as a musician). Most listeners are first able to recognize that there is a retrograde when they look at the musical score. Basically, in Fig. 1.5, the musical structure and intention considered by the musician, on the left-hand side, do not necessarily agree with the structure and intention perceived by the listener, on the right-hand side. However, there are cases in which, conversely, the listener actively creates structures and intentions that were not intended by the musician.

---

[26] The theme provided by Friedrich II for J. S. Bach's aforementioned 'The Musical Offering' is in C minor, in which the eleven notes apart from *B*♭ are used, yet in the variation of the same piece all twelve notes are used. Also, in 'The Well-Tempered Clavier Book I' the theme of No. 24 Prelude and Fugue in B minor is a melody using all twelve notes, truly displaying the significance of being 'well-tempered' in the final piece of the collection. It would not necessarily be improper to consider that the revelation behind Schoenberg's twelve-tone technique came from this composition which came two hundred years before. Later, the twelve-tone technique went on to pave the way for the attempt by Schoenberg's pupil Webern (Anton Webern, 1883–1945) to apply regulation to duration and volume as well as pitch (total serialism) and the musique sérielle created by Boulez (Pierre Boulez, 1925–2016) et al. A famous quotation from Boulez in this process is "Schoenberg is dead! Long live Webern".

[27] Hammerklavier Sonata.

Fig. 1.7 Example of retrograde in Beethoven's Piano Sonata (the numbers in circles are the number of bars from the beginning of the fourth movement. Upper extract: the theme begins from bar 16. Lower extract: the retrograde of the theme is from bar 152. The blue numbers 1–5 in the figure represent the corresponding bars). From http://imslp.org/, edited by Heinrich Schenker, published Vienna: Universal Edition (ca. 1920)

Structure received by listening is influenced by a human's short-term memory. It is said that a human's short-term memory can remember 7 ± 2 chunks[28] for from several seconds up to ten or so seconds [22]. If we convert this memory time into beats, in the case of 80 BPM (beats per minute), 4/4 tempo, it is approximately equivalent to between 10 and 20 beats, that is, from 2.5 to 5 bars. As chunks of pitch events are formed when several pitch events are retained simultaneously in the short-term memory, it is thought that a human can articulate and recognize a unity that is a phrase or passage of approximately four bars in length.

Assuming music theory is taking the musical structure that a listener can perceive as the target of analysis, this restriction of short-term memory would mean

[28] Chunk: a single unit of memory in short-term memory. Even a complex subject can be recognized/remembered comparatively easily if one can make it into chunks (chunking) by some sort of grouping or association.

the length of a musical composition could be no longer than a phrase or passage at the most. However, in standard music theory books, one can often find examples of melodies from twenty bars to over forty bars being analyzed as single structures (for instance, see [11, p. 250]). Judgment of discrimination or identity of pitch events which occur over a length of time that exceeds short-term memory retention time inevitably becomes vague. It is more natural to think that, when listening to a melody of a length that cannot be stored in short-term memory, the cognitive mechanism at work differs from that at work when listening to a short melody. Accordingly, it is appropriate to think that the structure of long melodies corresponds to the musical structure and intention given not by the listener, but by the musician or composer at the time of creation. To explain this in terms of Molino's trichotomy, when Beethoven composed his piano sonata, it was with a certain intention that he introduced the retrograde melody. Meanwhile, the majority of the listeners who heard the aforementioned composition for the first time probably comprehended and appreciated (received) the piece without realizing that it includes a retrograde melody. A few listeners, by listening to the piece in the knowledge that it includes a retrograde melody, would surely comprehend the composition in a different way.

1.8 Understanding Music that Imitates Understanding Language

To explore the meaning of music, or simply as a point of scientific interest, various similarities and differences between language and music have been compared and discussed [1, 3, 8, 18, 21]. In language, because we are clearly conscious of the distinction of surface-level signs and the meaning of vocabulary and characters, from long ago many theories have been proposed to explain what sort of relationship exists between surface-level signs and their meanings.

In Peirce's semiotics, mentioned previously, a rigorous distinction was carried out regarding the target indicated by a sign. In accordance with this, we, the authors of this book, considered that pitch events (and groups thereof) in a musical composition are signs (triggers) that reference other parts of the composition (targets). In this way of thinking, it is necessary to refer to the semiology of the Swiss linguist Saussure.[29] In Saussure's work, he calls the synchronic social application of language, i.e., vocabulary, grammar, and so on, *la langue*, which he distinguishes from personal language application, or *la parole*. Saussure considers that la langue is a system of signs (signe), composed of two components: *signifiant* (the signifier; symbolic representation = the thing representing) and *signifié* (the signified; symbolic content = the thing being represented). For example, the sequence of letters or pronunciation of 'apple' corresponds to the signifier, while the red, round fruit that comes into one's mind upon hearing or reading the word 'apple' corresponds to the signified. When people communicate using language, the symbolic representation or

[29] Ferdinand de Saussure, 1857–1913.

word 'apple', which is distinguished from other words, and the symbolic content or perception of apple, distinguished from other perceptions, are arbitrarily connected and the substance or meaning of apple is shared between the communicators. Thus, Saussure asserted, in this way language creates a peculiar system using signs.

When it comes to the concepts of sharing and communication, we must pay attention to the considerations of the Austrian philosopher Wittgenstein.[30] First of all, humans surmise rules from countable examples. If a small child is shown an 'apple', which is a countable thing, the child can discern 'apple' from things that are not apple and so articulate the world by means of this word. This kind of acquirement of vocabulary can be thought of as comprehension of a common rule in human society, but, because this learning process is carried out in individuals, it cannot be proved that vocabulary is definitely being shared in society. For a start, it is unclear how many apples a certain child will need to be shown before the child can acquire the concept. After having been shown a sufficient number of apples, it is still uncertain whether the child will recognize another apple as an apple. To give an extreme example, even though colors such as 'red' and 'blue' may be completely different to different people, the words become a common protocol when carrying out communication.[31] In his later period, Wittgenstein realized that such formation of rules cannot be regarded as a definite contract, and that the application of language is something in which rules may change dynamically, in the same way that children play games according to perfunctory rules. Thus, he called this concept a *language-game*. Hence, communication in society is a language-game itself.

The approach that truly revolutionized linguistics was Noam Chomsky's[32] generative grammar.[33] In the framework of Chomsky's generative grammar, he asserts that in the lead up to a person generating a sentence there is a relationship between surface-level structure, deep-level structure, and theoretical structure. First, let us consider a situation in verbal communication in which a speaker is trying to convey content with some certain meaning to a listener (Fig. 1.8). The speaker conceives the content he wants to convey, chooses vocabulary, then firstly constructs the deep-level structure within his mind. This then undergoes application of the standards of grammar to become a surface-level structure, and so becomes a phonological structure. The listener takes in the phoneme, analyzes the grammatical structure in order to accept it as a sentence, then tries to draw out the meaning from within that sentence. In this process, when the listener (sentence structure analyst) has been able to reproduce the same structure as the speaker (sentence structure generator), it is considered that the message content has been conveyed.[34] The three structures,

[30] Ludwig Wittgenstein, 1899–1951.

[31] Wittgenstein's investigation of such sensory sharing goes further, to consider, for example, "Is another person's sense of pain the same thing as my own sense of pain?" There is scientific evidence that the situation of being in 'pain' is at least the same reaction in any individual, yet there is no means of sharing 'how painful' or 'in what way it is painful.'

[32] Noam Chomsky, 1928–.

[33] *cf.* Chap. 3.

[34] In the way of thinking called generative semantics, meaning is the content conceived by the speaker and is the intention of what the speaker wants to convey. In contrast, in conceptual semantics,

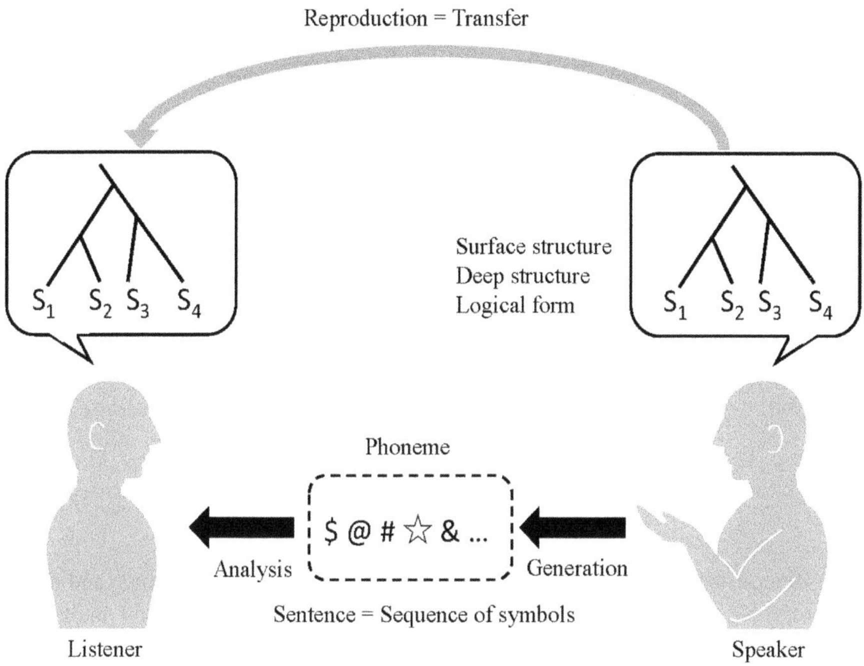

Fig. 1.8 Chomskian language communication

surface level, deep level and logic, in the diagram, have been discussed as tree structures for many years since Chomsky [5, 12, 25]. Sentence analysis progresses as shown in Fig. 1.9a. Considered in terms of Molino's trichotomy, this corresponds to the direction of reception. On the other hand, the direction in which a sentence is generated corresponds to the opposite direction to the analysis shown in Fig. 1.9a. The speech intention is expressed by the components of meaning and goes on to transform into deep-level structure and surface-level structure, which is equivalent to transformation giving meaning to a sentence.

The music theory GTTM also asserts that people who listen to music comprehend music by hierarchically constructing a tree structure, by analysis (Fig. 1.9b[35]). In GTTM also, the operation of generating a musical composition is, in the same way as in Schenkerian theory, called decoration or elaboration (or instantiation). For the sake of comparison, we have demonstrated the flow of analysis in Schenkerian theory in Fig. 1.9c. It can be seen that the fundamental structure of Schenkerian theory corresponds to the tree structure of GTTM.

---

meaning is the interpretation that the listener can give in relation to the surface-level speech. This contrast between generative semantics and conceptual semantics can be likened to the contrast between the tree structure intended by the speaker and the tree structure interpreted by the listener (*cf.* Chap. 3).

[35] For an explanation of the time-span tree and extension tree in the figure, please see Chap. 6.

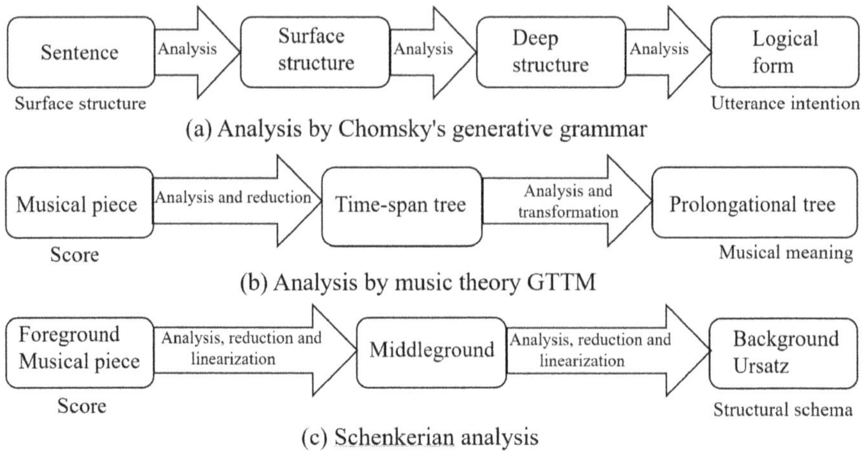

Fig. 1.9 Framework for comprehending meaning given to sentences and musical compositions

As demonstrated in Fig. 1.9, in the sense of analyzing a given sentence and musical composition to obtain a tree structure, both analysis of sentences and analysis of musical compositions follow the same outline. However, in actuality, there is a significant difference between analysis of sentences by Chomsky's generative grammar and analysis of musical compositions by GTTM. In Chomsky's generative grammar, analysis is carried out using the grammatical rules for generating the surface-level sentence. In contrast, in GTTM the referential relationships among phrases and melodies are expressed with a tree structure, and grammatical rules are used in the generation of that tree structure. Fred Lerdahl and Ray Jackendoff, two advocates of GTTM, say the following:

> We have found that a generative music theory, unlike a generative linguistic theory, must not only assign structural descriptions to a piece, but must also differentiate them along a scale of coherence, weighting them as more or less 'preferred' interpretations (that is, claiming that the experienced listener is more likely to attribute some structures to the music than others). Thus the rules of the theory are divided into two distinct types: *well-formedness rules*, which specify the possible structural descriptions, and *preference rules*, which designate out of the possible structural descriptions those that correspond to experienced listeners' hearings of any particular piece. The preference rules,[36] which do the major portion of the work of developing analyses within our theory, have no counterpart in standard linguistic theory; their presence is a prominent difference between the forms of the two theories [11, p. 9].[37]

From what does this difference between language and music originate? In the case of language, the existence of generative grammar rules means that erasable

[36] The rule that decides which is most preferable from among the multiple tree structures that are candidates for the analysis result.

[37] The modern composer Xenakis stated that "I do not think that any attempt to consider music like a language can be successful. The sub-structure of music is much closer to the sub-structure of space and time. Music is purer, much closer to the categories of the mind" [14, p. 89].

unimportant components, such as syntactic expletives, interjections and pauses, are few. Therefore, in language the concept of reduction is not as important as in music. Also, one tree structure corresponds to one sentence.[38] This is because the category or form assigned to the terminal symbol and midway nodes of a tree structure function as limitations when a valid tree structure is generated. Accordingly, it can be considered that the sentence, which is the surface-level structure, contains a sufficient amount of information for it to be manipulated or calculated directly.[39] In contrast, in music, because sufficient categories or forms are not assigned to the terminal symbols or midway nodes of tree structures, valid tree structures are generated in sets of multiples (selected according to preference rules), and in general more than one tree structure corresponds to one piece of music. In other words, the 'pseudo' generative rules of GTTM give birth to a structure that has a far greater degree of freedom than language. For this reason, we can consider that the musical score or composition, which is the surface-level structure, contains indefinite information for direct manipulation, and the operation of reduction, removing branches that are less important, becomes meaningful.[40]

1.9 Cognitive Reality

If you use a certain concept or model when rationally explaining a cognitive or psychological phenomenon, we say that concept or model has cognitive reality (which can also be called perceptual ubiquity). There is a stronger contention, which is the case of cognitive reality by means of a psychological phenomenon manifested based on the mechanisms of the brain. For example, the human mind is equipped with hardware called short-term memory, and it is well known that this is used in the cognition of relatively short pitch event series [22]. Cognition of pitch and cognition of harmony are relatively stable and have consistency. When assuming the existence of short-term memory to rationally explain why this is so, the existence of short-term memory is actually being confirmed. At this time, we can say that there is cognitive reality.[41]

---

[38] There are also cases in which two or more tree structures correspond to one sentence. For example, consider the sentence "I saw a girl with a telescope." There are two possible interpretations, one being that the speaker saw a girl holding a telescope, the other being that the speaker saw the girl through a telescope. The parse tree corresponding to each interpretation differs.

[39] Surely, this must be one of the reasons that machine learning functions extremely well in the processing of natural language.

[40] The ambiguity that originates from this point is a factor that makes computer processing of analysis based on GTTM, or Schenkarian analysis, difficult.

[41] 'Grounding' is a term that has a deep relationship to cognitive reality. When the relationship between a sign used within a sign system and the real-world object or concept to which that sign refers is correctly maintained even after the system operates and its state transitions, we say that the sign is correctly grounded. In particular, when the sign is expressing a cognitive or psychological

For us to realize music analysis that has stability and consistency, we argue that we must attach importance to cognitive reality and construct a relevant procedure and mechanism. The British music cognition scholar Geraint Wiggins and his associates make a similar assertion:

> Systems which aim to encode musical similarity must do so in a human-like way [24].

We argue that there is also cognitive reality in the tree structure obtained as the result of musical analysis (however, this only applies when the peculiarities of musical genre, style, etc. have been appropriately limited). In actuality, there are several works of research claiming that tree structures have cognitive reality. For example, in the DOP model, based on the hypothesis that, in the same way as people generate tree structures when they hear words, people also generate tree structures when they listen to music, that process is modeled and the memory to store fragments of melody is combined with a rule system [2]. Lerdahl and Jackendoff also assert that when people recognize music, hierarchical structures (time-span trees and extension trees) are generated [11, pp. 2, 105–112, 332].[42] An experiment has actually been conducted to confirm whether the aforementioned time-span tree has cognitive reality [5]. It was discovered that pitch events in tonal music are heard in a considerably strict hierarchical order, and it was concluded that a time-span tree, as an internal representation, has sufficient cognitive reality. Furthermore, Krumhansl showed the experimental results of cognitive reality on the tonal hierarchies that have the properties common to time-span tree [9]. Patel also discussed the time-span tree that forms a pitch event hierarchy based on structural prominence of a pitch event [20]. Following this, Wiggins et al. bring the argument around to tree structures in music, and state:

> the tree structures generated by generative language theories in music are more about semantic grouping than they are about syntactic grouping: the syntax serves the semantics [25].

We aim to construct a music theory that can be executed as a program on a computer, which realizes a music system which analyzes music given as an input and outputs the meaning as a tree structure. So far, we have introduced the concepts that will become the keys to realizing such a music system, efforts to pursue the structure and meaning of music, and comparison with natural language. Thus, we have laid out our thinking. We may not yet have found the answer to the big question of what music is, but we have probably come to see one path that approaches the answer. Hereafter, in this book, we will conduct a close investigation into the concepts and endeavors that pave that path.

---

phenomenon, that sign being correctly grounded is almost synonymous with the sign system having cognitive reality.

[42] *cf.* Sects. 1.8, 6.1.4, and 7.2.

References

1. R. Aiello, Music and language: parallels and contrasts, in *Musical Perceptions*, ed. by R. Aiello, J.A. Sloboda (Oxford University Press, 1994), pp. 40–63
2. R. Bod, A unified model of structural organization in language and music. J. Artif. Intell. Res. **17**, 289–308 (2002)
3. N. Cook, Perception: a perspective from music theory, in *Musical Perceptions*, ed. by R. Aiello, J.A. Sloboda (Oxford University Press, 1994), pp. 64–95
4. J.B. Davies, *The Psychology of Music* (Hutchinson, 1978)
5. N. Dibben, Cognitive reality of hierarchic structure in tonal and atonal music. Music Percept. **12**(1) (Fall), 1–25 (1994)
6. M. Hamanaka, K. Hirata, S. Tojo, Musical structural analysis database based on GTTM, in *Proceedings of ISMIR 2014* (2014), pp. 325–330
7. M. Hamanaka, K. Hirata, S. Tojo, Implementing "A generative theory of tonal music". J. New Music Res. **35**(4), 249–277 (2007)
8. R. Jackendoff, Parallels and nonparallels between language and music. Music Percept. **26**(3), 195–204 (2009)
9. C.L. Krumhansl, Rhythm and pitch in music cognition. Psychol. Bull. **126**(1), 159–179 (2000)
10. R. Leibowitz, *Schoenberg* (Éditions du Seuil, 1968)
11. F. Lerdahl, R. Jackendoff, *A Generative Theory of Tonal Music* (The MIT Press, 1983)
12. F. Lerdahl, Genesis and architecture of the GTTM project. Music Percept. **26**(3), 187–194 (2009)
13. A. Marsden, Generative structural representation of tonal music. J. New Music Res. **35**(4), 249–277 (2006)
14. N. Matossian, *Iannis Xenakis* (Kahn and Averill, 1986)
15. G. Mazzola, *The Topos of Music—Geometric Logic of Concepts, Theory, and Performance* (Birkhäuser Verlag, 2002)
16. L.B. Meyer, *Emotion and Meaning in Music* (University of Chicago Press, 1956)
17. J. Molino, *Fait Musical et Śemiologie de la Musique* (Musique en Jeu 17, 1975)
18. J. Molino, Toward a evolutionary theory of music and language, Chap. 11, in *The Origins of Music*, ed. by N.L. Wallin, B. Merker, S. Brown (2000), pp. 165–176
19. G. Nierhaus, *Algorithmic Composition: Paradigms of Automated Music Generation* (Springer, 2009)
20. A.D. Patel, Language, music, and the brain: a resource-sharing framework, in *Language and Music as Cognitive Systems*, ed. by P. Rebuschat, M. Rohmeier, J. Hawkins, I. Cross (The Oxford University Press, 2012), pp. 204–223
21. J. Sloboda, *The Musical Mind—The Cognitive Psychology of Music* (Oxford University Press, 1985)
22. B. Snyder, *Music and Memory* (The MIT Press, 2000)
23. D. Sperber, D. Wilson, *Relevance: Communication and Cognition* (Wiley-Blackwell, 1995)
24. G.A. Wiggins, Semantic gap?? Schematic Schmap!! Methodological considerations in the scientific study of music, in *11th IEEE International Symposium on Multimedia 2009*, pp. 477–482
25. G.A. Wiggins, D. Müllensiefen, M.T. Pearce, On the non-existence of music: why music theory is a figment of the imagination. Music. Sci. Discuss. Forum **5**, 231–255 (2010)

Chapter 2
The Mathematics of Ebony and Ivory Keys

> 'Ebony and Ivory' is a joint masterpiece of Paul McCartney and Stevie Wonder, representing black and white. 'Is there any question?' The lecturer asked the audience. One famous pianist raised his hand. 'Why the black keys and the white keys are arranged as such?' [2, p. 1]

In order to answer the above question, we need to get back to the ancient Greece. Pythagoras was born in the small island of Samos in the Aegean sea, circa 580 B.C. Nowadays, we categorize him as a mathematician, but at that time, there was no such profession; all the secular scholars at that time are now called as philosophers.

We nowadays associate the name of Pythagoras immediately with Pythagorean proposition. In his school, however, there was a doctrine that any number was represented by a ratio of two integers, namely by a rational number. As is known to this day, Pythagorean proposition cannot be valid without employing root numbers that are irrational, not shown by ratios of two integers.

Because this proposition is too famous, it masks his fame as an inventor of a musical scale. It is said that he noticed the tone interval of the perfect 4th, 5th, and the octave when he heard a blacksmith was hammering. Pythagoras verified his experience; he hung four strings with the same length with the different weights, and investigated the tone pitches when they were vibrating, though as usual this kind of legend may not be a historical fact.

2.1 Scale with 2 and 3

Pipes, strings, and drums are the primordial forms of musical instrument. Now let us observe if two tones are consonant when two strings are picked at the same time; then Why two tones made by two strings, one is the half length of the other, sound harmonized? When we pick a tensed string with fixed ends, it moves up and down, or left and right, and vibrates the air very rapidly, and the position of oscillation from the center of the string becomes a sinusoidal wave along with the time axis. Thus, one cycle of vibration, that is one round trip of a string, makes one period of a sinusoidal wave; usually a tone consists of hundreds of cycles per second.

K. Hirata et al., *Music, Mathematics and Language*,
https://doi.org/10.1007/978-981-19-5166-4_2

The magnitude of sinusoidal wave represents amplitude, the temporal length of a wave cycle is a period, and the inverse of the period becomes the frequency. The fast vibration means a high pitch, and the amplified up and down (left and right) makes a big sound. The timbre is made of the combination of multiple various sinusoidal waves. Even though these sinusoidal waves are multiply added, we can define the base wave length that corresponds to its own pitch. Thus, we can create various tones with various timbres of the same pitch.

Now, let us consider the situation picking multiple strings simultaneously, and pay attention to the 'nodes' of sinusoidal waves, that are the temporal points the waves cross the time axes. If such a node of a sinusoidal wave encounters that of the other wave so often, it implies that the two sinusoidal waves synchronize well and the two tones sound harmonized. If a string with a certain tension is snapped with another with the half length of the same tension, the nodes of the longer one meets that of the shorter one, once in twice; it means the octave. The inverse of the period of a cycle is the frequency. The longer string vibrates slower, that is its period is longer and its frequency is smaller, meaning the lower pitch. On the contrary, the shorter string makes the higher pitch. We define the octave as a pair of tones whose ratio of frequency is one to two. We call the tone with double frequency harmonic overtone (Fig. 2.1).

The period of a wave cycle is in proportion to the length of strings if they are in the same tension, and the ratio of their frequency (the inverse of the period) becomes a simple rational number, results in proximity [3]. If we consider the consonance of the octave, that is the ratio is 1:2, then, the ratio of 1:3 makes another pair of consonant notes. This is the G note of one higher octave. We call a *pitch class* a collection of notes by the difference of octaves. Thus, pitch class C refers to various notes C with the double/half frequency.

If we employ the notion of pitch class, the note G that has the triple frequency of the base C can be put inside of one octave, as the note with 3/2 times of C. Here, 'inside' means that the frequency of the note does not exceed the double of the base C.

Next, we can introduce another note, named D, as the note with 3/2 times frequency of G.

$$1 \times \frac{3}{2} \times \frac{3}{2} \times \frac{1}{2} = \frac{9}{8}$$

Thus, we can continue this procedure;

1. Introduce a new note with 3/2 times more frequency, and
2. If it exceeds 2 (the double of base C), divide by 2.

Let us name the succeeding note of D as A, then next E, and so on. The following is the table of frequency defined from C $\times 3/2 \times (1/2)^*$ (where $*$ means an appropriate number to put it in the scope of the octave, that is, $1 < (3/2)^n/(1/2)^* < 2$).

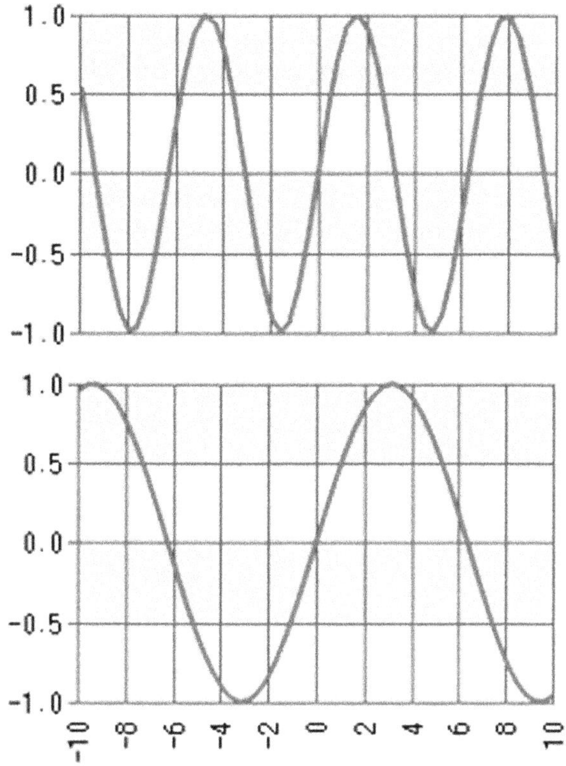

Fig. 2.1 Two waves with the difference of octave

$$
\begin{aligned}
&\mathrm{C}: 1\\
&\mathrm{G}: 1 \times \left(\frac{3}{2}\right)^1 = \frac{3}{2}\\
&\mathrm{D}: 1 \times \left(\frac{3}{2}\right)^2 \times \frac{1}{2} = \frac{9}{8}\\
&\mathrm{A}: 1 \times \left(\frac{3}{2}\right)^3 \times \frac{1}{2} = \frac{27}{16}\\
&\mathrm{E}: 1 \times \left(\frac{3}{2}\right)^4 \times \left(\frac{1}{2}\right)^2 = \frac{81}{64}\\
&\mathrm{B}: 1 \times \frac{3}{2} \times \frac{3}{2} \times \frac{1}{2} \times \frac{3}{2} \times \frac{3}{2} \times \frac{1}{2} \times \frac{3}{2} = \frac{243}{128}\\
&\mathrm{F}\sharp: 1 \times \frac{3}{2} \times \frac{3}{2} \times \frac{1}{2} \times \frac{3}{2} \times \frac{3}{2} \times \frac{1}{2} \times \frac{3}{2} \times \frac{3}{2} \times \frac{1}{2} = \frac{729}{512}\\
&\quad\vdots
\end{aligned}
$$

What does this naming convention as C, G, D, A, ..., mean? This is simply because the resultant scale becomes A, B, C, D, E, ... So, the introduction by 3/2 times frequency first, and the names are the hindsight.

We have invented the first five tones, only by 3/2 and 1/2. This five tones are quite common in the world, called *pentatonic*, and are known to be sufficient for us to sing simple songs. Actually, almost in the same era of Pythagoras, Jing Fang (BC78–BC37) of ancient China found that the two-thirds length of a bamboo pipe made a consonant sound. This is exactly the same as G. After the bamboo was cut to 2/3, he spliced 1/4 onto the 2/3, that is $2/3 \times 4/3$ of the original length, to invent a new note. This method is called *sanfen sunyi-fa*[1] though the procedure is in principle the same as that of Pythagoras.

Pythagoras continued the process from the original C by $3/2 \times (1/2)^*$. Now the fraction is $3^m/2^n$, and thus let us disregard the difference by 2^n and pay attention only to 3^m. Now the pitch classes are introduced as follows.

$$
\begin{array}{ll}
\text{C}: & 3^0 = 1 \\
\text{G}: & 3^1 \equiv 3/2\ (< 2) \\
\text{D}: & 3^2 \equiv 3^2/2^3 = 9/8 \\
\text{A}: & 3^3 \equiv 3^3/2^4 = 27/16 \\
\text{E}: & 3^4 \equiv 3^4/2^6 = 81/64 \\
\text{B}: & 3^5 \equiv 3^5/2^7 = 243/128 \\
\text{F}\sharp: & 3^6 \equiv 3^6/2^9 = 729/512 \\
\text{C}\sharp: & 3^7 \equiv 3^7/2^* \\
\text{G}\sharp: & 3^8 \equiv 3^8/2^* \\
\text{D}\sharp: & 3^9 \equiv 3^9/2^* \\
\text{A}\sharp: & 3^{10} \equiv 3^{10}/2^* \\
\text{F}: & 3^{11} \equiv 3^{11}/2^*
\end{array}
$$

When Pythagoras invented the 12th tone, namely he made the note of $3^{12}/2^*$ (again, $*$ is some appropriate number to make $1 < 3^{12}/2^* < 2$) from the base C, the resultant frequency becomes

$$1 \times 3^{12} \times \left(\frac{1}{2}\right)^{18} = \frac{531{,}441}{262{,}144} = 2.0278652954101562\ldots.$$

This value slightly exceeds 2, however, is a good approximation of 2. If we continue the process of $(3/2)^n \times (1/2)^*$, we never meet the exact 2 because 3 is prime to 2. In addition, our human auditory sensor cannot notice such a subtle difference. Thus, Pythagoras found our first compromising scale, that is, to regard the 12th note as the same pitch class as the original C, and thus the scale includes 12 notes in an octave.

Let us remind that the note with double frequency harmonizes very well with the original note, and thus we have given the same name on them as one common pitch

[1] *sanfen* means a division by three and *sunyi* means loss and gain. The final *fa* means 'method'.

class. Then, we are reconciled to name the slightly different notes the same pitch class according to Pythagoras.

Later, however, we encounter the various inconvenience by this subtle approximation of $2 \approx 2.027865\ldots$. This difference causes recognizable dissonance in some occasions. This 12th note is slightly higher than the double frequency, and we name this difference of ratio, 2.027865 versus 2, as **Pythagoras comma**.

$$\frac{531{,}441}{262{,}144 \times 2} = 1.013643265\ldots.$$

We contend again that 2 and 3 are prime to each other and $(3/2)^n \times (1/2)^*$ never becomes 2.

$$\left(\frac{3}{2}\right)^m \cdot \left(\frac{1}{2}\right)^n \neq 2$$

But, we can seek for better approximations since there are infinitely many pairs of such (k, l) as

$$\frac{3^k}{2^l} \approx 2.$$

When we have considered 12 tone scale

$$\frac{3^{12}}{2^{18}} = 2.0278652954101562\ldots,$$

but if we prefer better approximation we can employ

$$\frac{3^{53}}{2^{83}} = 2.0004180628082172345\ldots.$$

The 53rd note, obtained after 3^{53} divided by 2^{83}, becomes nearer to the double frequency, and the scale includes 52 notes in one octave. It is easily imagined that the difference of adjacent notes are far beyond human sensitivity, and such a musical instrument is unrealistic, however the piano with 53 keys in an octave was actually made. If you are not yet satisfied with this, the next better approximation is 665 keys in an octave.

2.2 Revised Pythagoras Scale

From now on, we employ only '♯' for half tone, forgetting '♭'. Pythagoras scale is constructed by the successive process of $(3/2)^n$ and occasionally the division by 2.

$$\mathrm{C} \underset{\times\frac{3}{2}}{\rightarrow} \mathrm{G} \underset{\times\frac{3}{2}}{\rightarrow} \mathrm{D} \underset{\times\frac{3}{2}}{\rightarrow} \mathrm{A} \underset{\times\frac{3}{2}}{\rightarrow} \mathrm{E} \underset{\times\frac{3}{2}}{\rightarrow} \mathrm{B} \underset{\times\frac{3}{2}}{\rightarrow} \mathrm{F}\sharp \underset{\times\frac{3}{2}}{\rightarrow} \mathrm{C}\sharp \underset{\times\frac{3}{2}}{\rightarrow} \mathrm{G}\sharp \cdots$$

Let us name F, that is the 11th member of the scale, as

$$G\sharp \underset{\times\frac{3}{2}}{\rightarrow} D\sharp \underset{\times\frac{3}{2}}{\rightarrow} A\sharp \underset{\times\frac{3}{2}}{\rightarrow} F.$$

Here if we approximate the 12th tone as C, the interval between F and the final C becomes narrow. Remember that real 3/2 note from F is beyond 2 in frequency, and is 2 plus Pythagoras comma. But, this is not preferable since F and C play important roles in a scale, and we expect that they harmonize well.

If we are to use Pythagoras scale, we should *shift* the occurrence of the comma somewhere else, not between the 11th (F) and the 12th (C), to hide the approximation to the interval less noticeable. One prevalent solution is to combine the notes until G♯ which made by $(3/2)^n$ upward and the remaining tones made downward by $(2/3)^n$ until D♯.

$$D\sharp \underset{\times\frac{2}{3}}{\leftarrow} A\sharp \underset{\times\frac{2}{3}}{\leftarrow} F \underset{\times\frac{2}{3}}{\leftarrow} C$$

Now we obtain the sequence of 12 tones, but the residual Pythagoras comma is confined between G♯ and D♯; in other words, the interval between them is less than 3/2, results in so-called the *wolf* fifth since it sounds like an unpleasant roaring voice of wolves. Why here? No rational reason; simply because it suffices many practical cases.

$$C \underset{\times\frac{3}{2}}{\rightarrow} G \underset{\times\frac{3}{2}}{\rightarrow} D \underset{\times\frac{3}{2}}{\rightarrow} A \underset{\times\frac{3}{2}}{\rightarrow} E \underset{\times\frac{3}{2}}{\rightarrow} B \underset{\times\frac{3}{2}}{\rightarrow} F\sharp \underset{\times\frac{3}{2}}{\rightarrow} C\sharp \underset{\times\frac{3}{2}}{\rightarrow} G\sharp \underset{\text{(narrow)}}{\leftrightarrow} D\sharp \underset{\times\frac{2}{3}}{\leftarrow} A\sharp \underset{\times\frac{2}{3}}{\leftarrow} F \underset{\times\frac{2}{3}}{\leftarrow} C$$

Here, we omit the half tones and show the diatonic collection by Pythagoras. Note that only F is introduced by the gimmick using the power of -1.

$$\begin{array}{cccccccc}
C & D & E & F & G & A & B & C \\
1 & (\frac{3}{2})^2 & (\frac{3}{2})^4 & (\frac{3}{2})^{-1} & \frac{3}{2} & (\frac{3}{2})^3 & (\frac{3}{2})^5 & 2 \\
 & \times\frac{1}{2} & \times(\frac{1}{2})^2 & \times 2 & & \times\frac{1}{2} & \times(\frac{1}{2})^2 & \\
 & \Downarrow & \Downarrow & \Downarrow & & \Downarrow & \Downarrow & \\
 & \frac{9}{8} & \frac{81}{64} & \frac{4}{3} & & \frac{27}{16} & \frac{243}{128} &
\end{array}$$

The completed Pythagoras scale possesses the following intervals.

$$\begin{array}{ccccccccccccccc}
C & & D & & E & & F & & G & & A & & B & & C \\
1 & & \frac{9}{8} & & \frac{81}{64} & & \frac{4}{3} & & \frac{3}{2} & & \frac{27}{16} & & \frac{243}{128} & & 2 \\
 & \times\frac{9}{8} & & \times\frac{9}{8} & & \times\frac{256}{243} & & \times\frac{9}{8} & & \times\frac{9}{8} & & \times\frac{9}{8} & & \times\frac{256}{243} &
\end{array}$$

In this scale, the half tone is not half; the whole tone is 9/8 and the half tone is 256/243, and thus,

$$\begin{cases} 9/8 = 1.125 \\ 256/243 \times 256/243 = 1.10986\ldots \end{cases}$$

implies that the whole tone is larger than two half tones.

In the above, we have considered only a diatonic collection but when we consider a chromatic collection, e.g., including C♯, D♯, and so on, there exist two different half tones. In the construction process of Pythagoras scale, C♯ appears at 7th multiple of 3/2. Then, C versus C♯ becomes $(3/2)^7 \times (1/2)^4 = 2187/2048 = 1.0679\ldots$. In the diatonic scale, B is defined by 243/256 and F is defined by 2/3, both from upper C. So the two half tones in the scale become the common value, but are narrower than the other half tones in the chromatic scale. Below, we show the intervals by half tones where $a = 2187/2048 = 1.0679\ldots$ and $b = 256/243 = 1.05349\ldots$.

$$
\begin{array}{ccccccccccccccccccccccccc}
\mathrm{C} & & \mathrm{C}\sharp & & \mathrm{D} & & \mathrm{D}\sharp & & \mathrm{E} & & \mathrm{F} & & \mathrm{F}\sharp & & \mathrm{G} & & \mathrm{G}\sharp & & \mathrm{A} & & \mathrm{A}\sharp & & \mathrm{B} & & \mathrm{C} \\
& \times a & & \times b & & \times b & & \times a & & \times b & & \times a & & \times b & & \times a & & \times b & & \times b & & \times a & & \times a &
\end{array}
$$

2.3 Just Intonation—Introduction of 5

Pythagoras scale was made only from two prime numbers 2 and 3, since the sound waves harmonize well and the ratio of frequency becomes simple. The next small integer 4 is not a prime but a multiple of 2, that is already included in Pythagoras scale. The next prime integer is 5. Let us consider introducing 5, which would make us feel also harmonic.

We should notice that

$$
\left(\frac{3}{2}\right)^4 = \frac{81}{16} = 5.0625 \simeq 5.
$$

Then, let us replace $(3/2)^4$ with 5, when it appears in Pythagoras scale below

$$
\begin{array}{cccccccc}
\mathrm{C} & \mathrm{D} & \mathrm{E} & \mathrm{F} & \mathrm{G} & \mathrm{A} & \mathrm{B} & \mathrm{C} \\
1 & \frac{3^2}{2^3} & \frac{3^4}{2^6} & \frac{4}{3} & \frac{3}{2} & \frac{3^3}{2^4} & \frac{3^5}{2^7} & 2
\end{array}
$$

and thus we obtain the following.

$$
\begin{array}{cccccccc}
\mathrm{C} & \mathrm{D} & \mathrm{E} & \mathrm{F} & \mathrm{G} & \mathrm{A} & \mathrm{B} & \mathrm{C} \\
1 & \frac{9}{8} & \frac{3^4}{2^4}\cdot\frac{1}{2^2} & \frac{4}{3} & \frac{3}{2} & \frac{3^4}{2^4}\cdot\frac{1}{3} & \frac{3^4}{2^4}\cdot\frac{3}{2^3} & 2 \\
 & & \Downarrow & & & \Downarrow & \Downarrow & \\
 & & 5\cdot\frac{1}{2^2} & & & 5\cdot\frac{1}{3} & 5\cdot\frac{3}{2^3} & \\
 & & \| & & & \| & \| & \\
 & & \frac{5}{4} & & & \frac{5}{3} & \frac{15}{8} &
\end{array}
$$

Let us calculate the ratios between each adjacent tones.

$$\begin{array}{ccccccccccccccc} C & & D & & E & & F & & G & & A & & B & & C \\ 1 & & \frac{9}{8} & & \frac{5}{4} & & \frac{4}{3} & & \frac{3}{2} & & \frac{5}{3} & & \frac{15}{8} & & 2 \\ & \times\frac{9}{8} & & \times\frac{10}{9} & & \times\frac{16}{15} & & \times\frac{9}{8} & & \times\frac{10}{9} & & \times\frac{9}{8} & & \times\frac{16}{15} & \end{array}$$

The new scale possesses very simple ratios between notes as follows, keeping the ratio of octave as 1:2.

C:E = 4:5, E:G = 5:6, F:G = 3:4, C:G = 2:3, C:A = 3:5

Every combination of two tones in this scale sounds quite consonant. This new scale is called **Just Intonation**.

The ratio of the triad of major third, e.g., CEG that is I of C major, becomes 4:5:6. The second inversion in the order of GCE becomes 3:4:5, meaning the sharper resonance than the non-inverted form, since it consists of smaller integers. The triad of minor third becomes 10:12:15.

Such scales that include the ratio 4:5 were already proposed by Didymus in the first century B.C. and by Ptolemios in the second century A.D. [1]. Comparing the ratio of C/E, between 64:81 in Pythagoras scale and 4:5 in just intonation, we call the difference

$$\frac{81}{64}/\frac{5}{4} = \frac{81}{80}$$

Syntonic comma. Also, we call the ratio between syntonic comma and Pythagoras comma, that is (53,141:524,288)/(81:80), *schisma*.

In compensation for this beautiful harmonization of just intonation, it owes the following defects.

- There exist two different whole tones: 9/8 and 10/9.
- The two half tones do not become either of the two kinds of whole tone, as $(16/15) \times (16/15) = 256/225$. Each of the above two whole tones is smaller than the two half tones, as

$$10/9 = 1.111\cdots \; < \; 9/8 = 1.125 \; < \; 256/225 = 1.13777\cdots.$$

So far, we have talked about the diatonic collection of just intonation, however, if we need to add half tones to the scale we need to consider various choices.

2.4 Eitz's Notation

In order to represent a temperament graphically, we employ Eitz's notation that consists of triangles, the nodes of which are notes; the bottom line of the triangle is the perfect 5th, the upper right diagonal is the major third, and the upper left diagonal is the minor third (Fig. 2.2).

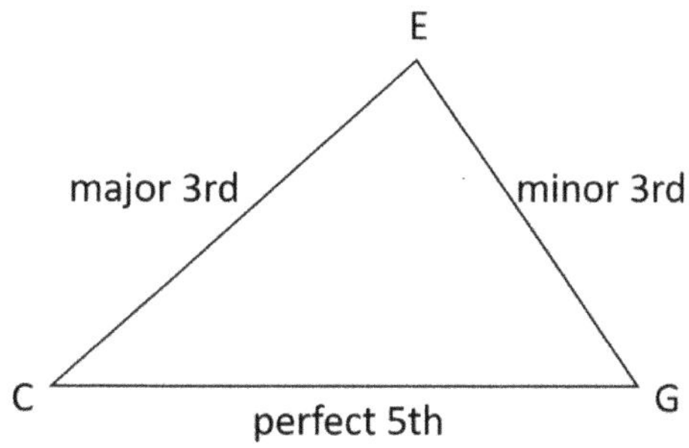

Fig. 2.2 Eitz's notation

In this notation, each pitch is that of Pythagoras temperament, but is corrected by the number of syntonic commas shown at the pitch name's upper right. For example, E of just intonation is $(81/80)^{-1}$ of that of Pythagoras, and thus we write E^{-1}. Below is the case of the major scale of just intonation.

$$\begin{array}{cccccccc} & A^{-1} & & E^{-1} & & B^{-1} & \\ F^0 & & C^0 & & G^0 & & D^0 \end{array}$$

In order to adjust the pitch of chromatic half tones in just intonation, which do not appear in its diatonic collection, many famous scientists proposed various ideas to realize more comfortable harmony, e.g., Johannes Kepler, astronomer who studied the movement of planets (1571–1630), Marin Mersenne, known by Mersenne prime number (1588–1648), Leonhard Euler, the mathematician (1707–1783), Jean-Jaques Rousseau, philosopher as well as composer (1712–1778). Furthermore, of course, many musicologists, like Alexander Malcolm (1685–1763), Friedrich Wilhelm Marpurg (1717–1795), Johan Phillip Kirnberger (1721–1783), and so on, have contributed to this issue.

Another graphic representation concerning only harmonic overtones by 3 and 5 is called Euler lattice; the horizontal row of which represents overtones by 3 (i.e., perfect 5th in just intonation) and the vertical column that by 5 (major third in just intonation). Since Pythagoras scale does not employ the prime of 5, only one horizontal line by 5^0 appears. As for just intonation, we employ $(5^0, 3^2)$ for D instead of $(5^1, 3^{-2})$ by definition of the temperament while we do $(5^1, 3^0)$ for E.

	3^{-3}	3^{-2}	3^{-1}	1	3	3^2	3^3
5^2	B	F♯	C♯	G♯	D♯	A♯	E♯
5^1	G	D	A	E	B	F♯	C♯
$5^0 = 1$	E♭	B♭	F	C	G	D	A
5^{-1}	C♭	G♭	D♭	A♭	E♭	B♭	F
5^{-2}	A♭♭	E♭♭	B♭♭	F♭	C♭	G♭	D♭

In this diagram, a cadence is considered to be a shift from right to left.

A^-	E^-	B^-	$F\sharp^-$	$C\sharp$	$G\sharp$	$D\sharp$
F^-	C^-	G^-	D^-	A	E	B
$D\flat^-$	$A\flat^-$	$E\flat -$	$B\flat^-$	F	C	G
$B\flat\flat^-$	$F\flat^-$	$C\flat^-$	$G\flat^-$	$D\flat$	$A\flat$	$E\flat$

2.5 What Is Overtone?

Thus far, we have considered the harmonic overtone with the three primes of 2, 3, and 5. Here, tentatively let us introduce a multiple by 7, named as B♭. Then, we obtain a consonant set of B♭:C = 7:4 = 1.75, C:E:G:B♭ = 4:5:6:7. However, A♯ in just intonation (later, we regard $B^\flat$ and $A^\sharp$ are one and the same in equal temperament), B♭:C = 16/9 = 1.777 ... becomes unstable, and the chord strongly requires the solution to tonic. Overtones by 8 ($= 2^3$), 9 ($= 3^2$), 10 ($= 2 \cdot 5$) are represented by multiples with primes of 2, 3, and 5. Therefore, overtones by $2^n \cdot 3^m$ have corresponding pitch classes both in Pythagoras scale and just intonation, and overtones by 5 appear only in just intonation. The following table further includes the overtones by 11 and 13.

Multiple by	
2	Octave higher C
3	Octave higher G in Pythagoras scale and just intonation
4	2 octaves higher C
5	2 octaves higher E in just intonation
6	3 octaves higher G in Pythagoras scale and just intonation
7	Near to 2 octaves higher A♯ in just intonation
8	3 octaves higher C in Pythagoras scale and just intonation
9	3 octaves higher D in Pythagoras scale and just intonation
10	3 octaves higher E in just intonation
11	Near to 3 octaves higher F♯
12	3 octaves higher C in Pythagoras scale and just intonation
13	Near to 3 octaves higher A
14	Octave higher the overtone by 7
15	3 octaves higher B
16	4 octaves higher C

The overtone by 11 is by definition $11/2^3 = 1.375$ when placed in one octave (divided by 2). The nearest pitch in Pythagoras scale, F♯ is $3^6/2^9 = 1.4238\ldots$ while $64/45 = 1.4222\ldots$ in just intonation. The overtone by 13 is by definition $13/2^3 = 1.625$. The nearest pitch A in Pythagoras scale is $3^3/2^4 = 1.6875$ while $5/3 = 1.6666\ldots$ in just intonation.

2.6 Meantone

Pythagoras scale started with the overtone by 3, and thus C:G = 2:3. Just intonation, in addition, included 5, by which we have obtained a harmony of C:E = 4:5. The construction of Pythagoras scale was simple; we have only employed 2 and 3, without 5. On the other hand, we cannot modulate pieces, that is, cannot change keys in just intonation because each interval in the scale is not even. The reconciliation between the two scales was found in the following **meantone**, which sacrifices C:G = 2:3, to save C:E = 4:5.

The note E in Pythagoras scale appears at the 4th 3/2, viz., the pitch from C is $(3/2)^4 \times (1/2)^*$. Since

$$\left(\frac{3}{2}\right)^4 \cdot \left(\frac{1}{2}\right)^2 = \frac{5}{4} \cdot \frac{81}{80},$$

E in Pythagoras scale is higher by one syntonic comma (81/80) than our target 5/4. Then, for each 3/2, if we lower 1/4 of a syntonic comma (i.e., to multiply the inverse of the fourth root of the syntonic comma), we obtain 5/4 after we have multiplied it 4 times. Let new G in meantone be

$$\frac{3}{2} \times \sqrt[4]{\frac{80}{81}}.$$

Then, we obtain new E as

$$\left(\frac{3}{2} \times \sqrt[4]{\frac{80}{81}}\right)^4 = \left(\frac{3}{2}\right)^4 \times \frac{80}{81} = \frac{5}{4} \times 2^*.$$

Or, it may be easier for us to think conversely; let the ratio of new G versus C be variable x. We obtain our target E, 5/4, by

$$x^4 \times \frac{1}{2^2} = \frac{5}{4},$$

that is, $x^4 = 5$. Thus,

$$x = 5^{\frac{1}{4}} = \sqrt[4]{5} \left(= \frac{3}{2} \times \sqrt[4]{\frac{80}{81}}\right) = 1.4953487\ldots$$

Fortunately, this value is not very different from 3/2 = 1.5.

Next, let us calculate the ratio of the two adjacent whole tones in meantone. If we divide C:D:E evenly, 1:($\sqrt{5}/2$):5/4. Then, we apply the same ratio to the sequence of F:G:A:B, namely, each interval becomes 1:$\sqrt{5}/2$. We need yet to fill two half tones in octave. Let y be the ratio of the half tone, then five whole tones and two half tones compose an octave, as

$$\left(\frac{\sqrt{5}}{2}\right)^5 \cdot y^2 = 2.$$

Therefore, $y = 8/5^{\frac{5}{4}}$. As a result, the meantone becomes as follows.

C	D	E	F	G	A	B	C
1	$\frac{\sqrt{5}}{2}$	$\frac{5}{4}$	$\frac{2}{5^{\frac{1}{4}}}$	$5^{\frac{1}{4}}$	$\frac{5^{\frac{3}{4}}}{2}$	$\frac{5^{\frac{5}{4}}}{4}$	2

The below is Eitz's notation of meantone. Note that the new G is $G^{-\frac{1}{4}}$ and E is the same E^{-1} as just intonation.

$$\begin{array}{ccccccccc} & E^{-1} & & B^{-\frac{5}{4}} & & & & & \\ C^{0} & & G^{-\frac{1}{4}} & & D^{-\frac{1}{2}} & & A^{-\frac{3}{4}} & & E^{-1} \\ & & & & & F^{+\frac{1}{4}} & & C^{0} & \end{array}$$

In meantone, especially, the 5th is not beautiful. From sixteenth century to eighteenth, again various musicologists proposed different compromising plans, considering the probable key shifts and at the same time avoiding the distortion in harmony, as Andreas Werckmeister (1645–1706), Johann Georg Neidhardt (1685–1739), Thomas Young (1773–1829), known by coherence of light, Francesca Antonio Vallotti (1697–1780), and so on [1]. Of course, there could not be a versatile solution. Whether a given scale is admissible depends on the function of musical instruments and human cognition.

2.7 Issue on Modulation

Now, let us turn our interest to the importance of **modulation**. It is a key change, for example, from C major to A minor or to G major, to change ambiences in the midst of music. Consider you play a melody beginning from C, and at some time later you'd like to repeat the same melody beginning from G. Then the initial sequence of C–D–E–F–$\cdots$ must be shifted in parallel to G–A–B–C–$\cdots$. Here, we notice our requirement; the interval from C to D must be identical to that from G to A, so as D to E be A to B, and so on.

The keyboard instrument consists of fixed keys where each key is tuned beforehand and its pitch cannot be changed. As we have seen, just intonation provides us very harmonized chords, however, the interval of C and D (9/8) is different from that of D and E (10/9); then, the melody begins from C cannot be transposed to a parallel one from D. In just intonation, if we try to modulate a melody, each interval of the melody needs to be changed. Otherwise, the melody would be distorted as well as the accompanied chords.

When we use half tones, the situation is far worse. As we have already shown, the half tone of just intonation is 16/15, and this is not the half of either of two kinds of whole tones, that are 9/8 or 10/9. Therefore, C♯ and D♭ become

$$\begin{aligned} C\sharp &= \tfrac{16}{15} = 1.067\ldots \\ D\flat &= \tfrac{9}{8} \times \tfrac{15}{16} = 1.054\ldots \end{aligned}$$

So that we cannot use one black key between C and D on the keyboard. The situation is the same between D and E as follows.

$$\begin{aligned} D\sharp &= \tfrac{9}{8} \times \tfrac{16}{15} = 1.2\ldots \\ E\flat &= \tfrac{9}{8} \times \tfrac{10}{9} \times \tfrac{15}{16} = 1.172\ldots \end{aligned}$$

How about employing the meantone? Then, we can ensure that the intervals between all the whole tones are the same, however yet, its half tone is not the half of the whole tone. That is, even though a black key between two white keys is tuned to just half between the white keys, it is still different from the existing half tones on white keys, that appear between E/F and B/C.

2.8 Equal Temperament

All the discussed above has been a prelude toward equal temperament. From now on, we introduce a temperament which has abandoned every pure harmonization. Instead, the temperament is quite versatile in modulation, where all the whole tones are the same interval and the half tone is exactly the half of a whole tone, as follows.

$$Do \underbrace{\ -\ }_{\text{whole}} Re \underbrace{\ -\ }_{\text{whole}} Mi \underbrace{\ -\ }_{\text{half}} Fa \underbrace{\ -\ }_{\text{whole}} Sol \underbrace{\ -\ }_{\text{whole}} La \underbrace{\ -\ }_{\text{whole}} Ti \underbrace{\ -\ }_{\text{half}} Do.$$

In Fig. 2.3, we show that the diatonic scale of C major marked by black circles can be easily shifted to D major marked by white circles, because of the uniform and impartial intervals in keys.

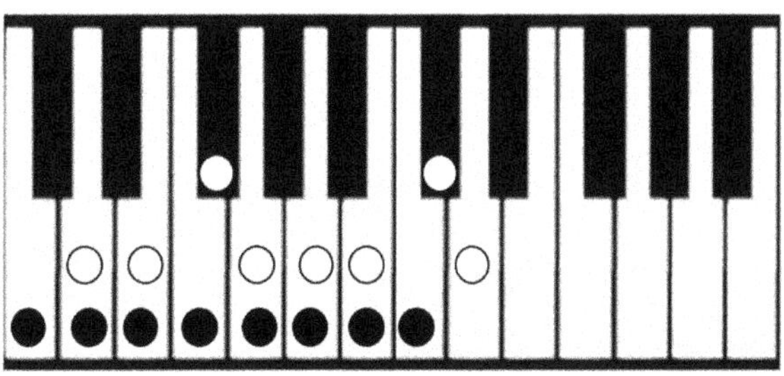

Fig. 2.3 C major (black circle) and D major (white circle)

Here, we recapitulate the significance of equal temperament. The temperament sacrifices the harmony made by the simple ratio of wave frequency but eases modulation; actually, worldwide music have been mapped onto this scale and we nowadays entertain its prevalence.

Solving $x^{12} = 2$

According to the tradition, an octave consists of five whole tones and two half tones, and if the half is the exact half of the whole tone, we need to divide one octave by 12 half tones (5 whole tones $\times$ 2 + 2 half tones). If we assume all the intervals are the same, the ratio of the frequency of two half notes must be $\sqrt[12]{2}$ since $(\sqrt[12]{2})^{12}$ becomes the ratio of octave, that is 2.

The next question is how *impure* the harmonies are in equal temperament in comparison to other temperaments. The following numerical evaluation may help us to understand the situation.

	Just intonation	Equal temperament
C:E	$5/4 = 1.25$	$\sqrt[12]{2^4} = 1.2599$
C:F	$4/3 = 1.333$	$\sqrt[12]{2^5} = 1.3348$
C:G	$3/2 = 1.5$	$\sqrt[12]{2^7} = 1.4983$
C:A	$5/3 = 1.667$	$\sqrt[12]{2^9} = 1.6818$

In order to clarify the difference in temperaments furthermore, let us introduce **cent**, introduced by Alexander J. Ellis (1814–1890). Let one octave be 1200 cents, where the whole tone and the half tone in equal temperament are 200 cents and 100 cents, respectively. Then, we obtain the following table.

	C/D	D/E	E/F	F/G	G/A	A/B	B/C
Equal temperament	200	200	100	200	200	200	100
Meantone	193	193	117	193	193	193	117
Just intonation	204	182	112	204	182	204	112
Pythagoras scale	204	204	90	204	204	204	90

Then, we add up the above ratios to show the height of each pitch, as below.

	C	D	E	F	G	A	B	C
Equal temperament	0	200	400	500	700	900	1100	1200
Meantone	0	193	386	503	697	890	1083	1200
Just intonation	0	204	386	498	702	884	1088	1200
Pythagoras scale	0	204	408	498	702	906	1110	1200

Influence of Equal Temperament

Now, let us remember our original question placed at the beginning of this chapter; why the black keys and the white keys are arranged as such on the piano? In order to answer this, we have considered Pythagorean 12 tones, harmonization of two tones, feasibility of modulation, and so on, and we have reached equal temperament.

The physical width of keys and the physical height of black keys of a keyboard instrument must have been standardized after trial and error, being the average lengths of human fingers considered. The colors of black and white were not obligatory. In seventeenth century, the colors of keys on the harpsichord were in the reverse between black and white, but it was said to be unfavorable by performers.

By the way, the five-line stave of the score to this day reflects the historical convention of intonation. The music score is a blueprint for us to render audible music, and to specify the temporal order of notes to be played. Conceivably, five or any number of lines may have represented different strings on an instrument, and a blob on a string had specified a timing to pick it. Such blobs had been arranged according to a time line so that the temporal duration of a note may have been represented by a spatial (horizontal) interval to the next blob, though later note notations with different duration, instead of blobs, were invented to save vacant spaces. Once upon a time, someone introduced an intermediate pitch between two lines (strings) to enrich music. Since the pitch of each line was already fixed, composers needed to write a blob between lines. Those lines and spaces represent different pitches in accordance with the difference of temperament, and thus, strictly speaking, we need to add the temperament information on the staves; but nowadays it is of equal temperament by default, and has overwritten the various obsolete pitches. Even after we obtained the equal temperament, we have been forced to use the five-line stave where the lines and the spaces are not homogeneous. How long should we need to endure this inconvenience?

Also, this is another issue of 12 tone equal temperament. Nowadays, every popular music is composed only by this temperament. So far so good, however, every other scales of ethnic music in the world is well mapped onto the equal temperament. This affair may be advantageous as we can easily introduce world music on our current instruments, but at the same time we should notice that this versatility of equal temperament absorbs the subtle difference of pitches on the original scale and would expel the existing diversity.

Clock Dial and Spiral

First, we give an easy visualization to understand the 12-tone equal temperament by a clock dial, on which 12 numbers are arranged with equal intervals. Since an octave consists of 12 tones, an interval between two half notes is shown by $360° \div 12 = 30°$. If we consider the position of the noon as C and the duration of one hour as the ratio of half tone, we can arrange each note on the clock dial as in Fig. 2.4.

In this clock dial, the frequency of the higher C, after making one round, obtains the twice of that of the original C. What is the meaning of 30° by one half tone, in other words, what is the gain in frequency by 30°? By simple comparison, 360°:30° = 2:x so that $x = 1/6$.

- Then, C♯ becomes 1/6 of the original? If so, the pitch is far reduced!

Fig. 2.4 12-tone clock

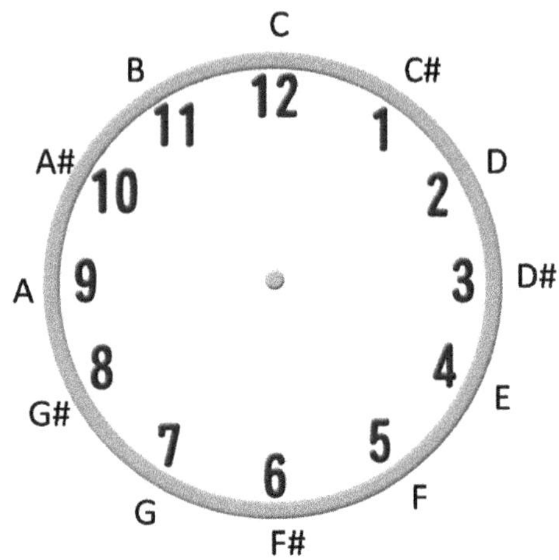

- Then, C♯ has gained extra 1/6; the frequency becomes $(1 + 1/6)$ times of C? If so, D♯ gained extra 3/6, meaning 1.5 times higher frequency from C only by three half tones!

Of course, the above are wrong. Clock dial is shown by *addition* of half tones, as half + half = whole tone. But, the ratio works by *multiplication*, as pitch × ratio = new pitch. So that 360:30 = 2:1/6 does not mean anything; the left-hand side is the ratio by the addition and the right-hand side is that of the multiplication. The correct statements are, since 360:30 = 12:1,

- C♯ has gained extra 1/12, that is, the frequency is $(1 + 1/12)$ times of C.
- The higher C has gained extra 12/12, that is the frequency is $1 + 12/12 = 2$ times of the original C.

Now, let us improve the clock dial and visualize the pitch height, employing a spiral. Prepare a cylinder and imagine we roll a paper of a triangle with a right angle onto it, where the length of the bottom edge of the triangle is identical to the circumference of the cylinder. One roll of a triangle represents that the pitch is raised by one octave (Fig. 2.5). If we continue to roll the same triangles successively, each from the height of the last triangle, every C comes to the same vertical line; so does C♯, D, D♯, and so on. This is the notion of pitch class, by which all the C's with different pitches are one and the same category. In that figure, if we roll the triangle by 30° degree counter-clockwise, the pitch becomes higher by a half tone, that gains 100 cents and the frequency becomes $(1 + \sqrt[12]{2})$ times larger. Thus, one roll results in 360°, 1200 cents, and twice the height.

Please note that the height on the surface of the cylinder is not the frequency itself. The sequence of frequency becomes a geometric progression, since for each step by half tone, the frequency is multiplied by $\sqrt[12]{2}$. However, in our case, the diagonal

Fig. 2.5 Spiral of 12-tone

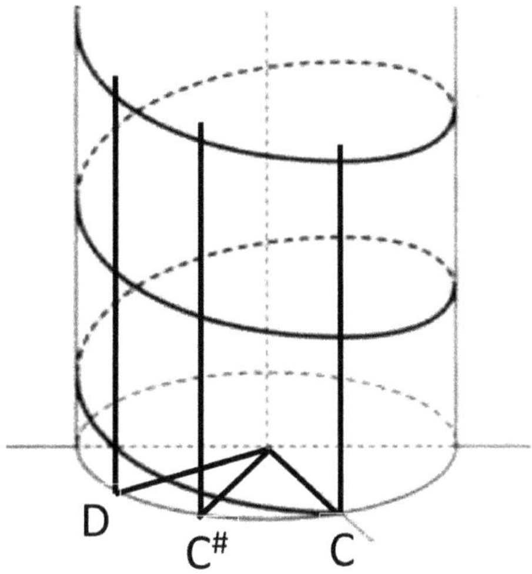

edge of the right triangle is linear.[2] Therefore, this linear climbing on the cylinder means the constant ratio, retrieved by logarithm.

$$\log \sqrt[12]{2} = \frac{1}{12} \log 2$$

This log 2 is the coefficient of the linear progression, that is the translation of multiplication by $\sqrt[12]{2}$. In our daily cognition, we don't need to care about the frequency. Thus, we are not conscious of logarithm. We only need to comparef pitch heights by steps, that is by the number of whole tones and half tones, as addition and subtraction.

2.9 Scale, Mode, and Key

We have talked about temperament which restricts each pitch of notes in a scale, that is employed for composing a certain piece of music. The *diatonic collection* is a set of notes in a scale; on the contrary, a scale is a collection of diatonic notes, put in order by pitch from the lower tone to the higher. However, there had been another manner to employ a scale when composing music.

Given a diatonic scale, this manner concerns the selection of *finalis* (currently became tonic), that is the final note of the music. Until sixteenth century, four *Gregorian modes* became prevalent, where the finalis was chosen among D, E, F, and G, each of which is called Dorian, Phrygian, Lydian, and Mixolydian, respectively.

[2] If we depict the absolute pitch by frequency, the height becomes $A(\sqrt[12]{2})^n$ for the nth pitch from some base pitch A; thus, the diagonal edge of the triangle becomes exponential.

Thus, the mode is a variety on the sequence of whole tones and half tones, to regulate the melody which are supposed to end up by a finalis. Gregorian modes were used in two ways according to *ambitus* (pitch register); one was to use the notes fully up to octave from the finalis, called *authenticus*, and the other was to use the notes up to 5th and down to 3rd from the finalis, called *plagalis*, though in both cases the register was confined in one octave. Later in the sixteenth century, there added two other modes; Aeolian beginning from A and Ionian from C. After then, since the instruments were improved and music became complicated, the register exceeded one octave, and thus, the distinction of authenticus and plagalis became meaningless. Thereafter, several modes had died away, either because they included quite dissonant intervals like the augmented 4th from finalis or because the 7th note was the whole tone from the finalis and was amended to half tone as subtonic (leading tone). As a result, Ionian and Aeolian have survived; nowadays the former is called a major scale and the latter a minor scale.

Music by mode was revived by Miles Davis in 1950s who tried to escape from those music fully regulated by the chord sequence, to make the most of melody.

2.10 History of 12-Tone Equal Temperament

Let us further get back to the old era. *Gregorian chant* appeared in the ninth century in the middle ages in Europe. The music was not accompanied by instruments and thus *monotonic*. Later, counter-melody began to be employed, called *organum*, and the music becomes *polyphonic*.

In the Gothic age of ca. the twelfth–thirteenth century, professional composers in Nôtre Dame school appeared and their masterpieces were left in various *neumatic* notation. In the fourteenth century, composing techniques were summarized as *Ars Nova*, and there appeared an extinguished composer Guillaume de Machaut (ca 1300–1377). In Renaissance era, Josquin Des Prez (1450/55–1521) in the Flanders school won the fame, and Palestrina (1525–1594) in later Renaissance, Claudio Monteverdi (1567–1643) in the Venetian school, and so on, contributed to the development of music.

The prime objective to pray in the church is to transmit the words in the holy script to the God, and music was its medium. Therefore, the music in Europe has developed together with language, at that time, Latin. However, after the invention of typographic printing by Johannes Gutenberg (1400–1468), the holy bibles were translated into German and began to be read widely. Until the sixteenth century, the center of music had been Italy where Baroque music bloomed, however, there occurred the culture of music also in Germany; Heinrich Schuütz (1585–1672) had written a mass in German.

In the end of Baroque era, Jean-Philippe Rameau (1683–1764) summarized the systematic theory of chords and tonality. Then, the music style was destined to shift from polyphony to *homophony*, where a melody line is supported by a sequence of harmonic chords. At this age, Johann Sebastian Bach (1685–1750) had written two volumes of '24 preludes and fugues for well-tempered clavier' which consists of all 12 major and 12 minor keys.[3] The theme of the 24th fugue, B minor, of volume II consists of all the 12 notes.[4] After these masterpieces, such composers as Chopin, Buzoni, Rachmaninov, Scriabin, Shostakovich, and so on, composed a series of pieces which consists of 24 keys, paying homage to J. S. Bach.

After J. S. Bach, Baroque music ended and after a while many famous classical composers had appeared successively; first, Vienna classicist (Haydn, Mozart, Beethoven), early romanticist (Schubert, Schumann), followed by late romanticist (Wagner, Brahms, Mahler). By the beginning of the twentieth century, almost all known classical composers emerged only within 150 years. What triggered this sudden emergence of many talents and achievements? One of the most convincing answers must be the completion of 12-tone equal temperament followed by the completion of keyboard instrument.

The music after this era was, in a sense, devoted to the effort to escape from equal temperament. Claude Debussy (1862–1918) proposed a scale dividing an octave by seven whole tones. This scale scarcely suggests concrete tonality; we cannot expect the succeeding progression of melody and feel left in a vague atmosphere. Bartók Béla (1881–1945) collected the melodies of the middle Europe (Hungary, Slovakia, Romania), which were basically pentatonic though with slightly different pitches, and rearranged them in the framework of Western tonal music which produced a unique lyricism with a new kind of vigor. Igor Stravinsky (1882–1971) introduced multiple tonality with irregular beat, and the style was called *primitivism*.

Vienna was the center of classical music, where Arnold Schoenberg[5] (1874–1951) was born earlier than Bartók and survived longer. He first composed very romantic music like *Verklärtnacht* or *Gurrelieder*, then followed by atonal era, and thereafter, he tried to maximize the impartiality of 12 tones. He invented *Dodecaphony* (12-tone music) where a main theme consists of all the 12 tones, each of which appears only once. This theme is inverted, retrogrades, or is inverted and retrogrades in a piece. He formed the new Vienna school together with two gifted disciples of Alban Berg (1885–1935) and Anton Webern (1883–1945), who greatly influenced the later composers.

Schoenberg said that people would whistle music by 12-tone music in the twenty-first century, but his expectation has never been fulfilled. Why must he deny tonality so harshly? In Arnold Schoenberg Center in Vienna, his word is shown, saying "As long as we take a compromising way, we never reach Rome."[6] After Schoenberg, Webern proposed *total serialism*, that gives other norms on 12-tone theme, succeeded by *musique sérielle* by Pierre Boulez (1925–2016). After this, has music still evolved?

---

[3] Nowadays, it is known that this 'well-tempered' does not necessarily mean equal temperament. Some musicologists say the well-temperament is a kind of revision of meantone.

[4] J. S. Bach also composed *Musikalischesopfer* (The Musical Offering), where again the theme to Friedrich II includes all the 12 notes except for B♭. This piece is in C minor, and thus B should accompany ♭, but why, here ♮ is attached.

[5] Originally Schönberg, but after he moved to USA he had changed his name in English spelling.

[6] "Der Mittelweg ist der einzige Weg, der nicht nach Rom führt."

2.11 Symmetry

Equal temperament is a result of effort to treat 12 notes in an octave equivalently. The easiest way to grasp this equivalence is to consider the symmetry.

Interval

By convention, the interval between the identical two notes is defined to be the 1st *degree*, not zero. The most conspicuous feature of equal temperament is the augmented nth is equal to the diminished $n + 1$st. For example, the augmented 4th is equal to the diminished 5th, that is *tritone*. However, of course, the augmented 4th and the diminished 5th have different meanings. The former is the 4th but by some reason an extra half tone is added. Also, the latter is the 5th but is reduced by a half tone. In other temperaments, for example, the augmented 2nd may have different pitch from the diminished 3rd.

In pitch classes, we disregard the difference of octaves. Thus, if the addition of two intervals is 9th degree, we regard the two intervals exchangeable. The following table shows the symmetric pairs of intervals.

Perfect 4th	⇔	Perfect 5th
Major 2nd	⇔	Minor 7th
Major 3rd	⇔	Minor 6th
Augmented 2nd	⇔	Diminished 7th
Augmented 3rd	⇔	Diminished 6th

In 12-tone equal temperament, a major 3rd plus a minor 3rd makes the perfect 5th and three major 3rd or four minor 3rd makes an octave, Then, we can arrange 12 pitch classes on the torus as in Fig. 2.6.

Group Theory

Symmetry is characterized by group theory. Let us consider several operations on a figure. An equilateral triangle is identical for the rotation by 120° and 240° as well as 0° = 360° while an isosceles is only by 0°. However, both triangles are axially

Fig. 2.6 12-tone torus

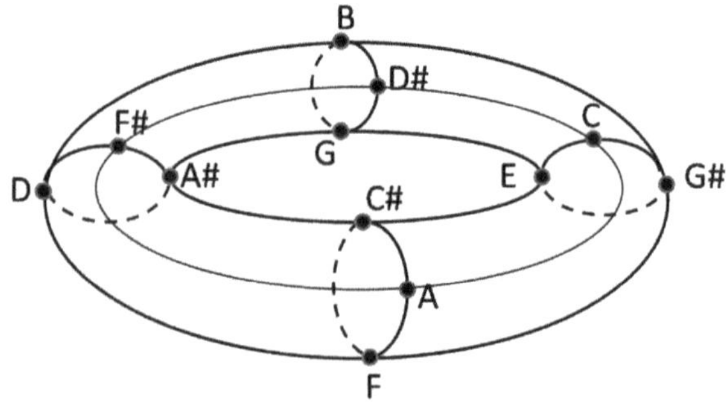

symmetric, that is, the reversed figure becomes the same. Now, let us define a set of such operations as rotation or reversion.

Here, we give the definition of group.

1. Operations in a set are *closed*, that is, a concatenation '$\circ$' of two operations belongs to the same group.
2. Operations are *associative*. Given three operations σ, τ, and υ, $(\sigma \circ \tau) \circ \upsilon = \sigma \circ (\tau \circ \upsilon)$. Then, the set is called semigroup.
3. When the semigroup includes an operation preserving identity, it is called a *monoid*.
4. For each operation in the monoid, if there exists an inverse operation, the set is a group.

The concept of group is introduced by Évalist Galois (1811–1832), after Abel–Ruffini Theorem claiming that the quintic equation with rational coefficients does not have a general solution, in terms of the radicals.

For example, the inversion of triad is a group. Let ρ be an operator for a chord c; then $\rho(c)$ is the first inversion, $\rho^2(c)$ is the second inversion, and $\rho^3(c) = c$. Let σ and τ be the inversion and the retrograde of a série of 12-tone music. Then, $\{e, \sigma, \tau, \sigma\tau\}$ is a group. Given a série s, $\sigma^2(s) = s$, $\tau^2(s) = s$, $\sigma\tau(s) = \tau\sigma(s)$, and so on.

Cyclic Group of Equal Temperament

Let an operation to raise by a half tone be ρ. Given C, all the other notes are generated as follows.

$$\begin{array}{llllll}
e(\mathrm{C}) & = \mathrm{C} & \rho(\mathrm{C}) & = \mathrm{C}\sharp & \rho^2(\mathrm{C}) & = \mathrm{D} \\
\rho^3(\mathrm{C}) & = \mathrm{D}\sharp & \rho^4(\mathrm{C}) & = \mathrm{E} & \rho^5(\mathrm{C}) & = \mathrm{F} \\
\rho^6(\mathrm{C}) & = \mathrm{F}\sharp & \rho^7(\mathrm{C}) & = \mathrm{G} & \rho^8(\mathrm{C}) & = \mathrm{G}\sharp \\
\rho^9(\mathrm{C}) & = \mathrm{A} & \rho^{10}(\mathrm{C}) & = \mathrm{A}\sharp & \rho^{11}(\mathrm{C}) & = \mathrm{B} \\
\rho^{12}(\mathrm{C}) & = \mathrm{C} & & & &
\end{array}$$

where $\rho^{12} = e$. In this way, a group generated by e and another operation ρ with its power is called *cyclic group*. Since $\rho^n = \rho\rho^{n-1}$, we can easily notice that G is 7 half tones upward from C, as well as 5 half tones downward.

$$G = \rho^7(\mathrm{C}) = \rho^{-5}(\mathrm{C}) = \mathrm{G}.$$

In general,

$$\rho^n(x) = \rho^{(n-12)}(x).$$

We can assign a bigger number than 12 on the shoulder of ρ since it can be reduced to under 12. For example, 54 times ρ implies that

$$\rho^{54}(x) = \rho^{12\times4+6}(x) = \rho^6(x),$$

namely, the result is the 6th in chromatic scale in the 4th upper octave. We employ '$\equiv$' for congruent *modulo* by 12, as follows.

$$7 \equiv -5 \pmod{12}$$
$$-3 \equiv 9 \pmod{12}$$
$$54 \equiv 6 \pmod{12}$$

Then, we can represent all the integers only by $\{0, 1, 2, 3, 4, 5, 6, 7, 8, 9, 10, 11\}$.

$$\begin{aligned} 0 &\equiv \cdots - 12, 0, 12, 24, 36, \cdots \\ 1 &\equiv \cdots - 11, 1, 13, 25, 37, \cdots \\ 2 &\equiv \cdots - 10, 2, 14, 26, 38, \cdots \\ 3 &\equiv \cdots - 9, 3, 15, 27, 39, \cdots \\ &\vdots \end{aligned}$$

We denote this number system as $\mathbf{Z}_{/12}$, that is, all the integers Z is divided by 12 and we are only concerned with their remnants, as follows

$$\mathbf{Z}_{/p} = \{0, 1, 2, \ldots, p-1\}.$$

Note that

$$\rho^a \rho^b = \rho^{a+b} = \rho^b \rho^a,$$

thus the operators ρ^a is *commutative*. A commutative group is called Abel group named after Niels Henrik Abel (1802–1829).

Note that the circle of fifths (Fig. 2.7) is a group of 12 members, generated by ρ^7; that is intrinsically the same as ρ but the order becomes

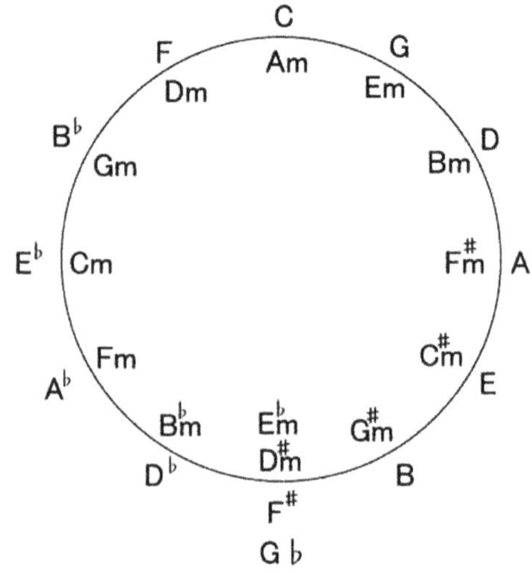

Fig. 2.7 The circle of fifths

$$e(\mathrm{C}) = \mathrm{C},\ \rho^7(\mathrm{C}) = \mathrm{G},\ \rho^{14}(\mathrm{C}) = \rho^2(\mathrm{C}) = \mathrm{D}, \ldots$$

and so on. Or, if we consider counter-clockwise circle,

$$e(\mathrm{C}) = \mathrm{C},\ \rho^{-7}(\mathrm{C}) = \rho^5(\mathrm{C}) = \mathrm{F},\ \rho^{-14}(\mathrm{C}) = \rho^{10}(\mathrm{C}) = \mathrm{B}\flat = \mathrm{A}\sharp, \ldots$$

organizes the circle of fourths. Let us define a new operator $\rho^7 = \xi$, then the sequence of

$$e, \xi, \xi^2, \xi^3, \xi^4, \xi^5, \ldots$$

is to compose the circle of fifths, that is, exactly the primitive process by Pythagoras and Jing Fang to invent a scale. On the contrary,

$$e, \xi^{-1}, \xi^{-2}, \xi^{-3}, \xi^{-4}, \xi^{-4}, \xi^{-5}, \ldots$$

renders the circle of fourths.

Our first example of intervals is now put in the relation of $\rho^m = \rho^n$ with $m + n = 12$.

Perfect 4th ($\rho^5 = \xi^{-1}$)	$\Leftrightarrow$	Perfect 5th ($\rho^7 = \xi$)
Major 2nd (ρ^2)	$\Leftrightarrow$	Minor 7th (ρ^{10})
Major 3rd (ρ^4)	$\Leftrightarrow$	Minor 6th (ρ^8)
Augmented 2nd (ρ^3)	$\Leftrightarrow$	Diminished 7th (ρ^9)
Augmented 3rd (ρ^4)	$\Leftrightarrow$	Diminished 6th (ρ^8)

References

1. D. Benson, *Music: A Mathematical Offering* (Cambridge University Press, 2007)
2. T.A. Johnson, *Foundation of Diatonic Theory* (Scarecrow Press, Inc., 2008)
3. C.L. Krumhansl, *Cognitive Foundations of Musical Pitch* (Oxford University Press, 1990)

Chapter 3
Music as Formal Language

> What's so special about music? First, all known cultures have had music – even those that have lacked a written language. It is as close to a universal human trait as you could hope for. Second, music – unlike, say, cooking, farming, talking, raising a family – doesn't obviously have any benefit. Of course, we love it, it makes us joyful or transports us into tears, rapture, and dance, but it bears no obvious, tangible evolutionary advantage. (Ball [2])

We often say birds' chirping as *singing*; such a metaphor has no meaning for them. From the viewpoint of birds, they try to communicate with each other, or more specifically male birds are wooing females. Thus, this is a language, as a method of communication. If we feel a chirping is a song, this is because we can find a tonal up and down and a certain rhythm in it. Birds utter through *syrinx* and hear by ears. As their beaks cannot change shape, the variety of their utterance is restricted to pitch and stress. On the contrary, we human beings have soft lip and flexible tongue, which enable further variety of consonants and vowels.

Here, we may ask ourselves an intrinsic question. Could music and language exist independently? Definitely, *no*. Nowadays, it is widely accepted that the origin of music and language is one and the same [22]. Music is a primitive form of communication, and thus, the origin of language is music.

> As neither the enjoyment nor the capacity of producing musical notes is faculties of the least direct use to man in reference to his ordinary habits of life, they must be ranked amongst the most mysterious with which he is endowed. They are present, though in a very rude and as it appears almost latent condition, in men of all races, even the most savage.
>
> It appears probable that the progenitors of man, either the males or females or both sexes, before acquiring the power of expressing their mutual love in articulate language, endeavored to charm each other with musical notes and rhythm. (Charles Darwin: *The Descent of Man* (1871)) [3]

Even now, in some aspects, music and language are inseparable. Chançon should be sung in French. Canzone must be sung in Italian. Beethoven (1770–1827) embedded the accent of 'Muss es sein? Es muss sein!' in German into the theme of the 4th movement of his 16th string quartet. We make language accents on vowels by up–down, long–short, or strong–weak beats that are innate in each language. Note that these notions are exactly the specification of musical notes in the score. Then,

K. Hirata et al., *Music, Mathematics and Language*,
https://doi.org/10.1007/978-981-19-5166-4_3

we can easily understand that the language is strongly related to the country music, that is, sung and played by an ethnic scale and local instruments.

Written music represented on the stave consists of a chronological sequence of notes. In this meaning, it is quite similar to natural language, consisting of a sequence of characters. At the same time, obviously, music and language are different. In natural language, there are units like morphology, lexical item (word), and sentence clearly indicated by full stop. However, we cannot find corresponding articulation in music. Then, how shall we contrive the analogy between music and language? Can we find latent grammar in it? Can we apply then, in the similar way, a syntactic parser to music?

3.1 Chomsky and Generative Grammar

Linguistics, after Ferdinand de Saussure (1857–1913) and Ludwig Wittgenstein (1889–1951), has been developed by Noam Chomsky (1928–). His linguistic theory is divided into the following five stages [8].

In 1950s in the USA, the linguists called the American school studied syntax, mainly based on Immediate Constituent (IC) analysis, where either a word syntactically dominates adjacent other words or is subject to its neighbors, to compose the whole sentence. This idea is generalized as *phrase structure grammar*; adjacent lexical items compose a larger phrase, and these neighboring phrases are further combined into a larger phrase to be a sentence.

Let us illustrate simple English grammar as below.

$$
\begin{aligned}
&\text{S} \rightarrow \text{NP VP}\\
&\text{NP} \rightarrow \text{Det N}\\
&\text{VP} \rightarrow \text{IV}\\
&\text{VP} \rightarrow \text{TV NP}\\
&\text{N} \rightarrow \text{dog, cat, man, girl, fish, house,} \ldots\\
&\text{Det} \rightarrow \text{the, a, an}\\
&\text{TV} \rightarrow \text{eat, love,} \ldots
\end{aligned}
$$

The rules state that S (Sentence) consists of two components; NP (Noun Phrase) as a subject and VP (Verb Phrase) as a predicate. NP consists of Det (Determiner) and N (Noun). VP is either by a single IV (Intransitive Verb), or TV (Transitive Verb) accompanied by NP as an object. Notice that in each rule the non-terminal symbol on the left-hand side of '→' occur independent of context. As a result, we can obtain such a *tree* as in Fig. 3.1. We call each rule a **production rule**.

Chomsky claimed in [7] that the finite number of vocabulary can be combined with the finite generative rules recursively, to generate infinite variety of sentences. Also, he bespoke that a long distance dependency could not be grasped by IC analysis; e.g., in

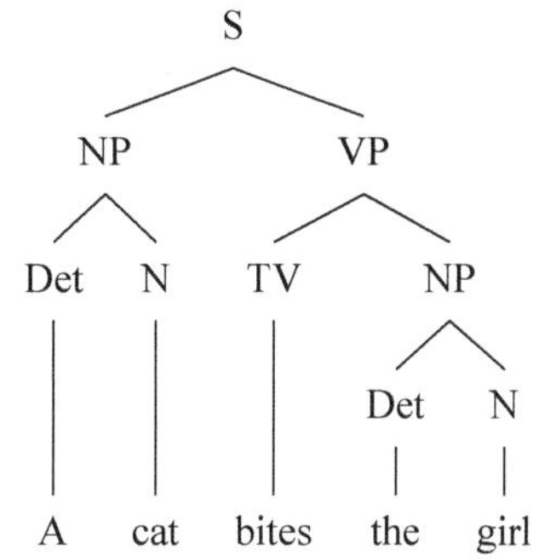

Fig. 3.1 A parse tree of an English sentence

What did you buy yesterday?

'buy' and 'what' must be in the relation of direct domination but are not adjacent. He considered that the two words must have been coalesced together when the speaker first had the intention of this utterance; so that these words are superficially detached later to make a question form. Namely, Chomsky considered that such query or negative sentences were *transformed* from the original declarative sentences. If we assume that the generative rules for question and negation independently, the number of rules increases too much and complicates their combinations. Even when IC analysis was prevalent, there existed such a meta-rule as the conjunction by 'and'. Thus, he considered that setting up meta-rules for transformation should be also admissible.

Another bold and outstanding hypothesis by Chomsky in this stage was that we human beings were born with the innate *language acquisition device* (LAD) [7].

Standard Theory [4] represents the second stage in 1960s when he proposed the distinction between the *deep structure*, that is the declarative sentence before transformation, and the *surface structure* after transformation. In this era, the innate grammar of LAD was named *universal grammar* (UG). Also, he suggested the embedding marker when a natural language sentence was embedded into another sentence as a clause recursively.

Extended Standard Theory in 1970s represents his third stage. In the grammar formalism, every phrase structure rule and transformation rule is abstracted to X-bar theory, by which

$$\overline{\overline{X}} \rightarrow \text{Spec } \overline{X}$$
$$\overline{X} \rightarrow X \text{ Comp}$$

though in his original notation, the bar is represented by ($'$) as

$$X'' \rightarrow \text{Spec } X', \;\; X' \rightarrow X \text{ Comp}.$$

Let X be a *head*, that is the prime constituent of a subtree, or the parent category is chosen from its daughter categories. The larger the number of bars, the higher the category locates in the tree. Spec is a specifier or a modifier of the head, and Comp is its complement. For example, a noun phrase NP accompanied by a determiner Det is represented as

$$\text{NP} \rightarrow \text{Det}\, N,$$

where if we consider the noun N is the head, N is X and Det is Spec, as

$$\overline{N} \rightarrow \text{Det}\, N,$$

however, for the convenience of syntactic analysis, we often consider the determiner is the head. For another example, a verb phrase VP accompanied by an objective noun phrase is, with a transitive verb TV,

$$\text{VP} \rightarrow \text{TV NP},$$

and thus, if we consider V is the head and NP is Comp,

$$\overline{V} \rightarrow V\ \text{NP}.$$

The order of the head and the specifier or the complement is flexible in universal grammar, but the parameter for this order is determined when an infant is tuned to its mother language.

In this Extended Standard Theory, all the transformation rules for movements (phenomena that a lexical item moves to another place in the sentence) were uniformly named '*Move* α'. In general, cased noun phrases governed by a predicate verb become the arguments of the verb, and the verb and the sequence of arguments form a case structure. When a cased noun phrase is moved to another case position in the structure, we call *A-movement*. For example, the transformation for passive voice is the A-movement since an objective noun is moved to a subject position. When a cased noun is moved to an extra position other than that of cased nouns, we call *A'-movement*. Such an extra position includes, for example, that of wh-interrogatives as *what, who, which*, and so on. We consider A'-movement leaves a *trace* at the original position though there remains no lexical/phonological item.[1]

During this stage, the semantics began to be discussed. George Laykoff (1941–) proposed the *generative semantics*, which represents the speaker's intention including the scope of negation or quantification, that was more abstract structure than the deep structure. Ray Jackendoff (1945–) proposed the interpretation of utterance, upon the surface structure of sentence, as the *conceptual semantics*.

[1] A missing element is in general called a *gap*; however, we name *trace* especially for such a gap after a movement. For example, in 'Which books did you file t without reading e?' t is the trace replaced by 'which' and e is the *parasitic* gap for the empty trace. Another missing element is a 'PRO' for the ellipsis of a pronoun (in both subject/object positions) in adjunct clauses. Especially, the ellipsis of a subject pronoun is often found in Romance languages/Japanese is shown by lowercase 'pro'.

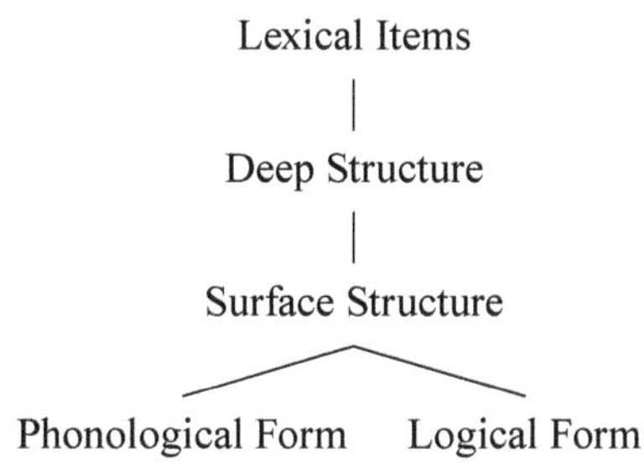

Fig. 3.2 Government and Binding theory

The fourth stage is the **Government and Binding** theory [5], which is the further rigorous formalization of the Extended Standard Theory, shown in Fig. 3.2. As a result, the whole theory was partitioned into six sub-theories with one principle.[2]

Later, Chomsky abandoned the X-bar theory, and all the combinations of juxtaposed categories have been explained as **recursive merge**. Also, **constituent control** explained that one daughter category governed another sister category, including all her descendants.

Minimalist Program [6] is the fifth and the final stage of Chomskian linguistics. The language is considered to be an interface between phonetics and semantics. Then, the role of syntax is to minimize the restrictions on this interface. The principle itself is thus simple; however, it is a philosophy or a rationale concerning linguistics, rather than a linguistic theory.

3.2 Formal Language and Automata

Chomsky Hierarchy was proposed in 1956 to give a hierarchy of complexity of formal language. When we say *formal* instead of natural language, the sentence is generated from a set of generative grammar, and only those generated by grammar rules are sentences. A generative rule is a rewriting system, where a symbol on the left-hand side of a production rule is replaced by the symbols on the right-hand side. Since this system gives a definite set of sentences, we can employ it for the definition of syntax of a logic or a programming language.

Among the hierarchy, the simplest *Regular Grammar* has a model of computation by *Finite Automata*, and the second simplest *context-free grammar* is modeled by *Push-Down Automata*, as explained below.

Finite Automata

A finite automaton consists of a finite set of *states* and *transitions* between them. In Fig. 3.3, a state is represented by a circle, and a transition an arrow. The states

[2] *Bounding theory*, *government theory*, *θ-theory*, *binding theory*, *case theory*, *control theory*, and *projection principle*.

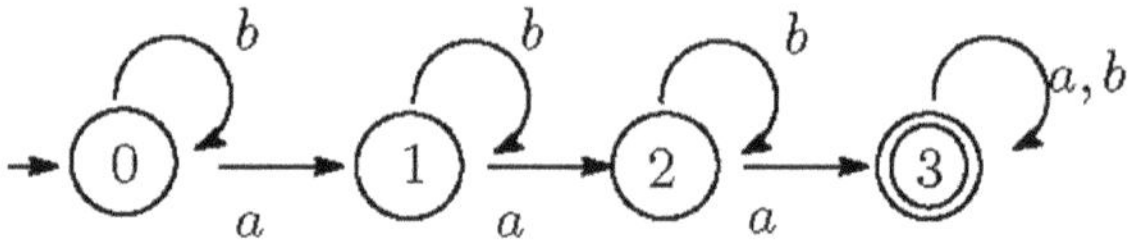

Fig. 3.3 Finite automaton

are indexed from 0 to 3. A transition is made by an input of one character, that is either a or b. The leftmost short arrow indicates the initial state, and the final state is shown by a double circle. An input sequence is processed from left to right, one character by another. For example, $abaa$ is processed in the following way. The first and leftmost character a triggers a transition $0 \to 1$, the next b makes a shift $1 \to 1$, and so on, and by the fourth a the automaton reaches the final state 3. We call such a sequence that reaches the final state a *sentence* acceptable by this automaton. Thus, we define a language as a set of sentences, accepted by a given automaton.[3]

By this automaton

$$aaa,\ aaba,\ abbbabbbabb,\ \ldots$$

are acceptable, but bba or aa is not a sentence. Actually, this automaton only accepts those sentences with three or more a's.

Instead of a graphic representation like Fig. 3.3, we can employ the following table. Each number shows a destination state, aligned by current states and input characters. The arrow shows the initial state and F the final state(s).

		a	b
$\to$	0	1	0
	1	2	1
	2	3	2
	$3F$	3	3

We say a finite state automaton is *deterministic* when δ is a function, that is, the destination uniquely exists for any combination of a current state and an input character. Otherwise, we say the automaton is *non-deterministic*. For any non-deterministic automaton, there exists an equivalent deterministic automaton that accepts the same language. Indeed, we can construct a corresponding deterministic finite automaton from a given non-deterministic automaton by a technique called *subset construction*.[4] The acceptance condition by a non-deterministic automaton is to look for all the possible transitions exhaustively to arrive at a final state; even though we can-

[3] Formally, a finite automaton is defined by a tuple $(Q, \Sigma, \delta, s, F)$; Q is a finite set of states, Σ is a set of input characters, $\delta : Q \times \Sigma \to Q$ is a transition function, $s \in Q$ is the initial state, and $F \subseteq Q$ is a set of the final states. In the example of Fig. 3.3, $Q = \{0, 1, 2, 3\}$, $\Sigma = \{a, b\}$, $s = 0$, $F = \{3\}$, and $\delta(0, a) = 1,\ \delta(1, a) = 2,\ \delta(2, a) = 3,\ \delta(3, a) = 3,\ \delta(0, b) = 0,\ \delta(1, b) = 1,\ \delta(2, b) = 2,\ \delta(3, b) = 3$.

[4] We regard the whole set of destination by an input character a one new state in the target deterministic machine.

not reach a final state after a choice of destination from a certain state by a given character, we need to try another destination if any.

Regular Language

Let α be a character, $\alpha_1\alpha_2$ be a concatenation of two characters, $\alpha_1 + \alpha_2$ be an exclusive choice of either of the two characters, and α^* (Kleene star) is a reprise more than 0 times of α. Now, given $\{a, b\}$ for α,

$$ab^*a$$

represents such a set of sentences that the first is a, followed by any number (including 0) of b, and a again, that is,

$$\{aa,\ aba,\ abba,\ abbba,\ abbbba, \ldots\}.$$

Such a representation is called a *regular expression* and the generated language is called a *regular language*. More formally, the regular expression has a syntax, given by Backus–Naur Form (BNF). The α on the left-hand side of ':=' is recursively defined by those on the right-hand side where '|' is an exclusive choice.

$$\alpha ::= \varnothing \mid \varepsilon \mid a \mid b \mid \alpha\alpha \mid \alpha + \alpha \mid \alpha^*$$

where $\varnothing$ shows α is empty and ε is a string with 0-length.

The finite automaton in Fig. 3.3 has an equivalent regular expression

$$b^*ab^*ab^*a(a + b)^*.$$

In general, there exists a regular expression for a deterministic finite automaton and vice versa.[5]

If we consider a regular language a set of sentences, we may call it a *regular set.* Let Σ be a set of characters; then, Σ^* is the concatenations of arbitrary numbers of characters in Σ. If $A \subset \Sigma^*$ is a regular set $A^c = \Sigma^* \setminus A$ (a complementary set of A for Σ^*) is also a regular set; for the automaton accepting A, construct a new automaton where the final states of A be non-final and the non-final states be final, then it accepts A^c. Also, if $A, B \subset \Sigma^*$ are regular, both $A \cap B$ and $A \cup B$ are regular.

Context-Free Grammar

Let N be a finite set of **Non-terminal symbols** (variables) and Σ be that of **Terminal symbols** (constants). As was mentioned in the explanation of phrase structure

[5] Let α and β be two regular expressions, and let M_α and M_β be corresponding automata, respectively. A new automaton for $\alpha\beta$ would be such that a final state of M_α issues an arrow to M_β, that is, a sequential concatenation of M_α and M_β. Also, $\alpha + \beta$ would be such a machine that a new initial state leads to two of M_α and M_β, and a final state in either of them leads to a newly added final state. Finally, to construct an automaton for α^*, we add a new arrow from a final state of α to its initial state, to enable repetition.

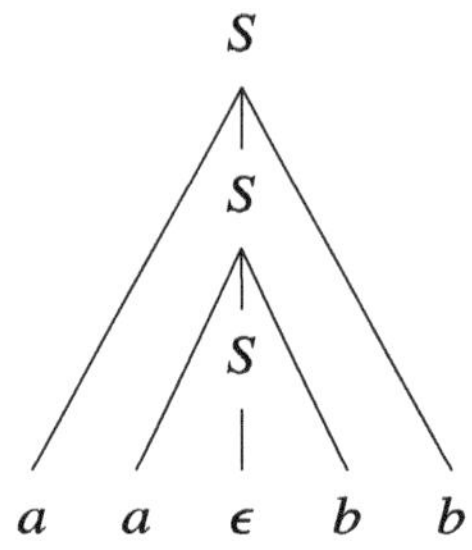

Fig. 3.4 Parse tree by CFG

grammar, a production rule replaces the left-hand side of '→' with its right-hand side.

In context-free grammar (CFG), only one non-terminal symbol $A \in N$ appears on the left-hand side of '→', to be replaced with a finite sequence in $(N \cup T)^*$ as

$$A \rightarrow \alpha_1 \alpha_2 \ldots.$$

Since the rule can be applied to every occurrence of A, disregarding its preceding or succeeding symbols, we say the situation context-free. Thus, we call such a rule a *context-free* grammar rule. A context-free grammar consists of a tuple (N, Σ, P, S), where P is a finite set of context-free rules and S is a specialized non-terminal symbol employed as the starting symbol.

For example, let $\Sigma = \{a, b\}$ and S consists of

$$S \rightarrow aSb,$$
$$S \rightarrow \varepsilon$$

where 'ε' is an empty symbol. We write '$S \rightarrow aSb \mid \varepsilon$' in short, with the '|' for the selection of rules. The S symbol first becomes either aSb or ε, and in the former case, the middle S would recursively be replaced by the same rules. Note that, even though the number of recursion is arbitrary, the number of a's and b's eventually becomes the same. We shown in Fig. 3.4 a *derivation* of string *aabb* from the given grammar, which becomes a tree.

Every CFG can be transformed into two different *normal forms*. Let A, B_i $(i = 1, 2, \ldots)$ be non-terminal symbols and a be a terminal one.

Chomsky Normal Form the right-hand side is restricted to either two non-terminal symbols or one terminal symbol.

$$A \rightarrow B_1 B_2 \mid a$$

which does not produce 'ε'.

Greibach Normal Form the right-hand side is headed by one terminal symbol followed by an arbitrary finite number (including zero) of non-terminal symbols.

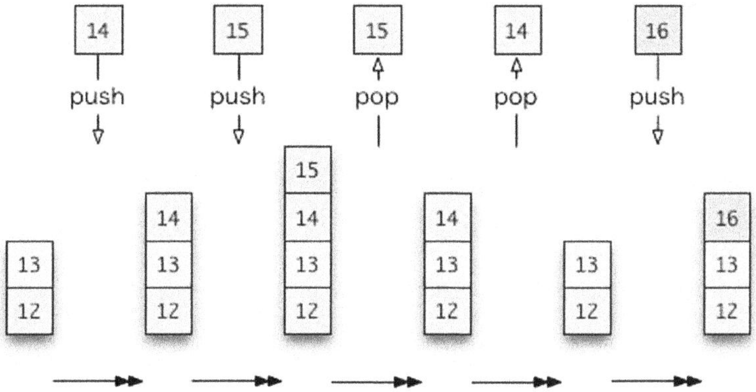

Fig. 3.5 Push-down stack

$$A \to aB_1B_2 \ldots B_k$$

A set of sentences produced by CFG is *context-free language* (CFL). Let Σ^* be a set of finite sequences of terminal symbols. Then, when $A, B \subset \Sigma^*$ are CFLs, $A \cup B$ and A^* become CFL. On the contrary, $A \cap B$ and $A^c = \Sigma^* \setminus A$ may not necessarily be context-free. If either one of A or B is regular, $A \cap B$ is context-free [13].

Push-Down Automata

A *push-down stack* is a virtual memory which works 'first-in last-out'; that is, the memorized first item is retrieved at last as is shown in Fig. 3.5. An automaton which possesses such a memory called Push-Down Automata (PDA).[6] This memorizing action is called *push*, and the retrieving action is called *pop*.

PDA changes its internal state for each input symbol of input strings, being similar to finite state automata, but at the same time, pushes or pops a corresponding symbol in the stack. Thus, the transition function δ needs a stack-top symbol, as well as an input character and the current state. Accordingly, its output becomes a pair of a new state and a new stack-top, though this new stack-top may consist of multiple stack symbols.

To define the acceptance of an input sentence, we can consider two possibilities; one is the acceptance by empty stack and the other is that by reaching a final state. However, actually, we can construct an equivalent automaton that accepts sentences by empty stack, given an automaton with acceptance by final state, and vice versa.[7]

[6] PDA consists of tuple $(Q, \Sigma, \Gamma, \delta, s, \perp, F)$ where Q is a finite set of states, s is the initial state, $F \subset Q$ is the final states, Σ is a finite set of input symbols, Γ is a finite set of stack symbols, $\perp \in \Gamma$ is the initial symbol of the stack. δ is a transition function $Q \times (\Sigma \cup \{\epsilon\}) \times \Gamma \to Q \times \Gamma^*$.

[7] Given an automaton which accepts sentences by empty stack, we can redefine a new final state, adding ϵ moves from those states with empty stack to this new final state. Given an automaton which accepts sentences by final states, we can add new transitions to clean the remaining symbols in the stack.

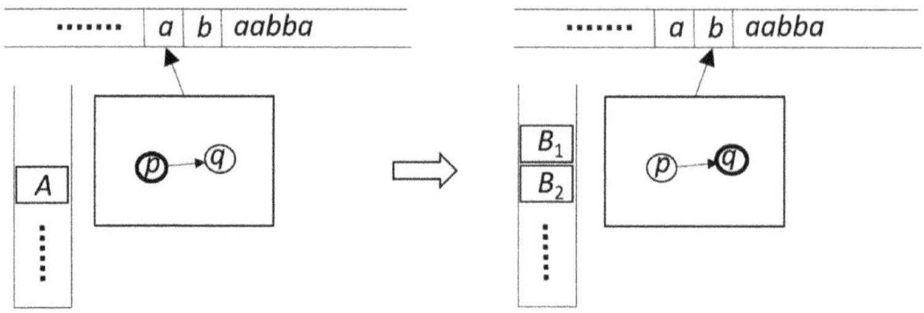

Fig. 3.6 A transition, given an input symbol a at state p, pops A and pushes $B_1 B_2$, and shifts to state q

For PDA, there is a possibility that the stack may become vacant, or reaching a final state, during reading the input sentence halfway. Therefore, we need to investigate if the stack becomes vacant, or having reached a final state, just when the input symbols are consumed. Such PDA with exhaustive search for acceptance is called Non-deterministic Push-Down Automaton (NPDA) (Fig. 3.6).

Any NPDA can be transformed to an NPDA with only one state.[8] Since only one state cannot distinguish the difference of states, we can disregard the existence of state, writing it as '_'. Any one-state NPDA accepts CFL, because any CFG has corresponding Greibach Normal Form

$$A \rightarrow c\ B_1 B_2.$$

Let $A,\ B_1,\ B_2$ be stack symbols, c be an input character, and the derivation be the transition, viz. this transition pops A after reading a and pushes $B_1 B_2$, as

$$\delta(\_, c, A) = (\_, B_1 B_2).$$

There might be multiple outputs for $\delta(\_, c, A)$; that is, there might be multiple grammar rules for the combination of A and c, as

$$A \rightarrow c\beta_1 \mid c\beta_2 \mid c\beta_3,$$

and thus CFL becomes the language NPDA accepts.

Chomsky Hierarchy

For example, such sentences as $a^n b^n$ (a, b appear at the same times) or wcw^R (palindrome: When $w = ab$, $w^R = ba$, centered by c) cannot be expressed by RG but can by CFG. Noam Chomsky has given a strict distinction between classes of formal language.

[8] We can embed all the state information into stack symbols. For example, given a transition $\delta(p, c, A) = (q_0, B_1 B_2)$, we can guess a possible destination after p, q_0. If they are $q_1,\ q_2$ we change the transition function as $\delta(\_, c, \langle pAq_2\rangle) = (\_, \langle qB_1q_1\rangle\langle q_1B_2q_2\rangle)$ [13].

type-0 grammar Phrase Structure Grammar $\Longleftrightarrow$ Turing Machine
type-1 grammar Context-Sensitive Grammar $\Longleftrightarrow$ Linear Bounded Automata
type-2 grammar Context-Free Grammar $\Longleftrightarrow$ Non-deterministic Push-Down Automata

$$\begin{cases} A \rightarrow aB_1B_2 \cdots \\ A \rightarrow a \end{cases}$$

type-3 grammar Regular Grammar $\Longleftrightarrow$ Finite State Automata

$$\begin{cases} A \rightarrow aB \\ A \rightarrow a \end{cases}$$

The name context-free means that the non-terminal symbol on the left-hand side of '$\rightarrow$' appears independently of its context. On the contrary, in Context-Sensitive Grammar, the occurrence of the left-hand non-terminal symbol depends on the context, e.g., $aXb \rightarrow Y\ Z$.

A state change of a finite state automaton has an equivalent production rule, the states being regarded as non-terminal symbols and the input characters as the terminal ones, as follows.

$$\delta(a, A) = B \Longleftrightarrow A \rightarrow aB$$

As a result, a regular language is translated into a context-free language. Note that the above rule is in Greibach Normal Form with the length of non-terminal symbols on the right-hand side is limited to 1.

The higher the language class is, the smaller number of type index becomes, and the more complex language the virtual machine can compose.

3.3 Human Language in the Hierarchy

The chirp of domestic finch is said to possess a grammar, and since the transitions from a phoneme to another is diagrammed by a finite state automaton; that is, the grammar is regular. On the contrary, our human language is said to belong almost to a class of context-free grammar. From now on, we regard that one word is an input symbol to our automaton instead of a phoneme.

Let us consider a sentence 'We go to Broadway to see a musical.' Then there is a dependency between 'go' and 'to Broadway', and 'to see' and 'a musical.' In principle, the dependency does not cross each other in one sentence in human language. In Fig. 3.7, a dependency is shown by a directed arrow. Because of the prohibition against crossing arrows, we cannot say 'We go to see to Broadway a musical.'

Now, let us regard that the beginning point of an arrow and the ending point are the open and the close parenthesis, respectively. Then, the prohibition of dependency crossing is stated as 'We must not close a parenthesis before closing the most recently opened parenthesis'. This situation also corresponds to the push-down stack. The opening action of a parenthesis corresponds to 'push' and the closing action to 'pop'. Namely, the following three conditions become one and the same restriction.

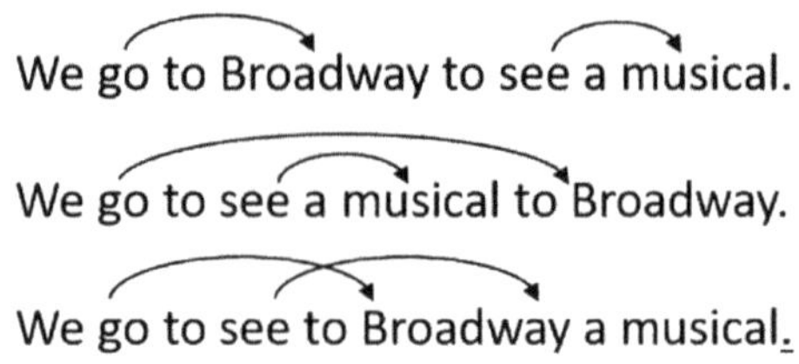

Fig. 3.7 Dependency

- No crossing of dependency
- Well-balanced parentheses
- Working memory by push-down stack.

According to the definition in the previous section, therefore, our human language belongs to the class of context-free grammar (CFG).

However, there are known a few exceptions in which dependency crosses. For example in Dutch, the postposed verbs in a subordinate violate this restriction. According to the prohibition of dependency crossing, 'Henry feeds' should be embedded within the structure of 'Fred helps'; however, Dutch says preserving the original word order.

Hij zegt dat ik Fred Henry de nijlpaauder zag helpeu voeren.
He said that I Fred Henry the hippos saw help feed.
(He said that I saw Fred helps Henry feed the hipos.)

In French, the order of personal pronouns between *object direct* and *object indirect* alternates, perhaps by smoothness of pronunciation.

- Je vous la présente. (Je la présente à vous.)
  I introduce her to you.
- Je la lui présente. (Je la présente à lui.)
  I introduce her to him.

In natural language syntax, one relation of dependency composes a subtree, and the whole sentence is a tree constructed from such subtrees recursively. In order to recognize such dependency, we utilize a tentative memory exactly modeled by a push-down stack in our brain. This dependency works as expectation as follows. When we catch a subject word in the other's utterance, we predict a predicate would follow. If we hear a determiner, we expect a noun or noun headed by an adjective. It is said that only human beings employ such working memory to recognize sentences, and thus we understand the hierarchical syntax.

Now let us consider that we listen to music by our ears as well as language, and we sing songs with our tongues and throats in the similar way to utter sentences. How can our recognition process of language and music not be common? We can presuppose that there should be the same expectation realization model even in recognizing a piece of music.

3.4 Language Class of Chord Progression

3.4.1 Context-Free Syntax of Cadence

Cadence (*Kadenz* in German) is a sequence of chords with which we feel the end of the piece. Let us write the scale degrees by uppercase roman numerals for major triads while lowercase roman for minor triads. We say 'I' possesses the function of *tonic*; similarly, we say 'V' has the *dominant* and 'IV' has the *subdominant* function, respectively. Note that V is the perfect 5th up from I and IV is the perfect 4th up, that is the perfect 5th below. The dominant function makes us feel tense while the succeeding tonic makes us relaxed. Therefore, the typical patterns of cadences become as follows.

$$
\begin{aligned}
&\mathrm{I} \rightsquigarrow \mathrm{V} - \mathrm{I}\\
&\mathrm{I} \rightsquigarrow \mathrm{IV} - \mathrm{V} - \mathrm{I}\\
&\mathrm{I} \rightsquigarrow \mathrm{IV} - \mathrm{I}
\end{aligned}
$$

The last one is called the *plagal* cadence. In the above, V becomes often tetrad, written as V_7. Here, '$\sim$' means a rather free passage though in many cases it preserves the memory of the initial tonic.

A cadence is embedded recursively into another cadence. For example, the sequence of V–I makes us feel the end of a piece, and in order to stress the ending, we can make II precede V. Since II is the perfect 5th below V, we can regard that the sequence II–V is embedded recursively instead of V in V–I and results in II–V–I. Such II (a major triad) is called the double dominant (*Doppeldominante* in German). Note that II includes a note out of the major scale; e.g., in C major, the minor triad ii consists of D, F, A; however, II includes D, F♯, A. If we regard this as the embedding, we should regard that the sequence of cadence consists of CFG. Only for those simple cadences, we can write a finite automaton in chord progression, that is of Regular Grammar, but when we refer to more complicated cadence structure we need to consider CFG.

Chord Progression Rules by Winograd

To write down a set of CFG rules for chord progression was tried by [23]. The first sentence of this paper, quoted below, is quite impressive.

> Fifteen years ago, linguistics was the private preserve of a small number of anthropologists and philosophers, along with an occasional language teacher or intrepid psychologists.

This statement seems to claim that linguistics in 1950s, that was before Chomsky, was not an established science though, of course, nowadays it is widely accepted as an important branch of science.

Anyway, this paper describes such rules of chord progression as follows.

cadence → plagal | authentic
authentic → dominant tonic
dominant → V
$V \rightarrow V_{seventh} \mid V_{triad}$
$V_{seventh} \rightarrow V_7 \mid V^6_5$

In this paper, the classification trees of tonality as well as triads and tetrads on scale degree appeared and they were applied to the analysis of several classical masterpieces; a sequence of pitch events was given to a LISP program, and output a sequence of scale degrees with tonality.

This style of chord analysis now seems common; anyone with a certain knowledge of cadence and CFG can implement this kind of parser. However, the cadence is not rigid and also the interpretation of chord in terms of key and degree is often equivocal. Therefore, this naïve method cannot ensure the precision or accuracy of chord identification.

Analogy of Language/Music by Bernstein

Leonard Bernstein, a highly famed composer and one of the most talented conductors, gave a sequence of lectures in Harvard University in 1976, called 'The Unanswered Question.' In which, he made an intriguing analogy between Chomsky's generative syntax and music. He showed that a simple English sentence could bear various different meanings, including negative or interrogative views, when the prosody was given. He exemplified this prosody by a sequence of chords. For example, the upward progression gives an expression of doubt and when it is accompanied by the triad of minor third the sentence wears a negative nuance. That is exactly the explanation of the early Chomskian school; i.e., a negative or an interrogative form is derived from a root form of declarative sentence. He tried to map several linguistic notions as morpheme, word, clause, and sentence onto such music notions as note, phrase, and so on. Some of those mappings may not necessarily be agreeable; however, even now, this lecture series gives us an important opportunity to reconsider the syntactic similarity between language and music.

3.4.2 Generative Syntax Model

The progression of chords, independent of rhythmic and melodic progression, has been also proposed by Rohmeier [19] as Generative Syntax Model (GSM).

There are highly acceptable and less acceptable (well-formed and ill-formed) chord sequences among a huge variety of possibilities, and this raises a question if we can reveal underlying formal principles of the sequences. According to this motivation, he proposed a core set of grammatical rules to cover the fundamental features of the recursive structure of tonal harmony.

The *dependency principle* connects each element (chord) to its preceding or succeeding chord (group), and each group recursively distinguishes a *functional head* on which the other group of chords are dependent. Chords are classified into functional categories which describe their tonal function, dependent on their contexts.

First, we prepare such sets as follows.

$\mathbb{P} = \{\text{piece}, P\}$	A set of music pieces
$\mathbb{K} = \{C\text{maj}, C\text{min}, C\sharp\text{maj}, C\sharp\text{min}, \ldots\}$	A set of keys
$\mathbb{R} = \{\text{TR}, \text{SR}, \text{DR}\}$	A set of regions
$\mathbb{F} = \{t, s, d, \text{tp}, \text{sp}, \text{dp}, \text{tcp}\}$	A set of functions
$\mathbb{S} = \{\text{I}, \text{II}, \ldots, \text{VII}, \text{V/I}, \ldots, \text{VII/I}, \ldots\}$	A set of scale degrees
$\mathbb{O} = \{\text{Cm}, \text{F}^7, \text{B}\flat^{M7}, \text{Am}^{\varnothing 7}, \ldots\}$	A set of chord symbols

In the phrase level, a piece as a sequence of phrases and a phrase generates a tonic seed (tonic region).

$$\text{piece}_{\text{key}=x\in\mathbb{K}} \rightarrow P^+,$$
$$P \rightarrow \text{TR}.$$

A piece may be generated by a single tonic seed, as

$$\text{piece} \rightarrow \text{TR}_{\text{key}=x\in\mathbb{K}}.$$

In the functional level, functional expansion rules are the following left-branching rules. TR (tonic regions) generates DR (dominant region) and SR (subdominant region), and then t (tonic), d (dominant), s (subdominant). t, d, s generate tp (tonic parallel), tcp (tonic counterparallel), dp (dominant parallel), and sp (subdominant parallel) which Hugo Riemann (1849–1919) had proposed, respectively (Fig. 3.8).

$\text{TR} \rightarrow \text{DR}\ t$	$\text{TR} \rightarrow t$	$t \rightarrow \text{tp}$
$\text{DR} \rightarrow \text{SR}\ d$	$\text{DR} \rightarrow d$	$t \rightarrow \text{tcp}$
$\text{TR} \rightarrow \text{TR DR}$	$\text{SR} \rightarrow s$	$s \rightarrow \text{sp}$
$\text{XR} \rightarrow \text{XR XR} \quad (\text{XR} \in \mathbb{R})$		$d \rightarrow \text{dp}$

Note that TR TR TR is ambiguous since it can be parsed in two ways.

The modulation rules enable local changes of key, with which each functional region may become a local tonic (with a new key feature), for $X \in \mathbb{F}$, $y \in \mathbb{K}$. The modulation function $\psi(f, k)\colon \mathbb{F} \times \mathbb{K} \rightarrow \mathbb{K}$ works, e.g.,

$$\psi(d, \text{B}\flat\text{maj}) = F\text{maj or } \psi(\text{tp}, \text{A}\flat\text{maj}) = F\text{min}.$$

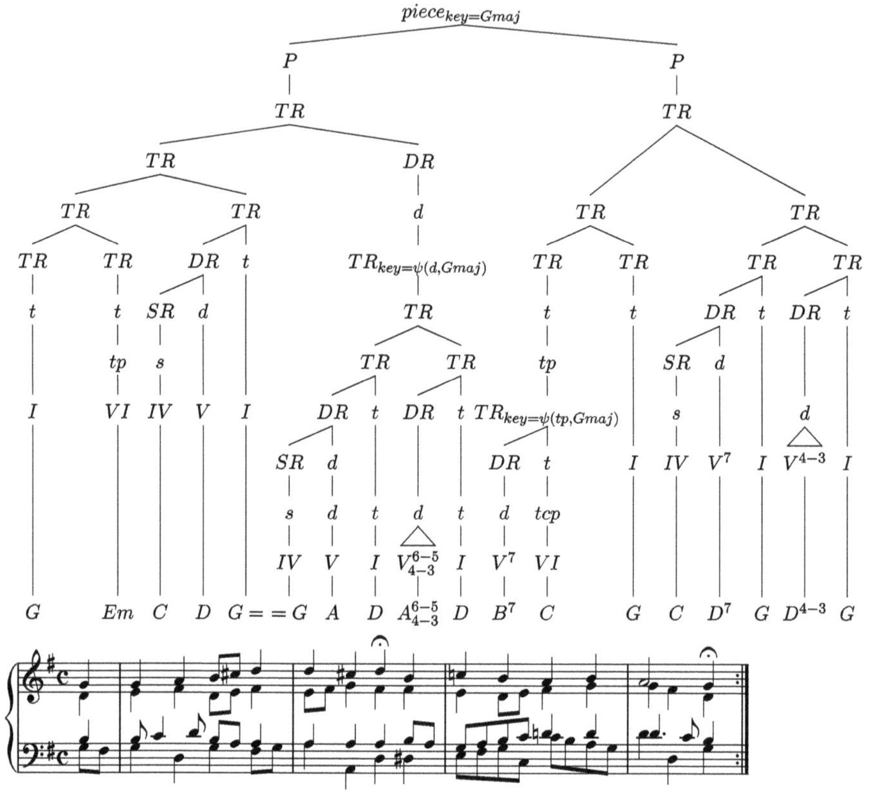

Fig. 3.8 Beginning part of Bach's chorale 'Ermuntre Dich, mein schwacher Geis', appears in [19]

$$X_{\text{key}=y} \rightarrow \text{TR}_{\text{key}=\psi(X,y)}$$
$$X_{\text{key}=y\,\text{maj/min}} \rightarrow X_{\text{key}=y\,\text{min/maj}}.$$

The secondary dominant rules are

$$X \rightarrow D(X)\ X \qquad (X \in \mathbb{S})$$
$$X \rightarrow \Delta(X)\ X \qquad (X \in \mathbb{S})$$
$$D(X) \rightarrow \begin{cases} \text{V/VI}/X \mid \text{VII/VI}/X & (X\text{: diminished triad}) \\ \text{V/X} \mid \text{VII}/X & \text{(otherwise)} \end{cases}$$

$D(X)$ is a chord of perfect fifth above X while $\Delta(X)$ is also a fifth above X but may not be dominant seventh.

The rules for the interface between functional level and scale degree level are those express the scale degree representations of Riemannian functions

$$t \to \mathrm{I} \qquad \mathrm{tp} \to \begin{cases} \mathrm{VI} & \text{major} \\ \mathrm{III} & \text{minor} \end{cases}$$

$$t \to \mathrm{I}\ \mathrm{IV}\ I \qquad \mathrm{dp} \to \mathrm{VII} \quad \text{minor}$$

$$s \to \mathrm{IV} \qquad \mathrm{sp} \to \begin{cases} \mathrm{II} & \text{major} \\ \mathrm{VI}\flat \mid \mathrm{II} & \text{minor} \end{cases}$$

$$d \to \mathrm{V} \mid \mathrm{VII} \qquad \mathrm{tcp} \to \begin{cases} \mathrm{III} & \text{major} \\ \mathrm{VI} & \text{minor} \end{cases}$$

Functional symbols may be sent to more strictly typed scale-degree representations, e.g., dominant seventh or *sixte ajoutée*,

$$d \to \mathrm{V}^7 \text{ or } s \to \mathrm{IV}^6.$$

Typing controls parsing ambiguity and is dependent on a specific musical style.

Finally, those types are replaced by the surface level. The key feature and scale degree information are used to derive the surface representation, e.g.,

$$\mathrm{V}^7_{\text{key}=\mathrm{E}\flat\,\text{maj}} \to \mathrm{B}\flat^7.$$

Any surface chord may be repeated as

$$X \to X^+ | \text{ for any } X \in \mathbb{O},$$

but does not reenter the recursive generation process.

3.4.3 Probabilistic Context-Free Grammar

We can assign a probability for each generation rule of context-free grammar (CFG), that is the probabilistic context-free grammar (PCFG). Let N be a set of non-terminal symbols, and E be an arbitrary sequence of terminal and non-terminal symbols. When there are multiple generations from $A \in N$, we assign a probability $[p_i]$

$$A_i \to E_i\ [p_i]\ (0 \le p_i \le 1)$$

so as to be $\sum_i p_i = 1$.

Let us consider the following grammar rules

S → NP VP	[0.8]
S → Aux NP VP	[0.1]
S → VP	[0.1] (+
	1.0
NP → Pronoun	[0.2]
NP → Proper-noun	[0.2]
NP → Det nominal	[0.6] (+
	1.0
Nominal → Noun	[0.3]
Nominal → Nominal noun	[0.2]
Nominal → Nominal PP	[0.5] (+
	1.0
VP → Verb	[0.2]
VP → Verb NP	[0.5]
VP → VP PP	[0.3] (+
	1.0
PP → Prep NP	[1.0]

Also, let us assign the probability of occurrence for each word in order that the sum for the whole vocabulary may be 1.0.

Det → the [0.6] | a [0.2] | that [0.1] | this [0.1]
Noun → book [0.1] | flight [0.5] | meal [0.2] | money [0.2]
Verb → book [0.5] | include [0.2] | prefer [0.3]
Pronoun → I [0.5] | he [0.1] | she [0.1] | me [0.3]
Proper-noun → Houston [0.8] | NWA [0.2]
Aux → does [1.0]
Pref → from [0.25] | to [0.25] | on [0.1] | near [0.2] | through [0.2]

Then, we can obtain two different parse trees for 'Book the flight through Houston' as in Fig. 3.9.

Let us compare the adequacy of the two trees. The probability p_1 of the plausibility of the tree in Fig. 3.9 is

$$p_1 = 0.1 \times 0.5 \times 0.5 \times 0.6 \times 0.6 \times 0.5 \times 0.3 \times 1.0 \times 0.2 \times 0.2 \times 0.5 \times 0.8$$
$$= 0.0000216$$

while that in Fig. 3.9 is

$$p_2 = 0.1 \times 0.3 \times 0.5 \times 0.6 \times 0.5 \times 0.6 \times 0.3 \times 1.0 \times 0.5 \times 0.2 \times 0.2 \times 0.8$$
$$= 0.00001296.$$

The occurrence of this sentence becomes the addition of the two probabilities as

$$p_1 + p_2 = 0.0000216 + 0.00001296 = 0.00003456.$$

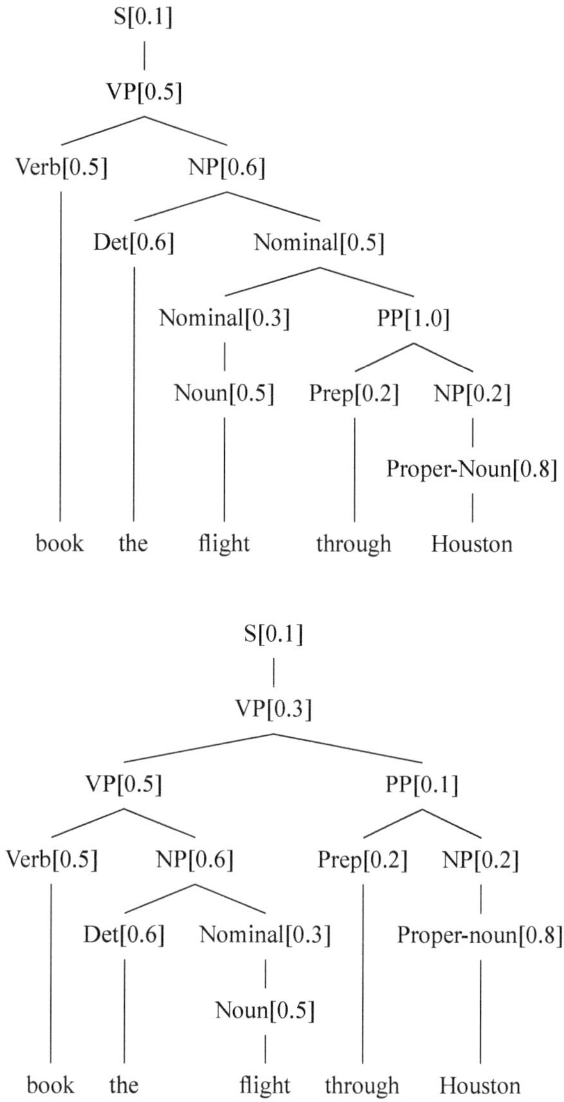

Fig. 3.9 Two parse trees of 'Book the flight through Houston'

We can apply PCFG directly to the chord progression. The following is the probability of cadence formation from the chord functions, appearing in the major pieces of Bach [18].

start:	
$S' \rightarrow$ A S F	[0.3]
$S \rightarrow$ S F	[0.7]
Anacrusis:	
$A \rightarrow$ ana v	[0.7]
$A \rightarrow$ ana i	[0.3]
Phrases:	
$S \rightarrow T\ S_1\ D\ T\ S$	[0.35]
$S \rightarrow$ T D T S	[0.25]
$S \rightarrow$ T M D T S	[0.07]
$S \rightarrow T\ S_1\ S_2\ T\ S$	[0.07]
$S \rightarrow S_1\ T\ D\ T\ S$	[0.07]
$S \rightarrow$ D T S	
$T \rightarrow$ i [0.8] | iii [0.1] | vi [0.1]	
$S_1 \rightarrow$ iv [0.7] | ii [0.2] | vi [0.1]	
$D \rightarrow$ v [0.4] | v_7 [0.3] | vii° [0.2] | iii [0.1]	
$M \rightarrow$ iii [1.0]	
$S_2 \rightarrow$ vi [1.0]	
$F \rightarrow$ T D T	[0.7]
$F \rightarrow T\ S_1\ T$	[0.3]

The probability distribution reflects the characteristics of Bach. Even for the same set of rules, if the assignment of probability is different, the character will be lost. Also, this assignment can be applied not only to composers but also to genre, era, region, and so on.

3.4.4 Head-Driven Phrase Structure Grammar

G, or V in C major, consisting of G, B, and D, has variations like tetrad V_7 (G, B, D, F) or inversion V_6. It is convenient for us if we can represent them are all V, but have different internal features. Such grammar with internal features is the Head-driven Phrase Structure Grammar (HPSG) [20].

Feature Structure

We call those various attributes such as gender, number, case, tense, and so on *features*. A feature structure is a form where a pair of a feature and its value is written in a row, and such pairs are listed in a column. The value can be another feature structure recursively. Two feature structures can be unified into one feature structure as long as there is no inconsistency in feature-value pairs. When the value consists of multiple candidates, we list them as '$\langle \ldots \rangle$'. The below is an example of a feature structure of a certain noun, where the whole structure is classified as 'Noun' shown by the label headed by '$\sim$', and we say the structure is *type*d to Noun.

$$\begin{bmatrix} \sim \text{Noun} & \\ \text{NUM} & \langle \text{sgl(singular), plr(plural)} \rangle \\ \text{GENDER} & \langle \text{masculine, feminine} \rangle \\ \text{PERSON} & \langle \text{1st, 2nd, 3rd} \rangle \\ \text{CASE} & \langle \text{subj, obj}, \cdots \rangle \end{bmatrix}$$

Head, Daughter, and Rules

In the tree structure, the upper node is called a parent and the lower node is called a daughter. In Chomsky's X-bar theory (p. 51), one of the daughters is considered to play a principle role to form their parent, as

$$\begin{cases} X' \rightarrow \text{Spec } X & \text{(Spec: specifier)} \\ X' \rightarrow X \text{ Comp} & \text{(Comp: complement)} \end{cases}$$

where X is called a *head-daughter*. For example, the noun is the head-daughter of a noun phrase,[9] and so the verb that of a verb phrase.

$$\begin{cases} \text{V}'' \rightarrow \text{N}' \text{ V}' & (\text{S} \rightarrow \text{NP VP}) \\ \text{V}' \rightarrow \text{V N}' & (\text{VP} \rightarrow \text{V NP}) \end{cases}$$

Each node in the phrase structure tree, that is a non-terminal symbol in production rules of context-free grammar, is called linguistically a *category*. A category can be given also by a typed feature structure; e.g.,

$$[\sim \text{V}''] \rightarrow [\sim \text{N}'][\sim \text{V}'].$$

Then, note that even such a generative rule itself can be written in a typed feature structure.

$$\begin{bmatrix} \sim \text{V}'' & \\ \text{HEAD-DTR} & [\sim \text{V}'] \\ \text{SPEC} & [\sim \text{N}'] \end{bmatrix}$$

Such a rule is called ID (Immediate Dominance) rule, especially ID-*schema* when shown by a feature structure.

Principles

A principle states conditions which an ID-schema must satisfy.

Head Feature Principle HEAD features concerning *agreement* in the parent must be inherited to, and be consistent to that of the head-daughter.

Subcategorization Principle A head-daughter is said to *subcategorize* its sisters. To define an ID-schema is to specify this subcategorization relation. Since a head-daughter recursively subcategorizes its sisters, the HEAD features are merged and unified into upper structures.

We employ indices '$\boxed{i}$' to refer to a feature structure; then, we can integrate such rules with the difference of agreements, as

[9] However, it is often practical to regard the determiner is the head-daughter of a noun phrase syntactically.

$$\begin{array}{l} \mathrm{V}''[\mathrm{sgl}, 1\mathrm{st}] \to \mathrm{N}'[\mathrm{sgl}]\ \mathrm{V}'[\mathrm{sgl}, 1\mathrm{st}] \\ \mathrm{V}''[\mathrm{sgl}, 2\mathrm{nd}] \to \mathrm{N}'[\mathrm{sgl}]\ \mathrm{V}'[\mathrm{sgl}, 2\mathrm{nd}] \\ \mathrm{V}''[\mathrm{sgl}, 3\mathrm{rd}] \to \mathrm{N}'[\mathrm{sgl}]\ \mathrm{V}'[\mathrm{sgl}, 3\mathrm{rd}] \\ \mathrm{V}''[\mathrm{plr}, 1\mathrm{st}] \to \mathrm{N}'[\mathrm{plr}]\ \mathrm{V}'[\mathrm{plr}, 1\mathrm{st}] \\ \qquad\qquad \vdots \end{array}$$

into one ID-schema

$$\begin{bmatrix} \sim \mathrm{V}'' & \\ \mathrm{HEAD} & \boxed{\mathrm{i}} \\ \mathrm{HEAD\text{-}DTR} & \begin{bmatrix} \sim \mathrm{V}' & \\ \mathrm{HEAD} & \boxed{\mathrm{i}} \end{bmatrix} \\ \mathrm{SPEC} & [\sim \mathrm{N}'] \end{bmatrix}$$

where $\boxed{\mathrm{i}}$ points to a common HEAD feature structure, consisting of number, person, and so on.

The parsing process of HPSG is based on these two principles; each lexical items possesses its own HEAD information, and when ID-schemata are applied to two adjacent lexical items, the parser applies the principles to unify them into a parent category. If a top category typed S (sentence) is formed, the parser could have parsed the given sentence.

Head and Subcategorization in Music

Now, let us get back to our original objective, that is, to represent a chord in a feature structure, with such internal features as 7th or inversion. In ii–V progression, ii can be considered to be a specifier for V. and in V–I, V is a specifier for I. On the contrary, in I–I, the latter I is a complement of the preceding I. Let category S (subdominant) be a specifier for D (dominant), and D for T (tonic). Then, we can provide the following lexicon.

$$\boxed{1} \begin{bmatrix} \sim \mathrm{T} & \\ \mathrm{HEAD\text{-}DTR} & [\sim \mathrm{T}] \\ \mathrm{COMP} & [\sim \mathrm{T}] \end{bmatrix}, \quad \boxed{2} \begin{bmatrix} \sim \mathrm{D} & \\ \mathrm{HEAD\text{-}DTR} & [\sim \mathrm{D}] \\ \mathrm{SPEC} & [\sim \mathrm{S}] \end{bmatrix}, \quad \boxed{3} \begin{bmatrix} \sim \mathrm{T} & \\ \mathrm{HEAD\text{-}DTR} & [\sim \mathrm{T}] \\ \mathrm{SPEC} & [\sim \mathrm{D}] \end{bmatrix}, \cdots$$

An example of analysis is shown in Fig. 3.10. Each chord holds internal features and, combining with adjacent chords by ID-schemata a parse tree is constructed for the sequence of C–$\mathrm{A_m}$–F–$\mathrm{D_m}$–G–C [21].

3.4.5 *Combinatorial Category Grammar*

Reductionism is a fundamental principle in modern science; that is, the character of the whole can be reduced to its components (atoms). In linguistics, this attitude

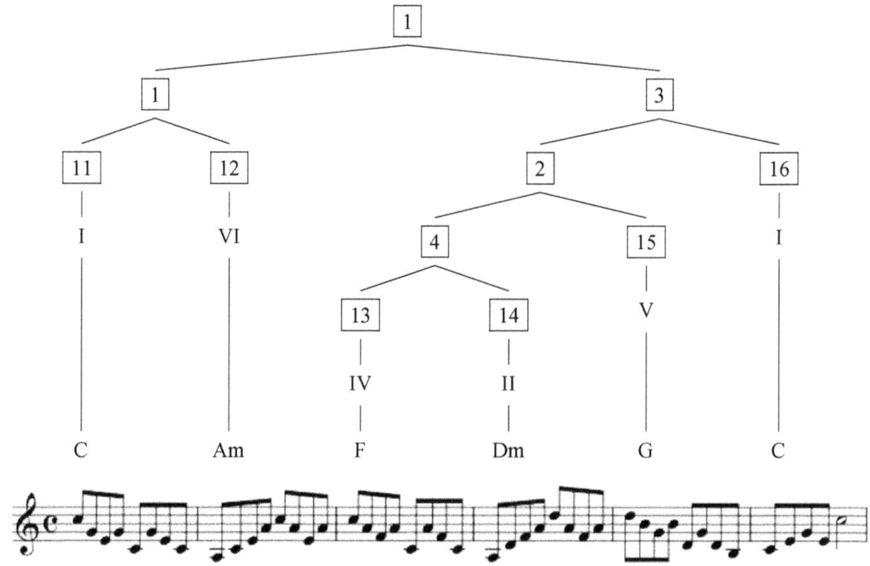

Fig. 3.10 Cadence recognition by HPSG

appears as *compositionality* or Frege's principle,[10] where the whole meaning of a sentence is composed by combinations of lexical items.

Category and Concatenation

In the syntactic rule

$$S \rightarrow \text{NP VP},$$

VP is considered to be a head to become S as was mentioned in X-bar theory, and thus, when VP 'bites' the adjacent NP they compose S. Then, NP is an argument to VP, writing with the reversed arrow:

$$S \leftarrow \text{NP } S/\text{NP}.$$

The process to compose S is therefore written as a proof below.

$$\frac{\text{NP } S/\text{NP}}{S}$$

We can reduce the number of category names, simply replacing them with '/' (slashes). Let e (entity) and t (truth value) be the fundamental categories for an individual and a sentence, respectively. Then, we can define the following categories.

[10] F. L. Gottlob Frege, 1848–1925.

Sentence	S	t
Common noun	CN	t/e
Verb phrase	VP	t/e
Intransitive verb	IV	t/e
Transitive verb	TV	$(t/e)/e$
Proper noun	PN	e
Verb adverb		$(t/e)/(t/e)$
Sentence adverb		t/t
Conjunction		$(t/t)/t$

In this categorization, a common noun should be considered to be t/e since it bites an individual and returns true or false. Then, a noun phrase for subject becomes $t/(t/e)$ by the process called '*type raising*'. We give this biting/bitten relation directions; i.e., the argument comes from the left-hand side or from the right-hand side as follows.

$$A \;\; B\backslash A \rightarrow B$$
$$\mathrm{B/A} \;\; A \rightarrow B$$

Now, we can compose a sentence from given vocabulary as follows [1].

$$\dfrac{\text{John}: e \qquad \dfrac{\text{runs}: t\backslash e \qquad \text{fast}: (t\backslash e)\backslash(t\backslash e)}{\text{runs fast}: t\backslash e}}{\text{John runs fast}: t}$$

Montague Semantics

Combinatory Categorial Grammar (CCG) was adopted by Richard Montague (1930–1971) as a tool to translate a part of English into the first-order logic. In this formalism, he translated such quantifiers as 'every' and 'a (an)' into '∀' and '∃', respectively, and showed a grammar called Proper Treatment of Quantifier (PTQ). With this, we can give two interpretations to 'Every man loves a woman.' as follows, simply changing the order of the composition of translated lexical items (λ-terms).

$$\forall x[\mathrm{man}(x) \rightarrow \exists y[\mathrm{woman}(y) \wedge \mathrm{love}(y, x)]]$$
(For any man, there exists his special lover.)
$$\exists y[\mathrm{woman}(y) \wedge \forall x[\mathrm{man}(x) \rightarrow \mathrm{love}(y, x)]]$$
(There is an idol girl, and every man loves her.)

Furthermore, this grammar employed modal logic and distinguished the intension (a conceptual mapping from a word to various possible worlds) from the extension (a concrete object in a certain possible world). For example, 'John seeks a friend.' can be read in two ways; 'a friend' is a virtual one or is a concrete person [9].

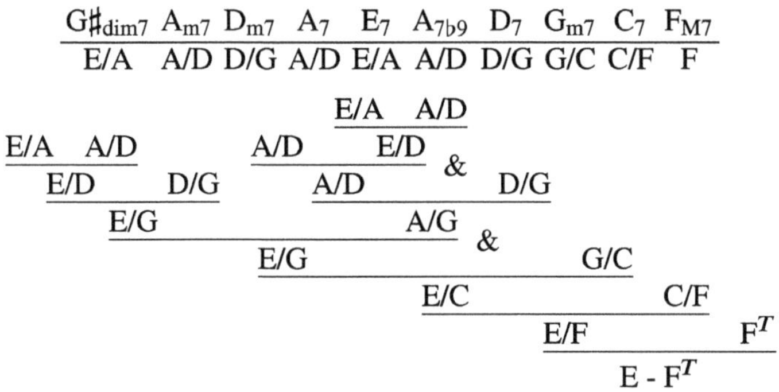

Fig. 3.11 Chord analysis by CCG [10]

$\text{seek}(\text{john}, \hat{}\lambda Q\exists x[\text{friend}(x) \wedge Q\{x\}])$

(John is looking for someone who would be his new friend.)

$\exists x[\text{friend}(x) \wedge \text{seek}(\text{john}, \hat{}\lambda P[P\{x\}])]$

(John has an appointment in front of the station.)

Jazz Chord Analysis by CCG

Now, we consider the syntactic analysis of the jazz chord sequence by CCG [10, 11]. For chord sequence D_{m7}–G_7–C, we can give two different cadences. First, when we regard D_m is the perfect fifth below G, D_m–G and G–C are a concatenation of two cadences. Second, when we regard D_m as a substitute of F^6, F–G–C (IV–V–I) is another cadence. If a sequence of A_7 D_{m7} G_7 is embedded before the solution of D_{m7} G_7, these two both resolved by the final C.

C(D_{m7} G_7)(A_7 D_{m7} G_7)C

with the coordination rule, noted by '&'.

In Fig. 3.11, we write X^D when X wears the dominant function. X/Y denotes that Y is the perfect fourth upper than X. Y on the right-hand side can be tonic or another dominant; then the situation is written as $Y^{D|T}$ (dominant or tonic). In Fig. 3.11, we show an example [10, 11], where $X^D/Y^{D|T}$ is written as X/Y for simplicity.

3.4.6 *Parsing Algorithms*

Thus far, we have discussed static representation of grammar in music; however, the dynamic algorithms are another intrinsic issue.

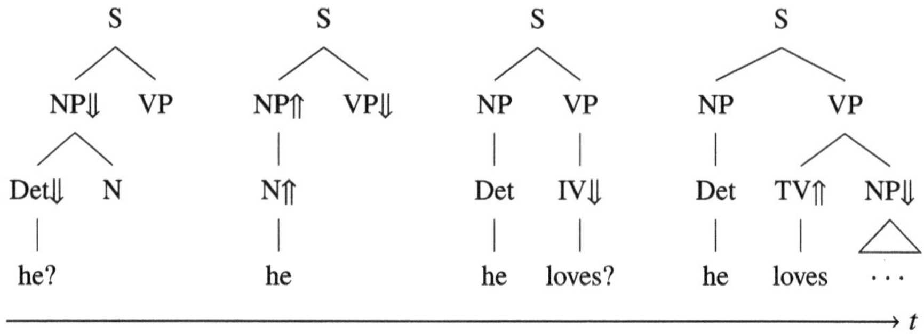

Fig. 3.12 Earley's algorithm

Expectation

In this chapter, we have claimed that we can hypothesize context-free grammar (CFG) in music. If so, we need to consider the long-distance dependency in a music piece. Namely, if we hear a pitch event we expect a dependent pitch event in the future. In case of I-R model [16, 17], an implication expects a realization. Or, it may be tension/relaxation in prolongation analysis in GTTM [14]. It may be simply the dominant motion, that is from dominant to tonic.

Now, let us consider to parse 'He loves a woman' by the following English grammar.

S → NP VP
NP → Det N | N
VP → IV | TV NP

The parsing proceeds from left to right in Fig. 3.12.

1. Start from S, then try to observe NP.
2. Category NP expects DET or N, in the top-down way.
3. When the parser finds 'He' as N, 'NP → N' is satisfied in the bottom-up way.
4. Then, in 'S → NP VP,' VP is expected to come.
5. Then, either IV or TV is expected.
6. When the parser finds 'loves', TV is satisfied.
7. Then, the parser expects that NP will follow TV, and so on.

In general, the parser tries to observe the leftmost category on the right-hand side of '→' in the top-down way. When the category is realized, it immediately generates an expectation that the second category on the right-hand side will follow. When a parent category (the left-hand side of '→') is realized, it may suffice an expectation in upper levels of the tree, in the bottom-up way. This repetition of observation, expectation, and realization is called Earley's algorithm (Fig. 3.12) employed in chart parser [12].

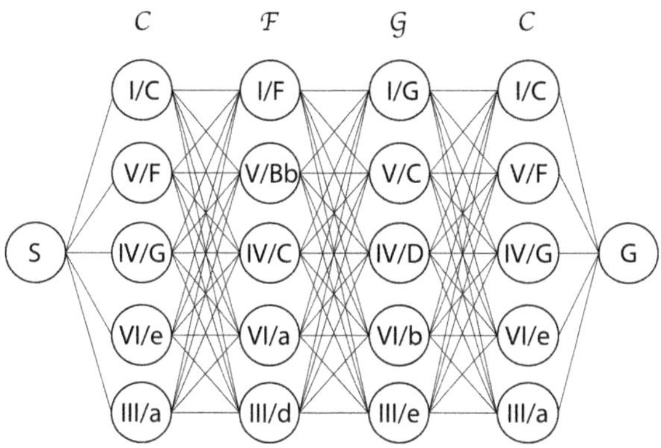

Fig. 3.13 Viterbi algorithm in chord progression

Local N-gram

In the above, we have paid attention to a global dependency by branching in CFG. However, if we consider only a local progression of chords, the N-gram is far easier and would achieve the high likelihood. In Fig. 3.13, we consider a problem to identify the key and local modulation, and to assign scale degrees on chord sequence: C–F–G–C. This example shows that the calculation of the distance in chords by Tonal Pitch Space (TPS) [15] with Viterbi algorithm, using hidden Markov model (HMM), and the path with the minimum distance should be considered to be the most probable interpretation.

References

1. J. Allwood, L. Andersson, O. Dahl, *Logic in Linguistics* (Cambridge, 1977)
2. P. Ball, BBC, 23 Apr 2014, http://www.bbc.com/future/story/20140423-is-music-really-all-about-sex
3. P. Ball, *The Music Instinct* (Vintage Books, 2010)
4. N. Chomsky, *Aspects of the Theory of Syntax* (The MIT Press, 1965)
5. N. Chomsky, *Lectures on Government and Binding* (Foris Publications, 1981)
6. N. Chomsky, *Minimalist Program* (The MIT Press, 1995)
7. N. Chomsky, *Syntactic Structures* (Mouton & Co., 1957)
8. V.J. Cook, M. Newson, *Chomsky's Universal Grammar: An Introduction* (Blackwell Publishing, 2007)
9. D.R. Dowty, R.E. Wall, S. Peters, *Introduction to Montague Semantics* (D. Reidel Publishing Company, 1981)
10. M. Granroth-Wilding, M. Steedman, Statistical parsing for harmonic analysis of Jazz chord sequences, in *Proceedings of ICMC2012* (2012)
11. M. Granroth-Wilding, M. Steedman, A robust parser-interpreter for Jazz chord sequences. J. New Music Res. **43**, 354–374 (2014)
12. M. Kay, Algorithm schemata and data structures in syntactic processing, in *Readings in Natural Language Processing*, ed. by B.J. Grosz, K.S. Jones, B.L. Webber (1986), pp. 35–70
13. D.C. Kozen, *Automata and Computability* (Springer, 1997)

14. F. Lerdahl, R. Jackendoff, *A Generative Theory of Tonal Music* (MIT Press, Cambridge, MA, 1983)
15. F. Lerdhal, *Tonal Pitch Space* (Oxford University Press, 2001)
16. E. Narmour, *The Analysis and Cognition of Basic Melodic Structures: The Implication-Realization Model* (The University of Chicago Press, 1990)
17. E. Narmour, *The Analysis and Cognition of Melodic Complexity: The Implication-Realization Model* (The University of Chicago Press, 1992)
18. S. Perchy, G. Sarria, Musical Composition with Stochastic Context-Free Grammars, in *Proceedings of 8th Mexican International Conference on Artificial Intelligence* (2009)
19. M. Rohmeier, Towards a generative syntax of tonal harmony. J. Math. Music **5**(1), 35–53 (2011)
20. I.A. Sag, T. Wasow, E.M. Bender, *Syntactic Theory* (CSLI Publications, 2003)
21. S. Tojo, Y. Oka, M. Nishida, Analysis of chord progression by HPSG, in *AIA'06 Proceedings of the 24th IASTED International Conference on Artificial Intelligence and Applications* (ACTA Press, 2006)
22. N.L. Wallin, B. Merker, S. Brown (eds.), *The Origins of Music* (The MIT Press, 2000)
23. T. Winograd, Linguistics and the computer analysis of tonal harmony. J. Music Theory **12**(1), 2–49 (1968)

Chapter 4
Berkleee Method

4.1 Berklee Method

The Berklee method originated as the music theory that was being taught at Berklee School of Music[1]. The Berklee method is primarily a theory that organizes and systemizes the relationship of harmonic progression and melody, and provides a methodology to express music symbolically and manipulate it mechanically.

Music was understood, from an early stage in its history, to be the result of the configuration of notes (phonemes), which are the components of music, in a two-dimensional space made up of time and pitch. The history of the development of music theory and sheet music lies in the repeated process of trial and error carried out to solve the problem of how to write down on paper, as symbols, this information of a phoneme itself and the information that positions it in the two-dimensional time × pitch space. *Symbolization of music* means segmenting and extracting the concepts produced in relation to music, such as the melodies, harmonies, rhythms, and styles that appear in a musical composition, then assigning an order to these concepts and either writing them down as symbols on paper, or rendering them as a form that can be managed by a computer [1][2]. In this chapter, from within the course of history of the symbolization of music, we consider the Berklee method.

[1] In Boston, in 1945, Lawrence Berk founded Schillinger House as the first school in the whole of America to teach jazz, which at the time was categorized as popular music. In 1954, the establishment was renamed Berklee School of Music. In 1970, it transitioned to become a university of music and was renamed Berklee College of Music. Notable graduates include Quincy Jones, Harvey Mason, John Scofield, Steve Vai, Dream Theater, Toshiko Akiyoshi, and Sadao Watanabe.

[2] Also called abstraction, mechanization, or digitalization.

K. Hirata et al., *Music, Mathematics and Language*,
https://doi.org/10.1007/978-981-19-5166-4_4

4.2 Degree

When two notes sound at the same time, classification of degree by consonance or dissonance is assigned, based on the principle of harmonic sequence (Table 4.1). In Table 4.1, Uni represents unison (the same note), Mn represents major nth, and mn represents minor nth. For example, M3 represents the major third, while m3 represents the minor third. In the same way, Pn expresses perfect nth. Lastly, '+4' expresses the degree of augmentation.

It is said that the simpler the frequency ratio, the more the two notes are heard to be in consonance (no beat tone) (Table 4.1, left side). Of course, in human sense of consonance and dissonance there are personal differences and differences in education, culture, and so on, which must surely make it difficult for all people to agree on the ordering of concepts. Accordingly, in the Berklee method, the dissonance levels shown in the right-hand table in Table 4.1 are imposed as an axiom. The Berklee

Table 4.1 Frequency ratio and dissonance level of degrees

Pitch	Frequency ratio	
Uni	1:1	
m2	15:16	
M2	8:9	
m3	5:6	
M3	4:5	
P4	3:4	
+4	45:64	
P5	2:3	
m6	5:8	
M6	3:5	
m7	9:16	
M7	8:15	
P8	1:2	
Dissonance level	**Description**	**Degree**
1	Consonant	M3, m3, M6, m6
2	Neutral, stable	Uni, P8, P5
3	Inorganic	P4
4	Moderately dissonant	M2, m7
5	Acutely dissonant	m2, M7
6	Unstable	+4

method calls frequency ratio a classical sense of harmony, while calling consonance level a modern sense of harmony. It should be noted that symbolization in this chapter refers to a concept that also includes assignment of order in a certain scale[3].

4.3 Chords

When it comes to chords in Western tonal music, various laws of composition (selection of notes and configuration of notes) have been conceived. Chords in the Berklee method are introduced as follows (Fig. 4.1): comprising between three and seven notes sounding simultaneously, ignoring difference in octave of the harmonic tones and considering only *pitch class* (regarding pitches of which only the octave difference varies as the same), and built up from the first (root) in degrees of a third (M3 or m3). In other words, pitch classes of harmonic tones are rearranged into the order of root, third, fifth, seventh, ninth, eleventh, thirteenth. Regarding the pitch class series produced as a result of this, the triad, composed of the root, third and fifth, and the tetrad, composed of the root, third, fifth, and seventh, are taken as the fundamental forms of chords. Furthermore, regarding tetrads, the ninth, eleventh, and thirteenth can be added as options. These notes are called tensions. Chords that include harmonic tones that have the same pitch class but differing octaves are called *inversions*, yet in the Berklee method inversions are all regarded as the same equivalence class and referred to by the same chord name. In actual practice, the sound of an inversion differs (slightly) from the sound of the original chord, but calling it by the same chord name is equivalent to asserting (coming to the clear decision) that an inversion has the same function as the original chord.

Next, notation is conferred on the fundamental chord forms and *tensions*. Figure 4.2 presents the format for writing chords and gives examples[4]. First, the root is written on the left, then the form of the chord is written in the lower right. The area contained within the dotted lines in the upper right is the area used when writing that, as an option, there is a ♭5 or −5. To the right of the form of the chord, is an area for adding a tension, as an option. In Fig. 4.2 we provide the layout of parts in chord name notation; for example, we write $\mathrm{G}\sharp_{7}$, $\mathrm{E}\flat_{M7(\flat 9,13)}$, and $\mathrm{A}_{m}^{\flat 5}$. To write the name of the pitch class of the root, it is necessary to decide which of the harmonic tones is the root (first degree), from the information of the key in which the chord appears and the preceding and succeeding chords. To put it another way, this means that the person describing the chord name carries out harmonic analysis. However, what is

[3] As mentioned previously in Sect. 1.4, according to the semiotics of Peirce (Charles Sanders Peirce, 1838–1914), in the signification yielded from the connection of a sign and a target, there are three types: icon (iconic similarity), index (physical causality) and symbol (unmotivated). From among the three types, symbolization in this chapter corresponds to index.

[4] This is just one school from among the many ways of writing that are in actual use. Various ways of writing, besides this one, are also being used.

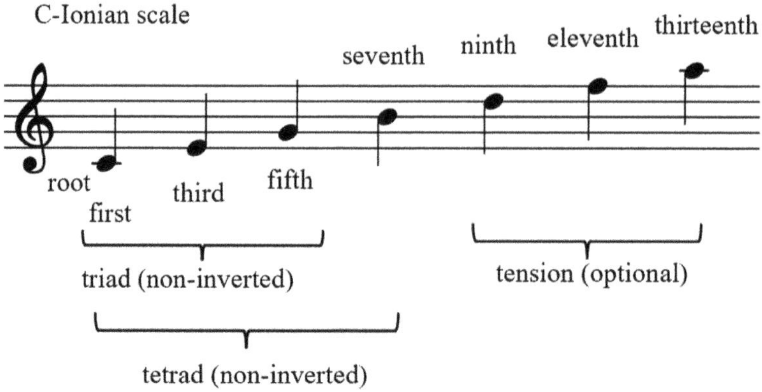

Fig. 4.1 Basic forms and options of chords

Fig. 4.2 Layout in writing chord names

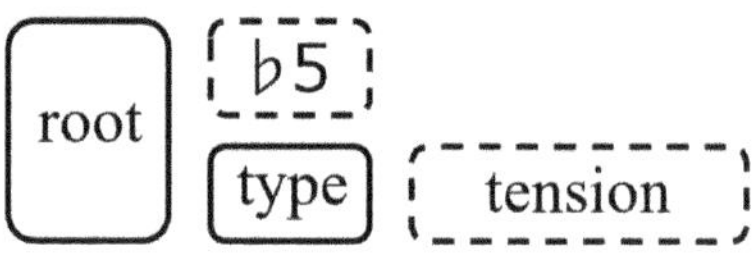

notated in a chord name is the name of the pitch class of the root; what degree that root is within the key is not described[5].

Designating the third, fifth, seventh harmonic tones in an Ionian chord (e.g., in C major this would be E, G, B) as zero change (0), the correspondence between the change of the third, fifth and seventh harmonic tones and the form of the chord is shown in Table 4.2. In the table, change '+1' means a rise of one semitone, while '−1' means a fall of one semitone. '[_]' means that 'nothing is to be written'. For example, the triad composed of the harmonic tones C, E, G can be notated as either C, or C_{Δ}, or C_{M}. Conversely, when the chord name of any one of these three styles is displayed, it uniquely means the chord composed of the harmonic tones (pitch class) C, E, G (In actual performance, there are also inversions, so multiple arrangements of the harmonic tones can be considered). In notation of tetrads including a seventh, the change of the seventh is not notated separately, instead it is notated as a combination with the change of the third. For example, the triads C and C_{Δ} both mean the chord composed of C,E,G, but in the tetrads C_7 and $C_{\Delta 7}$, the former means that the seventh is an interval of 10 semitones from the root note (B♭), while the latter means that the seventh is an interval of 11 semitones (B). 'ϕ' is called a half-diminished chord, and is a chord in which the third and fifth simultaneously change by only −1. To give an example, $C_{\phi 7}$ means the chord composed of C, E♭, G♭, B♭.

From the rules explained so far, in the fundamental form of chords in the Berklee method it is conjectured that the harmonic tones of the root, third, fifth, and seventh are all assembled. However, in actuality, there are cases in which a chord is composed

[5] When describing the root (first degree) in chord names in analysis of classical music, in most cases the degree in tonality (I, IV, V etc.) is used.

Table 4.2 Principle notations of changes of each harmonic tone and chord type

Change	Third	Fifth	Seventh
+1		+, +5, aug	
0	[_], Δ, M	[_]	Δ7, M7, maj7, mM7
−1	m, min	♭5, −5, ϕ	7, m7, min7, ϕ7

of two notes, or the third is intentionally removed to produce an ambiguous sound that is difficult to place as being in either a major or minor key. There are also cases of the seventh being removed. In principle, the Berklee method cannot express those kinds of chord. Therefore, in reality, when assigning chord names, the method conducts a harmonic analysis to guess the harmonic sound that may be missing (it is possible for there to be multiple chord names that can be assigned). Furthermore, there are instances of the introduction of heuristics related to notation, such as 'omit 3'. Conversely, if, for example, the harmonic tones of a tetrad are all assembled, the chord name and the harmonic tones correspond one-to-one. As the Berklee method does not care about what degree the root note is within a key (because we abstain from identifying the key by harmonic analysis), chord notation in the Berklee method is decided depending on the pitch class of the harmonic tones alone, thus it is not directly dependent on the key in which that chord appears (although, strictly speaking, because the key is involved when deciding the root, notation is indirectly dependent on the key). Accordingly, the chord G_7, for example, can be notated as G_7 regardless of what key it appears in. The French-born Canadian music scholar Nattiez[6] gives thirty-three different examples of how to interpret the Tristan chord [2], yet, because the Berklee method does not notate the degree of the root in relation to the key, the Tristan chord can be notated uniquely with the name $F_{\phi 7}$.

Even in the Berklee method, as in harmonic analysis of Western tonal music, when you want to express an interpretation that includes tonality, you can notate the root note's degree in the key, instead of its note name. For example, the triad C,E,G in C major can be notated as any one of I, I_{Δ} or I_{M}.

4.4 Chord Names and Rules of Functions

In the majority of textbooks and manuals relating to harmonic theory, after instruction on the fundamental construction of chords, like that given in the previous section, comes an explanation of chord sequences. At that point, concepts such as dominant motion, substitute chords, tension, and so on are introduced, and the explanation proceeds to the construction of more complex chords, or the arrangement of chords, and the psychological effect that can be obtained from this. That content is beyond the scope of this book, therefore we confine ourselves to presenting a summary of

[6] Jean-Jacques Nattiez, 1945 -.

Table 4.3 Group I: Table of diatonic chords / function tensions in major/minor scales

Chord name	Function	Tension		
		9th	11th	13th
I (I_6, $I_{\Delta 7}$)	T	$\natural 9$	[–]	(6th)
I_m (I_{m6}, I_{m7}, I_{mM7})	Tm	$\natural 9$	$\natural 11$	(6th)
II_{m7}	S	$\natural 9$	$\natural 11$	[–]
$II^{\flat 5}_{m7}$	Sm	$\natural 9$/Major Key	$\natural 11$	$\flat 13$
$III\flat_{\Delta 7}$ ($III\flat_6$)	T	$\natural 9$	$\sharp 11$	(6th)
III_{m7}	T	[–]	$\natural 11$	[–]
$IV_{\Delta 7}$ (IV_6)	S	$\natural 9$	$\sharp 11$	$\natural 13$
IV_7	S	$\natural 9$	$\sharp 11$	$\natural 13$
IV_{m7} (IV_{m6})	Sm	$\natural 9$	$\sharp 11$	(6th)
V_7	D	$\flat 9$, $\natural 9$, $\sharp 9$	$\sharp 11$	$\natural 13$, $\flat 13$
V_{m7}	Dm	[–]	$\natural 11$	[–]
$VI\flat_{\Delta 7}$	Sm	$\natural 9$	$\sharp 11$	$\natural 13$
VI_{m7}	T	$\natural 9$	$\natural 11$	[–]
$VI^{\flat 5}_{m7}$	Tm	$\natural 9$	$\natural 11$	$\flat 13$
$VII\flat_7$	Sm	$\natural 9$	$\sharp 11$/Major Key	$\natural 13$
$VII^{\flat 5}_{m7}$	D	[–]	$\natural 11$	$\flat 13$
$VII_{\Delta 7}$	D	[–]	$\natural 11$	$\flat 13$

Reproduced from [1, p. 165, p. 177]. Partially revised to conform to the notation of this book

the functions allocated to each chord, and the possible tensions, in Table 4.3, and Table 4.4. We concede more detailed explanation to an appropriate music theory book (e.g. [3, 4], etc.). In the table, Tm, Sm, Dm express a tonic minor chord, subdominant minor chord, and dominant minor chord, respectively. '[–]' expresses that use of a tension should be avoided.Provisional tonic in the table expresses whether the preceding provisional tonic, resolved by the secondary dominant †, is in either a major or minor key. For example, III_7 is resolved by VI, a fourth above, but because it is generally VI_m in the diatonic environment†, it becomes D (m).

The rules given in these tables about the tensions that are possible and those that should be avoided are applicable to any points within a musical composition. In other words, like Japanese chess pieces, tensions can be added whenever and wherever, so long as the rules allow[7]. As we have seen so far, because the Berklee method basically expresses chords and chord sequences by pitch class only, and not the harmonic tones actually being played, the method cannot express melodies that require octave information. Also, in simple sequences of chord names, the key in which those chords appear is not specified, thus the function of the chords (the degree with regard to the key) is not notated. Nevertheless, it is intentional that the Berklee method notates harmonies as sequences of chord names. This is done to separate

[7] This is called **puzzle gamification** of harmonic theory [1].

Table 4.4 Group II: Dominant and secondary dominant

			Tension		
Chord name		Function (provisional tonic)	9th	11th	13th
Dominant	V$_7$	D	♭9, ♮9, ♯9	♯11	♮13, ♭13
	II♭$_7$	D	♮9, ♯9	♯11	♮13
Secondary dominant	II$_7$ etc.	D (M)	♭9, ♮9, ♯9	♯11	♮13, ♭13
	III$_7$ etc.	D (m)	♭9, ♯9	♯11	♭13
	VI♭$_7$ etc.	D (M)	♮9, ♯9	♯11	♮13
	VII♭$_7$ etc.	D (m)	♮9	♯11	♮13

the melody and harmony contained in music, and to leave room for the musician to interpret a piece of music in order to identify the key. As a result, this dependence on interpretation enables more diverse interpretation by the musician, which helps to stimulate creative activity, such as *reharmonization*, i.e. putting a different harmony to the same melody, and *ad lib*, i.e. putting a different melody to the same harmony.

Such creative activity has given birth to music that transcends or departs from the concept of tonality, such as modal jazz music, or the music from impressionism and after in classical music, and has come so far as to penetrate into popular music. Expressing harmony in these kinds of music as a series of functions is difficult, but, if we use a sequences of chord names, expression is possible in most cases. This is probably one of the reasons that the Berklee method is still in general use even now.

4.5 Historical Significance

The Japanese jazz musician Naruyoshi Kikuchi[8] and the music critic Yoshio Otani[9] say, in their book, that "in musical history, there have been multiple periods in which music was symbolized, or people have tried to treat music as symbols" [1, p. 18]. They argue that twelve-tone equal temperament, the Berklee method, and the MIDI standard† are the three main innovations in the symbolization of music. As that same book has parts that position those innovations within musical history from the birth of music to the present, we have cited those parts [1, pp. 248–250] and summarized them in a list, having made alterations and additions in accordance with the content of this book :

[8] 1963–.

[9] 1972–.

- At the time of the birth of music, music is, probably, only one huge sound; there is only one pitch.
- Melody is born (Gregorian hymns, ancient Christian folk songs), but exists in analog isolation, with no temperament or tonality. There is slight intonation, subtle pitch, and so on, but these cannot be symbolized.
- Melody is configured on a type of grid, according to meter and scale.
- Fourth and fifth chords are born.
- Free modulation becomes possible in twelve-tone equal temperament. For example, in 'The Well-Tempered Clavier' (Bach, 1722).
- In rhythm, the technique is established of producing groups by repeating the smallest units, and adding accents.
- The technique is established of using chord changes to make music progress.
- After Bach, the popularization of music begins with late Baroque (seventeenth to eighteenth century). Symbolization makes acquisition of musical scores easy, and it becomes possible to reproduce a piece of music in any kind of place.
- (Jumping ahead to two hundred years after Bach) popular music based on functional harmony (having only the three functions T, D, S) is born in twentieth-century America. The Berklee method renders mass production of popular music possible.
- The way of thinking called mode is imported via ethnic music into harmonic music (chordality) in Europe.
- The influence of mode appears as modal jazz in the 1960s and funk in the 1980s.
- In 1981, the MIDI 1.0 standard is established. It becomes possible for a computer to carry out synthesizer performance and operation, as competently as a human, thus removing the restrictions of time and place on musical performance.

Achievements of the Berklee Method

The greatest achievement of the Berklee method is that it unrelentingly pressed forward with the symbolization of harmony, melody, and especially chord progression, known as functional harmony, and established an arrangement technique at the symbolic level. The harmonic and melodic theories that preceded this were a collection of practical heuristics for musicians, which were not sufficiently systematized. In contrast, the Berklee method described harmonic theory exactly like the rules of a game and changed creation of chord progression into something resembling an amusing puzzle. As the Berklee method is described by comparatively strict rules, there have also been many cases of information science research involving the implementation of those rules on a computer [5–10].

The jazz style bebop, which happened to be born in New York at the same time as the Berklee method, was characterized by a high degree of compositionality and linguistic descriptiveness in composition and performance, and having few ambiguities. It had a style in which improvised performance unfolds, just like a sport in which players compete in accordance with competition rules. Bebop and the Berklee method were highly compatible from the start, but the Berklee method developed in order to analyze bebop, then bebop in turn witnessed an increase in its logicality

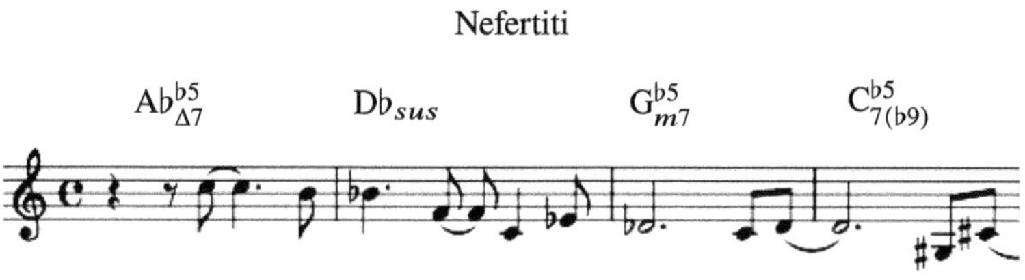

Fig. 4.3 Sample score in the Berklee method notation

and power of expression when the Berklee method was applied. It is said that, in this way, bebop developed until it became the first style within jazz music that it was thought should be taught at universities, due to its logical system.

Berklee Method and the MIDI Standard

As something that both the Berklee method and the MIDI standard have in common, we can raise the point that they both dealt with the tradeoff, arising from the technological capability of the time, between power of expression and cost of description. To reflect one's intention on a musical composition or performance, it is necessary to control the details of each individual note, but this generally takes both time and effort. In other words, increasing the level of expression incurs description cost. On the other hand, if rough instructions produced at an abstract level can be translated into control of each individual note by a machine, description cost can be reduced. However, realizing high-quality translation is critical. To put it simply, it is difficult to realize a high level of expression without incurring description cost. Therefore, reduction of description cost and improvement of power of expression are generally in a tradeoff relationship.[10]

Let us examine how the Berklee method and the MIDI standard overcame this tradeoff between power of expression and description cost. First, in the standard sheet-music composition of the Berklee method, a monophony is written on one stave of five lines and the chord name sequence (chord progression) is written directly above those five lines. The Berklee method describes any piece of music in this format. If you compare this to how sounds to be played are recorded note by note, on two staves in a piano score, or on multiple five-line staves in the case of an orchestral score, the description cost has been greatly reduced. Thus, the performer analyzes and performs a piece of music based on the chord name notation method and chord progression interpretation method given by the Berklee method. This gives a large degree of freedom to the performer's interpretation of a piece of music and the result of that interpretation is reflected in the performance. Nevertheless, unless the chord name notation method and chord progression interpretation method are learned and comprehended, it is difficult to capitalize on that freedom (Fig. 4.3).

The MIDI standard digitalized keypress information from a keyboard (position, timing, strength) and control information from a synthesizer (switch, button, event

[10] This corresponds to the flexibility-usability tradeoff related to systems (Sect. 1.3).

time, parameter value, etc.), enabling communication between a computer and synthesizer. Using conventional piano scores and orchestral scores, it was impossible to reproduce or record a performance that was exactly the same in regard to timing on a millisecond scale or loudness of volume on a dB scale. The introduction of the MIDI standard enabled not only performance of electronic instruments, but also digitalization of musical score information. As a result, performance information and score information were, for the first time, digitally symbolized instead of being recorded as audio signals. The MIDI standard, in the sense that it rendered information of both performance and score processable by a computer, gave people a new power of expression. In this way, as a result of the vast reduction in the cost of accurate recording of playing, and reproduction (performance), music genres such as technopop and dance were born and popular music came to be mass produced and mass consumed, thus furthering the popularization of music. At the same time, this also produced a great number of amateur musicians.

Valid Symbolization

Discovering appropriate symbolization is actually an extremely difficult task. Once you know the concepts behind equal temperament and the Berklee method and the MIDI standard, they seem so natural that it feels as though they must have existed since before (!) the birth of music. However, it is precisely because somebody conceived and gave shape to the matter of all those concepts that they generally pervaded and became popularized. If we assume the existence of computers, discovering appropriate symbolization means formally expressing knowledge, experience, concepts etc. on a computer. This does not mean simply writing a program that works, but also involves imbuing the behavior of that program with cognitive reality.[11] Based on the slogan 'knowledge is power', knowledge engineering, which was promoted from the 1970s to the 1980s, was able to demonstrate the usefulness of **formalized** knowledge on a computer, yet it also made it clear that the task of efficiently extracting and formalizing knowledge presented a major obstacle. In recent years, deep learning, which is currently receiving great attention, has been ground-breaking in that it has cleared the path for automation of the extraction and formalization of knowledge.

4.6 Merits and Demerits of Symbolization

Since Aristotle, for over two thousand years, continuous attempts have been made to formalize a part of human intelligence as a symbolic operation. In recent times in Europe, in particular, the pursuit of an approach that understands things by returning them to symbols, has resulted in great strides and great progress being made in the fields of science, the arts, society, culture, etc. In music too, over 99% of the music that we currently listen to is Western tonal music or a derivation thereof. One of the

[11] *cf.* Sect. 1.9.

reasons why music that was originally no more than one kind of ethnic music in the Western world was able to acquire this hegemony, is its drastic symbolization.

In this world, there are too many types of ethnic music to count, yet by the introduction of equal temperament and the invention of the Berklee method it became possible to imitate or simulate the majority of ethnic music using the syntax of Western tonal music. As a result, Western tonal music easily incorporated the components or characteristics of most ethnic music and succeeded in producing new compositions, genres and styles. Then, drastic symbolization, through the isolation of musical composition (melody and rhythm) from performance, gave Western tonal music an efficient and highly versatile musical score. In general, because the progression of music and the progression of the musical score were concurrent, the versatility of Western tonal music also increased. For example, central-European composers such as Dvorak[12] and Smetana[13] were able to produce music imbued with ethnic color, as a form of musical nationalism because they were able to map the musical modes of their regions onto twelve-tone equal temperament. Later Bartok[14] was able to use those indigenous modes to bring new color to the music of functional harmony, which seemed to have reached its limits. The success of these composers owes a great deal to the versatility of Western tonal music. In contrast, in music which has strong improvisational elements, like Indian music, the kind of musical score that accurately describes every phoneme to be performed did not develop. Also, in scores for traditional Japanese music, which pursues the expressiveness of phonemes to its very limits, the phonemes, the musical composition, and the performance are intentionally left as undifferentiated and tacit knowledge.

As demonstrated, the approach that segments and reduces the phenomena and concepts of music, then comprehends them in combination with symbols, (composition) is very strong. However, if you continuously move forward with symbolization, making it ever more precise and complex, will you ultimately be able to analyze and comprehend every kind of musical phenomenon and concept? Take, for example, Jean-Jacques Nattiez's work 'Music and Discourse: Toward a Semiology of Music', which presents multiple interpretations of the Tristan chord, played in the opening of Wagner's 'Tristan and Isolde' [2]. The first performance of 'Tristan and Isolde' was in 1865. Over the years spanning 1879 to 1981, thirty-three ways of interpreting the Tristan chord have been proposed. That the dispute has continued so long and that so many interpretations are possible is surely evidence that, even if we try to express the chord strictly according to the symbolic way of thinking, there is a part that cannot be captured by symbols.

In the music production scene also, there are sometimes periods of avidly pressing forward with symbolization in order to differentiate from other works or contentions. For example, in late bebop in the 1950s or fusion in the 1970s, music was being created that contained such a vast number of symbols and such complex structures as to render performance very difficult or almost infeasible. Within this music, pieces

---

[12] Antonin Leopold Dvorak, 1841–1904.

[13] Bedrich Smetana, 1824–1884.

[14] Bartok Bela Viktor Janos, 1881–1945.

were also composed that were difficult for an audience to comprehend. Kikuchi and Otani say that "to perform symbolization means to create a system of differentiation, and is a game with no end" [1, p. 268]. They also express this as 'gourmet-fication' or 'Berklee sickness'.

4.7 Virtualization

So far, we have used the word symbolization, but from the point of view of computer science we think it more fitting to call it virtualization. Generally, virtualization means abstracting the physical structure or limitations of the resources involved in computation (CPU, memory, network, input/output device, etc.), making them into a logical existence or object, and absorbing minor differences that exist in reality to provide only substantial functions. Virtualization differs from fictitiousness, on the point that it is modeled on a physical entity. The advantage of virtualization is that sorting, integrating, copying, and converting resources becomes both easy and flexible.

There are various names for the concept of virtualization, depending on the context or purpose in regard to which it is used. For example, regarding hardware that attaches importance to the interoperability of network protocol and accessories, etc., the words standardization and normalization are used, which have the meaning of extracting only substantial functions and making them common, in order to control a target. Concerning software, to enable easy reuse or to separate interface from implementation, the terms modularization, abstract data type and object orientation are used. These have a deep connection to the word formalization, used in the field of computer science. Commonly, *formalization* is the expression of a target as a mathematical model or system. The advantage of formalization is the realization of discrimination, inference (simulation) and prediction by the system. To conduct formalization, it is essential to correctly select the parameters for modularization, wherein lies a problem with the same root as symbol discovery or knowledge representation[15]. Nowadays, 'cloud' is a word you often hear, but the reason that the cloud is gathering attention is that, when securing the necessary computational resources, the quality and quantity can be regulated by the user's own hand, exactly like water, electricity or gas, and can be processed (materialized) freely by the user. Virtualization is the operation for cloudifying these computational resources that physically exist.

Let us consider virtualization in music. Twelve-tone equal temperament involves virtualizing every pitch in a scale, deciding on a semitone as the fundamental increment, and assigning an order. People often cite the advantage that, musically, modulation became both easy and free, but from the computer science viewpoint, for twelve-tone equal temperament as virtualization, there are various other advantages that can be cited. First of all, when all pitches are lined up evenly spaced, anybody can

[15] *cf.* Sect. 4.5.

reproduce the same piece of music anytime, anywhere, using any kind of instrument; ensemble performance of all kinds of instruments or songs becomes simple; simulating music from other genres becomes simple; incorporating music from other genres into one's own music (and occasionally plagiarizing) becomes simple; preparation for producing sound, or learning how to perform, becomes more efficient and playing instruments becomes simpler. By virtualization of rhythm, tactus was regulated as beat and tempo, Chronos time (physical time concept) was introduced, and repeated structures, i.e., bars and phrases, and hierarchical structure were brought in. The characteristics of chord notation in the Berklee method are: expression by pitch class, which does not directly consider key; the introduction of the fundamental form of stacked thirds; and classification of chords according to function. These being equivalent to virtualization of chords, they endowed harmony with the same advantages as twelve-tone equal temperament. Meanwhile, the MIDI standard was originally intended for virtualization of keyboard instruments or standardization of electronic instruments, but, because it was an exceedingly valid form of virtualization, not only keyboard instruments but also string instruments, percussion instruments, and so on became targets for virtualization. As a result, almost all activity connected to performance, recording etc. became controllable by computer using the MIDI standard, and restrictions of time and place ceased to be a problem, which changed the shape of performance and music production forever.

What is fascinating, is that the concept of virtualization, while it played a major part in aiding the development of computers, also played an important role in the development of Western tonal music. Virtualization is essential for humans, who are imperfect beings, to use tools both efficiently and with complete mastery. A computer is a tool for simulating a person's thought, while music is a tool for producing expression that influences a person's emotion. The human intelligence used to master these tools has physical limitations regarding the speed, capacity and accuracy of thought, memory, cognition, etc. This is why the flexibility-usability tradeoff and the tradeoff of expressiveness and description cost arise. When that happens, we can consider that standardization, abstraction, etc. brought about by virtualization, are compensating for the imperfection of humans.

4.8 Jazz, Classical and Pop Music

Twelve-tone equal temperament, the Berklee method and the MIDI standard, which are the three principle innovations of symbolization (Sect. 4.5), can be thought of as forms of symbolization that emerged in classical music, jazz and popular music. So, are there any other innovations that are common to classical music, jazz, and pop music? First, let us summon the American jazz trumpeter Miles Davis[16]. At a banquet held in 1987 to celebrate Ray Charles, Miles Davis turned to the couple next to him, a white politician and his wife, and said "I've changed music five or

[16] Miles Dewey Davis III, 1926–1991.

six times" [11]. In this section, we focus on the changes that are thought to be most important among those five or six times, which are the proposal of modal jazz (1959) and the combination of jazz with rock and R&B. Modal jazz is the way of thinking which says that transformation of the color of the sounds created by melody and chords produces propulsion of music (transitioning from a stable to an unstable state (tension), relaxing back into a stable state). In actual practice, transformation of the color of sound is produced by changing the scale (mode) being used, but this can also be done by basically creating melodies and chords using any of the notes contained within a scale. Before mode, it was thought that change of chords produced musical propulsion, thus melodies were created based on the limitations of the internal structure of a chord and the connection between chords. Davis' 1959 album 'Kind of Blue' is a monumental work that contains solely modal jazz pieces. Although modal jazz method gave musicians freedom and expressiveness, it also increased the difficulty of composition and performance.

Next, approximately twenty-five years after the Berklee method and ten years after modal jazz, Davis achieved the fusion of jazz and rock and R&B in his 1969 album 'Bitches Brew'. Listened to with modern ears, it sounds a little unrefined but still resembles an ordinary jazzy instrumental piece[17] at present, so it may be hard to believe that at the time it made Davis the enemy of all traditional jazz fans, who believed that true jazz was bebop. Incidentally, it is said that the rock musician Davis was particularly interested in then was Jimi Hendrix[18], while in R&B he looked to James Brown[19].

Jazz-style rock or rock-style jazz are not what we call fusion. These are just cases of playing a rock song melody while maintaining the syntax of jazz, or vice versa. In contrast, the fusion of jazz and rock and R&B refers to a new syntax being invented that is neither jazz nor rock nor R&B, and enabling the existence of musical compositions that could not be expressed or performed without that new syntax. In other words, the new syntax can express pieces composed in the old syntax, but when the old syntax cannot express pieces composed in the new syntax, that is when we realize that it is a new syntax. When version 2.0 of certain software is released, if data files executed on version 1.0 can also be used on version 2.0, we say version 2.0 has compatibility (especially downward compatibility). In contrast, there are often cases in which version 1.0 software cannot operate data files from version 2.0. In this case, we say that the version 1.0 software does not have compatibility (especially upward compatibility). Here, a new syntax corresponds to the version 2.0 software[20]. Genres newly born after the combination of jazz, rock and R&B include fusion and black contemporary. Miles Davis apparently had great confidence in this new music genre,

---

[17] a piece with only instruments and no singing.

[18] Jimi Hendrix, 1942–1970.

[19] James Brown, 1933–2006.

[20] Various Creole languages are the results of language mixture; when two language groups collide, they happen to construct new language norms which may affect the syntax. However, simple word adoption does not change the original language. Sushi or kimono seem nowadays common in English, but they are still compatible in English syntax.

stating in an interview with Rolling Stone magazine (December, 1969) "I could put together the greatest rock and roll band you ever heard."

Now, in classical music, the innovation equivalent to modal jazz that creates musical driving force by changing the color of sound is probably the appearance of impressionism around the year 1900[21]. The composers Debussy and Ravel, who pressed forward with the departure from functional harmony, are representative of the impressionist movement. Their work is characterized by bringing a sense of flotation to melody, and by the adoption of the diatonic scale and the elimination of the leading-tone[†]. The innovation in classical music that equates to the fusion of jazz and rock and R&B is probably the birth of new melodies, harmonies, and rhythm forms brought about by the introduction of ethnic music in around 1910. As representative composers, there are Bartok, and Stravinsky[22], who composed 'The Firebird', 'Petrushka', and 'The Rite of Spring', in his primitive period (around 1910–1913). Of course, there is no doubt that, as classical music is the senior of jazz, jazz musicians would have introduced its essence into jazz after having learned the theory and development of classical music.

In classical music, atonal music was advanced by Schoenberg et al. in around 1910, with the aim of expanding expressive power. In jazz also, in the 1960s a musical style called free jazz appeared, which, regarding melody, harmony, and rhythm (moreover, timbre), was free from the forms, styles, and theories of conventional jazz, that is to say, of Western tonal music. As explained in Chap. 5, when people listen to music, at a conscious or unconscious level they make the journey from implication to realization, and in doing so people comprehend music. However, in atonal music or free jazz, it is difficult to travel from implication to realization in melody, harmony, or rhythm; or the music may even sometimes sound like non-sense to a general audience. Accordingly, even if a piece wears the mantle of program music, understanding the meaning of that music is still extremely difficult. For that reason, even now, this music has not managed to attain popularity.

Up until now, we have made a rough comparison of the transition of jazz music and classical music. When a style change, such as modal jazz or genre fusion, occurs in a certain musical genre, we believe a specific pattern can be seen. As mentioned in Sect. 4.6, when musicians relentlessly press on with symbolization, to discriminate between other works and performances, they proceed ever further into complication and ultimately reach saturation. Therefore, in reaction to complication you should once again return music to an existence that accords with its original aim, and seek ideas from the uncomplicated style at the primary stage. In doing so, simple music will be created that has characteristics completely opposite to having huge numbers of symbols and complicated structure. Then, finally, complex music and simple music are dialectically sublated (aufheben) to the next stage. Within jazz music and classical

---

[21] *cf.* Sect. 2.10.

[22] Igor Stravinsky, 1882–1971.

music, this kind of style change has been repeated many times, but it feels as though the more recent the music genre, the shorter the interval between style changes is becoming. So, how much shorter will those intervals become in the future? It's a source of endless fascination.

References

1. N. Kikuchi, Y. Otani, in *The School that Taught Melancholy and Sensuality—A Bird's Eye View of Twentieth Century Commercial Music History through the Berklee Method* (Kawade Bunko, 2004). (in Japanese)
2. J.-J. Nattiez, Musicologie générale et sémiologie, Christian Bourgois Editeur (1987)
3. T. Hojnacki, J. Mulholland, in *The Berklee Book of Jazz Harmony* (The Berklee Press, 2013)
4. P. Schmeling, in *Berklee Music Theory Book 1, Basic Principles of Rhythm, Scales, and Intervals*, 2nd ed. (The Berklee Press, 2005)
5. M. Chemillier, Toward a formal study of jazz chord sequences generated by Steedman's grammar. Soft Comput. **8**(9), 617–622 (2004). (Sept.)
6. W.B. de Haas, R.C. Veltkamp, F. Wiering, Tonal pitch step distance: a similarity measure for chord progressions, in *Proceedings of the 9th International Society for Music Information Retrieval Conference, ISMIR 2008,* 14–18 September 2008, Philadelphia, PA, USA [Online]. Available: dblp. http://dblp.uni-trier.de/db/conf/ismir/ismir2008. Accessed: 3 Nov. 2016
7. H.V. Koops, J.P. Magalhaes, W.B. de Haas, A function approach to automatic melody harmonisation, in *Proceedings of the 1st ACM SIGPLAN Workshop on Functional art, Music, Modeling & Design* (Boston, US-MA, 2013). [Online]. Available: ACM-Degital library. http://dl.acm.org. Accessed: 3 Nov 2016
8. F. Pachet, Computer analysis of jazz chord sequence: is solar a blues?, in *Readings in Music and Artificial Intelligence*. ed. by E.R. Miranda (Routledge, New York, 2000), pp.85–114
9. M. Steedman, The blues and the abstract truth: music and mental models, mental models, in *Cognitive Science*, ed. by A. Garnham, J. Oakhill (Mahwah, NJ, Erlbaum, 1996), pp. 305–318
10. B. Thom, BoB: an interactive improvisational music companion, in *Proceedings of the 4th Intermational Conference on Autonomous Agents (AGENTS'00)* (ACM, 2000), pp. 309–316
11. M. Davis (with Quincy Troupe, Co-author), Miles: The Autobiography, Simon & Schuster (1989)

Chapter 5
Implication-Realization Model

5.1 The Implication-Realization Model

The Implication-Realization model is an attempt to understand music by the network formed by notes (Sect. 1.4)[1] . In this chapter, we will start by explaining about gestalt which appears in music, upon which the Implication-Realization model stands. Multiple basic patterns are defined in the Implication-Realization model, and at a glance these can seem to have been constructed ad hoc, but we shall demonstrate that actually they are constructed systematically. Lastly, we will conclude the chapter by introducing a certain psychological experiment that demonstrates the cognitive basis of the Implication-Realization model.

5.2 Gestalt that Appears in Music

Meyer[2] proposed applying gestalt psychology to the understanding of music [1, 2]:

> Musical meaning arises when an antecedent situation, requiring an estimate as to the probable modes of pattern continuation, produces uncertainty as to the temporal-tonal nature of the expected consequent. [2, p. 416]

---

[1] There are largely two ways in which people understand things. One is putting things into a group with the same or similar properties and giving them a name, while the other is creating a connection between the thing one wants to understand and other things. In mathematical terms, the former corresponds to creating sets and the latter to binary relation. Conveniently for us, these also correspond to musical terms: the former to GTTM and the latter to the Implication-Realization model. Furthermore, since a set is equivalent to a membership function, and binary relation is equivalent to a logical function with two arguments, it may be that the world is ultimately made up of functions.

[2] Leonard B. Meyer, 1918–2007. American music scholar and philosopher.

K. Hirata et al., *Music, Mathematics and Language*,
https://doi.org/10.1007/978-981-19-5166-4_5

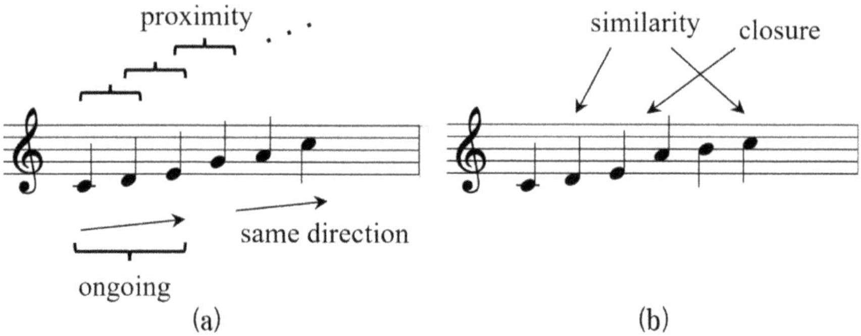

Fig. 5.1 Gestalt perceived in melody

In human perception or cognition, a phenomenon occurs in which the components themselves have no meaning or role, yet they come to have meaning by being combined with each other. This phenomenon is called gestalt[3]. Also, when people perceive, recognize, or appreciate music, this gestalt is generated in relation to pitch, duration, onset timing and harmony. As the properties (aspects) that produce gestalt, there are proximity, similarity, and same direction (Fig. 5.1).

In (a) in the figure, even if the major second (C-D or G-A) and the minor third (E-G or A-C) are present alongside each other, the progression continues, but, in (b) in the figure, when the perfect fourth (E-A) is introduced, it is not seen as one process and F or F-G-A, which is the implication of C-D-E, is denied and A-B-C is perceived as a new process. In other words, closure occurs at E. In this way, since the whole phrase has a meaning greater than the sum of its parts (known as totality), it can be understood that gestalt is not a simple bottom-up phenomenon. On the other hand, the properties at work in a top-down manner are good form, good continuation and optimum organization. Proximity, similarity, and same direction can be objectively defined and measured, whereas good form, good continuation and optimum organization cannot be objectively defined or measured. Meyer advocated an approach to cognitively grasp the meaning of music based on gestalt. Please note that Meyer's approach does not bring in an aesthetic or artistically interpretive viewpoint.

Narmour[4] developed and formalized Meyer's thinking and aimed to construct a theory to explain the relationship between locally adjacent notes. What makes the Implication-Realization model different from Schenkerian analysis and GTTM, which are the mainstream forms of music analysis, is, first of all, assuming that the form of melody itself expresses an Implication-Realization structure. In Ursatz in Schenkerian theory or the basic form of the GTTM prolongational tree etc., by reduction, one supposes a 'melody' at the level of chronologically distanced notes,

[3] *cf.* Sect. 1.3.

[4] Eugene Narmour, 1939-. American scholar of music theory and music perception and cognition.

but Narmour says that, since that abstract melody is not made of the actual sound that we hear with our ears, it is not important to consider such a melody[5].

Narmour asserts that music theory should simultaneously have two aims. The first aim is to seek, from the differing cases and phenomena relating to music, universal truths and simple and logical explanations. In this sense, music theory is a science, just like physics, chemistry, biology, and so on. The second aim is to discover the uniqueness of the composer, which takes us in the opposite direction to science[6]. The features or structure that make a certain work typical of the musician who created it are called **idiostructure**[7]. Musicians discover their idiostructures by themselves and introduce the idiostructures into works which musicians have already screened and emphasized on occasion. It can alternatively be said that musicians nurture their own idiostructures through their works.

5.3 The Principles of the Implication-Realization Model

Stepping off from the platform of gestalt, Narmour proposed two hypotheses of when people listen to music: 1. Suppose that one hears a note or group of notes, X, and next hears the same note or group of notes, X. Then, it is implied that one will further hear that same X next. This is expressed as X+X→X. 2. Suppose that one hears a note or group of notes, X, and next hears a different note or group of notes, Y. Then, it is implied that one will hear a further differing note or group of notes, Z. This is expressed as X+Y→Z.

Here we give a simple example of bottom-up gestalt. Let us consider the melody C–C in C major, i.e., a melody of which the pitch does not vary. If you hear C–C, most generally the next note implied is C and not D or F. If the third note is actually C, that implication is realized (i.e., C+C→C). Next, if we consider the melody C–D in C major, i.e., a melody that ascends by a major second, most generally the next note implied is E. If the third note is actually E, that implication is realized (i.e., C+D→E). Meyer and Narmour consider that emotion is not aroused in the case in which implication is realized. Now, let us consider the melody C–D–C, which actually often appears in C major. C–D ascends by a second, but since the third note reverses the direction, being C instead of E, a denial of implication occurs. In the same way, in the melody C–D–F, the direction of the third note is the same, but the gap between D–F extends to a minor third, thus here also a denial of implication occurs. In the case of the third note being E♭, the direction is the same and the gap between D–E♭ is a minor second, but the melody breaks out of the C major scale, causing

[5] Narmour in fact goes so far as to declare that "...current melodic analysis, with its emphasis on reduction to ever higher levels, has a very bad habit of ignoring all kinds of cognitively real melodic relations in favor of the supersummative agencies of tree-structured grammars." [3, p. xi].

[6] The discovered uniqueness of a composer may not constitute a scientific result, yet the methodology for discovering the composer's uniqueness can surely be scientific.

[7] The prefix idio means individualistic or unique.

a denial of implication. Meyer and Narmour consider that, by denial of implication, people's emotions are aroused regardless of whether or not they are conscious of it.

In this way, we can understand that the parameters for classifying a melody (or the parameters used when discussing the identity of a melody) are the pitch difference (interval) and movement direction (ascent, descent) of adjacent notes, and the pitch on the scale. Interval is not quantized in degrees of semitones, but is thought of only as three types: the first (zero pitch difference), an interval smaller than, or an interval larger than the diminished fifth (augmented fourth). In other words, a small interval is an interval of within five semitones and a large interval is an interval of more than seven semitones.

The Implication-Realization model is made up of two principles that generate the fundamental form produced by three locally adjacent notes, and implication.

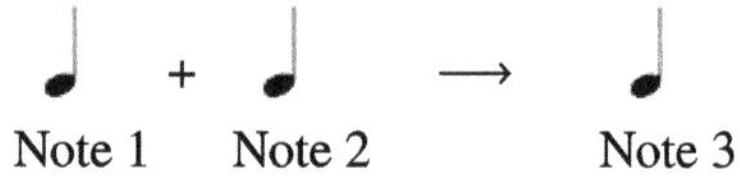

Principle of Registral Direction, PRD
When the interval between note 1 and note 2 is small, an interval of the same direction in note 3 is implied. When the interval between note 1 and note 2 is large, an interval of a different direction in note 3 is implied.

Principle of Intervallic Difference, PID
When the interval between note 1 and note 2 is small, an interval of the same degree (± 2 semitones) between note 2 and note 3 is implied. When the interval between note 1 and note 2 is large, a smaller interval between note 2 and note 3 is implied.

In the above figure, a single note is expediently expressed as a crotchet, but in the actual melody we can consider three note combinations that have various durations. Implication does not occur after hearing just the first note, but when the second note is heard implication occurs in accordance with the two principles (PRD, PID). On the third note, that implication is either realized or denied. When implication is realized there are three basic patterns (D, P, R, described hereafter). The two principles that generate implication are obtained from the aspects that produce gestalt, i.e., proximity, similarity and same direction, based on interval and the direction in which the notes move. Here, we want you to recall the gestalt psychology way of thinking, which says that even if individual components do not have meaning, meaning can be produced by combining those components. Also, as mentioned above, a small interval is an interval of within five semitones, and a large interval is an interval of more than seven semitones.

In the working of these two principles, it is said that there is an inherent/unconscious level and an acquired/self-conscious level[8]. In the same way as we have just

[8] Furthermore, the acquired level is divided into the valid style confined within a specific composition, and the valid style across multiple works. As an example of the former, there are cases in which a motif presented at the start of a piece appears many times within that piece. As an example of the latter, there are melodies created in accordance with the pentatonic scale of traditional Japanese popular ballads, or the hemitonic pentatonic scale (Okinawan scale).

described, attempts to investigate a scientific music theory primarily target the inherent/unconscious level, while attempts to discover idiostructure target the acquired/self-conscious level.

5.4 Basic Implication-Realization Patterns

All the patterns produced from the principles of the Implication-Realization model are presented in Fig. 5.2.

In this table, all combinations of all parameters are listed. The second column in the table (size of interval) is a combination of the interval between note 1 and note 2 and the interval between note 2 and note 3. S (short) represents 'within five semitones', L (long) represents 'more than seven semitones', and 0 represents 'same pitch' (first degree). Additionally, since the pattern, like the aforementioned C-D-C, in which note 2 moves by a small degree and note 3 returns to the same pitch as note 1, appears frequently in ordinary melodies, we treat this as a special case (expressed as 'aba' by Narmour [3]). The third column in the table (same direction) is a combination of the cases in which the direction from note 1 to note 2 and note 2 to note 3 is the same and not the same. All the parameters are produced from these second and third columns. The fourth and fifth columns express whether or not the Principle of Registral Direction (PRD) and the Principle of Intervallic Difference (PID) are satisfied. In the Implication-Realization model, patterns in which at least one of either PRD or PID is satisfied are given names (first column) and taken as the basic patterns[9]. Examples of each pattern to which a name is assigned are presented in Fig. 5.2. Incidentally, reverse patterns (upside down) that invert the ascent and descent of each pattern are also classified as the same pattern.

Narmour says that the movement of notes in the Implication-Realization model is like the movement of chess pieces. The pawn is a weak piece that can only move one square. When your opponent places his hand on a pawn so as to move it for his next turn, you can estimate to what square that pawn will move, and it will actually move as estimated. In this sense, the diminished second, for example, is like a pawn. In contrast, since the queen can move in any direction and any number of squares, by the rules of chess the possibility of a wide range of movements can be considered. However, in the middle of a game of chess, the positional relationship of you and your opponent's pieces only permits extremely limited movement. In this sense, a jump of an augmented sixth is like the movement of the queen, for example. In chess there are other pieces such as the knight and rook, and, as the next move, possibilities and options of a variety of strengths arise. Understanding the movement of notes in a piece of music by musical analysis is equivalent to investigating what pieces moved and in what way they moved to win a game.

Let us look at how a piece of music is actually analyzed using the basic patterns. Firstly, D (Duplicate) is the basic pattern of repetition (Fig. 5.3); in the figure, (a) is an example of when implication grows stronger by repetition. When we compare these 12 semiquavers to the case in which they are re-written as a single dotted half-note,

[9] We will touch on the origin of the name of each pattern where necessary.

Pattern	Intervals	Same direction	PID	PRD
D	0 0	yes	yes	yes
ID	S S (=)	no	yes	no
P	S S	yes	yes	yes
IP	S S	no	yes	no
VP	S L	yes	no	yes
-	S L	no	no	no
R	L S	no	yes	yes
IR	L S	yes	yes	no
-	L L	yes	no	no
VR	L L	no	no	yes

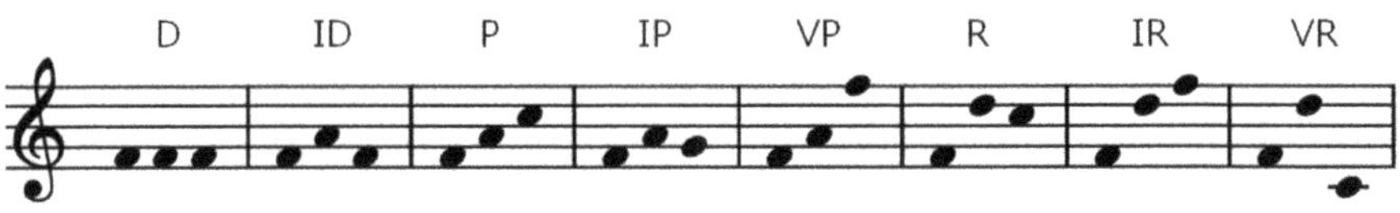

Fig. 5.2 Classification of Implication-Realization patterns

Fig. 5.3 Basic pattern D (duplicate). Reproduced from [3, p. 98]

the effect of repetition becomes clear. On the fourth beat, the implication of repetition is denied because the degree changes, however, the duration remains the same. The repetition in (b) in the figure can also be rewritten as a single dotted half-note. When the implication of repetition is denied on the fourth beat, not only the degree but also the duration has changed. Hence, the degree of denial is larger than in (a) and the listener is made strongly aware that it is the end of the repetition.

(c) J. S. Bach. Well-tempered clavier I no.6,5,10 Fugue

Fig. 5.4 Basic pattern P (process). Reproduced from [3, p. 101]

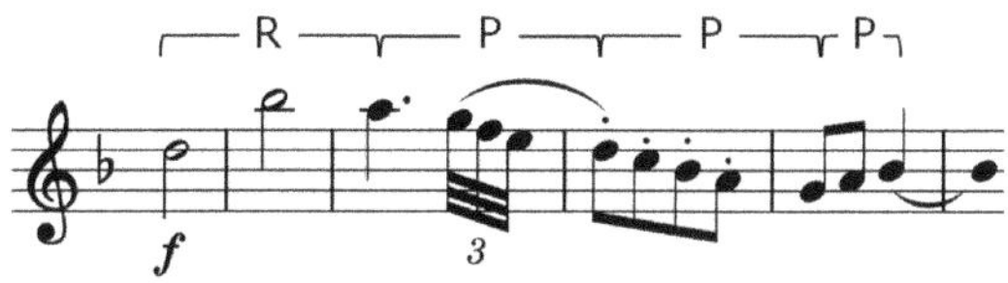

Mozart, Piano concerto K.459, third movement (Allegro assai) bar 287--90

Fig. 5.5 Basic pattern R (reversal). Reproduced from [3, p. 159]

P (Process) is the basic pattern of continuation, of which three examples are presented in Fig. 5.4. P is a pattern that is inherent and of which the listener is almost entirely unaware, and has the effect that even a person who does not know the piece of music can easily perceive the scale of the piece upon hearing P at the beginning. At the same time, people listen to music while also expecting other patterns with low possibility. However, a weak expectation will not leave a significant impact even if denied, and will soon be forgotten. It is common for a basic pattern other than P to be combined directly after P, thus the entirety of the melody accords with acquired and top-down knowledge. In the examples given in Fig. 5.4, a listener with prior knowledge relating to northern Germanic music, middle-period Baroque, harpsichord or choral music would probably expect that kind of peculiar phrase after P.

R (Reversal) is the basic pattern of reversal (Fig. 5.5). The ascent from D to B♭ in the example in the figure makes the listener feel the possibility of D minor and implies A, which is dominant, as the third note, an implication which is realized (in actuality the piece is in F major). This kind of motion appears very frequently in Western tonal music. As in the example in Fig. 5.5, in a pattern in which P follows on from R it can intuitively be understood that after a jump of more than a fifth a reversal occurs as an attempt to fill in the gap.

One question that rises in the FAQ[10] relating to the Implication-Realization model is how the start point of a basic pattern is chosen. The answer to this question is

[10] Frequently Asked Questions.

closure. Closure is the point at which implication does not arise from a note sequence heard so far, or the point at which implication becomes ambiguous, suppressed, or weakened. What this actually means is a time when degree, note direction or duration changes, a time when a rest or accented beat occurs, or a time when dissonance is resolved into consonance. In actual melody, these occur in composite and various strengths of closure are produced (Fig. 5.6).

The right end of the double arrow (->>-) in (a) in the figure is the end point of P and expresses the closure that occurs due to the change of degree, note direction and duration. At the same time, that point is the start point of the next basic pattern. In (b) in the figure, a large duration occurs at the right end of P (the note marked as '*'), producing the effect of attenuating the implication, which creates closure. In (c) in the figure is an example in which the end point of duplication becomes closure just as it is. The note at the right end of the opening D pattern is the end point of duplication and the note marked as 'currencydollar' expresses closure due to an accented beat. A further continuing pattern of P and ID also creates closure (the note marked as '*').

Another FAQ is whether basic patterns can be overlapped and the answer to this is yes.

In example i in Fig. 5.7, the patterns 'aba' (ID) and P overlap, and in the example ii the patterns IP, P and ID are overlapping. Motion that returns to exactly the same note is expressed as aba, motion close to that is expressed as aba^1 (note 1 a and note 3 a^1 are slightly different), and three notes that include P, which is made by distanced notes, are expressed as aa^1a^2 and bb^1b^2 (Narmour's notation is easily mistaken for footnote numbers and can thus be a little misleading, but here we prioritize the notation of the original author). This kind of motion of notes is called transformational (motion that ascends or descends in a linear manner). In the figure, 4 and 3 mean the fourth degree and the third degree, respectively. Below the staff, where 'Form' is written, one of the hypotheses recognized by gestalt is named 'A'. 'A' corresponds to 'X' on the left side of X+X→X. Then, 'A', which is not strictly the same note, is repeated twice. When the point '‡' arrives, the realization was not 'A'. Also, the structures aa^1a^2 and bb^1b^2 appear and, although the first three notes B♭-G-C form a basic pattern, implication is denied on the fourth note C. In example ii in Fig. 5.7, the third note F is the middle note in the ascending note series E♭-F-G and is not a note that produces the transitional P pattern G-F-E♭ (this E♭ is the E♭ that begins the second bar). In contrast, since the sixth note (the fourth beat) F is both the end point of the IP pattern G-C-F and is on an accented beat (marked as '†'), it becomes closure and is recognized as the second note of the P pattern G-F-E♭, marked in the uppermost level, above the staff.

Here we present an example of Narmour himself having analyzed a piece of music using the Implication-Realization model (Fig. 5.8).

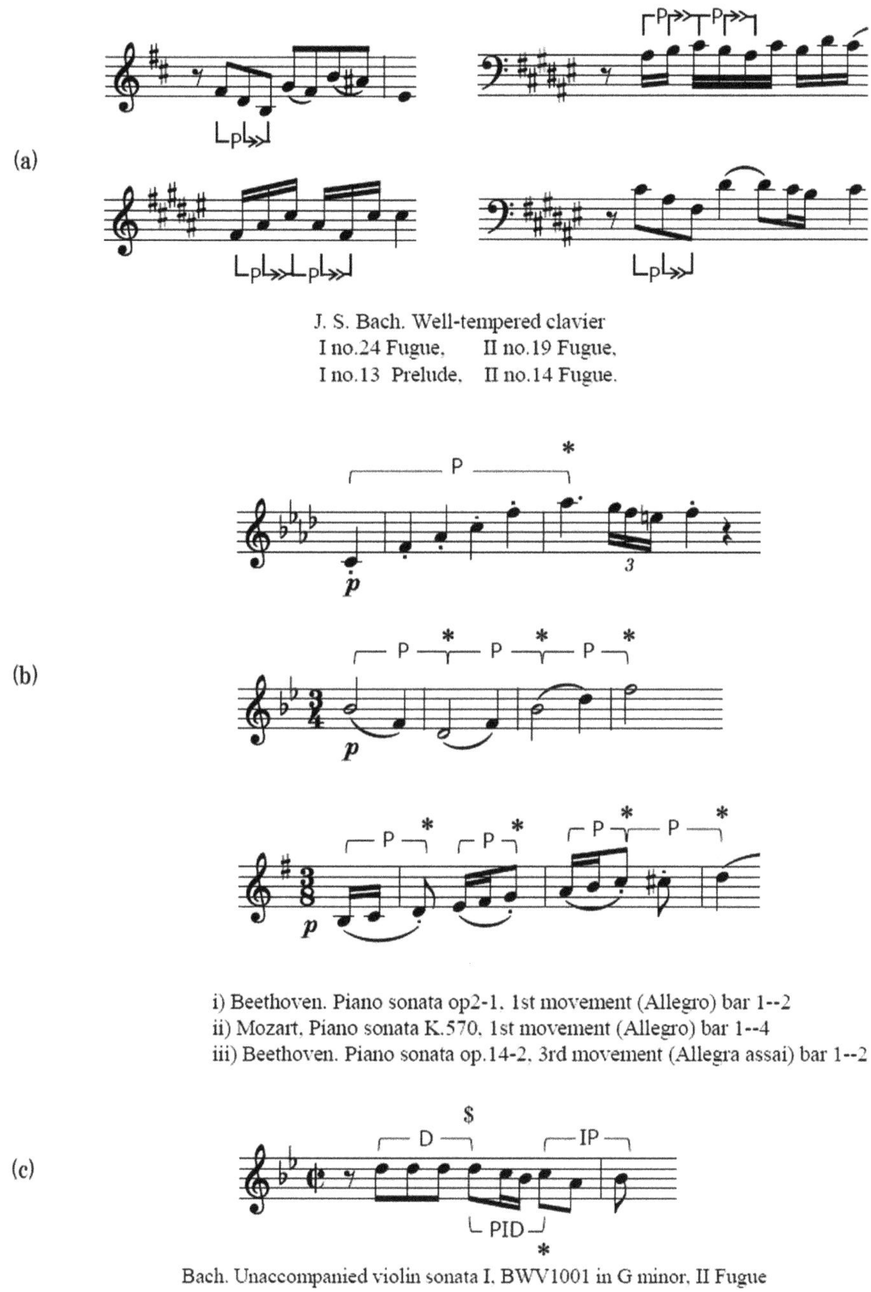

Fig. 5.6 Examples of closure. Reproduced from [3]

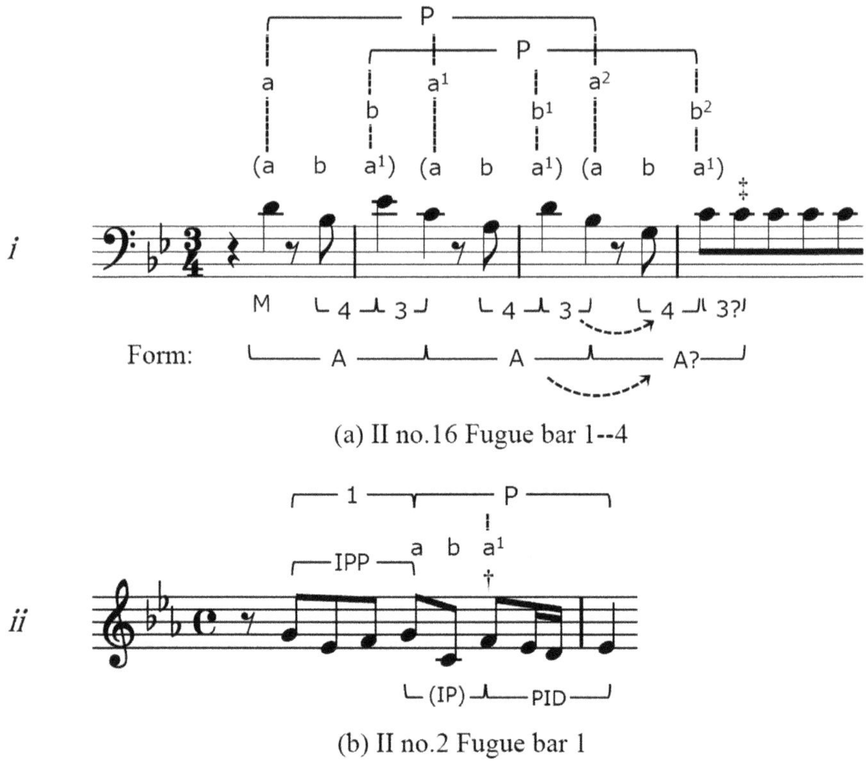

Fig. 5.7 Examples of superposition of basic patterns. Reproduced from [3, p. 133]

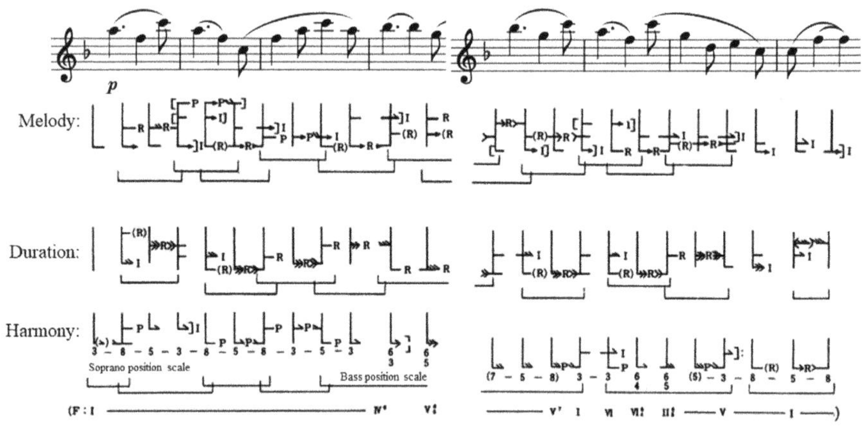

Fig. 5.8 Example of analysis, by Narmour himself, of the fifth movement of Beethoven's Symphony No. 6 in F major 'Pastoral'. Reproduced from [4, pp. 28–29]

Here, Narmour analyzes not only melody, but also duration and harmony. According to Murao, it was understood that "with the exception of the last bar, the parts with strong beats are recognized as structural notes" [4].[11]

5.5 Carlsen's Experiment and the Validity of the Implication-Realization Model

Let us touch on the experiment by James C. Carlsen, who is a proponent of the validity of the Implication-Realization model [6]. Although Carlsen's work was published more than 40 years ago, the results are clear and helpful to convince us of the validity. For subsequent studies, see [7–9], for instance.

Subjects are instructed to listen to two notes that promote expectation, then to sing the natural melody that follows those two notes. At this time, the first note of the sung melody is supposed to be the third note in an Implication-Realization pattern. The subjects are 91 first-year level students from music colleges in Hungary, Germany and America, aged between 15 and 23. The stimuli given to a subject, and the subject's response, are shown in Fig. 5.9, in which (a) represents the positions of metronome pulses, which are at a rate of 60 BPM. First there are two beats during which no note is played, then two stimulus notes are played (represented by o). In the seven seconds (seven beats) after that, the subject is made to sing the melody that naturally follows on from the two stimulus notes. At this time, the subject is instructed not to think about trying to make a good melody[12].

After one trial run ends in this way, there is a break of two to three seconds then the next run begins. In (b) in the figure, we present an example of two notes that were actually played to a subject, and an example of the melody that the subject proceeded to sing. The interval of the stimulus notes in this case (A in (b) in the figure) is the diminished third (three semitones), and the interval of the second stimulus note and of the first note in the response melody (B in (b) in the figure) is the diminished second (one semitone).

The experiment results are summarized in Table 5.1.

In the table, *stimulus interval* refers to the interval between the two stimulus notes (this corresponds to A in Fig. 5.9b), and *response interval* refers to the interval between the second stimulus note and the first note sung in response (this corresponds to A in Fig. 5.9b). Stimulus interval and response interval are in units of semitones. For example, -12 means a pitch descending by 12 semitones, which is equivalent to

[11] Regarding the development of the Implication-Realization model after Narmour's publications [3, 5], we recommend watching the video of Narmour's lecture given at the BKN25 Symposium held at McGill University (Montreal, Canada) in 2014 http://www.music.mcgill.ca/bkn25/videos/Narmour.mp4.

[12] The set-up in the initial preliminary experiment was that subjects sing not the melody that naturally follows but just one note that naturally follows. However, since doing so resulted in the frequent appearance of patterns that could be interpreted as authentic cadences or half cadences, the experiment task was improved to that of singing the naturally following melody [6, p. 25].

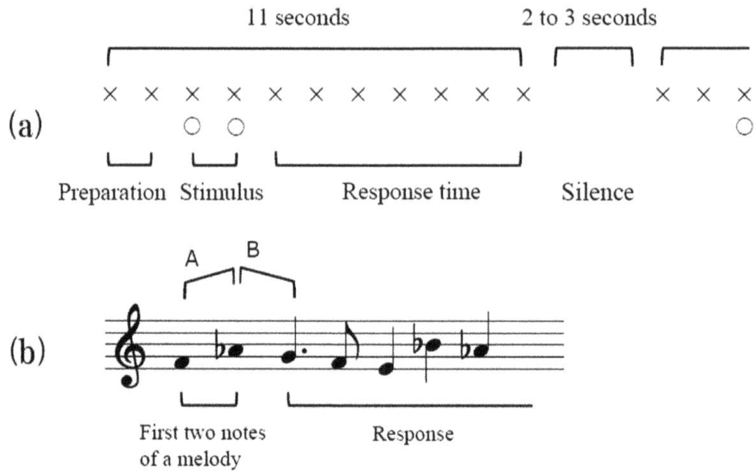

Fig. 5.9 Stimuli and response in Carlsen's experiment. Reproduced from [6, p. 15]

one octave down. Response intervals are presented ranked by frequency of appearance, up to the third most frequent[13]. Each cell on the response interval side contains three types of data, which are response interval, Implication-Realization pattern and frequency of occurrence. In stimulus interval -12, for example, the three items, 5 IR 13.1%, of the no.1 response interval, mean that the response interval is five semitones (ascent of a perfect fourth), in terms of the Implication-Realization model it is an IR pattern, and, among all the patterns obtained for this stimulus interval -12, the occurrence frequency of response interval 5 is 13.1%. A stimulus interval of ± 6 (augmented fourth, diminished fifth) is classified as a large interval and an Implication-Realization pattern is assigned. Carlsen calls the melodic beginning strength when occurrence frequency is over 40%, that when it is below 40% and above 25%, and that when it is below 25% 'strong' continuation, 'moderate' continuation and 'weak' continuation, respectively.

We will now indicate several focus points that support the Implication-Realization model.

- Bottom-up gestalt principles are at work and there is a trend in which both small stimulus intervals and large stimulus intervals are followed by a small response interval.
- When stimulus interval is 2 or -2 (the major second), the respective frequencies of response interval also being 2 or -2 are 64.3% and 46.1%, from which we can understand that the major second stimulus interval most strongly implies pattern P (Process).

[13] For the complete experiment results, please refer to Carlsen [6, p. 18].

Table 5.1 Results of Carlsen's Experiment

Stimulus interval	Response interval ranked by frequency of appearance								
	No. 1			No. 2			No. 3		
−12	5	R	13.1 %	2	R	13.0 %	−1	IR	10.5 %
−11	−1	IR	39.9 %	1	R	9.2 %	11	VR	7.6 %
−10	−2	IR	13.9 %	1	R	13.0 %	−1	IR	12.3 %
−9	−1	IR	33.8 %	2	R	11.1 %	7	VR	9.9 %
−8	1	R	26.9 %	−1	IR	11.1 %	−2	IR	10.3 %
−7	−1	IR	19.1 %	2	R	15.7 %	5	R	15.1 %
−6	−1	IR	23.9 %	1	R	23.7 %	6	VR	10.6 %
−5	2	IP	20.0 %	5	ID	15.3 %	−3	P	13.5 %
−4	2	IP	32.3 %	−1	P	17.7 %	−3	P	14.8 %
−3	−2	P	20.3 %	1	IP	16.1 %	−4	P	15.7 %
−2	−2	P	46.1 %	−1	P	32.1 %	2	ID	7.3 %
−1	−2	P	37.6 %	−1	P	29.9 %	1	ID	15.5 %
0	2	IP	32.4 %	0	D	21.7 %	−2	IP	9.7 %
1	1	P	48.5 %	2	P	27.7 %	−1	ID	9.1 %
2	2	P	64.3 %	1	P	20.5 %	−2	ID	5.1 %
3	−1	IP	28.7 %	4	P	23.1 %	2	P	13.9 %
4	3	P	38.4 %	1	P	23.9 %	−2	IP	16.9 %
5	−1	IP	22.1 %	2	P	17.7 %	4	P	16.9 %
6	1	IR	34.0 %	−1	R	20.7 %	−6	VR	7.9 %
7	−3	R	14.8 %	−1	R	12.7 %	2	IR	11.3 %
8	−1	R	44.7 %	1	IR	10.9 %	0	R	6.7 %
9	−2	R	35.8 %	−1	R	14.0 %	1	IR	11.0 %
10	−1	R	40.5 %	−2	R	20.3 %	0	R	7.0 %
11	1	IR	41.0 %	−1	R	16.8 %	−2	R	11.1 %
12	−1	R	30.8 %	0	R	12.1 %	−2	R	9.3 %

Reproduced and modified from [6, p. 18]

- The three most frequent patterns for both stimulus interval 12 (one octave up) and stimulus interval 10 (a minor seventh up) are all R (Reversal). Also, the frequency of R occurring after stimulus interval 8 (a minor sixth up) surpasses 50%. From this, it can be conjectured that in stimulus intervals 5 and 7 (perfect fourth and perfect fifth) the function as a threshold becomes weaker. For example, as R of stimulus interval 7, the frequency of response interval −3 is 14.8% and the frequency of −1 is 12.7%. As R of stimulus interval −7, the frequency of response interval 2 is 15.7% and the frequency of 5 is 15.1%.
- In contrast, after stimulus interval −7, the frequency of IR of response interval −1 is 19.1%, and after stimulus interval −7, the frequency of IR of response interval 2 is 11.3%. When we look at stimulus interval 5 or −5, there is no R in the top three,

but instead the frequency of ID is 15.3% (stimulus interval 5, response interval −5 occurs at 5.3% frequency, making it the eighth most frequent, thus we do not print it in this table).

We also see some results that do not conform to the Implication-Realization model.

- In stimulus interval 4 (major third), P of response interval 3 occurs at 38.4% frequency and IP of response interval −2 occurs at 16.9% frequency. However, in stimulus interval −4 this is reversed, and P of response interval −3 has only 14.8% frequency, while IP of response interval 2 has 32.3% frequency.
- In stimulus interval −12, the no.1 and no.2 response intervals are 5 and 2, occurring at 13.1% and 13.0% frequency, respectively, and both intervals are R. In contrast, in stimulus interval −11, no.1 is IR of response interval −1, at 39.9%, and no.2 is R of response interval 1 at 9.2%. Similarly, in stimulus interval −10 (descending minor seventh) also, IR of response interval −2 is no.1 at 13.9% frequency, while R of response interval 1 has 13.0% frequency. The same trend can be seen in stimulus intervals 11 and 12.
- In stimulus interval 6 (augmented fourth, diminished fifth), IR of response interval 1 occurs at 34.0% frequency and R of response interval −1 at 20.7%. In stimulus interval −6, response interval −1 occurs at 23.9% frequency, and R of response interval 1 at 23.7%.

As the reason why such results that partially do not conform to the Implication-Realization model were produced, we can consider the influence of scale-step[14]. When stimulus interval was −10, for example, it can be considered that the second note was recognized as the note that introduces an octave (leading note) and IR patterns largely occurred. In addition, it can be considered that in the case of response interval ±1 (ascent or descent of a minor second) after stimulus interval ±6 (ascent or descent of an augmented fourth), as a result of the second note having fulfilled its role as the leading note of the scale notes, the occurrence frequency of both response intervals 1 and −1 became higher. Also, it can be considered that the fact that P of stimulus interval 4, response interval 3 occurs at 38.4% frequency, and IP of stimulus interval −4, response interval 2 at 32.3% frequency, is due to the influence of scale-step. Besides this, there is the possibility that the context for dissonance or large stimulus intervals could not be established appropriately and no implication occurred in the first place, or the possibility that the subject had not carried out sufficient singing practice.

Finally, Carlsen concludes that, although the experiment results markedly reflected the styles, culture, knowledge, and so on that the subjects had so far experienced, the influence of register or music proficiency level was small.

[14] The scale that forms the basis of the music one is listening to. Most people use notes from the scale of the music genres to which they are used to listening, and are aware of the tonality of that scale while following a melody. For example, people used to listening to Western tonal music perceive, be it consciously or unconsciously, the notes of the diatonic scale (or its subsets) and the function of each note.

References

1. L.B. Meyer, in *Emotion and Meaning in Music* (University of Chicago Press, 1956)
2. B. Leonard, Meyer, meaning in music and information theory. J. Aesthetic Art Criticism **15**(4), 412–424 (1957)
3. E. Narmour, in *The Analysis and Cognition of Basic Melodic Structures: The Implication-Realization Model* (The University of Chicago Press, 1990)
4. T. Murao, Cognition in musical analysis, in *Music and Cognition*. ed. by G. Hatano (The University of Tokyo Press, 1987), pp.1–40. (In Japanese)
5. E. Narmour, in *The Analysis and Cognition of Melodic Complexity: The Implication-Realization Model* (The University of Chicago Press, 1992)
6. J.C. Carlsen, Some factors which influence melodic expectancy. Psychomusicology **1**, 12–29 (1981)
7. D. Deutsch, The processing of pitch combinations, in *The Psychology of Music*, 2nd edn (1999), pp. 349–411
8. T.M. Pearce, G.A. Wiggins, Expectation in melody: the influence of context and learning. Music Percept. **23**(5), 377–405 (2006)
9. E.G. Schellenberg, Expectancy in melody: tests of the implication-realization model. Cognition **58**(1), 75–125 (1996)

Chapter 6
GTTM and TPS

Schenkerian analysis claimed that there existed *Ursatz* (a fundamental structure) in each music piece, which was obtained by the process called *reduction*. If so, there should be a *hierarchy* among the notes with regard to their salience or importance, to survive in the process of reduction. This hierarchy is naturally represented by tree structure. Although Schenkerian analysis has been known to musicologists, a concrete analyzing process of such structure has scarcely been proposed. In this chapter, we present the *Generative Theory of Tonal Music* (GTTM) which externalized this process, accompanied by the complementing theory of *Tonal Pitch Space* (TPS).[1]

6.1 Introduction to GTTM

GTTM consists of the following four sub-theories. The *Grouping Analysis* is to articulate a music piece or to group notes to form phrases, finding structural boundaries. The *Metric Analysis* is to find the positions of repetitive beats. In these two processes, the authors of GTTM claim that there should be the notion of salience among notes; that is, some notes are more salient than others. The following *Time-span Analysis* constructs a *time-span tree*, reflecting such salience and analyzing them in the hierarchical way. Finally, the tree would be rearranged to reflect the chord functions in the *Prolongational Analysis*, to produce a *prolongational tree*.

Each sub-theory consists of well-formedness rules and preference rules. The former is the syntactic restriction which should be always satisfied. On the contrary, the latter states the preferences among admissible analyses.

[1] In this chapter, we directly refer to the figures in [1, 2], but those with page numbers are reproduced for this book.

K. Hirata et al., *Music, Mathematics and Language*,
https://doi.org/10.1007/978-981-19-5166-4_6

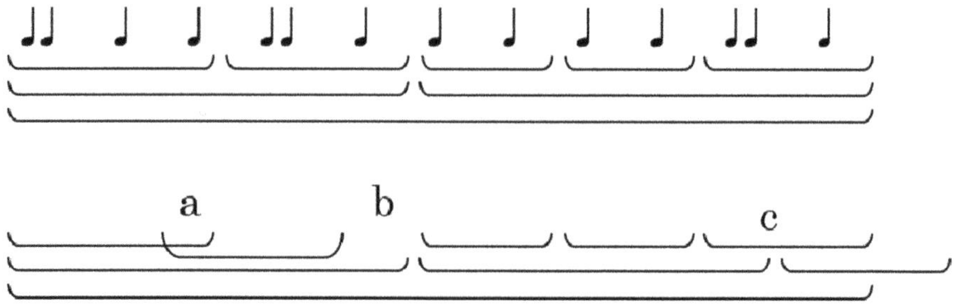

Fig. 6.1 Well-formed (upper) and ill-formed (lower) grouping structures

6.1.1 Grouping Analysis

A group is a sequence of notes or pitch events and is contiguous with each other. We can assign an intuitive meaning upon it, dependent on its length, as a motif, a phrase, a melody, and so on. However, such meanings are not always necessary; we simply divide or dissolve a piece into a sequence of groups, and the groups construct larger groups recursively, according to the given syntactic rules.

We summarize the Grouping Well-Formedness Rules (GWFR) as follows.

(GWFR1)	A group consists of a consecutive sequence of pitch events, and only contiguous sequences can constitute a group
(GWFR2)	A piece constitutes a group
(GWFR3)	A group may contain smaller groups
(GWFR4)	If an upper group contains part of a smaller group, it must contain all pitch events of the smaller group
(GWFR5)	If an upper group contains a small group, the upper group must be exhaustively partitioned into small groups

Obviously from GWFRs, the groups do not overlap each other. A sequence of smaller groups constitute a larger group hierarchically, and result in one large group, that is the whole music piece, as is shown in the upper figure of Fig. 6.1.

The groups in the lower figure of Fig. 6.1 are ill-formed at the following three positions.

a: A pitch event is included in multiple groups in the same level.
b: A pitch event is not included in any group in a level.
c: The upper boundary does not coincide with its lower boundary.

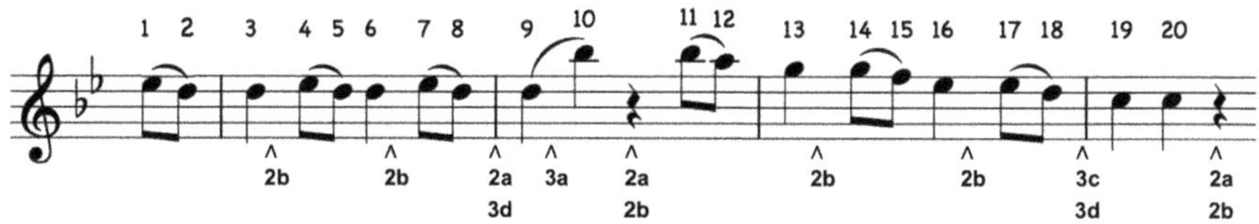

Fig. 6.2 Candidates of boundaries by (GPR2) and (GPR3) [1, p. 47]

Now, let us consider how we human recognize music structure. GWFRs restrict boundaries so as not to produce an ill-formed group, however, the following grouping preference rule (GPR) works more practically to identify intuitive boundaries.

(GPR1)	Strongly avoid a group consisting of a single pitch event
(GPR2)	We call *onset* and *offset* for the beginning time of a note and the ending time of the note, respectively. Consider any four consecutive notes. Then, if either (a) The interval between the offset of the second and the onset of the third notes, or (b) The interval between the onset of the second and the onset of the third notes is longer than that between the first and the second or the third and the fourth notes, they tend to be boundaries
(GPR3)	Between the second and the third notes in any consecutive four notes, when the differences of (a) Pitch (b) Dynamics (*forte*, *piano*, and so on) (c) Articulation (*staccato*, *legato*, and so on) (d) Duration Are larger than those between the first and the second or the third and the fourth, they tend to be boundaries
(GPR4)	The more salient the effects of (GPR2) or (GPR3) are, the more they tend to be boundaries of larger groups

Notice that (GPR2) and (GPR3) mention the concrete criteria of boundaries, while (GPR4) refers to the other rules. In the definitions of preference rules in GTTM, this kind of *meta*-rules often appear.

In Fig. 6.2, the candidates of boundaries based on (GPR2) and (GPR3) are shown with the rule names, though note that all the possible candidates are not presented. If multiples rules are applied, we employ (GPR4), where (GPR2) and (GPR3) are salient, and we construct larger groups. Notice also that in Fig. 6.3, there are no overlapping groups or no opening crevices between groups; a boundary of a larger group necessarily coincides with those of the smaller groups.

Fig. 6.3 Grouping analysis of the theme of the first movement, Mozart K.550 (Symphony No. 40 in g-minor) [1, p. 37]

As opposed to (GPR2) and (GPR3), the following (GPR5) and (GPR6) deal with relations in groups.

(GPR5)	(Symmetry) Any group is preferably divided into two groups of equal length
(GPR6)	(Parallelism) Group structure should reflect parallel parts of groups

Finally, (GPR7) refers to the results other than the grouping analysis.

(GPR7)	The grouping analysis prefers to be *stable* after the time-span analysis and the prolongational analysis

This is another meta-rule and is not self-contained. The time-span analysis and the prolongational analysis are supposed to be executed after this grouping analysis, so that this rule requires recursive analyses, but note that the notion of stability does not arise only from the grouping analysis.

6.1.2 *Metrical Analysis*

The metrical analysis is to obtain a metrical structure, which represents the correct positions of repetitive beats. If the input to the GTTM analyzer already possesses time signature like bars and meters, this analysis is not necessary. The whole theory, however, is planned to admit more general format of input data.

The metrical structure also possesses the notion of hierarchical level. If the meter is in four, the four positions of beats in a bar are abstracted to two positions of strong beats, that are every other beat position in four. Similarly, in the highest level, the strongest beat position in a bar occurs at every other strong beat.

Metrical Well-Formedness Rule (MWFR) consists of the following four rules.

(MWFR1)	Every attack point must be associated with a beat at the smallest level of metrical structure. For example, when the sixteenth is the shortest in the piece, the beat should be specified by the sixteenth
(MWFR2)	A beat in a certain level must be a beat in the lower level of metrical structure
(MWFR3)	A strong beat appears once in two or three beats
(MWFR4)	In each level, strong beats appear in equally spaced beats

The following is the Metrical Preference Rules (MPR).

(MPR1)	(Parallelism) Parallel groups receive a parallel metrical structure
(MPR2)	(Strong Beats Early) The strong beat in a group appears early in the group
(MPR3)	(Event) The positions of strong beats preferably coincide with the inception time of the pitch events. Inception positions of pitch events with no beats are shown by '$*$', and heard as syncopation
(MPR4)	(Stress) Stressed pitch events as accented notes (>, ^, *sf*, and so on) preferably occur at strong beats
(MPR5)	(Length) Those pitch events receive preferably strong beats, if they are longer in duration of dynamic, slur, pattern of articulation, harmony, and so on

Among the above, (MPR4) and (MPR5) have a strong relationship with linguistics, that is, each word possesses strong and weak syllables. In order to express such strong/weak distinction, we employ *forte/piano*, duration of vowels, or high/low pitches. These notions are especially salient in reading poems. However, those preference rules are not common between language and music. Rather, we should only admit that such musical notions reside within languages.

In Fig. 6.4, we represent the hierarchical level by the number of dots. Figure 6.5 shows an example of syncopation, where '$*$' appears at the inception of a pitch event.

Fig. 6.4 Metrical-structure analysis [1, p. 74]

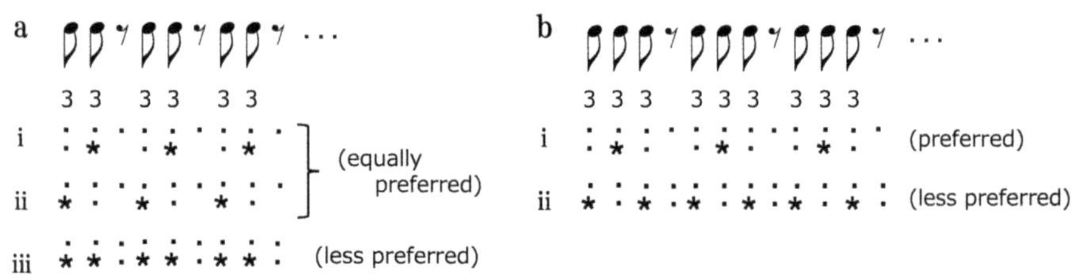

Fig. 6.5 Syncopation in metrical analysis [1, p. 77]

In addition to the above preference rules, the following rules are suggested.

(MPR6)	The stable bass
(MPR7)	The stable cadence
(MPR8)	Suspension at strong beats
(MPR9)	Optimality in time-span reduction
(MPR10)	Preference of every other strong beat

These (MPR6) to (MPR9) again refer to the notion of *stability* which includes the result of other analyses, and thus, they are not self-contained and not independent; so these rules are meta-rules.

6.1.3 Introduction to Reduction

The fundamental principle of GTTM is *redcution*. The reduction hypothesis states that

> Assigning relative salience on each pitch event, the listeners try to grasp the whole structure (*Geschtalt*) in the hierarchical way.

The Schenkerian analysis, however, defined the basic structure (*Ursatz*) is a sequence of Tonic–Dominant–Tonic, supporting a downward melody (*Urlinie*) toward Tonic. This notion seems rather too simple to explain actual complicated music. Therefore,

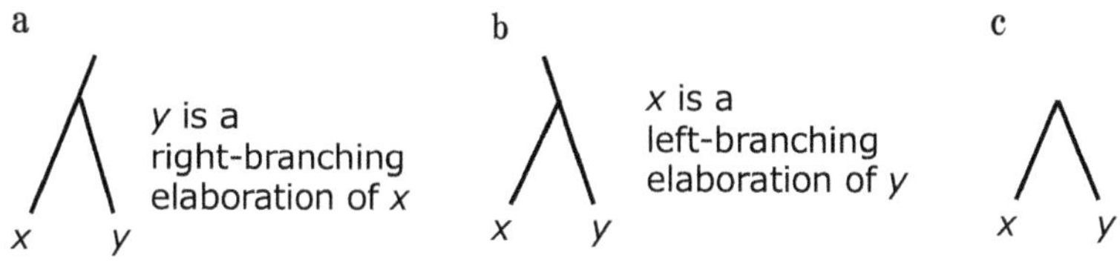

Fig. 6.6 Left/right branching [1, p. 113]

GTTM compares the salience of two adjacent pitch events and regards that the less salient one is subordinate to or elaboration of the more salient one. This situation is represented in Fig. 6.6 as the downward branching.

In general, the listeners seek for the stability of pitches, that is based on the consonant/dissonant chords, the base note and the inversion of triads, the circle of fifth, voice leading, and so on. As a result, the whole structure forms a tree; however, every tree is not necessarily felt stable if we only pay attention to pitches. In many cases, the stability relies on the structural accent, that is derived by rhythm. Such structural accent may not exist at the boundary of groups, nor necessarily possess strong beats. Therefore, we need to adequately merge the importance of pitch with that of rhythm. In order to do this, we first obtain *time-span segmentation* from the result of grouping analysis and that of metrical analysis, where the salience is recursively defined. Then, we acquire a time-span tree, which will be explained next, as a result of time-span segmentation.

Note that the time-span reduction does not reflect human cognitive aspects such as tension and relaxation. If we are to pay more attention to such psychologically stable structure, we need to consider the stability of harmony more, rather than the structural stability based on grouping and metrical analyses. The psychological structure often disregards the surface bars and meters, or time-span segmentation, since the influence of preceding chords *prolongs* beyond such boundaries. Thus, we name the psychological tree structure prolongation tree, and the process *prolongational reduction*. We explain these two reduction principles below.

6.1.4 Time-Span Reduction

We regard that a note which resides at both ends of a group, especially when it bears a strong beat, is salient. For four meters, for example, the note of the first beat in a bar is more salient than that of the third, and the third is more salient than the second and the fourth. In the time-span reduction, we compare such salience in the bottom-up way in a tournament. In this process, a less salient branch is absorbed and attached to the more salient branch, and finally the most salient branch survives and reaches at the root (top) of the *time-span tree*. This process, however, requires partially top-down operations to balance the whole tree, by the equal-length partitioning (GPR5) or parallelism (GPR6), to acquire the *stability*.

After the grouping analysis, the layered groups become hierarchical. As a result, the time-span analysis becomes hierarchical; namely the most salient pitch event is fixed in a local group and it survives to the next higher (larger) groups. In Fig. 6.7, the pitch event at level *a* is most salient, and those in level *b* follow the one in *a*. In accordance with this process, the number of pitch events is reduced. In the higher level, a music piece is also more abstracted and simplified.

The *the strong reduction hypothesis* tells us that we can assume there exists such a reduction process. In a psychological sense, a listener of music constructs such a skeleton of music, and in this mental process, we distinguish important notes from unimportant notes. These important notes form the basic structure while those unimportant notes are disregarded.

We show a process of reduction for a concrete piece in Fig. 6.8. In this figure, from level *c* to level *b*, among the five pitch events in level *c*, the second and the third ones are reduced. Note that the reducible branches are only those which have no more subordinate branches. At first, the first pitch event is compared with the third in the original score, and the first survives. Then, the first pitch event is compared with the seventh in the score and survives further. The final two pitch events survive into level *b*.

After the reduction, the survived pitch events do not reside at the same temporal position (onset–offset) nor possess the same duration. Each survived event, thus, represents a time interval within which the event is most salient and the duration is considered to be prolonged. Such an abstract pitch event thus represents a local key of the whole governing interval.

The Shenkerian analysis only shows the result of reduction while in the time-span analysis the process of reduction is shown in the tree, and thus, the time-span tree represents a rich datum of structure in terms of grouping and structural heads. On the contrary, the events in the reduced structure lose the original information as to the onset and the duration.[2] Therefore, we need another independent *rendering* process to realize a music piece from a tree structure.

In the time-span analysis, there exist *structural accents* of the phrase, that are relations from the structural [b]eginning to its [c]adence. Such [b] and [c] correspond just like 'ball-throwing' and its 'catching.' At the cadence, the two pitch events V-I are agglutinated to be one branch and are treated as one pitch event. The preceding pitch events to a cadence are considered to be subordinate. For this, we put an *egg-like* shape between two cadential events, to denote a position where its subordinate event is attached (Fig. 6.9).

Please see, for example, the theme of the first movement of Piano Sonata No.11 in A major by Mozart (Fig. 6.11). This theme consists of I-V and I-V-I as shown in Fig. 6.11a; when we pay attention only to the fourth bar, the tonic on the first beat seems more salient than others. Therefore, this analysis results in the tree in Fig. 6.11b. However, this is wrong. We need to consider the correspondence between [b] and [c], and the correct analysis would be Fig. 6.10 and thus results in Fig. 6.12.

---

[2] For example, the longest time-span possesses eight bars while the corresponding pitch event, a chord of A major in the eighth bar possesses only one beat and a half.

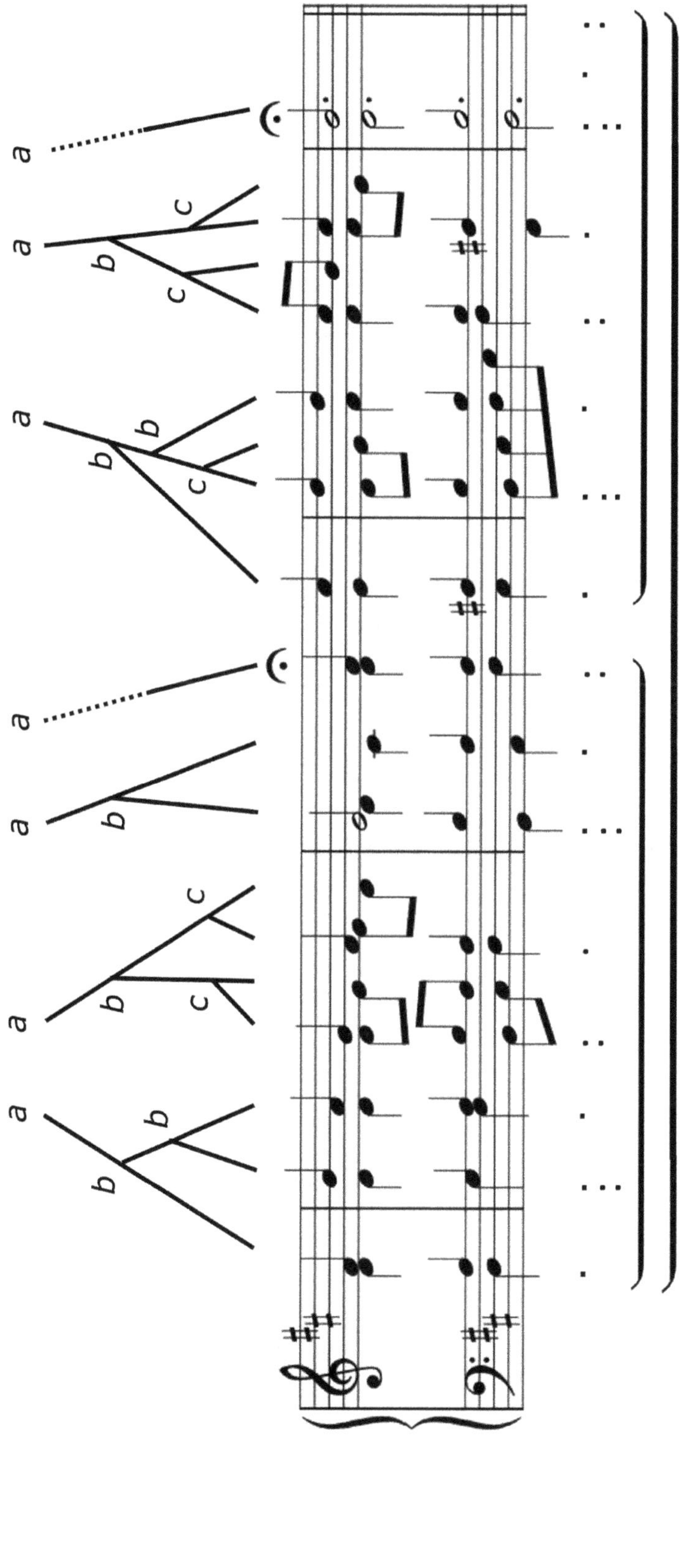

Fig. 6.7 Bottom-up process of time-span anal [1, p. 132]

Fig. 6.8 Time-span reduction for 'O Haupt voll Blut und Wunden' in St. Matthew Passion [1, p. 115]

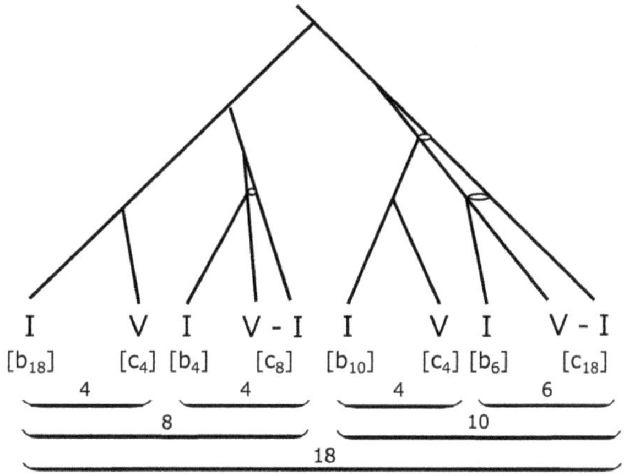

Fig. 6.9 Correspondence between **b** and **c** [1, p. 139]

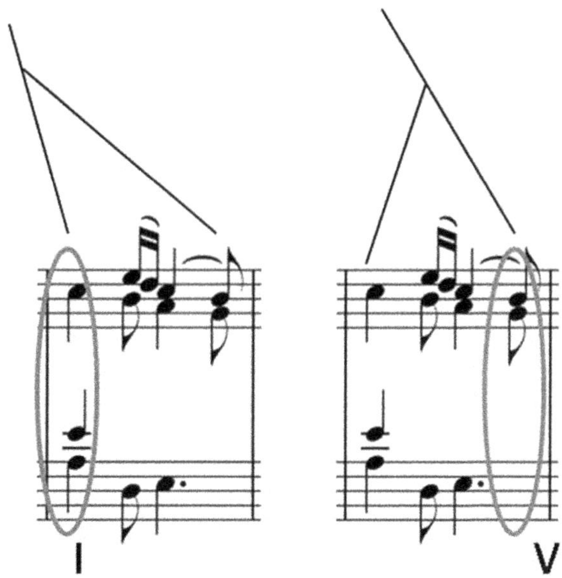

Fig. 6.10 Half-cadence of the fourth bar, 1st movement of K331

In the Schenkerian analysis, *Urlinie* $\hat{3} - \hat{2} - \hat{1}$ accompanies the sequence of chords of tonic-dominant-tonic. In this process, we need a concrete algorithm to choose this intermediate dominant. This most important dominant is called *structural dominant*. Let us consider the following progression.

$$\underbrace{\underbrace{\mathrm{I} \longrightarrow \mathrm{V}}\ \underbrace{\mathrm{I} \longrightarrow \mathrm{V\text{-}I}}}$$

We can find two dominants in the above, and a candidate for the structural dominant is to choose the one which is located near to the center, to divide the piece into equal

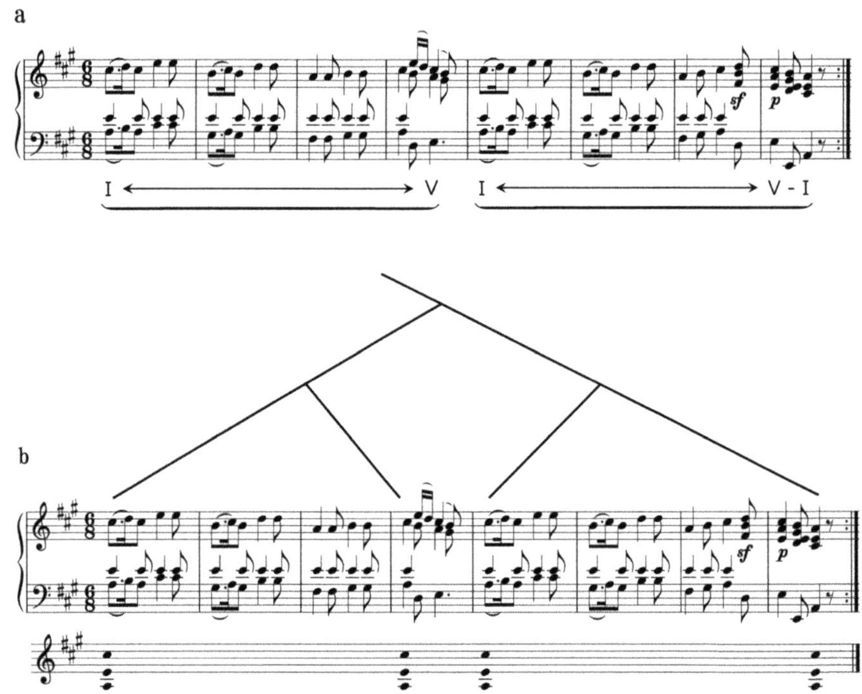

Fig. 6.11 Wrong analysis of **b** and **c** [1, p. 135]

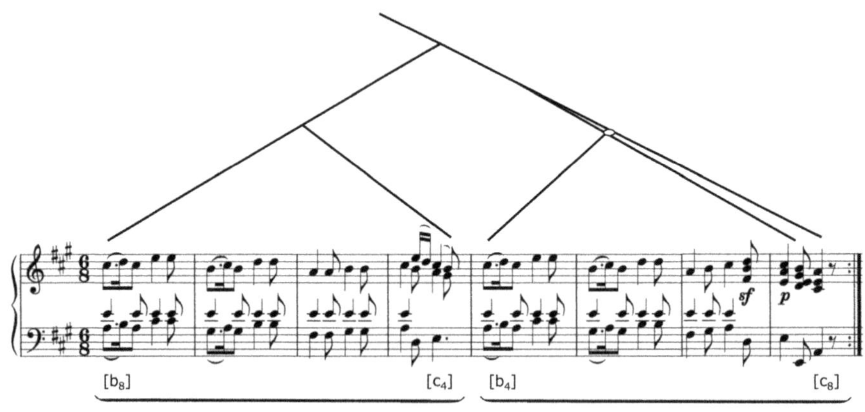

Fig. 6.12 Correct recognition of half-cadence [1, p. 141]

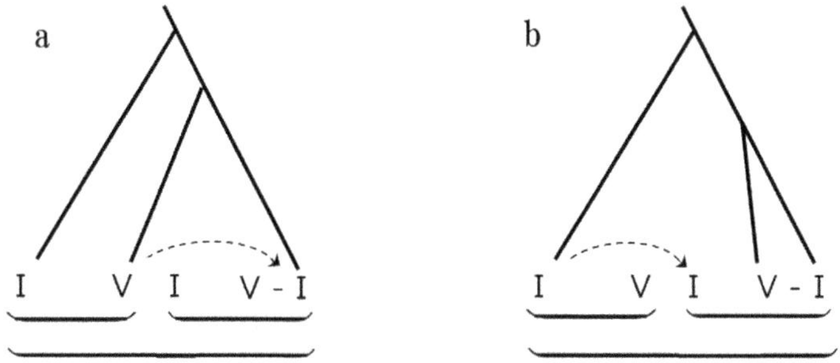

Fig. 6.13 Detection of structural dominant; dotted arrows show prolongations [1, p. 141]

length. However, such a center-located dominant may not always exist. Especially in minor keys, we often encounter III instead of V. And the prime reason by which we should avoid the center-located dominant is the effect of *prolongation*. If we consider the mid-V is the structural dominant, its effect prolongs to the final V (Fig. 6.13a). Therefore, we prefer Fig. 6.13b that reflects the fact that the opening tonic prolongs its effect by the next tonic.

Here, we summarize the concrete principles for the time-span analysis. The rules for the analysis consist of well-formedness rule (WFR) and preference rule (PR), as well as the grouping analysis and the metrical analysis.

(TSRWFR1)	There exists a head pitch event.
(TSRWFR2)	The leaves of a tree are pitch events.
(TSRWFR3)	In general, a head is chosen among the pitch events, existing in lower subtrees. However, the following exceptional operations may be included.
	Fusion: A chord in *arpeggio* is considered to be one pitch event.
	Transformation: We may insert a hypothetical chord.
	Cadential Retention: If two consecutive pitch events are regarded as cadence, they are agglutinated to be one event, which is retained to the upper level in the tree.
(TSRWFR4)	Between two consecutive events, the last event is more important than the penult one.

The selection of the head in a given time-span, we respect the following preference rules.

(TSRPR1)	Prefer an event with strong beat
(TSRPR2)	Prefer an intrinsically consonant event, and/or one close to the local tonic
(TSRPR3)	Weakly prefer a high pitch event in the melody line, or a low pitch event in bass
(TSRPR4)	Respect the parallelism
(TSRPR5)	Prefer an event to stabilize metrical structure
(TSRPR6)	Prefer an event which stabilize the prolongational reduction (a) Prefer an event with linear progression from/to the heads of adjacent time-spans (b) Prefer a harmonically smooth event from/to the heads of adjacent time-spans
(TSRPR7)	(Cadential retention) prefer consecutive events to form a cadence
(TSRPR8)	Prefer an event near to the beginning of a time-span, if the event functions as structural beginning [b]
(TSRPR9)	Prefer [c] to [b] as head

6.1.5 Prolongational Reduction

Since the time-span tree is obtained by the grouping analysis and the metrical analysis, the tree represents the rhythmic stability. On the contrary, the prolongational tree explained below represents the harmonic stability.

In the prolongational tree, the right-branching and the left-branching reflect the departure from tonic and the regression to tonic, respectively. Therefore, the former causes *tension* and the latter becomes *relaxation* (Fig. 6.14).

The notion of *prolongation* is the mental effect that a certain pitch event keeps sounding psychologically, beyond the original duration. The scope of this reverberation is assumed in the following three grades.

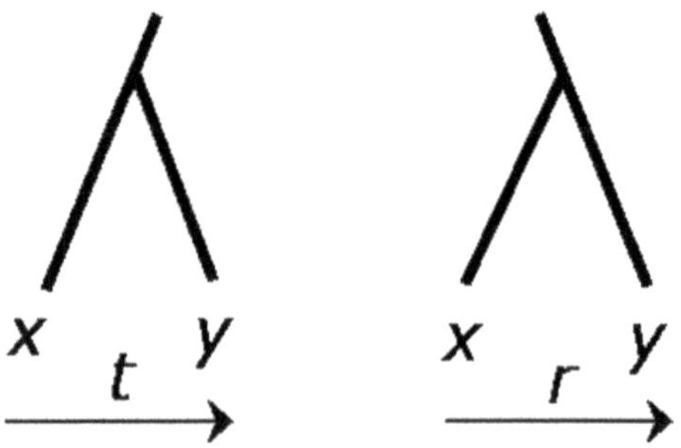

Fig. 6.14 Structures of tension and relaxation [1, p. 181]

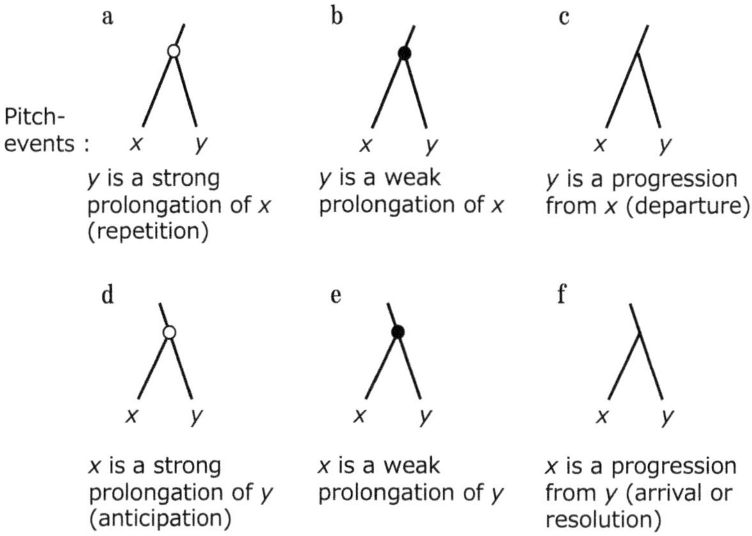

Fig. 6.15 Six patterns of tension and relaxation [1, p. 182]

Fig. 6.16 Basic form [1, p. 189]

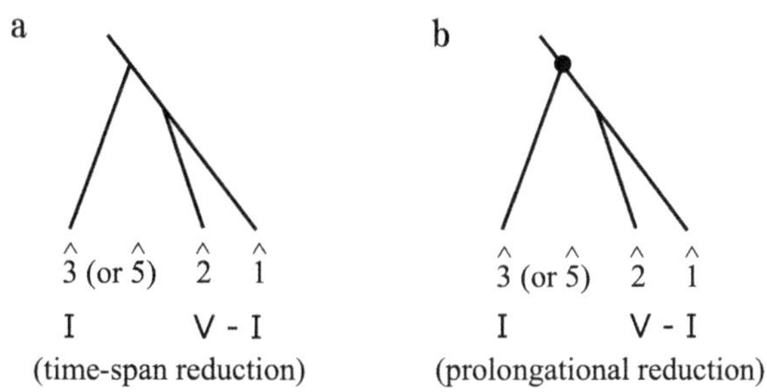

- Strong prolongation: The same root with the same bass of a chord, as well as the same melody tone, is maintained.
- Weak prolongation: The same root of a chord is maintained.
- Progression: It does not include the same third nor the fifth.

According to the previous distinction between the right-branching (tension) and the left-branching (relaxation), the distinction between the strong/weak prolongation and the progression are defined in the parallel way. Therefore, we obtain six different branching patterns as shown in Fig. 6.15.

GTTM assumes the *basic form*, a corresponding notion to *Urlinie* of Schenkerian analysis, which begins from a tonic by left-branching from the cadential tonic, followed by a left-branching dominant (Fig. 6.16).

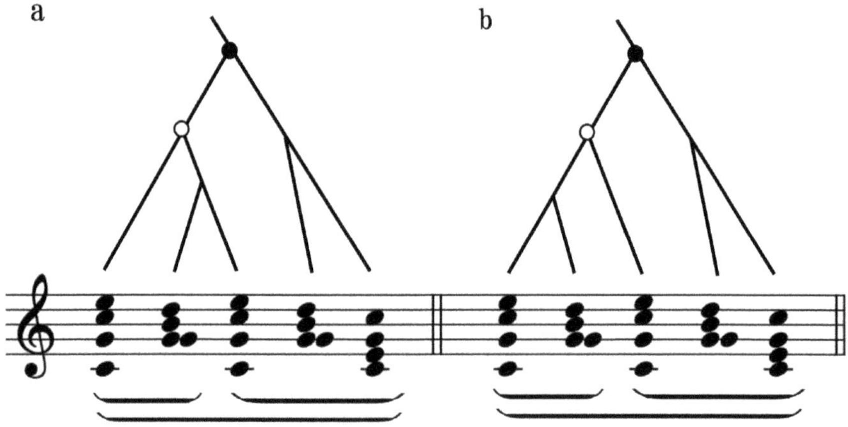

Fig. 6.17 Antecedent, consequence, and implication [1, p. 191]

Fig. 6.18 Cadential preparation [1, p. 192]

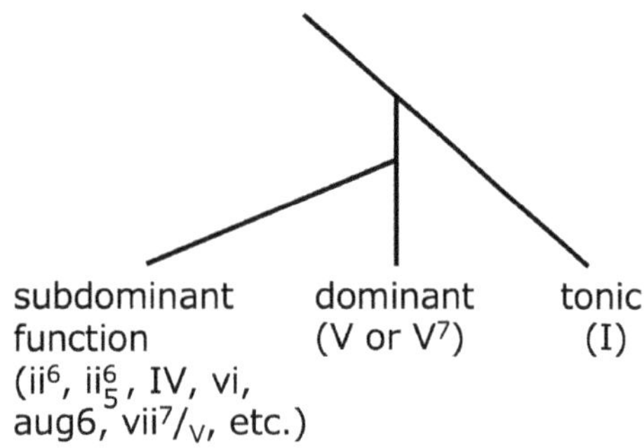

Let us look back to the structure of the following.

$$\underbrace{\underbrace{I \longrightarrow V}\ \underbrace{I \longrightarrow V\text{-}I}}$$

This is called an *interruption form* by a half-cadence, and the first half is called *antecedent* and the latter *consequence*; therefore, we regard the relation as an implication. Therefore, the tree of this structure, which reflects the prolongation, becomes Fig. 6.17b.

A sequence of subdominant, attached to a cadence (V–I) by a left-branching, is called a cadential preparation (Fig. 6.18).

In tonal music, we do not tolerate a structure consisting of a relaxation alone, of a tension alone, or of a tension after a relaxation (Fig. 6.19a, b, c, respectively). Usually, we require a relaxation after a tension (Fig. 6.19d). Such a structure is called a *normative structure*. Thus, a stable tree must respect both the basic form and the normative form.

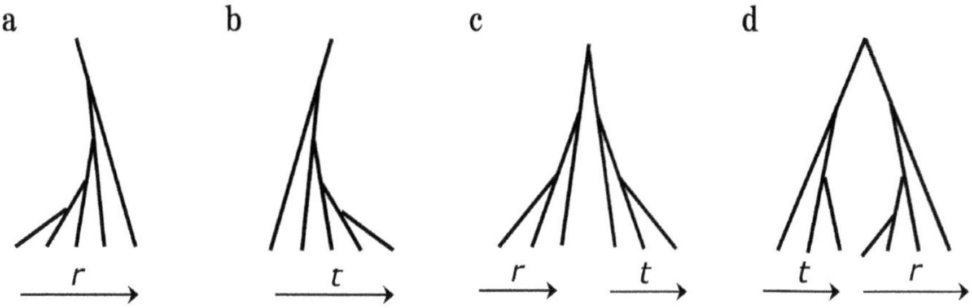

Fig. 6.19 Hypothetical variety of tension and relaxation [1, p. 198]

We introduce here the *secondary notation* to denote the prolongation directly on the score, connecting pitch events by slur. We employ a dotted line for a strong prolongation, and a hard line both for a weak prolongation and for a progression, in the hierarchical way (Fig. 6.20).

A prolongational tree is constructed, arranging an existing time-span tree, in the top-down way. First, we introduce well-formedness rules (PRWFR).

(PRWFR1)	There exists only one head per a prolongation
(PRWFR2)	A pitch event is an elaboration of another, and the junction is classified into three patterns of strong/weak prolongation, and progression
(PRWFR3)	An event in a prolongation is either a prolongational head or a recursive elaboration of the head
(PRWFR4)	Branches do not cross in the prolongational tree

Next, we summarize the prolongational reduction preference rules (PRPR).

(PRPR1)	In choosing the most important pitch event in the prolongational tree in some region, the event should be also the most important in the time-span in the same region

In Fig. 6.21, the tree in the left-hand side is a time-span tree, and the most important pitch event is the one from the final {C,E,G,C}. The next most important is the beginning {C,G,C,E}, and the one after next is the {G,G,B,D}.

(PRPR2)	In prolongational region $(e_i - e_j)$, suppose e_k is most prolongationally important. If there is a time-span including e_i and e_k but not e_j, let e_k be a subordinate branch to e_i. If there is a time-span including e_k and e_j but not e_i, let e_k be subordinate to e_j

Fig. 6.20 Secondary notation [1, p. 202]

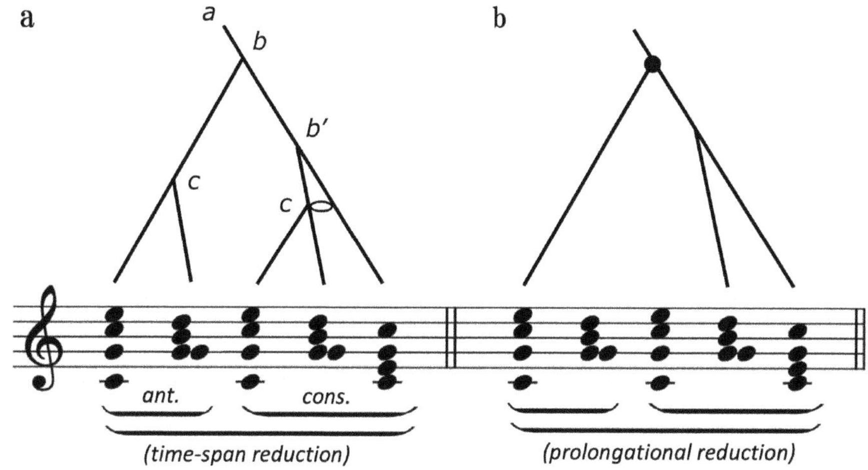

Fig. 6.21 Selection of the most important pitch event [1, p. 189]

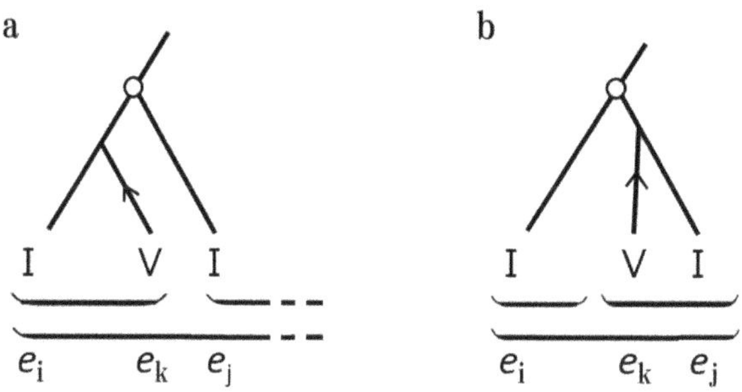

Fig. 6.22 Relation between time-span and prolongation [1, p. 221]

In Fig. 6.22, in the left tree, V is attached to the left I, but in the right tree, V is attached to the right I.

(PRPR3)	In prolongational region ($e_i - e_j$), in choosing the most prolongationally important event e_k, we employ the following criteria to stabilize the tree and e_k would be subordinate to either e_i or e_j

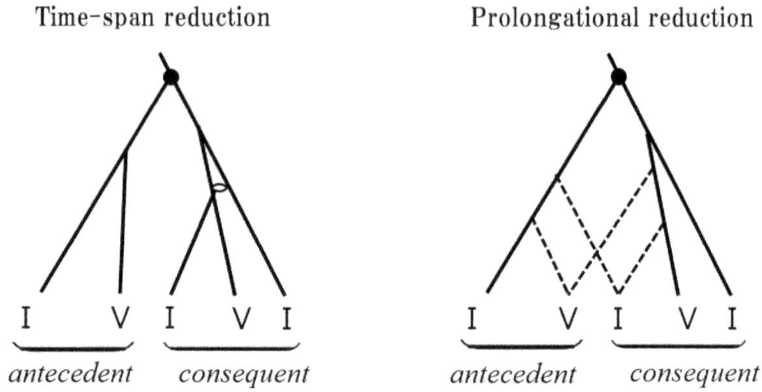

Fig. 6.23 Algorithm of prolongational reduction (1) [1, p. 223]

Stability conditions

Branching	Right-branching: Strong prolongation > weak prolongation > progression Left-branching: Progression > weak prolongation > strong prolongation
Diatonic collection	The connection of two pitch events is more stable when the two are included in or imply the same diatonic collection
Melody	The connection of two pitch events is more stable if the interval is smaller An ascending progression is more stable in the right-branching. A descending progression is more stable in the left-branching
Circle of fifths	In the connection of two chords, the smaller the distance in the circle of fifths is, the more stable In the right-branching, the ascending (clockwise) direction is more stable. In the left-branching, the counterclockwise direction is more stable

In Fig. 6.23, in the time-span tree in the left-hand side, the intermediate V and I are two candidates of the next prolongationally important event. Then, there are four possibilities as shown in the right-hand side. According to the stability conditions, this should be solved as in Fig. 6.24.

(PRPR4)	In prolongational region ($e_i - e_j$), the most prolongationally important event e_k should be attached to the more important event between e_i and e_j
(PRPR5)	Parallel passages should receive parallel analyses
(PRPR6)	The normative prolongational structure should include the following four (five) elements (a) A beginning of prolongation (b) An ending of prolongation chosen from one of the cadence (c) Optional: A right-branching of the beginning of prolongation, as the most important elaboration (d) A right-branching of the beginning of prolongation, as the next important elaboration (e) A left-branching subdominant progression, attached to the most important elaboration of the first element of cadence

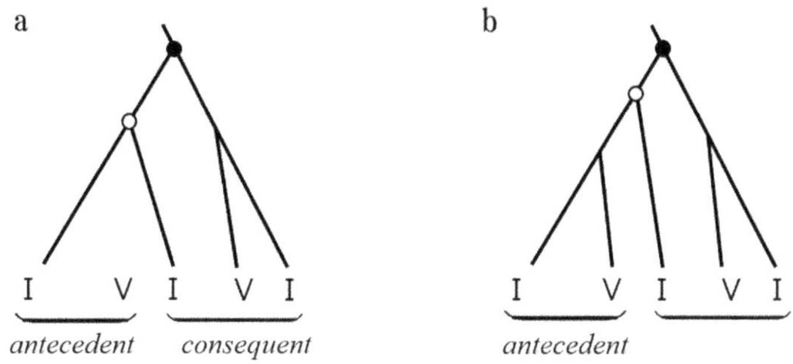

Fig. 6.24 Algorithm of prolongational reduction (2) [1, p. 224]

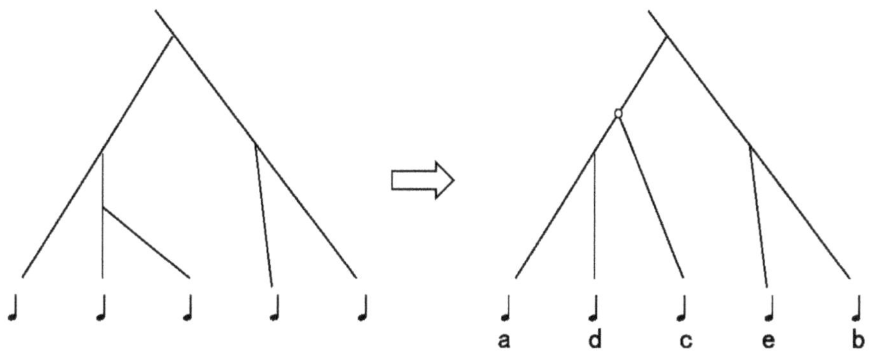

Fig. 6.25 Interaction principle principle

In some practical situations, the notion of the most prolongationally important event may contradict between (PRPR1) and (PRPR3). In order to solve this contradiction, we ease the condition of (PRPR1), as follows.

> In order to make as a sufficiently stable prolongationally connection, e_k must be chosen from the events in the two most important sub-levels of time-span reduction represented in $(e_i – e_j)$ [1, p. 228]

We call this **interaction principle**. In Fig. 6.25, the next important event in the time-span tree (the right-hand side) is either the second or the fourth note. However, the third note becomes the strong prolongation when attached to the first note, that is very stable, and thus, we adopt the third note in the sub-level after next. In the right-hand side, the prolongational tree is shown where a–e of (PRPR6) are annotated.

This process is a kind of compensation and is not a logical consequence, to apply the theory to actual situation.

6.2 Tonal Pitch Space

Cadence Detection in GTTM

Let us look back to the theme of Piano Sonata No.11 in A major by Mozart (K.331), in Fig. 6.11 (also in Fig. 6.12). In order to recognize the half-cadence in the fourth bar (Fig. 6.10), we need to analyze the chords and to find the sequence of V (dominant) and I (tonic). However in GTTM, the process is not mentioned. In this section, we introduce Tonal Pitch Space (TPS) [2] to discuss the relation between chords in tonal music. Tonality arises from a scale and chords on it, and the scale is fixed by various frequency ratios among pitches included in it. Nowadays, a scale consists of seven diatonic collection out of 12 tones in equal temperament which results in major/minor scales.

Distance in Pitch Class

Basic space consists of the following five levels, e.g., in the case of C major.

a) Octave level:	C											
(b) Fifth level:	C							G				
(c) Triadic level:	C				E			G				
(d) Diatonic level:	C		D		E	F		G		A		B
(e) Chromatic level:	C	D♭/C♯	D	E♭/D♯	E	F	G♭/F♯	G	A♭/G♯	A	B♭/A♯	B
Pitch class	0	1	2	3	4	5	6	7	8	9	10	11

Pitch proximity is measured both by vertical and by horizontal distances. The vertical distance is the depth of the level where the target pitch event first appears.

Depth	0	4	3	4	2	3	4	1	4	3	4	3
Pitch class	0	1	2	3	4	5	6	7	8	9	10	11

Next, the horizontal distance is measured by the number of in-between pitch classes in each level.

(a) $0 \rightarrow 12$ (C–C)
(b) $0 \rightarrow 7 \rightarrow 12$ (C–G–C)
(c) $0 \rightarrow 4 \rightarrow 7 \rightarrow 12$ (C–E–G–C)
(d) $0 \rightarrow 2 \rightarrow 4 \rightarrow 5 \rightarrow 7 \rightarrow 9 \rightarrow 11 \rightarrow 12$ (diatonic collection)
(e) Chromatic collection

For example in level (b), the horizontal distance between C and G is 1 while in level (c) C and E is 1. The horizontal distance from C means the smallest distance to reach C among various levels.

Ex. 5(F)$\rightarrow$ 0(C) = 1 (at level(d): 5(F)$\rightarrow$4(E)) + 1(at level(c): 4(E)$\rightarrow$0(C)) = 2.

Steps in												
(b)	0							1				
(c)	0				1			1				
(d)	0		1		2	3		3		2		1
(e)	0	1	2	3	4	5	6	5	4	3	2	1
Pitch class	0	1	2	3	4	5	6	7	8	9	10	11

The distance is defined by the addition of the vertical distance and the horizontal distance though '♯' is regarded to require two steps, e.g., C♯– D – C is distance 2.

(a)	C												(C)
(b)	C		⟵	⟵				G					(C)
(c)	C	⟵	⟵		E			G	⟶	⟶	⟶		(C)
(d)	C	⟵	D		E	F		G	⟵	A		B	(C)
(e)	C	D♭/C♯	D	E♭/D♯	E	F	G♭/F♯	G	A♭/G♯	A	B♭/A♯	B	(C)
Pitch class	0	1	2	3	4	5	6	7	8	9	10	11	

Distance	0	5/6	4	6/6	3	5	7/6	2	6/7	5	7/6	4
Pitch class	C	D♭/C♯	D	E♭/D♯	E	F	G♭/F♯	G	A♭/G♯	A	B♭/A♯	B

Chord Distance in the Same Key

The uppermost figure in Fig. 6.26 shows chord C, that is, I in C major. Let the height of chromatic collection (level (e)) be 0 and that of diatonic collection (level (d)) be 1. Then, pitch class 0 (C) is height 4, pitch class 7 (G) is 3, and pitch class 4 (E) is 2. Now, let us consider the operation to move this chord I to 4 steps toward the right, on the diatonic level (d), that corresponds to the upward shift by the perfect fifth. Note that if overflowed to the right they appear continuously from the left, counting by *modulo* 12. The diatonic collection consists of 7 notes, and thus, the shift by 4 to the right on level (d) is the same as the shift by 4 to the left. Finally, we obtain the bottom figure in Fig. 6.26 where newly arrived pitch events are renamed. We place underlines for those which changed the height.

Here, let us sum up the number of the *increased* height, as follows.

2 steps on pitch class 2
1 step on pitch class 7
1 step on pitch class 11

that is 4 in total. This number implies that

- If there are more common notes, the number becomes smaller.
- The root, the fifth, and the third notes are differently influential.

As we have observed thus far, the shift by the perfect fifth upwards is the nearest move. Then, we employ the chordal circle of fifths (Fig. 6.27) and define the distance

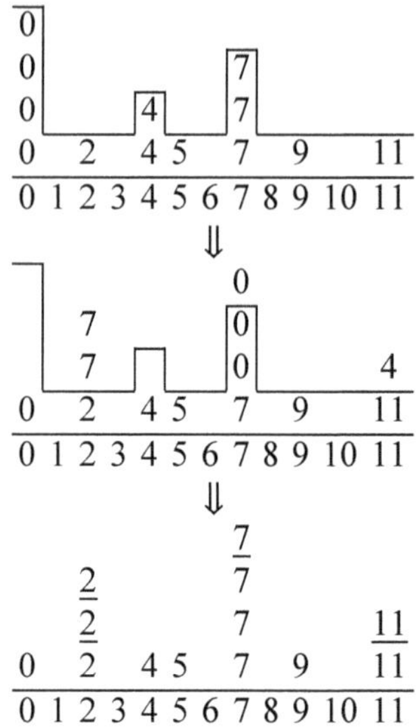

Fig. 6.26 Chord shift by 4 steps on diatonic collection to the right (left)

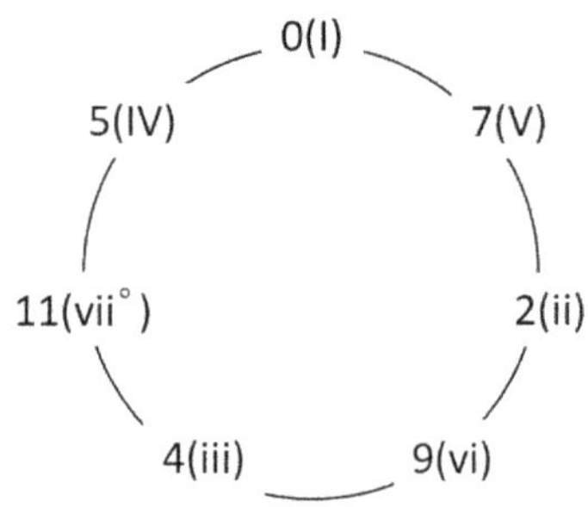

Fig. 6.27 Chordal circle of fifths in the same diatonic collection; the Arabic number is the pitch class while the roman number is the chord on the scale degree

from chord x to y in the same key (in the same diatonic collection) as the steps j in the chordal circle of fifths, plus the sum of the different number of height k in the basic space (Fig. 6.26).

$$\delta(x \rightarrow y) = j + k$$

Fig. 6.28 shows the distances between two chords in C major.

In major scales, the distances of triads from scale degree I are common and the same; we represent major triad by uppercase roman, minor triad by lowercase roman, and the diminished triad by '°'.

Chord degree	I	ii	iii	IV	V	vi	vii°
Distance	0	8	7	5	5	7	8

									9		
				4					9		
0				4					9		
0		2		4	5		7		9		11
0	1	2	3	4	5	6	7	8	9	10	11

$\delta(\text{vi/C} \rightarrow \text{vi/C}) = 0 + 0 = 0$

					$\underline{5}$						
$\underline{0}$					$\underline{5}$						
0					$\underline{5}$				9		
0		2		4	$\underline{5}$		7		9		11
0	1	2	3	4	5	6	7	8	9	10	11

$\delta(\text{vi/C} \rightarrow \text{IV/C}) = 3 + 4 = 7$

Fig. 6.28 Distances of chords in C major

Next, we align the chords by degrees in the following torus, that is the topside is connected to the bottom side as well as the right side is connected to the left side.

- vertically by fifth: $\cdots \rightarrow$ I $\rightarrow$ V $\rightarrow$ii $\rightarrow$ vi $\rightarrow$ iii $\rightarrow$ vii° $\rightarrow$ IV $\rightarrow$ I $\rightarrow \cdots$
- horizontally by third: $\cdots \rightarrow$ I $\rightarrow$ iii $\rightarrow$ V $\rightarrow$ vii° $\rightarrow$ ii $\rightarrow$ IV $\rightarrow$ vi $\rightarrow$ I $\rightarrow \cdots$

	⋮	⋮	⋮	⋮	⋮	⋮	⋮	
⋯	I	iii	V	vii°	ii	IV	vi	⋯
⋯	V	vii°	ii	IV	vi	I	iii	⋯
⋯	ii	IV	vi	I	iii	V	vii°	⋯
⋯	vi	I	iii	V	vii°	ii	IV	⋯
	⋮	⋮	⋮	⋮	⋮	⋮	⋮	

In earlier days, a progress of chords was limited only one-step to upward or downward, or one-step to rightward or leftward. The functional harmony to this day, established by Hugo Riemann (1849–1919) admits substitute chord; from I, IV, V to upward I→vi, IV→ii, V→iii, and to downward I→iii, IV→vi, V→vii°.

Chord Proximity in Related Keys

To define the distance in chords in related keys, we employ the circle of fifths, considering that dominant and subdominant keys are the nearest. First, we move the diatonic collection (level (d)) of the basic space by shifting 7 steps to the right (by the perfect fifth). In Fig. 6.29, the pitch collection {0, 2, 4, 5, 7, 9, 11} in C major (upper in the figure) is moved by 7 steps to the right (middle) and is renamed (bottom), to obtain the diatonic collection of F major {0, 2, 4, 6, 7, 9, 11} adopting 5 (F) instead of 6 (F♯).

Now we redefine the distance of chords in related keys as follows.

$$\delta(x \rightarrow y) = i + j + k$$

$$\begin{cases} i: \text{The number of steps in the circle of fifths of keys} \\ j: \text{The number of steps in the chordal circle of fifths in a key} \\ k: \text{The number of increased height in basic space} \end{cases}$$

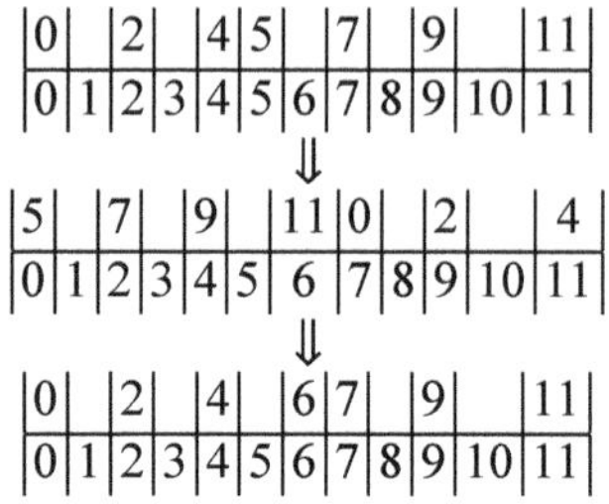

Fig. 6.29 Shift by the perfect fifth in the same diatonic collection

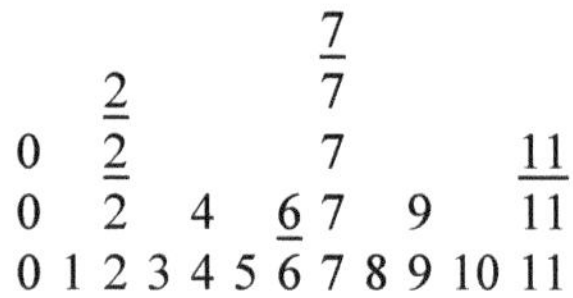

Fig. 6.30 Distance from I/C to I/G

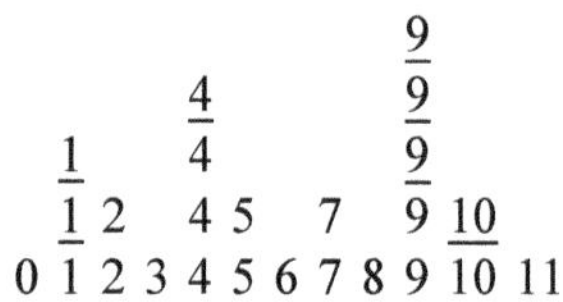

Fig. 6.31 Distance from I/C to V/d

The first i mentions the key shift by the circle of fifths. A difference of one in i means one change of the number of ♯ or ♭. For example, δ(I/C → I/G) becomes: i is 1 from C to G, j is 1 since the root shifted from C to G, and the sum of difference of height k is 5, and thus $1 + 1 + 5 = 7$ (Fig. 6.30).[3]

We need an extra care for the minor scale since there are three kinds of natural/harmonic/melodic minor scales. We employ the natural minor scale for the basic space; however, we use the harmonic minor scale only for V and vii°. In Fig. 6.31, the diatonic collection of the harmonic minor scale $\{1, 2, 4, 5, 7, 9, 10\}$ is employed instead of that of the natural minor scale $\{0, 2, 4, 5, 7, 9, 10\}$. As a result, $\delta(\text{I/C} \rightarrow \text{V/d}) = 1 + 3 + 7 = 11$.

Since we have assumed the distance in keys, two chords with the same chord name change their distance from another chord, as follows.

- {C,E,D} → {G,B,D} $\begin{cases} \delta(\text{I/C} \rightarrow \text{V/C}) = 0 + 1 + 4 = 5 \\ \delta(\text{I/C} \rightarrow \text{I/G}) = 1 + 1 + 5 = 7 \end{cases}$
- {C,E,D} → {D,F,A} $\begin{cases} \delta(\text{I/C} \rightarrow \text{ii/C}) = 0 + 2 + 6 = 8 \\ \delta(\text{I/C} \rightarrow \text{i/d}) = 1 + 2 + 7 = 10 \end{cases}$

We can measure the distance of keys by the circle of fifths for the related keys, but this principle is not applied to the distant keys as we may be able to track an unnecessarily long detour to reach the target key. To avoid this roundabout, we

[3] The original notation in [2] employs degrees also for keys, as I/V. For readability, we employ roman alphabet for keys, as I/G, where the major key is in uppercase and the minor key is in lowercase.

provide the *regional space* where keys are arranged in the two-dimensional diagram, as follows.

$$\begin{cases} \text{vertical: fifth} \\ \text{horizontal: alternation of parallel keys (C–c) and relative keys (a–C)} \end{cases}$$

The topside of the regional space is connected to the bottom side, and the right side is connected the left side; therefore, the space becomes toroidal. We restrict the shifts in keys to follow the shortest path in the regional space.

$$\begin{array}{ccccccccc} & \vdots & \vdots & \vdots & \vdots & \vdots & \vdots & \vdots & \\ \cdots & d\sharp & F\sharp & f\sharp & A & a & C & c & \cdots \\ \cdots & g\sharp & B & b & D & d & F & f & \cdots \\ \cdots & c\sharp & E & e & G & g & B\flat & b\flat & \cdots \\ \cdots & f\sharp & A & a & C & c & E\flat & e\flat & \cdots \\ \cdots & b & D & d & F & f & A\flat & a\flat & \cdots \\ \cdots & e & G & g & B\flat & b\flat & D\flat & d\flat & \cdots \\ \cdots & a & C & c & E\flat & e\flat & G\flat & g\flat & \cdots \\ & \vdots & \vdots & \vdots & \vdots & \vdots & \vdots & \vdots & \end{array}$$

Chord Proximity in Remote Keys

When the target chord resides not in related keys, we should not regard it as a borrowed chord but should consider the modulation. Then, we need to define the distance in keys in general. The first clue is to consider the proximity between the tonics in different keys. To this purpose, we first investigate the distance between tonics among the related keys.

$$\begin{array}{ll} \delta(\text{I/C} \rightarrow \text{I/G}) = 7 & \delta(\text{I/C} \rightarrow \text{I/F}) = 7 \\ \delta(\text{I/C} \rightarrow \text{i/d}) = 10 & \delta(\text{I/C} \rightarrow \text{i/e}) = 9 \\ \delta(\text{I/C} \rightarrow \text{i/a}) = 7 & \delta(\text{I/C} \rightarrow \text{i/c}) = 7 \end{array}$$

The above results show that the dominant/ subdominant keys of the relative key, e.g., e-minor and d-minor seen from C major, become rather small values (9 and 10 respectively). However, the dominant/subdominant keys of the parallel key, e.g., g-minor and f-minor seen from C major, are far. In Fig. 6.32, the box in the left-hand side shows the tonics of the related keys from C major while that in the right-hand side shows those from c-minor, and the distance between C major and c-minor is 7. Therefore, we distinguish the two boxes in Fig. 6.32, naming each box *pivot region*, and restrict the accessible keys to the six keys including itself within a box, excluding the parallel key. We call *pivot region tonic* for I in major keys, and for i in minor keys, each locates mid-right and mid-left in the pivot region, respectively. The move between pivot regions is only allowed between pivot region tonics.

Fig. 6.32 Proximity in tonics in related keys

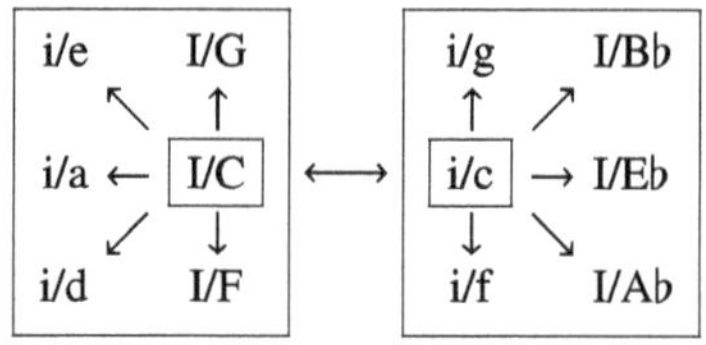

δ(I/C → I/G) = 7 δ(I/C → I/F) = 7 δ(I/C → i/d) = 10
δ(I/C → i/e) = 9 δ(I/C → i/a) = 7

δ(i/c → i/g) = 7 δ(i/c → i/f) = 7 δ(i/c → I/B♭) = 10
δ(i/c → I/E♭) = 7 δ(i/c → I/A♭) = 9

δ(I/C → i/c) = 7

When we cannot find the target chord in the same pivot region, we move to the adjacent pivot region via the pivot region tonics, though we must add the value 7 between them. For example, let us consider the case from C_1/R_1 to C_2/R_2 (C_i is a scale degree and R_i is a key) where R_1 and R_2 are in the different pivot regions. We define the distance Δ as follows.

$$\begin{aligned}\Delta(C_1/R_1 \rightarrow C_2/R_2) = & \ \delta(C_1/R_1 \rightarrow I/P_1) \\ & + \delta(I/P_1 \rightarrow I/P_2) + \cdots + \delta(I/P_{n-1} \rightarrow I/P_n) \\ & + \delta(I/P_n \rightarrow C_2/R_2)\end{aligned}$$

where R_1 and P_1 reside in the same pivot region. The move from P_i to P_{i+1} is a transition by pivot region tonics. In the final line, we assume P_n and R_2 are in the same pivot region. For example, $\Delta(\mathrm{I/C} \rightarrow \mathrm{i/c}^\sharp) = \delta(\mathrm{I/C} \rightarrow \mathrm{i/e}) + \delta(\mathrm{i/e} \rightarrow \mathrm{I/E}) + \delta(\mathrm{I/E} \rightarrow \mathrm{i/c}^\sharp) = 9 + 7 + 7 = 23$ (Fig. 6.33).

For convenience, we employ *combined geometrical space*, as follows, shown in Fig. 6.34.

- In the center, we place the I chord of the key, and we array other chords in the key vertically by the fifth and horizontally by the third.
- The matrices of the nine chords are then arranged so as that the center I chord forms the regional space.

The Principle of the Shortest Path

A progression from a pitch event to another pitch event is a path in the regional space, where we assume that the path should be shortest, that is, smallest in the distance. This implies that we should avoid useless modulation or migration in the regional space. This is exactly similar to physical phenomena where objects move along the shortest path in the gravity or in the electromagnetic field.

Let us illustrate this by a prolongational tree in Fig. 6.35.

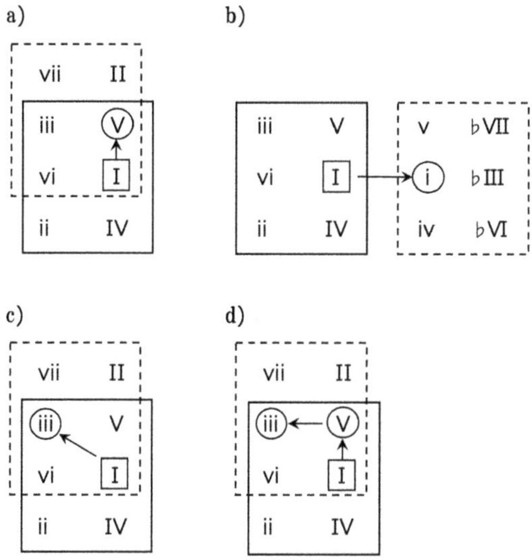

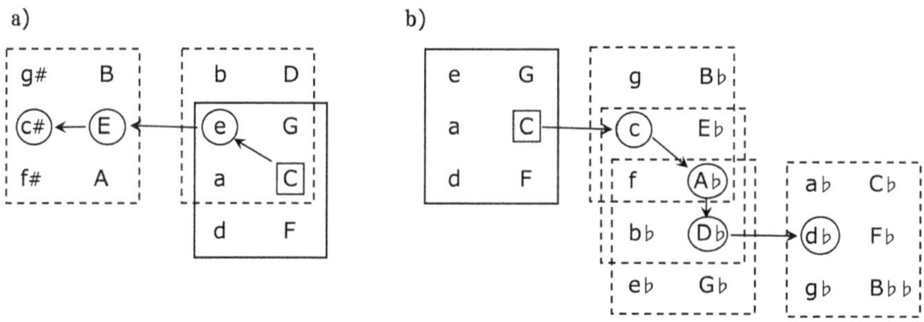

Fig. 6.33 Pivot region shift

Fig. 6.34 Combined regional space

III	V	vii°	iii	V	vii°
VI	i/e	III	vi	I/G	iii
ii°	iv	VI	ii	IV	vi
III	V	vii°	iii	V	vii°
VI	i/f	III	vi	I/C	iii
ii°	iv	VI	ii	IV	vi
III	V	vii°	iii	V	vii°
VI	i/d	III	vi	I/F	iii
ii°	iv	VI	ii	IV	vi

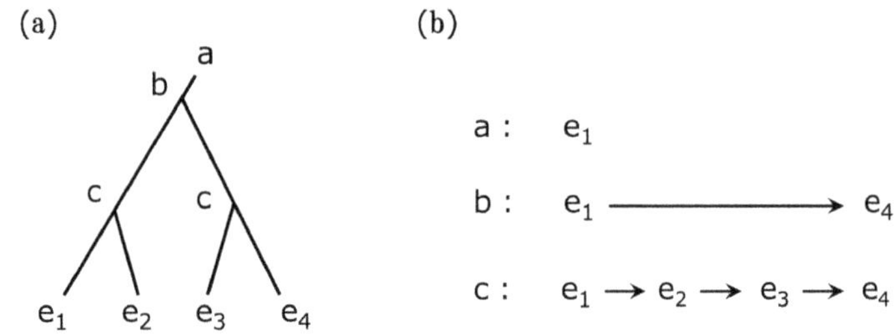

Fig. 6.35 Prolongational tree and level

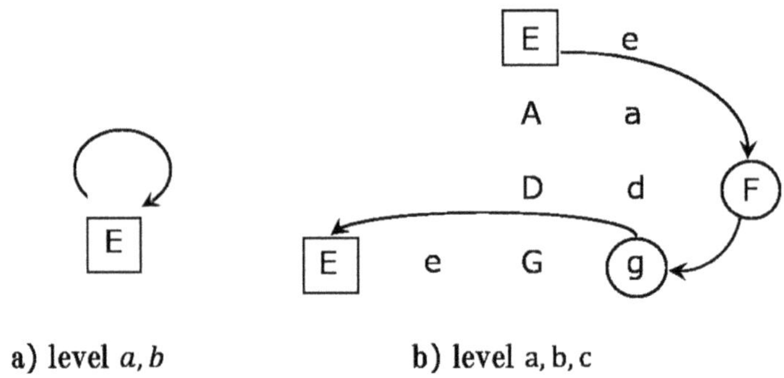

Fig. 6.36 Path in the different levels

1. Let a–b–c be the different depth or height in the tree, according to the level of prolongation.
2. We assume the prolongation of chords, depending on the height of tree, as follows.

   - In level a, every pitch event is under the influence of e_1.
   - In level b, a piece begins from e_1 and finishes by e_4.
   - In level c, the progression is $e_1 \to e_2 \to e_3 \to e_4$.

3. We show different paths dependent on the depth, in the combined regional space. The squared label shows either the start or the destination, and the circled events are those on the path, connected by directed arrows.
4. For example in Fig. 6.36, (a) shows level a and b, and (b) does level a, b, c.
5. In Fig. 6.37b,

   - The double line shows a pivot that appears on the score. In the center of the figure, C is surrendered by nine other chords, meaning it is I/C, and is interpreted immediately as V/F below in the figure.
   - The dotted arrow/double line suggests the path on the principle of the shortest. If V/E → V/C on the upper-left corner is interpreted as V/e → III/e, the path would be shorter.

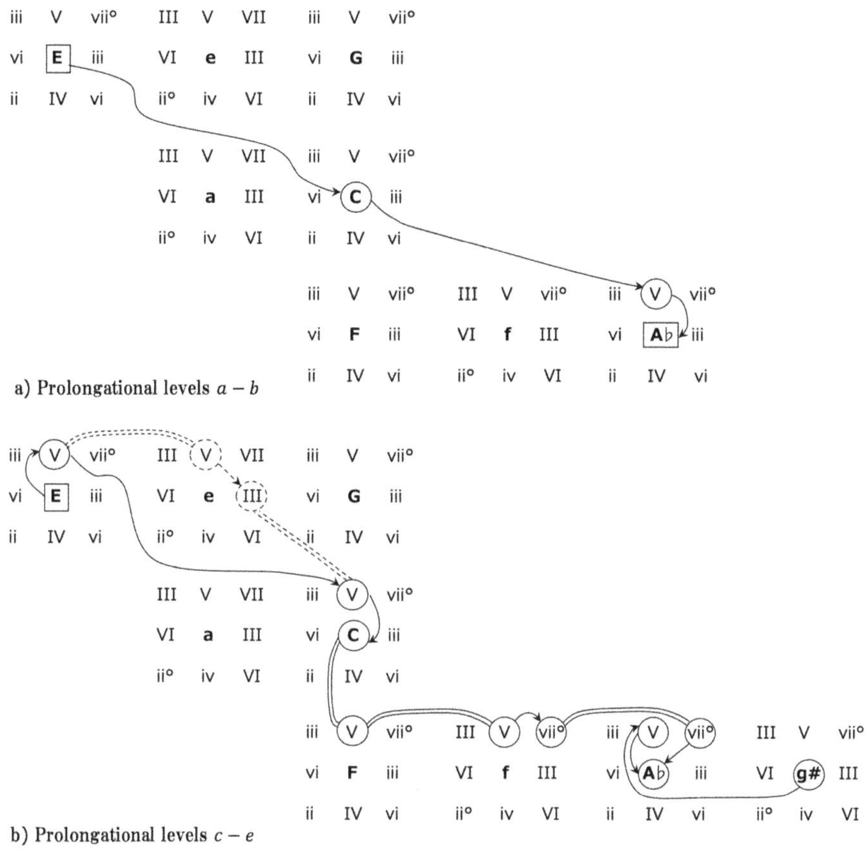

Fig. 6.37 Paths in the different levels in the combined regional space

6.2.1 *Tonal Tension and Attraction*

Tonal Tension

When two consecutive chords possess a big value in distance, it causes a tension. Thus, *sequential tension* T_{seq} is measured by the chordal distance. At the same time, a chord itself may possess its own tension because of inversion or non-chord tone, given by T_{diss}. Therefore, we define

$$T_{\text{seq}}(y) \stackrel{\text{def}}{\equiv} T_{\text{diss}}(y) + \delta(x_{\text{prec}} \to y)$$

where x_{prec} is a chord preceding y.

In general, a trained listener remembers the initial tonic and thus is sensitive in being distant from the tonic. Therefore, when there are two connected chords in the

Fig. 6.38 Melodic attractor

(4)	C												C
(3)	C				E			G					C
(2)	C		D		E	F		G		A		B	C
(1)	C	D♭/C♯	D	E♭/D♯	E	F	G♭/F♯	G	A♭/G♯	A	B♭/A♯	B	C

prolongational tree, if the second chord is farther away than the first one, the tension increases. On the contrary, when the second comes nearer to tonic, we feel relaxed. Then, we consider the global value of tension T_{glob} dependent on the position in the prolongational tree, that is the accumulation of the local tension T_{loc}.

$$T_{\text{loc}}(x \rightarrow y) = \delta(x \rightarrow y)$$
$$T_{\text{glob}}(y) = T_{\text{loc}}(x_{\text{dom}} \rightarrow y) + T_{\text{inh}}(x_{\text{dom}})$$

where x_{dom} is the chord which dominates y directly as an upper branch of y, and T_{inh} is the sum of the tension received from far more upper chords of x_{dom}.

Melodic Attractor

A trained listener is conscious of the digression from tonic also in melody, as well as that from tonic in harmony. Now, we evaluate the tendency toward tonic in melody, as *attractor*. First, we give melodic tension values as the depth of each note in Fig. 6.38. For example, C is 0, C♯ is 3 and so on. In the figure, B is a neighbor of A in the same level while G is a neighbor in a higher level. In this case, we regard that A is more strongly attracted or *anchored* to G. This anchoring strength is the parenthesized numbers in Fig. 6.38. Since C is 4, D is 2, and E is 3, D is anchored to E by $3/2$ while D is more strongly anchored to C by $4/2 = 2$.

We define the strength of melodic attraction as

$$\alpha(p_1 \rightarrow p_2) = \frac{s_2}{s_1} \times \frac{1}{n^2}$$

where s_i is the anchoring strength of p_i and n is the number of semitones between p_i's.

Weighted TPS

The above formalization of TPS should be examined in accordance with actual pieces of music. For example, the chordal proximity $\delta(x \rightarrow y) = i + j + k$ is a naïve addition but we could give more precise definition by weighted coefficients, as

$$\delta(x \rightarrow y) = w_1 i + w_2 j + w_3 k$$

Similarly, we could tune the original definition of tension $T_{glob} = T_{loc} + T_{inh}$ to

$$T_{glob} = w_1 T_{loc} + w_2 T_{inh}.$$

The evaluation of weights is the future work, based on the accumulated music data.

References

1. F. Lerdahl, R. Jackendoff, *A Generative Theory of Tonal Music* (The MIT Press, Cambridge, 1983)
2. F. Lerdhal, *Tonal Pitch Space* (Oxford University Press, Oxford, 2001)

Chapter 7
Formalization of GTTM

This book begins with the subsection title, "Music theory that enjoys the benefits of computers", and we state there "We believe that we can approach an answer to what music is if we can express this implicit knowledge as a computer program and execute the program" (Sect. 1.1). There are many types of information related to music, and there are various methods to represent such information, too. Among them, we assume the time-span tree of GTTM is promising for representing the listener's cognition and the composer's intention. In this section, we introduce the results of our research on formalizing the time-span tree and establishing an algebraic system for the time-span tree. Beyond this, we aim to construct a mathematical system to manage and/or manipulate music in the same way as we freely manage basic arithmetic and calculate numbers. Also, we believe that our attempts would be a milestone on the journey toward a certain style of computational musicology.

7.1 Putting Intention into Music

Creating or producing music is more technically difficult than recognizing or comprehending music. As attempts to analyze and theoretize the actual phenomenon of generating music or language, there is work such as Molino's trichotomy,[1] which we have touched on many times in this book, or Lakoff's theory of generative semantics.[2] Here, a problem is putting intention into music. *Intention* refers to some sort of meaning which is provided by a composer or speaker, in other words the person

[1] *cf.* Sect. 1.7.

[2] *cf.* Sect. 3.1.

K. Hirata et al., *Music, Mathematics and Language*,
https://doi.org/10.1007/978-981-19-5166-4_7

putting out content, and assigned to the content for some purpose.[3] Based on that intention, by selecting the components of a piece of music or a sentence and giving them a structure, we can expect an effect in which some kind of emotion or action is induced in the person receiving the content. If we were able to express intention independent of the content of a musical composition or sentence, we would surely simply be able to input the intention one is thinking of into a system, then transform and manipulate the intention on a computer. However, at present, as the basic principles and rules relating to intention put into content have not yet been formalized, the definition of its concepts and behaviors is ambiguous and incomplete. For this reason, it is difficult to realize a program that correctly operates in the same way as a human. Regarding the activity of a person assigning intention and producing music or language, there have been numerous proposals categorized as so-called composition methods or paragraph writing method. It would be more appropriate to classify these as practical methodologies or collected know-how for expressing intention directly as groups of musical notes or vocabulary.

As methods working on a computer for actually realizing or else supporting the operation of putting intention into content, there are editor, case-based reasoning, machine learning, the generate and test method, genetic algorithm, simulation, and so on. Editor is a tool for inputting the necessary letters or notations one by one, in order to produce the sentence or musical score that you want to express. This takes time, but it allows you to produce a sentence or musical score as per your intention. Case-based reasoning and machine learning are methods in which you present the system with existing sample content with an intention similar to the intention you want to include. Then, based on that content, the system reconstructs the content to be presented. In general, case-based reasoning performs reconstruction from one piece of existing content, while machine learning performs reconstruction from multiple (a large number of) pieces of existing content. Regarding generate and test method and genetic algorithms, these are methods that make use of a general rule because it is difficult to realize a system that directly generates the content with intention, but it is easier to provide a rule or function for evaluation or discrimination. In other words, even if putting intention into the content is difficult, it is comparatively easy to check whether or not the intention you wish to include has been included. Simulation is a method that uses the above methods in composite. Template can be seen as a method that fills in empty slots in a template with values generated by the above methods. All of the methods described above are methods that directly structure individual contents and present them, and as such these methods are limited by the trade-off, relating to system usage, between flexibility and usability.[4]

Actually, there is one more method for a computer to realize the process of putting intention into content. That method is a programming-style method which is carried

[3] In 1987, the American philosopher Bratman (Michael Bratman, 1945–) proposed the BDI (Belief–Desire–Intention) model as a model for human decision-making in the real world. The BDI model explains rational future-directed intention in a dynamic environment and provides a method for realizing this. Into this model is introduced the concept of intention relating to thought or activity.

[4] *cf.* Sect. 1.2.

out by a person freely combining either basic operations of which the properties are well-known, or basic functions with which the person is familiar. In this method, in the same way as a programmer, while programming, imagines the run-time behavior of the code he or she is writing, contents are created while imagining the intention and the final form of the content. With this programming-style method, it may be possible to find an optimal point in the trade-off between flexibility and usability regarding system usage. However, it should be noted that, as a basic premise for this method, one must be able to predict and imagine the overall properties and final form of the contents even during the creation process. Is it possible to realize a method for programming music based on reductionism in the sense of creating music in a bottom-up manner? Could we discover a computational system that would allow us to alter, transform and replace the tree structures that express the meaning of music in any way we wish.[5] in the same way as every kind of calculation can be realized by the four arithmetic operations included in a program, or every class of geometrical figure can be drawn if you have a ruler and compass?[6] As we discussed in Sect. 1.3, if we separate the fundamental layer that treats gestalt and intersubjective structures and properties from the higher layer that treats sensitivity, preference and artistic quality, we can appropriately configure the basic arithmetic operations, which may enable us to perform programming on music. In the section below, we will introduce our attempt at music generation, which applies the music theory GTTM [2–5, 11].

7.2 GTTM Analysis and Rendering

As shown in Fig. 7.1, what we mean here by musical analysis is the extraction of a time-span tree from a given musical score or performance. From a musical score, GTTM analysis examines and extracts the information not written on the score, in the form of a time-span tree. In the same way, when taking a performance of a piece of music as the target of analysis, relationships, and information that are difficult to pick up directly from performance are examined and extracted in the form of a time-span tree.[7]

Now, since the terminal leaves of a time-span tree are not actual notes, to listen to a time-span tree it is necessary to supplement the abstract sounds of time-span trees with information of onset and duration and convert them into actual notes. The operation of externalizing time-span tree information as a musical score and converting it into real notes that can be played or listened to in this way are called rendering. Rendering is an operation that is the reverse of musical analysis and which has the role of producing ambiguity at the surface level, i.e., the score.

[5] In the field of image processing, there is a cognition method based on reductionism called mathematical morphology [1]. An image (shape) is treated as a mathematical set, and comprehension of the meaning of the image is conducted by applying basic arithmetic operations to the set and transforming it.

[6] https://en.wikipedia.org/wiki/Straightedge_and_compass_construction.

[7] In Sect. 1.9, we argue that a time-span tree has cognitive reality.

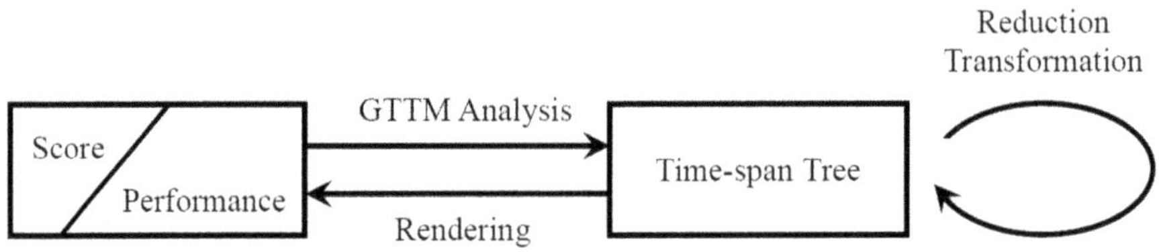

Fig. 7.1 Relationship between GTTM analysis and rendering

In GTTM analysis, since, in general, multiple time-span trees are extracted when a certain score or performance is provided, the analysis from score/performance to time-span tree is a 1:N projection [8]. Figure 7.2a is an example of two types of score which have been produced from the same melody but in which slur is applied in different ways. In accordance with the ways of applying slur, two types of time-span tree are generated. Even if exactly the same melodies occur at different places on the score, the meaning of those melodies differs depending on whether they appear, for instance, at the beginning of the composition or at the end, and thus those different interpretations can be expressed as different time-span trees. Furthermore, there are cases in which a melody that is exactly the same on the score is given different interpretations by multiple musicians, in which case it can, in the same way, be expressed as different time-span trees. On the other hand, as shown in Fig. 7.2b, rendering is also a 1:N projection. The principal reason for this is that, since the concept of rests is not included in a time-span tree, arbitrariness arises in the introduction of rests in rendering.

7.3 Formalization of Time-Span Trees

We have described the form of a time-span tree as expressing a situation in which the most important notes triumph, as in a tournament.[8] Within a time-span tree, as long as a certain pitch event keeps 'winning', it continues in a straight line, while the losing junctions become the peripheral nodes of that straight line. The pitch event that survives up to the primary root of a certain time-span tree is the most important pitch event and dominates the entirety of that time-span tree. In the same manner, for the two partial trees that are obtained by moving down by one step to either the right or left from the root, the pitch events that remain up to the root of the respective partial trees are the most important pitch events that dominate each of those partial trees. Division into these partial trees can be repeated until one recursively reaches the leaves.

Here, *maximum time-span* refers to the time-span (duration) at the ultimate junction within the time-span tree that a certain pitch event has survived up to. At the ultimate survived junction, the pitch event dominates the longest time-span. Then, we will consider two maximum time-spans of which one includes the other. Since

[8] *cf.* Sect. 6.1.4.

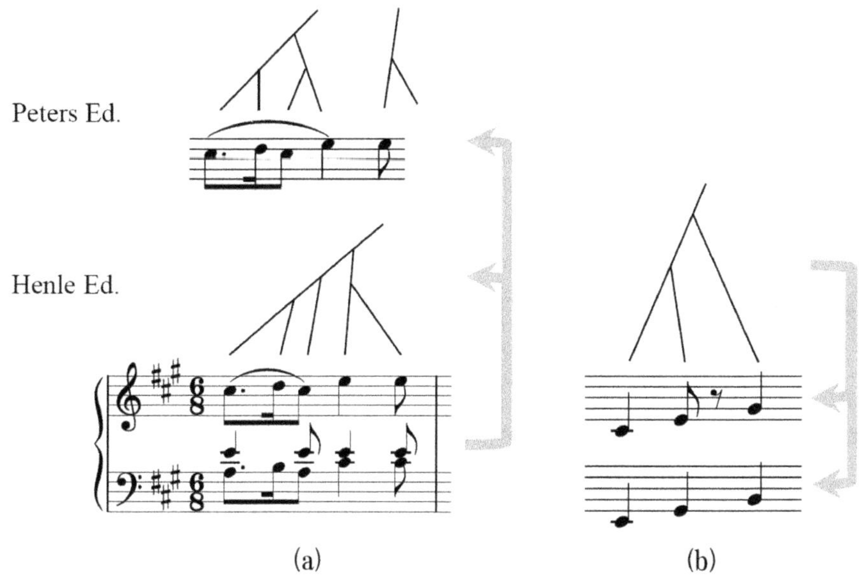

(a) 1-to-many mapping in GTTM analysis (score to time-span tree)

(b) 1-to-many mapping in rendering (time-span tree to score)

Fig. 7.2 Ambiguity in GTTM analysis and rendering

the longer maximum time-span dominates a longer range, it is assumed to contain more information. At this point, we introduce the hypothesis that if we reduce (eliminate) a branch including one pitch event, we lose the information corresponding to that maximum time-span. This is called the *maximum time-span hypothesis*. In the example in Fig. 7.3a, a certain melody is composed of the four pitch events e1, e2, e3, and e4, and each pitch event has a corresponding duration on the score: s1, s2, s3, and s4, respectively (indicated in thin lines in the figure). In Fig. 7.3b, that melody's time-span tree and the corresponding maximum time-spans mt1, mt2, mt3, and mt4 are illustrated (in bold lines). The relationship between the time-spans in Fig. 7.3a and the maximum time-spans in Fig. 7.3b is as follows. In the lowest level of the hierarchy, there are pitch events of which the time-span and maximum time-span are equivalent: mt2 = s2, mt3 = s3. In the level above, the relationship mt1 = s1 + mt2, mt4 = mt1 + mt3 + s4 = s1 + s2 + s3 + s4 is established. Here, if we take, for example, the duration of a quarter note to be 12 ticks,[9] the relationship becomes s1 = s2 = s3 = s4 = 12, mt2 = mt3 = 12, mt1 = 24, mt4 = 48. In other words, the whole time-span extends by the connection of adjacent time-spans in the lower level of the time-span tree. In summary, when all the time-spans in the lower level are connected, that becomes the maximum time-span.

[9] A tick means a unit of time used within music software or hardware systems. The term derives from the tick of a clock, i.e., the optical resolution (minimum time) when the clock hand marks time.

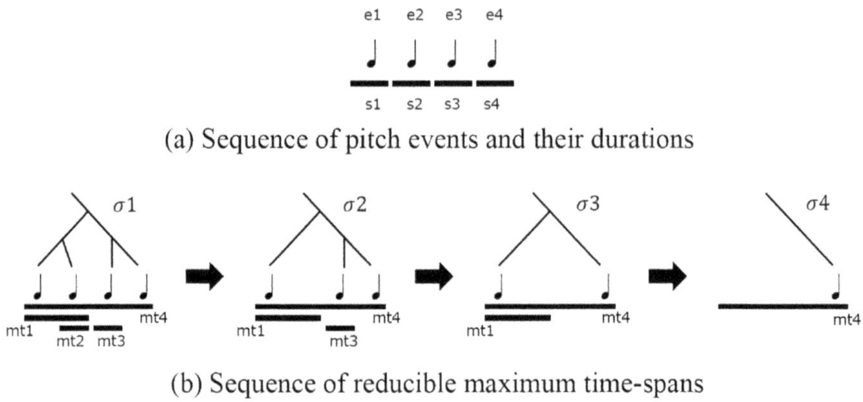

Fig. 7.3 Hierarchical structure of maximum time-spans, and their reduction

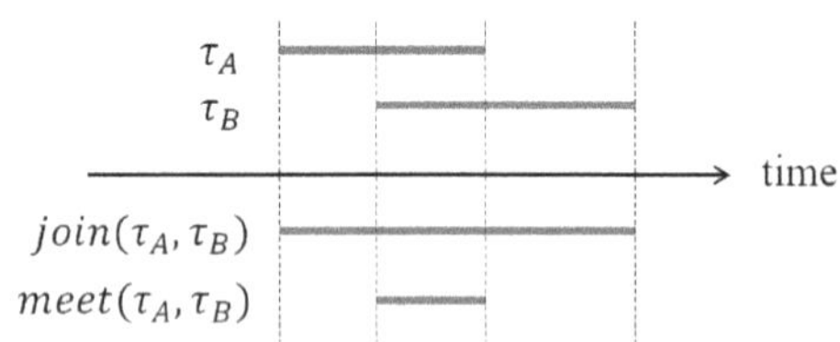

Fig. 7.4 Join and meet of time-spans

Let us consider the procedure for reducing a time-span tree. Reduction is the operation of eliminating one time-span included in a time-span tree, but time-spans cannot be eliminated arbitrarily. It is only the secondary time-spans at the terminals that can be eliminated. A *subsumption relationship* exists between the pre-reduction time-span tree and the post-reduction time-span tree. The subsumption relationship is the most fundamental relationship in knowledge representation.[10] In a certain time-span tree, there are generally multiple places at which it is possible to perform reduction. Therefore, since the execution procedure for reduction is not fixed, the set of the reduced time-span trees becomes a partially ordered set: a 'poset'.[11] Furthermore, if join and meet can be defined on a poset, we say the poset makes a lattice. To put it intuitively, join corresponds to the union of sets, while meet corresponds to the intersection of sets.

As a base case, we will consider the join and meet of the two time-spans τ_A and τ_B (Fig. 7.4).

If τ_A and τ_B are separate from each other (if there are no parts that overlap chronologically, or else connection is not possible), join does not exist and meet becomes empty (notated as $\perp$). This accords with the maximum time-span hypothesis which

[10] The study field called mereology takes as its theme the provision of a logical basis for the relationship between the parts and the whole.

[11] A poset (partially ordered set) satisfies reflexive, antisymmetric, and transitive relations.

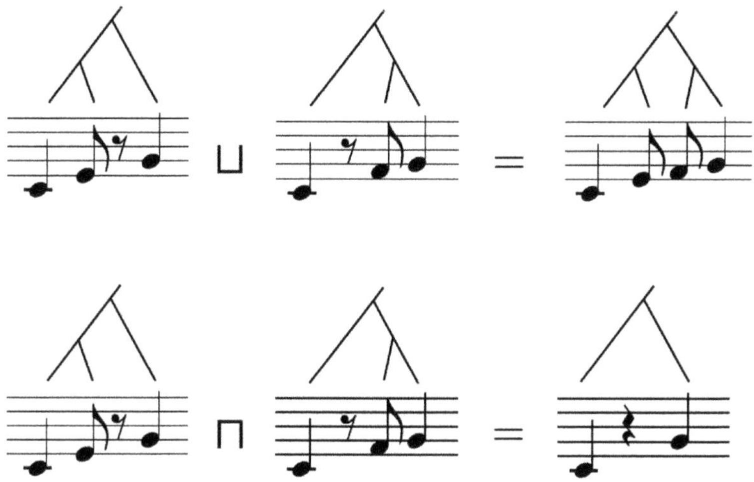

Fig. 7.5 Simple example of join and meet of time-span trees

states that a time-span that dominates a longer range contains more information.[12] Next, as an inductive case, we will consider the two time-span trees σ_1 and σ_2. When a branch corresponding to σ_1 occurs as a certain subtree of σ_2, we say that σ_1 is subsumed by σ_2.[13]

We define join and meet in a more formal way, as follows.

join: When a minimum y, such as $\sigma_1 \sqsubseteq y$ and $\sigma_2 \sqsubseteq y$, exists, we call this the join of σ_1 and σ_2 and write it as $\sigma_1 \sqcup \sigma_2$.

meet: When a maximum x, such as $x \sqsubseteq \sigma_1$ and $x \sqsubseteq \sigma_2$, exists, we call this the meet of σ_1 and σ_2 and write it as $\sigma_1 \sqcap \sigma_2$.

A simple example is presented in Fig. 7.5. The join operator $\sqcup$ and the meet operator $\sqcap$ are recursively applied to the time-span tree and, in the case of Fig. 7.5, ultimately the join and meet of an eighth note (partial time-span tree) and eighth rest are comuputed. Join and meet are operations relating to time-span trees, but to explain them simply let us view a time-span tree and a musical score as identical, so long as there is no ambiguity. In the join of an eighth note and eighth rest, we regard the eighth rest as $\bot$, thus the value of join becomes an eighth note. In contrast, since one side of meet is $\bot$, the value of meet becomes $\bot$. Accordingly, join computes the unification of the two trees given as arguments, while meet computes the common parts of the two trees. As there is no indeterminism in this process of computing join and meet,[14] join and meet exist uniquely. Therefore, the partially ordered set of the

---

[12] This idea is inspired by interval semantics of temporal logic.

[13] The subsumption relationship in this text is defined based only on the configuration of the time-span tree and the maximum time-spans and ignores the information of pitch event (pitch).

[14] That is, the scenario does not arise in which there exist multiple step candidates for which the next execution is possible; one candidate must be deterministically chosen before execution.

time-span tree becomes a lattice. On the lattice, when we have $x \sqsubseteq \sigma_A$, $\sigma_A \sqcup x = \sigma_A$ and $\sigma_A \sqcap x = x$ hold. Furthermore, when we have $\sigma_A \sqsubseteq \sigma_B$, for arbitrary x, $x \sqcup \sigma_A \sqsubseteq x \sqcup \sigma_B$ and $x \sqcap \sigma_A \sqsubseteq x \sqcap \sigma_B$ hold. On the type of algebraic lattice in which join and meet exist, the following kind of absorption laws also hold: $(\sigma_A \sqcup \sigma_B) \sqcap \sigma_A = \sigma_A$ and $(\sigma_A \sqcap \sigma_B) \sqcup \sigma_A = \sigma_A$.

Intuitively, some readers may think that join corresponds to a union, while meet corresponds to an intersection. In actuality, the maximum time-span and the join and meet operations between the two have been introduced in such a way that join and meet satisfy the properties corresponding to the standard union and intersection, respectively. As properties that do not conform, depending on the arguments given to join, the value of join is not defined; in other words, join is partial (when we explained about the base case in Fig. 7.4, we gave an example of there being no join), whereas meet is total.

In Tojo and Hirata (2012), we gave a time-span tree represented in feature structure without the concept of maximum time-span and provided an algorithm for join and meet, to be applied to the representation. In contrast, the system that we propose in this book employs join and meet whose domain is the set of time-span trees with introducing the concept of maximum time-span. As a result, we obtain the algebraic system in which join and meet are available [5]. Additionally, we consider that this algebraic approach is one of the realization methods for the simplicity that appears among the design principles proposed by Norman (Donald Norman, 1935–):

> Simplicity: The complexity of the information appliance is that of the task, not the tool. The technology is invisible. [9]

In other words, if a user were to attempt to realize certain complex processing, the user would realize this by combining the simple and intuitive operators such as join and meet. This is the same as how any calculation, no matter how complex, can be realized by combining the basic arithmetic operations.

7.4 Reduction Distance

Reducing a time-span tree means eliminating one time-span contained within that time-span tree,[15] At this time, the series of time-span trees obtained by eliminating time-spans one by one is called a reduction path. Since there are generally multiple branches for which reduction is possible, there are also multiple reduction paths. In accordance with the maximum time-span hypothesis introduced in the previous section, we use the fact that the same amount of information is lost as maximum time-spans eliminated by reduction, and define the distance of the time-span trees on the reduction path as equivalent to the sum of the eliminated maximum time-spans (we call this reduction path distance).

---

[15] The reverse operation to reduction is adding new branches, one by one, which is called elaboration.

Next, we generalize the concept of the distance between time-span trees on the reduction path as the concept of the distance between time-span trees on the lattice. Considering calculation of distance, we determine that the reduction of a branch is carried out one branch at a time. Branches are always reduced in a bottom-up manner, in other words we say that a branch is reducible when that branch has no sub-branches below it. However, we except the tree made of one pitch event, i.e., a tree comprising one branch.

First, we take $\varsigma(\sigma)$ as the set of pitch events included in time-span tree σ, take $\sharp\varsigma(\sigma)$ as the cardinality of the set, and take s_e as the maximum time-span of pitch event e. We define the distance $d_{\sqsubseteq}$ between two time-span trees such that $\sigma_A \sqsubseteq \sigma_B$ on the reduction path, in the following way.

$$d_{\sqsubseteq}(\sigma_A, \sigma_B) = \sum_{e \in \varsigma(\sigma_B) \setminus \varsigma(\sigma_A)} s_e.$$

In the example in Fig. 7.3b, since, when reduction is performed from $\sigma 1$ to $\sigma 4$ pitch events are eliminated in the order of e2, e3, e1, the distance between $\sigma 1$ and $\sigma 4$ becomes mt2 + mt3 + mt1. Now, even if e3 had been reduced first of all, followed by e2, the distance would not be changed. The distance between time-span trees can appear to be simply the sum total of the maximum time-spans of the eliminated branches. However, a correct distance can be obtained if branches must be eliminated in the correct order. As we want to provide a method to calculate the distance between two arbitrary time-span trees, for this purpose, first of all, we define the sum of the maximum time-spans for a time-span tree.

$$tmts(\sigma) = \sum_{e \in \varsigma(\sigma)} s_e,$$

We call this value *total maximum time-span*. If $\sigma_A \sqsubseteq \sigma_B$, it gives us $d_{\sqsubseteq}(\sigma_A, \sigma_B) = tmts(\sigma_B) - tmts(\sigma_A)$. As a special case, there is $d_{\sqsubseteq}(\bot, \sigma) = tmts(\sigma)$. Here there are two time-span trees, σ_A and σ_B. We consider the union $\sigma_A \sqcup \sigma_B$ and intersection $\sigma_A \sqcap \sigma_B$ of those trees. Evidently, since $\sigma_A \sqcap \sigma_B \sqsubseteq \sigma_A \sqcup \sigma_B$ is satisfied, we can consider two reduction paths from $\sigma_A \sqcup \sigma_B$ to $\sigma_A \sqcap \sigma_B$ that pass through σ_A and through σ_B. Now, we want to define the distance so that it can be determined uniquely as $d_{\sqsubseteq}(\sigma_A \sqcap \sigma_B, \sigma_A \sqcup \sigma_B)$. First, let us define the two types of distance measure.

$$d_{\sqcap}(\sigma_A, \sigma_B) \equiv d_{\sqsubseteq}(\sigma_A \sqcap \sigma_B, \sigma_A) + d_{\sqsubseteq}(\sigma_A \sqcap \sigma_B, \sigma_B)$$
$$d_{\sqcup}(\sigma_A, \sigma_B) \equiv d_{\sqsubseteq}(\sigma_A, \sigma_A \sqcup \sigma_B) + d_{\sqsubseteq}(\sigma_B, \sigma_A \sqcup \sigma_B)$$

From the above distance measures and the fact that reduction path distance is uniquely determined, we immediately obtain the *distance lemma*, $d_{\sqcup}(\sigma_A, \sigma_B) = d_{\sqcap}(\sigma_A, \sigma_B)$ (for proof, please see [11]). From this lemma, since we understand that the distance between σ_A and σ_B, $d(\sigma_A, \sigma_B)$, can be given uniquely, the expression $\{\sqcap, \sqcup\}$ is redundant. Therefore, we delete $\{\sqcap, \sqcup\}$ from the notation $d_{\{\sqcap, \sqcup\}}$ and simply write it as 'd'. Furthermore, regarding this definition of distance, the triangle inequality

$$d(\sigma_A, \sigma_B) + d(\sigma_B, \sigma_C) \geq d(\sigma_A, \sigma_C)$$

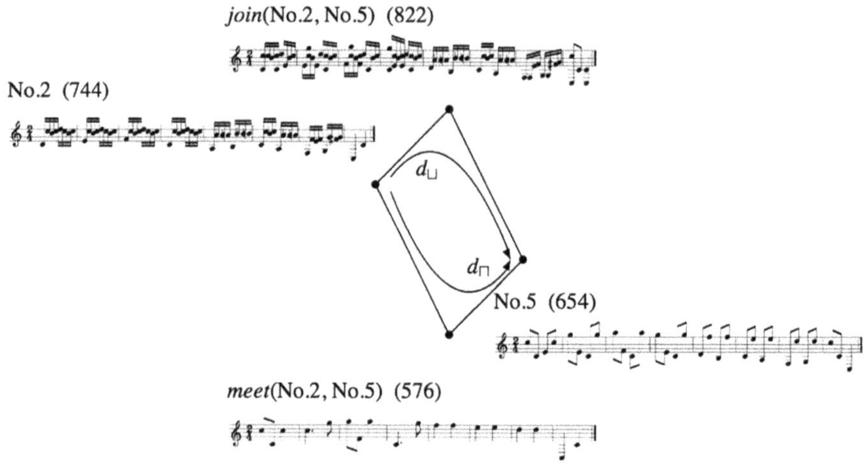

Fig. 7.6 Parallelogram formed by variations No. 2 and No. 5 and their join and meet. The numbers in brackets represent total maximum time-span (in units of ticks)

also holds. For more technical details, please see [11].

Now, to proceed, in Fig. 7.6 we present an example of giving two melodies and calculating the join and meet of those melodies. As the two melodies, we use variations No. 2 and No. 5 from Mozart's *Twelve Variations on 'Ah vous dirai-je, Maman'* K.265/300e (also known as the 'Twinkle Twinkle Little Star Variations'). The numbers in round brackets in the figure represent the total maximum time-spans defined in the previous section. In Fig. 7.6, if we determine a quarter note as 12 ticks, the total maximum time-span of variation No. 2 is 744 ticks, while the total maximum time-span of variation No. 5 is 654 ticks. Then, if we follow the definitions of the two kinds of distance measure, we can see that $d_\sqcap = (744 - 576) + (654 - 576) = 246$ and $d_\sqcup = (822 - 744) + (822 - 654) = 246$ are established. In the figure, since the opposite sides of the quadrangle formed by the four time-span trees are the same length, that quadrangle is a parallelogram. In the example in Fig. 7.6, we have shown that the distance lemma and triangle inequality of distance actually hold.

Join and meet could be calculated in the case of the time-span trees of variations No. 2 and No. 5 shown in Fig. 7.6, but, as we explained previously, in general it is not guaranteed that join can always be calculated. For calculating join properly, at all corresponding nodes of the two time-span trees given as arguments to join, the maximum time-spans must be connectable (Fig. 7.4). 'Connectable' means that there are overlapping parts between the given two time-spans. If two time-spans are connectable, the value of join can be calculated as a union. Also, join and meet must satisfy the absorption law and distance lemma. For further technical details, please see [3].

As mentioned in a footnote of the previous section, the subsumption relationship between time-span trees does not care about that between pitch events, all the pitch events e appearing in a time-span tree are viewed as identical; in other words, equivalently, $join(e, e) = meet(e, e) = e$. Hence, in calculating distance between melodies, distance between pitch events is not considered at present.

7.5 Experiment to Assess the Validity of the Time-Span Tree

To confirm to what extent the distance between time-span trees, introduced in the previous section, is the same as the psychological distance perceived when a person listens to the melodies, we conduct an experiment with subjects. As the set piece of music, we use Mozart's *Twelve Variations on 'Ah, vous dirai-je, maman'* K.265/300e. This composition comprises twelve variations, but in the experiment we use only the first eight bars of each variation (Fig. 7.7). The original compositions are polyphonies†, however, as our method can currently only handle monophony†, we arranged the original pieces into monophonies prior to the experiment. At that time, we extract the important notes from the right-hand and left-hand parts, select one note in the case of chords, and adjust the octave so that the melody flows smoothly. In the experiment, we create pairs of every combination of the theme and twelve variations (eight bars) (${}_{13}C_2 = 78$ pairs).

In the experiment using subjects, we gathered eleven university students (of which seven had experience of musical instrument performance). We notate the thirteen melodies to be listened to as m_i ($i \in \{0, 1, 2, \cdots, 12\}$, 0 stands for the theme, and 1–12 the variations) and have each subject listen to every pair $\langle m_i, m_j \rangle$ once, in an arbitrary order. Each time a subject listens to a pair, they answer a question on to what extent m_i is similar to m_j, on a five-level scale: Very similar $= 2$, Similar $= 1$, Neither similar nor dissimilar $= 0$, Not similar $= -1$, Entirely dissimilar $= -2$. When beginning the experiment, to avoid the problem of a cold start, the subjects listen to the theme and twelve variations (eight bars) all the way through, though they do not conduct evaluation of the melodies. To prevent the order effect, the subjects listen to the same pair, reordered, one more time later. That is to say, eventually the subjects always listen to both $\langle m_i, m_j \rangle$ and $\langle m_j, m_i \rangle$. We calculate the average from the evaluation scores given to the two pairs by a subject, then further calculate the average across all the subjects. In this way, we obtain the distance matrix that expresses the psychological distance between m_i and m_j.

In the experiment to calculate the theoretical value, we adopt the reduction distance introduced in the previous section. We use maximum time-span in the calculation of reduction distance, but, to enable us to deal with triplets as well, we decided on a third of a sixteenth note as the smallest unit of distance (we use the same unit in Figs. 7.3 and 7.6). To obtain the correct time-span trees for the theme and twelve variations, the trees were first created by one of the authors of the paper [5], after which they were cross-checked by another author.

It is no simple matter to examine and discover the correspondence relationship between the theoretical distance $d(\sigma_A, \sigma_B)$ and psychological distance expressed in the distance matrix. Therefore, we use *multidimensional scaling* (MDS) to visualize

Fig. 7.7 Opening eight bars of each variation, arranged into monophonies for the experiment

that correspondence relationship. MDS is a method that, when given the distance matrix of which the elements are the distance or discrepancy (opposite of similarity) between items, identifies the multiple axes (coordinate space) that most effectively explain the entire relative relationships of the distance, and presents items in the coordinate space. Accordingly, items that are closer in distance measure will also be positioned more closely in the coordinate space.

First of all, we express the distance among the thirteen melodies, using Torgerson Scaling MDS; however, we hardly found a clear correspondence relationship between the theoretical distance and degree of psychological similarity. Therefore, we reduced the targets to the theme and variations No. 1 to No. 9 (ten melodics in total) and redisplayed the graph by MDS (Fig. 7.8).

In the figure, 'theme' and the numbers i $(1 \ldots 9)$ correspond to the melodies in Fig. 7.7. Regarding the contribution rate of each axis in the MDS of theoretical distance shown in Fig. 7.8a, the first principal component is (x-axis) = 0.21 and the second principal component is (y-axis) = 0.17. In Fig. 7.8b, which shows the degree

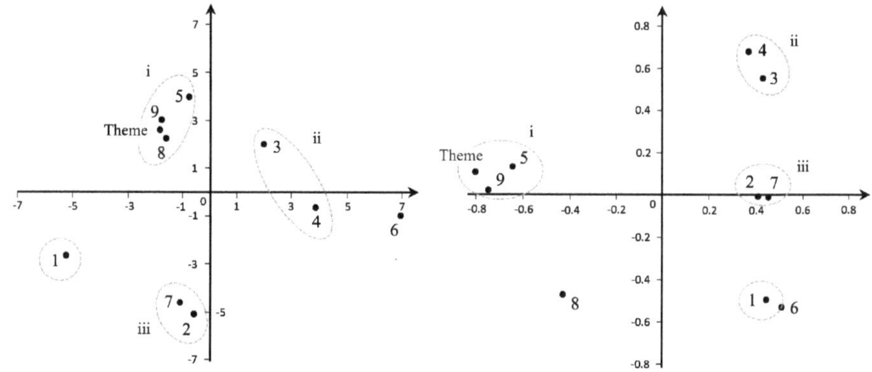

(a) Theoretical estimation (b) Human listener

Fig. 7.8 Expression of relative distance of melodies by multidimensional scaling

of human psychological similarity, the first principal component is (x-axis) = 0.32 and the second principal component is (y-axis) = 0.17.

In the figure, between (a) and (b), several interesting relationships can be seen regarding the ten melodies. Firstly, if we focus on the clusters that can be seen in both (a) and (b), the theme, No. 5, No. 8, and No. 9 form cluster *i*, No. 3 and No. 4 cluster *ii*, and No. 2 and No. 7 cluster *iii*. Furthermore, the relative positional relationship between clusters *i*, *ii*, and *iii* is also similar in (a) and (b). To consider a melody besides those mentioned above, the relative positional relationship between variation No. 1 and the other melodies is also similar. As there is not a large difference between the contribution rates of the first principal component and second principal component in (a), you may intuitively find the correspondence relationship between (a) and (b), if we rotate the coordinate system of (a) 90° anticlockwise. In contrast, as for the relative positional relationship of variation No. 6, no correspondence can be seen between (a) and (b). By this experiment, just by focusing on rhythmic structure,[16] it is revealed that there is a preferable correspondence relationship between reduction distance and psychological similarity. To make our methodology more elaborate, it would be necessary to investigate the similarity of pitch events. In addition, it is critical to make a comparison with conventional Levenshtein distance, earth mover's distance, etc., and clarify the unique characteristics of the distance that we are proposing.

[16] As described in the footnote in Sect. 7.3, a time-span tree is configured ignoring the information of pitch event.

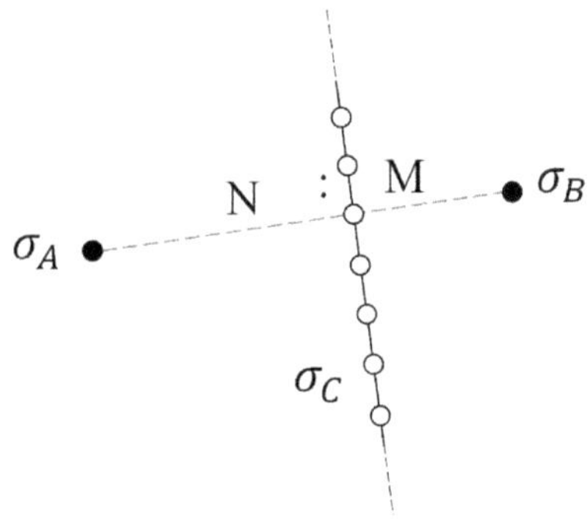

Fig. 7.9 Range of existence of compositions that fulfill conditions for morphing

7.6 Melody Morphing by Time-Span Tree

Originally morphing referred to an algorithm for generating an image that is the intermediate of two given images.[17] In music, in the same way, the algorithm that generates an intermediate melody from two given melodies is called morphing.

In this section, we will present the algorithm (morphing algorithm) that generates an intermediate melody when given two variation melodies composed from one theme. Firstly, we call the time-span trees of the two variations σ_A and σ_B, and the time-span tree of the morphing result σ_C. At this time, we demand that, on a certain distance space, σ_C will be a $M\colon N$ internal dividing point of σ_A and σ_B. Here, $M\colon N$ is the ratio relating to the total maximum time-spans *tmts* (Sect. 7.4). Attention should be paid to the fact that there are infinitely many points at the specific ratio of distance from σ_A to that from σ_B, $M\colon N$ (Fig. 7.9). Firstly, let us consider a line segment connecting σ_A and σ_B, called L, and a point that internally divides L into $M\colon N$, called P. Next, let us consider a line that is perpendicular to L and intersects P, called Q. Then, any point on Q satisfies the condition of ratio $M\colon N$ described above.

Therefore, we also demand that the morphing algorithm computes σ_C, which exists only on the line segment connecting σ_A and σ_B.

The morphing algorithm that we propose is presented below (Fig. 7.10) [3]:

1. Give two melodies σ_A and σ_B,[18] calculate $meet(\sigma_A, \sigma_B)$.
2. Consider the reduction path from σ_A to $meet(\sigma_A, \sigma_B)$, eliminate notes one by one from σ_A, obtain the time-span tree α that divides that reduction path into $N\colon M$.
3. In the same way, obtain the time-span tree β that divides the reduction path from σ_B to $meet(\sigma_A, \sigma_B)$ into $M\colon N$.
4. Calculate $join(\alpha, \beta)$.
5. Convert time-span tree $join(\alpha, \beta)$ into an actual composition (rendering of score).

[17] This was made famous by the official music video for 'Black or White' (1991) by the 'King of Pop' Michael Jackson (1958–2014) (morphing occurs from approximately 5 m 25 s onward in the video).

[18] Here, since time-span trees and melodies correspond one-to-one, we conveniently use the same notations for melodies and time-span trees as long as there is no ambiguity.

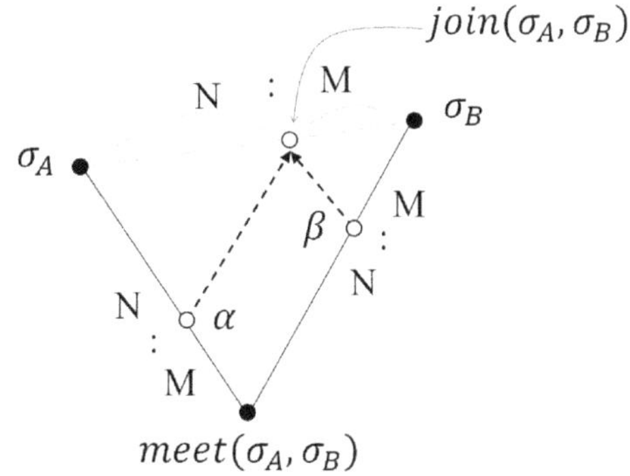

Fig. 7.10 Morphing algorithm

In the figure, there are the four time-span trees α, β, $meet(\sigma_A, \sigma_B)$ and $join(\alpha, \beta)$. These trees form a parallelogram like that in Fig. 7.6. It is clear that, regarding the distance between σ_A and σ_B, we have $d(\sigma_A, \sigma_B) = d(\sigma_A, join(\alpha, \beta)) + d(join(\alpha, \beta), \sigma_B)$. That is to say, the algorithm computes σ_C, which exists on the line segment connecting σ_A and σ_B: if $tmts(\sigma_A) \leq tmts(\sigma_B)$, we have $tmts(\sigma_A) \leq tmts(\sigma_C) \leq tmts(\sigma_B)$.[19]

We have three comments to add regarding the morphing algorithm. The first concerns the join of time-span tree nodes of which the directions of the branches differ (in other words, unification of left branching and right branching). In the current implementation of join, the nodes corresponding to the two time-span trees are simply overlapped, regardless of whether the direction of branching is the same or different. To put it simply, it is as though two states of branch are existing simultaneously. There is room for argument as to whether or not such superimposed nodes of which the branch directions differ should be handled in the same way as the current implementation.[20]

The second comment relates to the rendering algorithm. The rendering algorithm currently being implemented views each maximum time-span as a line segment expressing one note on a piano roll and converts the time-spans into notations on a musical score, in a top-down fashion from the upper level (closest to the root of the tree). There are cases in which the lower-level time-spans (closest to the terminals of the tree) partially or totally overwrite an upper-level time-span. As a result, the case can occur, for example, in which a maximum time-span, though it may be the most important pitch event, is totally overwritten by several lower-level time-spans and thus does not remain as a musical notation on a score. Accordingly, in the simplistic top-down algorithm, there are cases in which a valid melody (musical score) cannot be generated. To counter this, we can consider, for example, incorporating not only top-down but also some kind of bottom-up process into rendering, or application of GTTM analysis to incomplete results during the rendering process.

Concerning the first comment, if we allow superimposed nodes of which the branch directions differ as described above, the rendering method for such nodes also

[19] *tmts* is the total maximum time-span introduced in Sect. 7.4.

[20] We can also adopt the policy of not allowing these kinds of superimposed nodes.

becomes an issue. Simply at first, there is a method to decompose the superimposed nodes or subtrees, render them separately, and then superimpose the rendered ones again. As another implementation, there is, for example, an algorithm by which a score is rendered by sequentially picking up appropriate notes from superimposed nodes or subtrees in a transformational manner.[21] The question of rendering also leaves room for discussion.

The third comment is on whether we may improve the morphing algorithm so that it does not calculate join for the time-span trees of which the branch directions are different from each other. This would mean that, when for the arguments to join, two time-span trees of which the branch directions differ are selected from the reduction paths, the algorithm would backtrack[22] and select other time-span tree(s) from the reduction path(s). Alternatively, it is also possible to solve the problem using constraint programming,[23] in which we describe the constraint that demands not to calculate the join of nodes with different branch directions. In doing this, although there may still be a case in which it is difficult to generate output for some internal division ratios given to the morphing algorithm, we are able to avoid handling a data structure of which the interpretation is undecided.

7.7 Concluding Remarks

Through the experiments introduced in Sects. 7.5 and 7.6, we have considered the two questions of whether time-span trees are correctly expressing human musical cognition and whether we are correctly calculating time-span trees.

Looking at the relative distances between the variations (Fig. 7.7) and the relative distances between the morphing melodies (Fig. 9.7), it is very interesting that such good performance, in terms of discrimination, was achieved only by the configuration of a time span tree, without calculating differences in pitch events. However, if we think about it for one step further, since we consider pitch event information when generating a time-span tree, we can consider that pitch event information is indirectly reflected in the configuration of the time-span tree.

When we investigated the places where the distance obtained from the subjects and the theoretical distance did not match, we found that all the reasons for this were related to pitch events. One reason is that, for the two time-span trees of which

[21] This idea is associated with the transformation head of time-span trees [7, p. 155].

[22] Backtrack is invoked when an algorithm faces difficulties with running further, due to some contention or contradiction, in the midst of a computing process to find the answer to a problem. An algorithm rolls back (returns) a computing process to a certain previous point, reselects candidate solutions that differ from those used previously, and resumes a computing process from the return point.

[23] A type of programming paradigm in which, just by having a programmer declare the conditions that a variable or variables must fulfill (we call these constraints), a computer automatically discovers the values of the variables needed to satisfy those constraints. In short, there is no need for a programmer to describe the procedure of calculation step by step.

we measured the distance, although the configuration of the trees is almost similar, one is in a major key and the other is in a minor key; then the impressions of the melodies rendered from the two trees were greatly different from each other. Another reason is that, as we touched on in the footnotes in Sect. 7.2, since a proper subsumption relationship is not given to pitch events, in the current system, all pitch events are viewed as the same; that is, we have $join(e, e) = meet(e, e) = e$. Hence, if we take the two melodies of which the time-span trees have the same configuration yet the pitch events alone are different, the pitch event information in the two trees is degraded and lost at present, and the two trees become the same. Evidently, it is after all necessary to express information of pitch events appropriately as a time-span tree and calculate their distances.[24] The rendering algorithm also leaves much room for improvement. By rendering a time-span tree, a person becomes able to listen to the melody it expresses. Therefore, when that rendering can appropriately transform important pitch events into musical notations, we are for the first time able to evaluate whether a time-span tree correctly expresses human musical cognition. Accordingly, it follows that the quality of rendering influences the quality of experiment results.

References

1. H. Goutsias, H.J.A.M. Heijmans (eds.), *Mathematical Morphology* (IOS Press, Amsterdam, 2000)
2. M. Hamanaka, K. Hirata, Implementing methods for analysing music based on Lerdahl and Jackendoff's generative theory of Tonal music (Chapter 9), in *Computational Music Analysis*, ed. by D. Meredith (Springer, Berlin, 2016), pp. 221–249
3. K. Hirata, S. Tojo, M. Hamanaka, Algebraic mozart by tree synthesis, *Proceedings of Joint ICMC and SMC 2014*, pp. 991–997
4. K. Hirata, S. Tojo, M. Hamanaka, An algebraic approach to time-span reduction (Chapter 10), in *Computational Music Analysis* (Springer, Berlin, 2016), pp. 251–270
5. K. Hirata, S. Tojo, M. Hamanaka, Cognitive similarity grounded by tree distance from the analysis of K.265/300e, in *Proceedings of CMMR 2013* (October, 2013), pp. 415–430. Also in *Sound, Music, and Motion*, Lecture Notes in Computer Science (2015), vol. 8905, pp. 589–605
6. F. Lerdahl, *Tonal Pitch Space* (Oxford University Press, Oxford, 2001)
7. F. Lerdahl, R. Jackendoff, *A Generative Theory of Tonal Music* (The MIT Press, Cambridge, 1983)
8. A. Marsden, K. Hirata, S. Tojo, Towards computable procedures for deriving tree structures in music: context dependency in GTTM and Schenkerian theory, in *Proceedings of the Sound and Music Computing Conference 2013 (SMC2013)*, pp. 360–367
9. D. Norman, *The Invisible Computer* (The MIT Press, Cambridge, 1999)
10. SWI-Prolog, http://www.swi-prolog.org/. Accessed on 16 June 2022
11. S. Tojo, K. Hirata, Structural similarity based on time-span tree, *Proceedings of CMMR 2012*, pp. 645–660. Also in *From Sounds to Music and Emotions*, Lecture Notes in Computer Science (2013), vol. 7900, pp. 400–421

[24] For defining the subsumption relationship between pitch events, we think that Lerdahl's Tonal Pitch Space theory [6] is promising.

Chapter 8
Implementation of GTTM

8.1 Introduction of Implementing GTTM

To get a music theory to operate on a computer, however, we must overcome some widely recognized fundamental difficulties. One is giving an ambiguous concept a firm definition, and another is compensating for the lack of necessary concepts (externalization). For example, we may easily decide whether two melodies are similar to each other, but in general each of us likely makes a different decision, and it is difficult to fully explain why the melodies are similar. To write a program that replicates a human checking melodic similarity, we have to cope with the problem commonly known as knowledge acquisition [23]. Marsden [16] describes this problem, from a musicology point of view, as meeting the following requirements of a representation system for structural music manipulation:

- Musical symbols, objects, and concepts are all well-defined; a new one is defined by predefined ones.
- Musical symbols, objects, and concepts are all grounded to relevant ones in the real world; there must be a consistent, well-segmented correspondence between musical symbols, objects, and concepts in a representation system and those in the real world.

We think these requirements can play an important role in overcoming the above difficulties and mechanizing music theory.

Although many music theories have been proposed [2, 3, 15, 17, 24, 27], each theory is differently motivated, and the insight used as a starting point is different, as are the fundamental concepts and models. Furthermore, each theory is presented in a different description style; for example, one is presented totally in a descriptive style using sample scores, and another in a procedural style showing program fragments. Therefore, to offer efficient and precise definitions of the musical symbols, objects, and concepts involved in defining similarity while still satisfying the above requirements, we have to carefully examine music theories for their potential to operate on a computer and then select one as a starting point.

K. Hirata et al., *Music, Mathematics and Language*,
https://doi.org/10.1007/978-981-19-5166-4_8

We believe that the Generative Theory of Tonal Music (GTTM) [15] is the most promising theory for mechanizing and developing a support system, thanks to three of its features. The first is the use of rules to describe the musical insight and knowledge obtained by investigating in detail the musical structures and relations occurring in a piece of music. The rules of GTTM accumulate fundamental musical phenomena and concepts, define the relations between them, and prescribe the conditions to be satisfied as well as the desired situation. Originally, Lerdahl and Jackendoff employed the form of rules to express their results in a manner that ensures human readability, since rules can properly segment and organize musical introspection and knowledge so that a human can easily understand them. In addition, such rules can be translated into a computer program due to the modularity of knowledge.

The second feature is that GTTM is designed to consistently represent the multiple aspects of music in a single framework. This feature is important in the sense that when GTTM is executed in a mechanical way, contradiction should be prevented as much as possible. For instance, if we imagine a simple operation that splits a melody, the condition of applying the split operation may vary depending on the relevant musical structure. Therefore, it is preferred that the splitting position of a melody and that of an ornamented melody be essentially identical. Unless a system of consistent operations in terms of melody, rhythm, and harmony is developed, the resulting splitting positions may be different.

The third feature is that GTTM has been developed based on the concept of reduction, which we believe should be adopted as the proper way of taking into account deep structures [12, 25]. Reduction, in general, connects an original element and its ornamented one (complicated one), and it corresponds to an 'is-a' relation, the most fundamental relation in knowledge representation. Accordingly, deep structure would emerge from the network of concepts connected by relations involving 'is-a', where many knowledge representation techniques are available [23]. In contrast, conventional approaches to representing and comparing music mostly focus on surface information and do not introduce the 'is-a' relation. Thus, they unfortunately cannot handle deep structures or high-level musical knowledge properly.

Furthermore, Lerdahl and Jackendoff also recognized the advantages of mechanizing GTTM to some extent ([15], p. 55):

> Our theory cannot provide a computable procedure for determining musical analyses. However, achieving computability in any meaningful way requires a much better understanding of many difficult musical and psychological issues than exists at present.

We think that "many difficult musical and psychological issues" would encompass what we are trying to solve in this book.

In this chapter, we extend GTTM by full externalization and parameterization (Sect. 8.3.2) and propose exGTTM. This externalization in mechanizing GTTM includes introducing an algorithm for generating a hierarchical structure of the time-span tree in the mixed manner of top-down and bottom-up. Such an algorithm has not yet been presented for GTTM, and in fact it seems that researchers have not even recognized the need for this type of algorithm. The parameterization includes introducing a parameter controlling the priorities of rules to avoid a conflict among the rules, as well as the parameters for controlling the shape of the hierarchical time-span tree. It has been suggested that such control parameters are required in GTTM, but they have not been explicitly presented. On the other hand, we restrict GTTM and implement a subset of GTTM because mechanization has priority over all else. As an example of the restrictions, only a monophony is handled, and harmony is not taken into account. We provide a comprehensive summary of the detailed restrictions in Sect. 8.3.2.

Here, note that we distinguish two kinds of ambiguity in music analysis: one involves music understanding by humans, and the other concerns the representation of a music theory. The former kind of ambiguity derives from the ambiguity of music itself. The following is quoted from the book on GTTM ([15], p. 9) .

> In music, ⋯ grammaticality per se plays a far less important role, since almost any passage of music is potentially vastly ambiguous – it is much easier to construe music in a multiplicity of ways. The reason for this is that music is not tied down to specific meanings and functions, as language is. In a sense, music is pure structure, to be "played with" within certain bounds. The interesting musical issues usually concern what is the most coherent or "preferred" way to hear a passage.

For the latter type of ambiguity, related to GTTM, no concept needed for mechanization has been presented, or it has been presented only in an implicit way. Therefore, due to the former kind of ambiguity, we assume there are more than one correct result. We avoid the latter kind of ambiguity as much as possible by full externalization and parameterization.

The significance of full externalization and parameterization is twofold: precise controllability, and coverage of the human results. Whenever we find a correct result that exGTTM cannot generate, we introduce new parameters to exGTTM and give them proper values so that it can generate the correct result. In this way, we repeatedly externalize and introduce new parameters until we can obtain all of the results that humans consider correct. In total, we have introduced 15 parameters for grouping-structure analysis, 18 for metrical-structure analysis, and 13 for time-span reduction. It is eventually guaranteed that for every piece in a given set of pieces, by assigning certain values to these parameters, exGTTM can generate a correct analysis result. In other words, exGTTM can precisely control the analysis result by adjusting the parameter values, thus covering all of the correct analysis results. We think that full externalization and parameterization is an important intermediate step toward a fully automatic GTTM analyzer. Moreover, we think that full externalization and parameterization are significant regarding the testability of music theories. Temperley pointed this out as follows ([27], p. 14):

> If the parameters of the rules can be specified, the output of the rule system for a given input can be determined in an objective way, making the theory truly testable.

8.2 Previous Work on Implementing a Music Theory

Our primary concern is implementing a music theory. We do not compare GTTM with other music theories on their own merits, since musicological comparison is outside the scope of this book. The preference rule systems (PRS) [27] approach, along with its practical implementation, the Melisma system of Sleator and Temperley, is a pioneering work in implementing music theory. PRS analyzes music from six aspects: meter, melodic phrase, counterpoint, pitch spelling, harmony, and key. For each analysis, Temperley presents a set of well-formedness rules and the preference rules. The former defines the possible structures considered acceptable, while the latter chooses the optimal analysis out of the possible ones, as GTTM described in Sect. 6.1. In the following, we briefly describe the implementation strategy of PRS and the Melisma system.

The Melisma system basically employs dynamic programming to find the best-so-far partial analyses at every intermediate stage, and it finally reaches an entire analysis with the highest score. Temperley asserts that there are two kinds of problems in implementing the entire analysis. The first problem is how the PRS program is to evaluate individual possible analyses. The program analyzes a piece by assigning a numerical score to each analysis, which reflects how well it satisfies the preference rules. The second problem is how the program evaluates all possible well-formed analyses of a piece according to the preference rules and then finds the most plausible analysis, possibly with the highest score.

Let us examine an example of handling the first problem in meter analysis. To calculate the strength of a unit segment, we assume each note contained in the segment contributes a value, called effective length, which is either the maximum of its duration and its registral IOI (interonset interval to the following note within the line of texture) or 1.0, whichever is smaller. The total strength of a segment is calculated by the square root of its number of notes multiplied by its average effective length. Thus, the contribution of each note to the total strength is predetermined and fixed.

For the next example, we handle the first problem in melodic phrase analysis. The first step in devising the implementation is to determine a way of evaluating analyses by three rules: gap, phrase length, and parallelism. Here, correct weights for the three rules relative to one another were determined by a trial-and-error process beforehand, and for a given phrase, the score of each sub-phrase is further weighted by the length of the sub-phrase.

When the program searches for a globally optimal analysis based on the results of the local analyses, it must consider global analyses rather than simply choose the best analysis for each segment in isolation. Consequently, the second problem arises. Usually, even for a monophonic short melody, the number of possible local analyses may grow exponentially with the number of segments, and the size of the best-so-far analysis becomes extremely large. The Melisma system suppresses the explosion of analyses by properly eliminating less significant analyses by dynamic programming. Temperley argues that, to some extent, this searching process reflects the human moment-to-moment cognitive process of revision, ambiguity and expectation when listening to music.

As described above, in PRS, the weights of rules and parameter values are fixed during an entire analysis. Thus, a conflict of rule applications never occurs, and some analysis can be obtained in any event. However, the conflict is not always resolved appropriately, and a true analysis is not always acquired. We have an intuition that the proper rule weights and parameter values must vary dynamically, depending on the part of the piece being analyzed.

In our research, we do not consider the cognitive process itself. Since the GTTM rules already represent the cognitive process at a conceptual level, we focus on implementing the GTTM rules.

In Melisma, a hierarchical metrical structure is acquired as follows. First, the best location for a tactus beat within a range of 400–1600 ms is identified, using a variant of the dynamic programming technique. This forms the preferred tactus level for the piece that emerges from the meter analysis rules. Then, the program derives the upper levels then the lower levels; that is, the hierarchy is acquired in a middle-out manner. The regularity rule is given priority, at the upper levels, i.e., imposing a penalty for changes in the number of beats, rather than at the tactus level. Note that at the topmost level (the whole note level), to avoid the side effect of the length rule (preferring long notes as strong beats), Melisma simply ignores the length rule as heuristics. Temperley, however, argues that a substantial solution to this side effect is introducing a grouping rule.

In our research, to acquire the hierarchies of the GTTM analyses, we adopt a strategy of taking into account global and local information at the same time, in contrast to the middle-out approach in the meter analysis of PRS. To eventually obtain an optimal solution that satisfies as many preference rules as possible, we think our strategy is advantageous.

Stammen [26] implemented only the basic rules for a grouping structure and were unable to obtain a hierarchical grouping structure. Nord [18] implemented grouping, metrical, and time-span analyses, but the rule applications were done by hand.

Among the previous works not directly related to GTTM, the techniques for melody segmentation are well-developed, and there have been many attempts to propose algorithms for melody segmentation at boundaries [1, 4, 26, 27]. Conventional methods focus on identification of local boundaries but do not pay much attention to obtaining a hierarchical grouping structure for acquiring a time-span tree like in GTTM.

In research using a Voronoi diagram drawn on a piano roll score [9], a polyphony is analyzed in a hierarchical way. However, since the analysis lacks a musical basis, there are cases in which no appropriate hierarchical grouping structure is obtained. The methods based on beat tracking [5, 22] can also only acquire a hierarchical metrical structure in one measure, since they cannot consider such larger metrical structures as two measures, four measures, and so on.

8.3 Implementing GTTM on a Computer

Among music theories, GTTM is tractable for implementation on a computer, but many tasks remain toward building a working system. Toward this end, we briefly summarize the organization of GTTM and present the implementation problems involved. Then, we propose strategies for resolving these problems.

> GTTM is a music theory for describing the insight of an 'experienced listener,' and it consists of four sub-theories: grouping-structure analysis, metrical-structure analysis, time-span reduction, and prolongational reduction.

Among the four sub-theories, this chapter presents the methodology for implementing the grouping-structure analysis, metrical-structure analysis, and time-span reduction [8, 9, 9]. Since the prolongational reduction is still evolving and controversial, we do not implement it at present.

8.3.1 Problems in Implementing GTTM

As described above, when we make GTTM rules operate on a computer, we have to make an ambiguous concept into a firm definition and compensate for the lack of concepts. Roughly speaking, these tasks correspond to parameterization and externalization, respectively. Here, we discuss the problems occurring in the process of parameterization and externalization.

Ambiguous Rule Definition

As an example, the following is Grouping Preference Rule 4 (GPR4), regarding the extent to which GTTM intensifies the effects of GPR2 and GPR3:

> Where the effects extracted by GPR2 and GPR3 are relatively more pronounced, a larger-level group boundary may be placed

Here, GPR2 prescribes the relationship of onset (attack) and offset (release) timings and a group boundary. GPR3 prescribes the relationship of pitch interval, dynamics, note duration, and group boundary. That is, there are many factors influencing the determination of a group boundary. Accordingly, the meaning of the phrase "relatively more pronounced" in GPR4 is ambiguous, because we do not know how to normalize the effects of the factors or how to compare the effects with each other. Moreover, the phrase "may be placed" implies that at one time GPR4 holds, while at another time it does not. However, we do not know in what particular situation GPR4 holds.

Fig. 8.1 Simple example of conflict between rules

Conflict Among Preference Rules

Since preference rules stipulate situations where they preferentially hold, they may often conflict. However, there are no rules for resolving preference rule conflicts in GTTM.

For example, Fig. 8.1 shows the situation of conflicting preference rules. Here, GPR3a identifies a leap point in the melody as a group boundary (notes 3–4, notes 7–8, and notes 11–12), while GRP6 identifies an iterating point as a group boundary (notes 4–5, notes 8–9, and notes 11–12). Thus, GPR1 is as follows:

> Avoid analyses with very small groups

That is, there is a constraint to prevent a group consisting of a single note. Therefore, GPR3a and GPR6 conflict with each other at notes 4 and 8. If both group boundaries were adopted, we would obtain single-note groups and GPR1 would be violated. Consequently, we should adopt either GPR3a or GPR6 at notes 4 and 8; however, we do not know which GPR should be given higher priority.

Lack of Working Algorithm

Knowledge represented in the rule form is in general considered declarative, which is advantageous in the sense that a knowledge programmer does not need to take into account an algorithm for reasoning. Instead, a system is required to perform automatic reasoning on the knowledge declaratively described. In GTTM, unfortunately, there are few descriptions of the reasoning, and working algorithms needed to compute analysis results.

For example, GPR6 is as follows:

> Where two or more segments of the music can be construed as parallel, they preferably form parallel parts of groups.

GPR6 is motivated by the fact that the beginning and the end of a parallel segment may be heard as a group boundary. Therefore, we should design an algorithm to indicate the beginning and the end of every parallel segment occurring in a piece. Furthermore, the depth of a boundary must reflect the properties of a parallel segment, where the properties include the length, employing either pitch-oriented matching or timing-oriented matching, and the weighting of either the beginning or the end.

As a result, we will possibly obtain the bottom graph in Fig. 8.8. However, the GPR6 statement does not provide any procedural information for generating such a function.

Procedural information for constructing hierarchical structures for grouping-structure analysis and time-span reduction is not sufficient in GTTM. For example, GPR4 mentions which placement of a larger-level group boundary is preferable but does not state an algorithm for this placement. Moreover, when constructing a grouping structure, a working algorithm has to take into account not only GRP2 and GPR3, but also GPR5 and GPR6. GRP2 and GPR3 concern local structures and generate a grouping structure in the bottom-up manner; in contrast, GPR5 and GPR6 concern global structures and generate a grouping structure in the top-down manner. It would be difficult to design an effective algorithm incorporating these GPRs consistently. As another example, the preference rules of time-span reduction (TSRPRs) only mention which head should be selected, not how. To describe how to select a head, a working algorithm has to appropriately identify the set of head candidates from which a head is selected and then integrate bottom-up and top-down head selections, in a similar manner to GPRs.

8.3.2 Solution: Proposal of exGTTM

We present the design strategy of a machine-executable extension of GTTM, exGTTM. As described, the fundamental difficulties involve giving an ambiguous concept a firm definition and compensating for the lack of concepts. To overcome these difficulties, we employ full externalization and parameterization to yield precise controllability and coverage of the human results.

We are implementing a subset of GTTM. Before going into detail, it would perhaps be helpful for readers if we were to sum up the restrictions in implementing GTTM.

- Only a monophony is handled.
- Harmony (key and chord progression) is not taken into account.
- Only ordinary heads occur in a time-span tree.
- There is no feedback from the time-span reduction to the grouping- and metrical-structure analyses.
- The prolongational reduction is not mechanized.
- The input representation is a list of notes that corresponds to a monophonic piano roll.
- We divide the entire problem into identifying the domain of all possible answers and searching for the most preferred one; here, we only deal with the former sub-problem.
- We focus on implementing GTTM, but it does not consider the human process of perceiving and recognizing music.

Paradoxically speaking, what we have not implemented enables us to implement GTTM.

Table 8.1 Fifteen adjustable parameters for grouping-structure analyzer

$S_{\mathrm{GPR}R}$ $(0 \leq S_{\mathrm{GPR}R} \leq 1)$	Strength of each rule. The larger the value is, the stronger the rule acts in Eqs. (8.19) and (8.23). $R \in \{2a, 2b, 3a, 3b, 3c, 3d, 4, 5, \text{and } 6\}$
$\hat{\sigma}$ $(0 \leq \hat{\sigma} \leq 0.1)$	Standard deviation of a Gaussian distribution, the average of which is the boundary by GPR5. The larger the value is, the wider its skirt becomes in Eq. (8.14)
W_m $(0 \leq W_m \leq 1)$	Balance between temporal similarity of attack points and that of pitch difference in GPR6. The larger the value is, the more the system estimates the pitch difference in Eq. (8.15)
W_l $(0 \leq W_l \leq 1)$	Weight for the length of parallel phrases. The larger the value is, the more the length of parallel phrases is prioritized in GPR6 in Eq. (8.15)
W_s $(0 \leq W_s \leq 1)$	Balance determining whether the note i becomes the ending note of a group or the beginning note of the following group in GPR6. The larger the value is, the more the note tends to be the ending note in Eq. (8.16)
T_{GPR4} $(0 \leq T_{\mathrm{GPR4}} \leq 1)$	Threshold at which the effects of GPR2,3 are considered to be salient in GPR4. The smaller the value is, the more probably GPR4 is applied in Eq. (8.13)
T^{low} $(0 \leq T^{\mathrm{low}} \leq 1)$	Threshold in the lower-level boundary. The smaller the value is, the more salient the boundary becomes

Full Externalization and Parameterization

We appropriately supply lacking parameters and make implicit parameters explicit.[1] The parameters introduced by exGTTM are categorized into three categories: identified, implied, and unrecognized.

For the first category, a parameter is identified in GTTM but is not assigned concrete values. Hence, we valuate such a parameter. For example, since the resulting valuc of thc GPR2a application, D_{GPR2a}, is binary, if it holds, D_{GPR2a} makes 1, otherwise 0. On the other hand, since GPR6 is held indefinitely, the resulting value of GPR6, D_{GPR6}, also varies continuously between 0 and 1.

For the second category, a parameter is implied in GTTM. Hence, we make it explicit. For example, to resolve the preference rule conflict, we introduce parameters to express the priority for each preference rule ($S^{\mathrm{GPR}R}$ in Table 8.1, $S^{\mathrm{MPR}R}$ in Table 8.2, and $S^{\mathrm{TSRPR}R}$ in Table 8.3). Since each preference rule has its own priority, all of the priority patterns are realized. This is an example of full parameterization.

For the third category, we need to add parameters that are not recognized in the original theory, since some of them may almost completely lack any musicological meaning. For example, GPR6 in exGTTM needs to add parameters for controlling the properties of parallel segments, including the weights for pitch-oriented matching or timing-oriented matching.

[1] In the paper, the word 'parameter' is used not only for parameters used in controlling a system externally, but also for internal variables (intermediated variables) connecting submodules.

Table 8.2 Eighteen adjustable parameters for the metrical-structure analyzer

Parameters	Description
$S_{\text{MPR}R}$	Strength of each rule. The larger the value is, the stronger the rule acts in Eqs. (8.34), (8.35) and (8.38). $R \in \{1, 2, 3, 4, 5a, 5b, 5c, 5d, 5e, \text{and } 10\}$
$\acute{W}_m$ $(0 \leq \acute{W}_m \leq 1)$	Balance between temporal similarity of attack points and that of pitch difference in MPR1. The larger the value is, the more the system estimates the pitch difference
$\acute{W}_l$ $(0 \leq \acute{W}_l \leq 1)$	Weight for the length of parallel phrases. The larger the value is, the more the length of parallel phrases is prioritized in MPR1
$\acute{W}_s$ $(0 \leq \acute{W}_s \leq 1)$	Balance determining whether the note i becomes the ending note of a group or the beginning note of the following group in MPR1. The larger the value is, the more the note tends to be the ending note
$T_{\text{MPR}R}$	Value of the threshold that decides whether each rule is applicable in Eqs. (8.25), (8.28), (8.29), (8.30), (8.31). $R \in \{1, 4, 5a, 5b, \text{and } 5c\}$

Table 8.3 Ten adjustable parameters for time-span tree analyzer

Parameters	Description
$S_{\text{TSRPR}R}$	Strength of each rule. The larger the value is, the stronger the rule acts in Eqs. (8.46) and (8.47). $R \in \{1, 2, 3, 4, 5a, 5b, 5c, 5d, 5e, \text{and } 10\}$
$\grave{W}_m$ $(0 \leq \grave{W}_m \leq 1)$	The balance between the temporal similarity of attack points and that of the pitch difference in TSRPR4. The larger the value is, the more the system estimates the pitch difference
$\grave{W}_l$ $(0 \leq \grave{W}_l \leq 1)$	The weight for the length of parallel phrases. The larger the values is, the more the length of parallel phrases is estimated in TSRPR4
$\grave{W}_s$ $(0 \leq \grave{W}_s \leq 1)$	The balance determines whether the note i becomes the ending note of a group or the beginning note of the following group in TSRPR4. The larger the value is, the more the note tends to be the ending note

We add a comment to the domain of intermediate variables, denoted as D and B. The domain of all the intermediate variables is constrained within the range of 0 to 1, and for this purpose, those variables are normalized at every computing stage. Thanks to this property, exGTTM can flexibly combine any intermediate variables (and possibly parameters) and cascade as many weighted-mean calculations as needed. Accordingly, this facilitates precise controllability.

Algorithm for Acquiring Hierarchy

Among issues that require working algorithms, the problems for acquiring hierarchical structures in the grouping- and metrical-structure analyses and the time-span tree reduction can be all regarded as a constraint satisfaction problem (CSP). This is because only the properties to be satisfied for the hierarchical structures are represented in the form of a rule, that is, no constraint nor order of generating hierarchical structures is determined in advance.

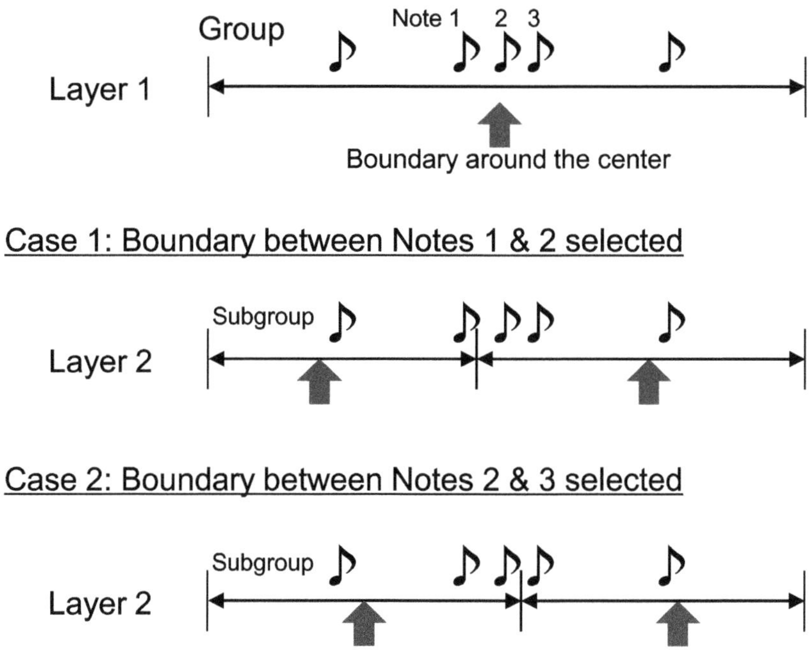

Fig. 8.2 Global constraints by GPR5

The constraints stipulated by the GTTM rules are divided into two categories: local and global. The former includes GPR2 (proximity) and TSRPR1 (strong metrical position), and the latter includes GPR5 (symmetry) and MPR1 (parallelism). We need to handle global constraints carefully when generating hierarchical structures. For the example of GPR5 in Fig. 8.2, given a group at Layer 1, an inner boundary likely occurs around the center of the group, that is, either between Notes 1 and 2 or Notes 2 and 3. Here, we can consider two cases as follows. In Case 1, the boundary between Notes 1 and 2 is selected, taking into account the effects of some other rules. Then in each subgroup in Layer 2, the inner boundary of the subgroup may occur in the left-hand side of a center note. On the other hand, in Case 2, the boundary between Notes 2 and 3 is selected. Therefore, the inner boundary may occur in the right-hand side of a center note. Consequently, in computing GPR5, the boundary position determined influences the identifications of remote boundaries in lower layers, and we have to take into account up-to-date global information every time. In other words, a global constraint is inevitably dynamic.

Based on the above consideration, we are developing algorithms for generating hierarchical structures for exGTTM so that nodes are generated either from the bottommost nodes or the topmost node incrementally, and that every time the nodes at a layer are calculated, global information is recalculated before moving onto an adjacent layer. We will describe these algorithms in more detail later (Sects. 8.4.2, 8.5.2, and 8.6.2).

8.4 Grouping Analysis

The algorithm of grouping analysis consists of the following steps.

1. Regard the whole piece as a group.
2. Apply those rules that are applicable to local structures.
3. Calculate local strength as boundaries.
4. Apply phrasal rules.
5. Calculate phrasal boundaries.
6. Divide the entire piece into two.
7. Repeat steps 4–6 as long as there is a local boundary.

Using this procedure, we can regulate the order of rule application and combine phrasal and local structuring.

We show the procedure in Fig. 8.3. We adopt MusicXML [20] for the input format since it is now prevalent for composition, analysis, and search; moreover, it can be easily converted to other formats. However, exGTTM does not use the information of key and meter provided by MusicXML. In addition, we have designed GroupingXML as an output format of the grouping structure.

In this procedure, we restrict the target of analysis to monophonic music.[2]

8.4.1 Application of Grouping Preference Rules

In this section, we explain ten grouping preference rules (GPRs), i.e., GPR_R ($R \in \{1, 2a, 2b, 3a, 3b, 3c, 3d, 4, 5, \text{and } 6\}$). The possibility that the i-th transition becomes a boundary by the R-th rule is denoted by $D_{\mathrm{GPR}_R}(i)$ ($0 \leq D_{\mathrm{GPR}_R}(i) \leq 1$, $R \in \{1, 2a, 2b, 3a, 3b, 3c, 3d, 4, 5, \text{and } 6\}$). In this study, we introduce the fifteen adjustable parameters shown in Table 8.1. Figure 8.4 shows the relation between the grouping preference rules and the parameters. Besides the above ten rules, GTTM includes GPR7 (time-span and prolongational stability), which prefers those structures by which the time-span reduction or the prolongational reduction become more stable. However, this rule requires the information of later processes, such as time-span/prolongational reductions, to be sent back to the earlier processes, and its details are not given in GTTM [15]. Consequently, we have not included GPR7 in this study.

Calculation of Basic Parameters

We first calculate six basic parameters from MusicXML, that is,

ρ_i the offset-to-onset interval (OOI)
ι_i the interonset interval (IOI)

---

[2] Monophonic music consists only of a melody line that is not accompanied by chords.

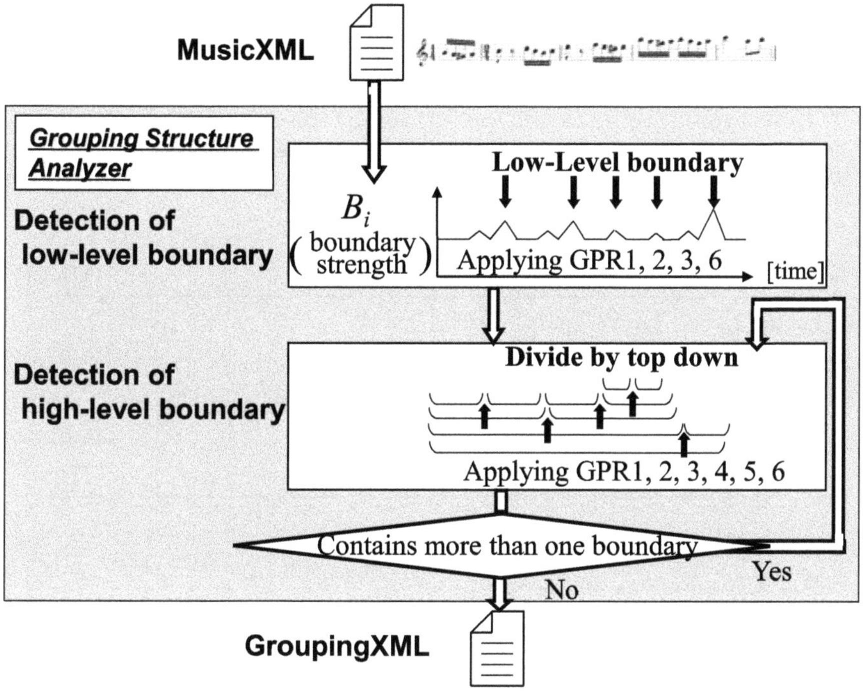

Fig. 8.3 Processing flow of grouping-structure analyzer

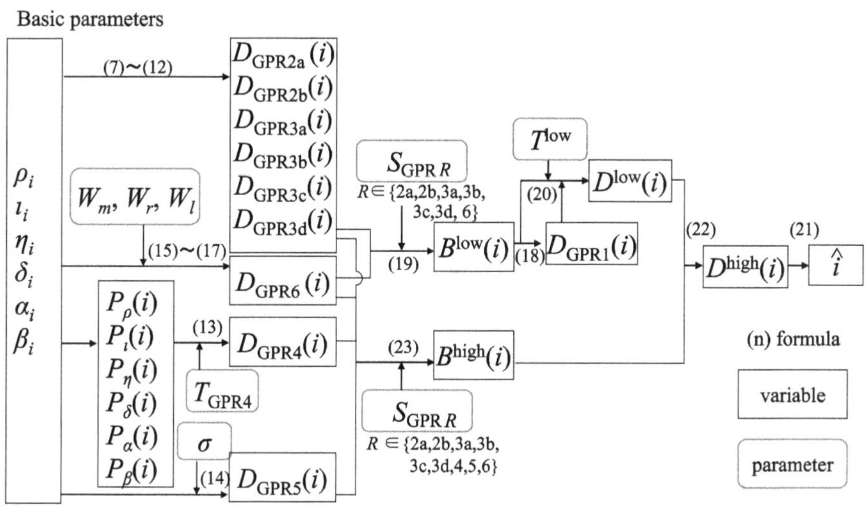

Fig. 8.4 Relationship between parameters and GPRs

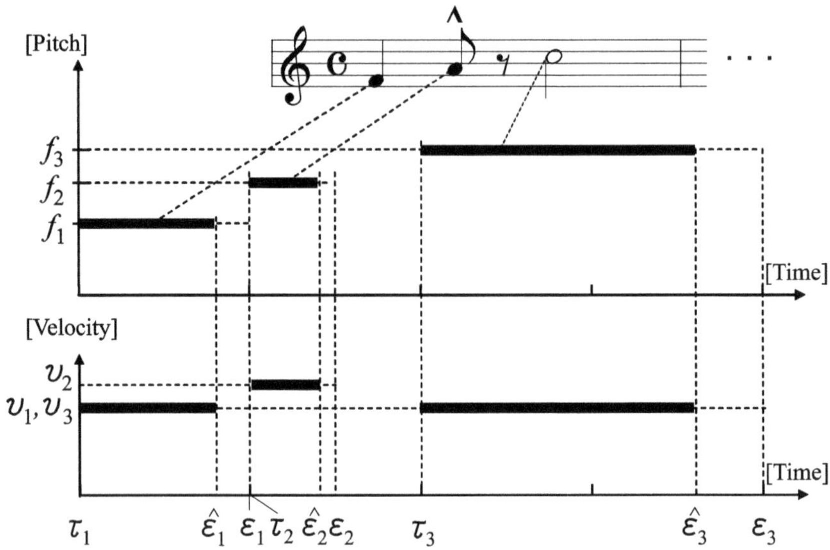

Fig. 8.5 Calculation of basic parameters

η_i the register (pitch difference)
δ_i the dynamics difference
α_i the difference in the ratio between the formal length of the note on the score and its real duration in performance
β_i the difference in duration

In Fig. 8.5, τ_i is the formal length of the i-th note on the score, ε_i is the formal offset time, $\hat{\varepsilon}_i$ is the real offset time, f_i is the pitch, and υ_i is the dynamic. The time unit is that of a quarter note, and the pitch is measured by a semitone (MIDI note number). We formally represent these basic parameters mathematically.

$$\rho_i = \begin{cases} \tau_{i+1} - \hat{\varepsilon}_i & \text{if } \tau_{i+1} - \hat{\varepsilon}_i \geq 0 \\ 0 & \text{otherwise} \end{cases} \tag{8.1}$$

$$\iota_i = \tau_{i+1} - \tau_i \tag{8.2}$$

$$\eta_i = f_{i+1} - f_i \tag{8.3}$$

$$\delta_i = |\upsilon_{i+1} - \upsilon_i| \tag{8.4}$$

$$\alpha_i = \left| \frac{\varepsilon_{i+1} - \tau_{i+1}}{\hat{\varepsilon}_{i+1} - \tau_{i+1}} - \frac{\varepsilon_i - \tau_i}{\hat{\varepsilon}_i - \tau_i} \right| \tag{8.5}$$

$$\beta_i = |\iota_{i+1} - \iota_i| \tag{8.6}$$

Application of GPR2, 3, and 4

GPR2, 3, and 4 are applied to the four consecutive notes n_1, n_2, n_3, n_4. The i-th transition, that is, the interval between the i-th note and the $i+1$-th, can be either a boundary ($D_{\mathrm{GPR}_R}(i) = 1$) or not ($D_{\mathrm{GPR}_R}(i) = 0$).

GPR2a (slur/rest) recognizes a boundary if the offset-to-onset interval (OOI) of n_2 and n_3 is longer than that of n_1 and n_2 and that of n_3 and n_4. Thus, GPR2a is formalized as follows.

$$D_{\mathrm{GPR2a}}(i) = \begin{cases} 1 \text{ if } \rho_{i-1} < \rho_i \text{ and } \rho_i > \rho_{i+1} \\ 0 \text{ otherwise} \end{cases} \tag{8.7}$$

GPR2b (attack point) recognizes a boundary if the interonset interval (IOI) of n_2 and n_3 is longer than that of n_1 and n_2 and that of n_3 and n_4. Thus, GPR2b is formalized as follows.

$$D_{\mathrm{GPR2b}}(i) = \begin{cases} 1 \text{ if } \iota_{i-1} < \iota_i \text{ and } \iota_i > \iota_{i+1} \\ 0 \text{ otherwise} \end{cases} \tag{8.8}$$

GPR3a (register) recognizes a boundary if the pitch difference between n_2 and n_3 is larger that of n_1 and n_2 and that of n_3 and n_4. GPR3a is formalized as follows.

$$D_{\mathrm{GPR3a}}(i) = \begin{cases} 1 \text{ if} |\eta_{i-1}| < |\eta_i| \text{ and } |\eta_i| > |\eta_{i+1}| \\ 0 \text{ otherwise} \end{cases} \tag{8.9}$$

GPR3b (dynamics) recognizes a boundary if there is a change in dynamics between n_2 and n_3, but no changes between n_1 and n_2 nor between n_3 and n_4.

$$D_{\mathrm{GPR3b}}(i) = \begin{cases} 1 \text{ if } \delta_{i-1} = 0,\ \delta_i \neq 0,\ \text{and } \delta_{i+1} = 0 \\ 0 \text{ otherwise} \end{cases} \tag{8.10}$$

GPR3c (articulation) recognizes a boundary if there is a change in articulation between n_2 and n_3, but no changes between n_1 and n_2 nor between n_3 and n_4. Because we could not find a definition of articulation in GTTM [15], we substitute it with the ratio between the formal length on the score and the real duration in performance. Thus, the definition becomes as follows.

$$D_{\mathrm{GPR3c}}(i) = \begin{cases} 1 \text{ if} \alpha_{i-1} = 0,\ \alpha_i \neq 0,\ \text{and } \alpha_{i+1} = 0 \\ 0 \text{ otherwise} \end{cases} \tag{8.11}$$

GPR3d (length) recognizes a boundary if the durations of n_2 and n_3 are the same while that of n_1 and n_2 and that of n_3 and n_4 are different. GPR3d is formalized as follows.

$$D_{\mathrm{GPR3d}}(i) = \begin{cases} 1 \text{ if } \beta_{i-1} = 0,\ \beta_i \neq 0,\ \text{and } \beta_{i+1} = 0 \\ 0 \text{ otherwise} \end{cases} \quad (8.12)$$

GPR4 (intensification) recognizes a boundary if the results by GPR2 and 3 are salient. To formalize GPR4, we consider whether $P_\rho(i)$, $P_\iota(i)$, $P_\eta(i)$, $P_\delta(i)$, $P_\alpha(i)$, $P_\beta(i)$ have larger values; that is, the results of GPR2a, 2b, 3a, 3b, 3c, 3d are salient. T_{GPR4} ($0 \leq T_{\mathrm{GPR4}} \leq 1$) is the threshold for judging whether GPR4 is applicable, i.e., whether the effects of GPR2a, 2b, 3a, 3b, 3c, 3d are salient.

$$D_{\mathrm{GPR4}}(i) = \begin{cases} 1 \text{ if } \max(P_\rho(i), P_\iota(i), P_\eta(i), P_\delta(i), P_\alpha(i), P_\beta(i)) > T_{\mathrm{GPR4}} \\ 0 \text{ otherwise,} \end{cases} \quad (8.13)$$

where

$$P_\rho(i) = \begin{cases} \rho_i/(\rho_{i-1} + \rho_i + \rho_{i+1}) \text{ if } \rho_{i-1} + \rho_i + \rho_{i+1} > 0 \\ 0 \quad \text{otherwise} \end{cases}$$

$$P_\iota(i) = \iota_i/(\iota_{i-1} + \iota_i + \iota_{i+1})$$

$$P_\eta(i) = \begin{cases} |\eta_i|/(|\eta_{i-1}| + |\eta_i| + |\eta_{i+1}|) \text{ if } |\eta_{i-1}| + |\eta_i| + |\eta_{i+1}| > 0 \\ 0 \quad \text{otherwise} \end{cases}$$

$$P_\delta(i) = \begin{cases} \delta_i/(\delta_{i-1} + \delta_i + \delta_{i+1}) \text{ if } \delta_{i-1} + \delta_i + \delta_{i+1} > 0 \\ 0 \quad \text{otherwise} \end{cases}$$

$$P_\alpha(i) = \begin{cases} \alpha_i/(\alpha_{i-1} + \alpha_i + \alpha_{i+1}) \text{ if } \alpha_{i-1} + \alpha_i + \alpha_{i+1} > 0 \\ 0 \quad \text{otherwise} \end{cases}$$

$$P_\beta(i) = \begin{cases} \beta_i/(\beta_{i-1} + \beta_i + \beta_{i+1}) \text{ if } \beta_{i-1} + \beta_i + \beta_{i+1} > 0 \\ 0 \quad \text{otherwise} \end{cases}$$

Application of GPR5 (Symmetry)

GPR5 prefers that a group be divided into two subgroups of the same length. Otherwise, the more similar the lengths of the two subgroups, the more preferable. In this study, we consider a function that gives priority to the symmetry of the two consecutive subgroups. As a representative of such functions, we employ a Gaussian distribution $D_{\mathrm{GPR5}}(i)$ with the standard deviation σ, the unit of which is a quarter note.

Figure 8.6a shows the distribution $D_{\mathrm{GPR5}}(i)$ of the probability of symmetry. After all of the GPRs are applied, the distribution in the lower grouping level becomes that in Fig. 8.6b. The nearer the standard deviation σ comes to 0, the narrower the skirt becomes, and the larger the value of $D_{\mathrm{GPR5}}(i)$ becomes. Thus, the midpoint of the upper group tends to be a boundary of subgroups. On the contrary, when σ is large, the boundaries of lower groups may deviate from the center of their higher group.

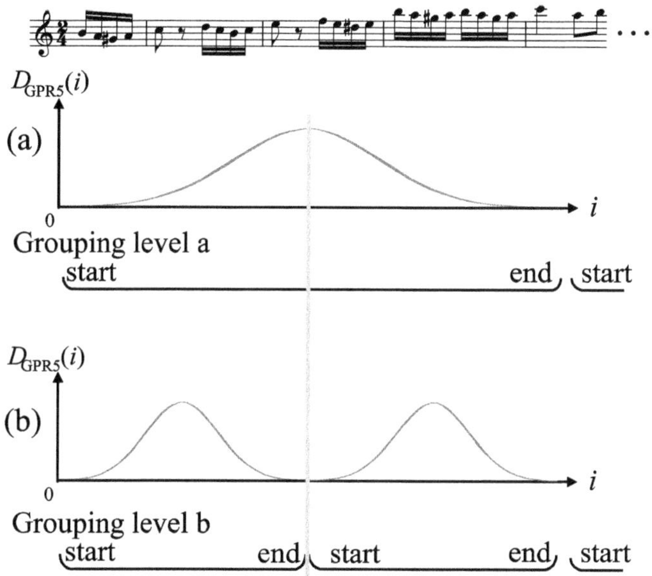

Fig. 8.6 Degree of symmetry $D_{GPR5}(i)$

$$D_{GPR5}(i) = \frac{1}{\sqrt{2\pi}\sigma} \exp\left\{\frac{-(\tau_i - \tau_{mid})^2}{2\sigma^2}\right\}, \tag{8.14}$$

where

$$\tau_{mid} = \frac{\varepsilon_{end} - \tau_{start}}{2},$$

and *start* is the first note of a group at the current grouping level and *end* is the ending note. *start* and *end* are renewed and new $D_{GPR5}(i)$ is calculated when the upper group is divided and its lower groups are generated.

The actual adjustable parameter of the system is not σ but $\hat{\sigma} \times (\varepsilon_{end} - \tau_{start}) = \sigma$; thus, the skirt of the Gaussian distribution becomes narrower in the lower grouping levels.

Application of GPR6 (Parallelism)

GPR6 concerns parallelism, that is, the melodic identity or similarity. Namely, if multiple parts in a musical piece include similar melodies, then the grouping structure should also reflect the same parallelism. Thus, when similar parts are found, both ends of the melody are highly likely to be boundaries. In this section, we discuss the parameter $D_{GPR6}(i)$ $(0 \leq D_{GPR6}(i) \leq 1)$, that is, the probability for the note i to be the beginning or the ending note of a parallel phrase. As a result, we expect that the highly probable positions of boundaries are clarified as in Fig. 8.7.

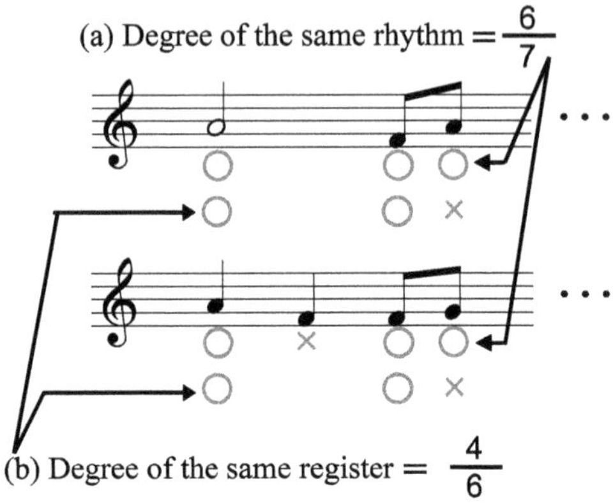

Fig. 8.7 Similarity of parallel phrases

$D_{\text{GPR6}}(i)$ is calculated as follows. First, we calculate the similarity between the interval from note i with length r and the one from j with the same length. Next, for such i, we calculate the similarity for all j's with the same length r. Because there is no description of the similarity of melodies in GTTM [15], we define our own similarity. Our adjustable parameters for this similarity include:

- W_m $(0 \leq W_m \leq 1)$ For each note, give a preference of the similarity of onset time to that of pitch.
- W_l $(0 \leq W_l \leq 1)$ Give a preference of the longer interval to the shorter one when parallel intervals overlap each other.
- W_s $(0 \leq W_s \leq 1)$ For each note, give a preference of being the beginning note of a group to being the ending note.

The similarity in this definition does not affect other parts of the system. Thus, we can substitute other methods (e.g., [11]) for our definition.

Let us first consider the example in Fig. 8.7. In the figure, three notes out of four coincide in regard to onset time. Two notes out of the three also coincide in regard to pitch. In our implementation, we regard a greater number of notes having the same onset time as indicating greater similarity of melodies. Furthermore, the more the number of notes of the same onset time have the same pitch, the more similar the melodies are.

We formalize the above discussion as follows. We assume that the beginning and the ending notes of a group possess beats and that the length of an interval r is a multiple of a beat. Also, we assume that parallelism cannot occur at such adjacent positions, say, as the distance of less than a quarter of a beat. Given a beat number m (≥ 1), we write the interval of r beats from m as $[m, m+r)$, which does not include the $(m+r)$-th. We define the basic parameters as follows.

- $N(m, r)$ the number of notes in $[m, m+r)$.
- $O(m, n, r)$ the number of notes of the same onset time in $[m, m+r)$ and $[n, n+r)$.
- $P(m, n, r)$ the number of notes of both the same pitch and same onset time.

We define the similarity between the interval $[m, m+r)$ and $[n, n+r)$ with these parameters:

$$G(m, n, r) = \left\{ \frac{O(m, n, r)}{N(m, r) + N(n, r)} \times (1 - W_m) + \frac{P(m, n, r)}{O(m, n, r)} \times W_m \right\} \times r^{W_l}, \tag{8.15}$$

where given the whole number of beats L, $1 \leq m, n \leq L - r + 1$ and $1 \leq r \leq L$. Beyond this domain, we consider that $G(m, n, r) = 0$.

Note that r^{W_l} becomes 1 when $W_l = 0$, and as r increases, r^{W_l} also increases as far as $W_l > 0$. Thus, as W_l comes close to 1, the similarity of longer intervals becomes significant.

However, there are also intervals that are meaningless for calculating the similarity. We have assumed that the beginning and the ending notes of an interval must be on certain beats, and thus, those intervals that do not satisfy this condition should be excluded. We introduce a predicate to determine whether the i-th note possesses a beat.

$b(i)$ i-th note is the beginning one of an interval.
$e(i)$ i-th note is the ending one of an interval.
$t(i)$ i-th note is either the beginning or ending one of an interval.

We employ the following definitions.

$head(m)$ returns the first note i in $[m, m+1)$.
$tail(m)$ returns the last note i in $[m, m+1)$.
$beat(i)$ returns m if i is in $[m, m+1)$.

Then,

$b(i)$ is true if $i = \text{head}(\text{beat}(i))$ and $i \neq \text{tail}(\text{beat}(i))$.
$e(i)$ is true if $i \neq \text{head}(\text{beat}(i))$ and $i = \text{tail}(\text{beat}(i))$.
$t(i)$ is true if $i = \text{head}(\text{beat}(i)$ and $i = \text{tail}(\text{beat}(i))$.

Next, we calculate the similarity of intervals beginning from the i-th note.

$$A(i) = \sum_{n=1}^{L} \sum_{r=1}^{L/2} \begin{cases} G(\text{beat}(i), n, r) \times (1 - W_s) \\ \quad \text{if } b(i) \text{ holds and } N(n, 1) \geq 1 \\ G(\text{beat}(i) - r, n - r, r) \times W_s \\ \quad \text{if } e(i) \text{ holds and } N(n, 1) \geq 1 \\ G(\text{beat}(i), n, r) \times (1 - W_s) \\ +G(\text{beat}(i) - r, n - r, r) \times W_s \\ \quad \text{if } t(i) \text{ holds and } N(n, 1) \geq 1 \\ 0 \text{ otherwise} \end{cases} \tag{8.16}$$

Because parallel intervals do not overlap each other, the length of an interval must be shorter than half of the whole number of beats L. As the final step, we normalize

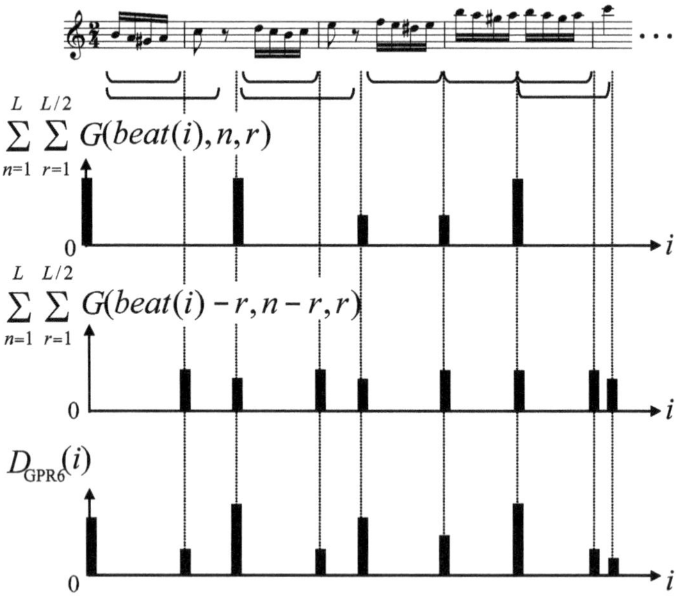

Fig. 8.8 Degree of parallelism $D_{\text{GPR6}}(i)$

$A(i)$. Let $A_{\max}$ be the maximum value among the notes included in the piece, that is, $A_{\max} = \max(A(1), A(2), \ldots, A(N(1, L))$. Then,

$$D_{\text{GPR6}}(i) = A(i)/A_{\max}. \tag{8.17}$$

Note that the value of $D_{\text{GPR6}}(i)$ is indifferent to the length of the entire piece. The greater the number of parallel sequences beginning, or ending, with i, the larger the value of $D_{\text{GPR6}}(i)$ is.

In Fig. 8.8, the uppermost graph denotes the possibility that each note can be the beginning of a parallel interval. Similarly, the middle graph shows the possibility of each note being the ending. The bottom graph is the result of combining the above two, together with the normalization.

Application of GPR1 (Alternative Form)

GPR1 prohibits one note from forming a group. GPR1 gives a criterion for whether the i-th transition can be a boundary ($D_{\text{GPR1}}(i) = 1$) or not ($D_{\text{GPR1}}(i) = 0$). In Fig. 8.9, $B^{\text{low}}(i)$ represents the local strength by a real number between 0 and 1; the larger the value is, the more likely the boundary is. $D_{\text{GPR1}}(i)$ is calculated in the following way.

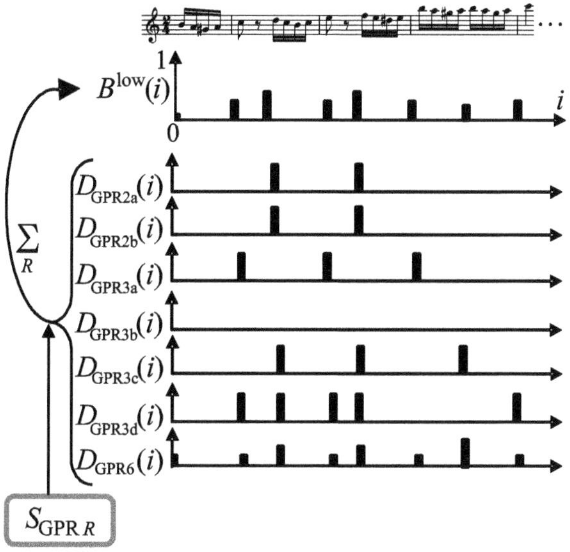

Fig. 8.9 Low-level strength of boundary $B^{\text{low}}(i)$

$$D_{\text{GPR1}}(i) = \begin{cases} 1 \text{ if } B^{\text{low}}(i-1) \leq B^{\text{low}}(i), \\ \quad B^{\text{low}}(i) \geq B^{\text{low}}(i+1), \\ \quad \text{and } D_{\text{GPR1}}(i-1) = 0 \\ 0 \text{ otherwise,} \end{cases} \tag{8.18}$$

where

$$B^{\text{low}}(i) = \frac{\sum_R D_{\text{GPR}_R}(i) \times S_{\text{GPR}_R}}{\max_{i'} \left(\sum_R D_{\text{GPR}_R}(i') \times S_{\text{GPR}_R} \right)} \tag{8.19}$$

and $R \in \{2a, 2b, 3a, 3b, 3c, 3d, \text{and } 6\}$.

8.4.2 *Acquisition of Hierarchical Grouping Structure*

Local boundaries are detected by $D_{\text{GPR1}}(i)$, $D_{\text{GPR2a}}(i)$, $D_{\text{GPR2b}}(i)$, $D_{\text{GPR3a}}(i)$, $D_{\text{GPR3b}}(i)$, $D_{\text{GPR3c}}(i)$, $D_{\text{GPR3d}}(i)$, and $D_{\text{GPR6}}(i)$. T^{low} is the threshold for determining whether the i-th transition becomes a boundary ($D^{\text{low}}(i) = 1$) or not ($D^{\text{low}}(i) = 0$). $B^{\text{low}}(i)$ is defined in Eq. (8.19).

$$D^{\text{low}}(i) = \begin{cases} 1 \text{ if } B^{\text{low}}(i) > T^{\text{low}}, \\ \quad \text{and } D_{\text{GPR1}}(i) = 1 \\ 0 \text{ otherwise} \end{cases} \tag{8.20}$$

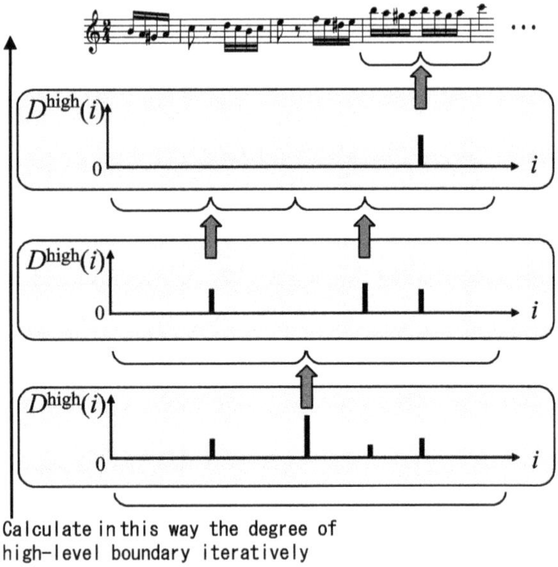

Fig. 8.10 Construction of hierarchical grouping structure

The hierarchical grouping structure is formed from the local boundaries $D^{low}(i)$ in the bottom-up way and also from $D_{GPR1}(i)$, $D_{GPR2a}(i)$, $D_{GPR2b}(i)$, $D_{GPR3a}(i)$, $D_{GPR3b}(i)$, $D_{GPR3c}(i)$, $D_{GPR3d}(i)$, $D_{GPR4}(i)$, $D_{GPR5}(i)$, and $D_{GPR6}(i)$ in the top-down way. $B^{high}(i)$ represents the strength of a boundary in a higher hierarchy as a real number from 0 to 1. $B^{high}(i)$ is different from $B^{low}(i)$ in that the former reflects the result of those rules that concern phrasal structure, that is, $D_{GPR4}(i)$ and $D_{GPR5}(i)$. When a group includes a local boundary in it, the boundaries of one upper level $\hat{i}$ are recursively detected by the following procedure (Fig. 8.10), where $B^{high}(i)$ is renewed at each level, since the value of $D_{GPR5}(i)$ will change at every grouping level.

Then we have a boundary

$$\hat{i} = \underset{i}{\operatorname{argmax}}\, D^{high}(i), \tag{8.21}$$

where

$$D^{high}(i) = D^{low}(i) \times B^{high}(i), \tag{8.22}$$

$$B^{high}(i) = \frac{\sum_R D_{GPR_R}(i) \times S_{GPR_R}}{\max_{i'} \left(\sum_R D_{GPR_R}(i') \times S_{GPR_R}\right)} \tag{8.23}$$

for $R \in \{2a, 2b, 3a, 3b, 3c, 3d, 4, 5, \text{and } 6\}$ and for all the i's included in the group.

See Fig. 8.5 for the full procedure of parameter calculation.

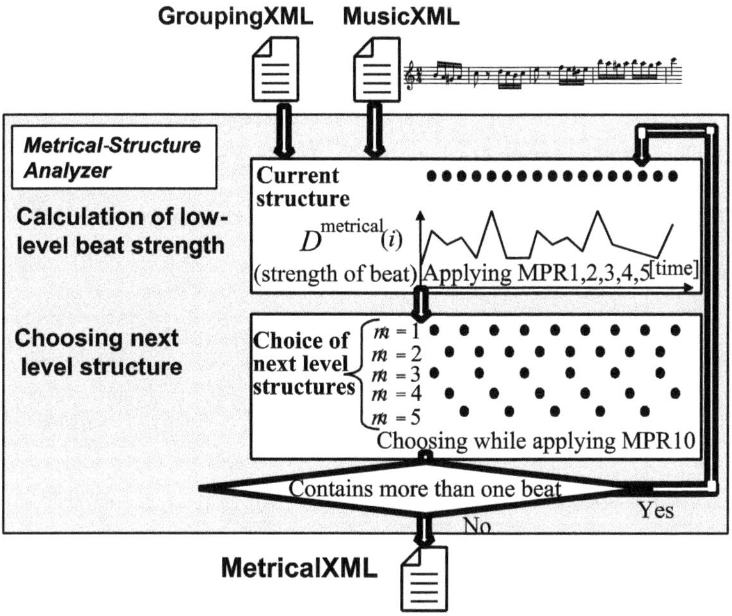

Fig. 8.11 Processing flow of metrical-structure analyzer

8.5 Metrical Analysis

The algorithm of metrical analysis consists of the following steps.

1. Regard all of the beats in the entire piece as a lowest-level (global) metrical structure.
2. Apply those rules that are applicable to local metrical structures.
3. Calculate local-level metrical strength.
4. Select the strongest metrical structure from the possible structures.
5. Repeat steps 2 to 4 as long as the current structure contains more than one beat.

By following this procedure, we can construct a hierarchical metrical structure.

Figure 8.11 shows the processing flow of the metrical analysis. As the primary input formats, we adopt MusicXML [20] and GroupingXML [7]. A hierarchical metrical structure is constructed in a top-down way, while the lower-level beat strength is detected in a bottom-up way. We then design MetricalXML as the export format for our system.

8.5.1 Application of MPRs

Here, we discuss the applications of MPR1, 2, 3, 4, 5, and 10. We do not include MPR9 because this rule requires sending the information to the later process of time-

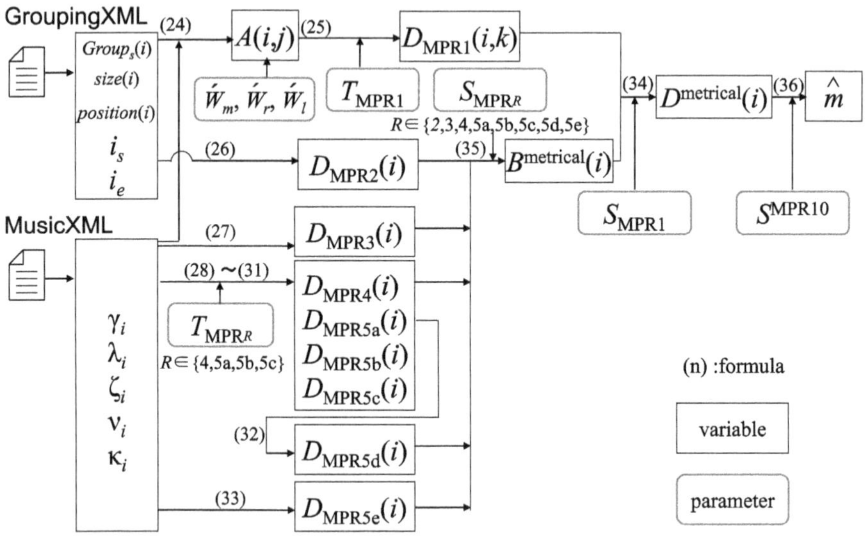

Fig. 8.12 Parameters in MPRs

span reduction and back to the earlier process of metrical analysis. Furthermore, we do not deal with MPR6, MPR7, or MPR8 because we restrict our target music to monophony. The strength of the beat dependent on each rule can be expressed by $D_{\mathrm{MPR}_R}(i)$ $(R \in \{1, 2, 3, 4, 5a, 5b, 5c, 5d, \text{and } 5e\})$, where $0 \leq D_{\mathrm{MPR}_R}(i) \leq 1$. As there is no strict order in applying MPR rules, ambiguities may result from the analysis. To solve this problem, we use adjustable parameters $S_{\mathrm{MPR}_R}(i)$ $(R \in \{1, 2, 3, 4, 5a, 5b, 5c, 5d, 5e, \text{and } 10\})$, which enable us to control the strength of each rule. Figure 8.12 shows the relationship between the parameters and MPRs. Our metrical-structure analyzer has 18 adjustable parameters, which include S_{MPR_R}, $\acute{W}_m$, $\acute{W}_r$, $\acute{W}_l$, and $T_{\mathrm{MPR_R}}$ (Table 8.2).

Calculation of Basic Parameters

From the input MusicXML, the following five basic parameters of the i-th beat in the current hierarchy of beats are calculated. When there is no note in the position of the i-th beat, each basic parameter becomes zero.

γ_i dynamic
λ_i length of note
ζ_i duration of dynamic
κ_i length of slur
ν_i pitch

Since GTTM [15] does not include the notion of 'duration of dynamic,' we define it as the length from one beat to the next beat or rest. The averages of the above basic parameters are denoted as $\bar{\gamma}$, $\bar{\lambda}$, $\bar{\zeta}$, $\bar{\kappa}$, and $\bar{\nu}$, respectively. From the result of GroupingXML, the two basic parameters i_s and i_e are the beginning and the ending, respectively, of the smallest group containing i and more than one beat, in the current structure.

Application of MPR1 (Parallelism)

MPR1 concerns the parallelism in metrical structures and prefers that a pair of parallel groups have similar metric structures. The similarity is evaluated basically in the same way as in GPR6 (Eq. 8.15), but the intervals to be estimated are different. In the case of GPR6, we have targeted all of the intervals with length r, while in MPR1 we apply the method only to the resultant groups of the grouping analysis. Then, the degree of parallelism $A(i, j)$ between the i-th beat in the interval $[m, m+r)$ and the j-th beat in $[m, m+s)$ becomes

$$A(i, j) = G(\text{group}_s(i), \text{group}_s(j), \text{size}(i)), \tag{8.24}$$

where $\text{group}_s(i)$ is the first beat of the group including i, and $\text{size}(i)$ is the number of beats of the group. When the value of $A(i, j)$ goes beyond the threshold T^{MPR1} after normalization, we judge that the i-th beat and j-th beat are parallel.

$$D_{\text{MPR1}}(i, j) = \begin{cases} 1 & A(i, j)/A_{\max} > T^{\text{MPR1}}, \\ & \text{and position}(i) = \text{position}(j) \\ 0 & \text{otherwise} \end{cases} \tag{8.25}$$

given

$$A_{\max} = \max(A(i, 1), A(i, 2), \ldots, A(i, L)),$$

where $\text{position}(i)$ is the temporal duration from the beginning of the group including the i-beat to the i-th beat itself.

Application of MPR2 and 3

MPR2 (strong beat early) has a weak preference for a metrical structure in which the strongest beat in a group appears relatively early in the group. We formalized $D_{\text{MPR2}}(i)$ so that the closer the strongest beat appears to the beginning of the group, the higher the value is

$$D_{\text{MPR2}}(i) = (i_e - i)/(i_e - i_s). \tag{8.26}$$

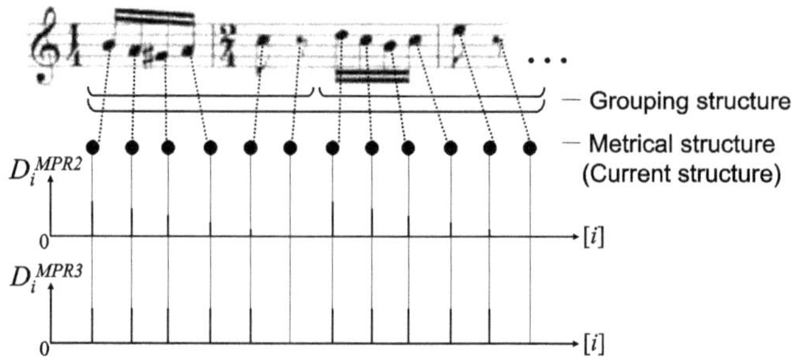

Fig. 8.13 Application of MPR2 and 3

MPR3 (event) prefers a metrical structure in which the inceptions of pitch events are on strong beats (Fig. 8.13). Thus, $D_{\text{MPR3}}(i)$ returns 1 if i has a beat, and 0 otherwise.

$$D_{\text{MPR3}}(i) = \begin{cases} 1 & \gamma_i > 0 \\ 0 & \gamma_i = 0 \end{cases} \tag{8.27}$$

Application of MPR4, 5a, 5b, and 5c

We introduced the adjustable parameters T_{MPR_R} $(R \in \{4, 5a, 5b, \text{and } 5c\})$ $(0 \leq T_{\text{MPR}_R} \leq 1)$ to control the threshold that determines whether each rule is applicable, i.e., $(D_{\text{MPR}_R}(i) = 1)$ or not $(D_{\text{MPR}_R}(i) = 0)$ (Fig. 8.14).

MPR4 (stress) prefers a metrical structure in which a relatively strong beat occurs at the inception of a stressed note. $D_{\text{MPR4}}(i)$ returns 1 if a stressed note has a strong beat, and 0 otherwise.

$$D_{\text{MPR4}}(i) = \begin{cases} 1 & \gamma_i > 2 \times \bar{\gamma} \times T_{\text{MPR4}} \\ 0 & \text{otherwise} \end{cases} \tag{8.28}$$

MPR5a (long pitch event) prefers a metrical structure in which a relatively strong beat occurs at the inception of a long note. $D_{\text{MPR5a}}(i)$ returns 1 if a relatively longer note possesses a strong beat, and 0 otherwise.

$$D_{\text{MPR5a}}(i) = \begin{cases} 1 & \lambda_i > 2 \times \bar{\lambda} \times T_{\text{MPR5a}} \\ 0 & \text{otherwise} \end{cases} \tag{8.29}$$

MPR5b (long duration of a dynamic) prefers a metrical structure in which a relatively strong beat occurs at the inception of a long duration of a dynamic. $D_{\text{MPR5b}}(i)$ returns 1 if a dynamically large note possesses a strong beat, and 0 otherwise.

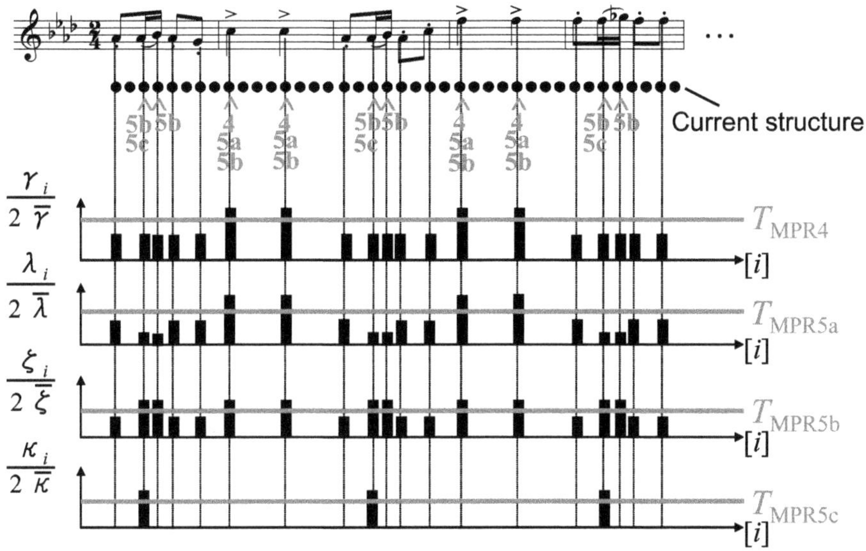

Fig. 8.14 Application of MPR4, 5a, 5b, and 5c

$$D_{\mathrm{MPR5b}}(i) = \begin{cases} 1 & \zeta_i > 2 \times \bar{\zeta} \times T_{\mathrm{MPR5b}} \\ 0 & \text{otherwise} \end{cases} \tag{8.30}$$

MPR5c (long slur) prefers a metrical structure in which a relatively strong beat occurs at the inception of a long slur. $D_{\mathrm{MPR5c}}(i)$ returns 1 if a relatively long slur possesses a strong beat, and 0 otherwise.

$$D_{\mathrm{MPR5c}}(i) = \begin{cases} 1 & \kappa_i > 2 \times \bar{\kappa} \times T_{\mathrm{MPR5c}} \\ 0 & \text{otherwise} \end{cases} \tag{8.31}$$

Application of MPR5d and 5e

MPR5d (long pattern of articulation) prefers that the relatively long repetition of the same articulation has a strong beat. Because we could not find a definition for this *repetition*, we regard it as the repetitive application of MPR5a according to the examples in GTTM [15]. $D_{\mathrm{MPR5d}}(i)$ returns 1 if MPR5a is consecutively applied, and 0 otherwise.

$$D_{\mathrm{MPR5d}}(i) = \begin{cases} 1 & D_{\mathrm{MPR5a}}(i) = 1 \text{ and } D_{\mathrm{MPR5a}}(i+1) = 1 \\ 0 & \text{otherwise} \end{cases} \tag{8.32}$$

MPR5e (long duration of a pitch) is the rule for pitch-repetition. $D_{\mathrm{MPR5e}}(i)$ returns 1 if the same pitch persists, and 0 otherwise.

$$D_{\mathrm{MPR5e}}(i) = \begin{cases} 1 & \nu_i = \nu_{i+1} \\ 0 & \text{otherwise} \end{cases} \tag{8.33}$$

8.5.2 *Acquisition of Hierarchical Metrical Structure*

Low-level beat strength $D^{\mathrm{metrical}}(i)$ is calculated by $D_{\mathrm{MPR1}}(i, j)$, $D_{\mathrm{MPR2}}(i)$, $D_{\mathrm{MPR3}}(i)$, $D_{\mathrm{MPR4}}(i)$, $D_{\mathrm{MPR5a}}(i)$, $D_{\mathrm{MPR5b}}(i)$, $D_{\mathrm{MPR5c}}(i)$, $D_{\mathrm{MPR5d}}(i)$, and $D_{\mathrm{MPR5e}}(i)$.

$$D^{\mathrm{metrical}}(i) = B^{\mathrm{metrical}}(i) + \sum_j (B^{\mathrm{metrical}}(j) \times S_{\mathrm{MPR1}} \text{ if } D_{\mathrm{MPR1}}(i, j) = 1), \tag{8.34}$$

where

$$B^{\mathrm{metrical}}(i) = \sum_R D_{\mathrm{MPR}_R}(i) \times S_{\mathrm{MPR}_R} \tag{8.35}$$

and $R \in \{2, 3, 4, 5a, 5b, 5c, \text{and } 5d\}$. $B^{\mathrm{metrical}}(i)$ represents the weighted summation of S_{MPR_R} and $D_{\mathrm{MPR}_R}(i)$, ($R \in 2, 3, 4$, 5a, 5b, 5c, 5d, and 5e), and $D^{\mathrm{metrical}}(i)$ represents the sum of $B^{\mathrm{metrical}}(i)$ and summation of $B^{\mathrm{metrical}}(j)$, where the i-th beat and j-th beat are parallel and consequently $D_{\mathrm{MPR1}}(i, j) = 1$.

A hierarchical metrical structure is constructed by iterating the calculation of the low-level strength of the beat $D^{\mathrm{metrical}}(i)$ for the current structure and choosing the next-level structure. When the current structure contains more than one beat, the next-level structure is chosen as follows. First, we assume that the piece is in simple duple time; then we compare among

$$\left\{ \sum_{\{i|i=2k-1\}} D^{\mathrm{metrical}}(i), \sum_{\{i|i=2k\}} D^{\mathrm{metrical}}(i) \right\} \tag{8.36}$$

($k = 1, 2, 3, \ldots$), and choose the larger one, i. e., either the odd i's or the even i's would organize the upper structure. In a similar way, when we assume that the piece is in simple triple time, is are collected in three different ways: $\{i|i = 3k - 2\}$, $\{i|i = 3k - 1\}$, or $\{i|i = 3k\}$ ($k = 1, 2, 3, \ldots$), and we choose the set by which

$$\sum_i D^{\mathrm{metrical}}(i) \times S_{\mathrm{MPR10}} \tag{8.37}$$

becomes largest. Note that **MPR10** prefers metrical structures in which every other beat is strong so that the simple triple time is deterred by S_{MPR10}.

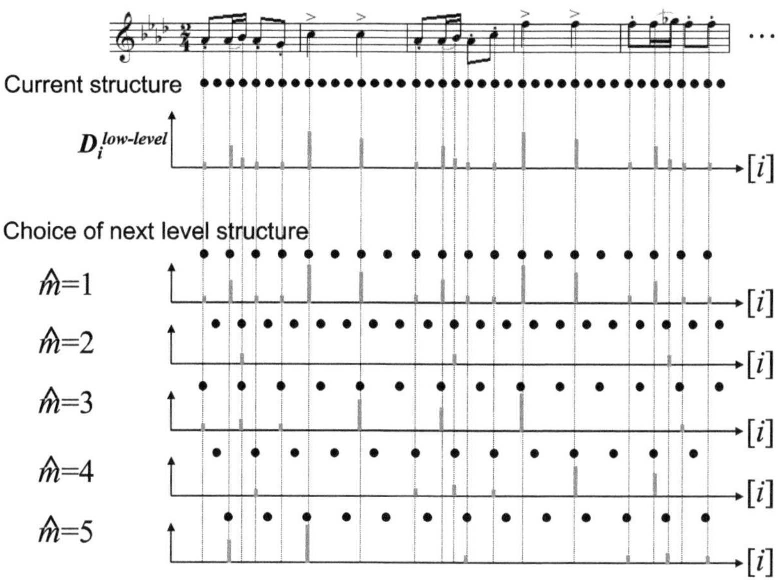

Fig. 8.15 Selecting the next-level structure

In (Fig. 8.15), $\hat{m}$ shows the choice of

$$\hat{m} = \begin{cases} 1 \text{ if } i = \{1, 3, 5, \ldots\} \\ 2 \text{ if } i = \{2, 4, 6, \ldots\} \\ 3 \text{ if } i = \{1, 4, 7, \ldots\} \\ 4 \text{ if } i = \{2, 5, 8, \ldots\} \\ 5 \text{ if } i = \{3, 6, 9, \ldots\} \end{cases} \tag{8.38}$$

including both simple duple and simple triple time.

As a result, each note or rest of a music piece is marked by a *dot* if it possesses a strong beat at a certain level of the hierarchy. According to the difference in levels and the strength of a beat, each note has a different number of dots.

8.6 Generation of Time-Span Tree

The time-span tree is constructed in the following way.

1. Consider all of the notes as heads.
2. Apply those rules that are applicable to local-level heads.
3. Calculate the head strength at a local-level.
4. Select the next-level head from each time-span.
5. Iterate steps 2 and 4 as long as the time-span contains more than one head.

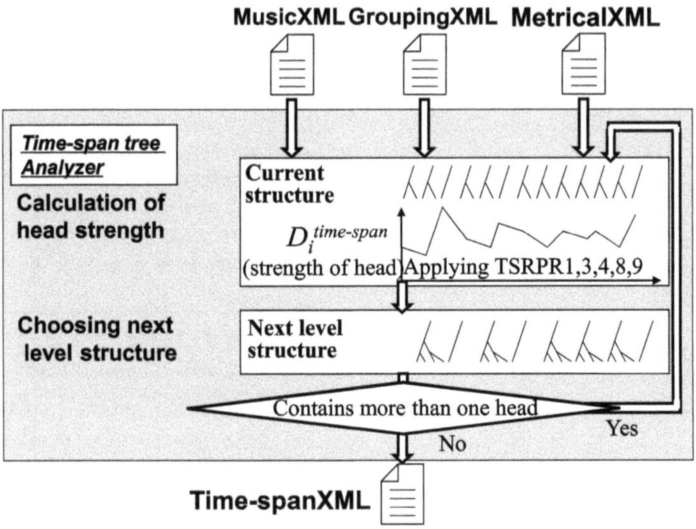

Fig. 8.16 Processing flow of time-span tree analyzer

Here, we employ the adjustable parameters S_{TSRPR_R} ($R \in \{1, 3a, 3b, 4, 8, \text{and } 9\}$), each of which is the strength of a time-span tree preference rule. Figure 8.16 shows the processing flow of the time-span reduction. As the input formats, we adopt MusicXML [21] , GroupingXML [7], and MetricalXML [8]. We then design Time-spanXML as the export format for our system.

8.6.1 Application of Time-Span Reduction Preference Rules

In this section, we explain our application methods of TSRPR_R ($R \in \{1, 3, 4, 8, \text{and } 9\}$). In this study, we restrict our target music to monophonic music, so we do not deal with TSRPR2 and TSRPR7. Furthermore, we do not implement TSRPR5 and TSRPR6 because they suggest a *reverse* flow of processing; i.e., they select a time-span tree that makes metric structures or prolongational reductions stable. $D_{\mathrm{TSRPR}_R}(i)$ ($R \in \{1, 3a, 3b, 4, 8, \text{and } 9\}$) indicates whether TSRPR_R holds. Since the priority among these TSRPRs was not shown in GTTM [15] as were GPRs and MPRs, we introduce adjustable parameters S_{TSRPR_R} ($R \in \{1, 3a, 3b, 4, 8, \text{and } 9\}$). Figure 8.17 shows the dependency between the application of TSRPRs. Our time-span tree analyzer has 13 adjustable parameters, which include $S_{\mathrm{TSRPR_R}}$, $\grave{W}_m$, $\grave{W}_m$, and $\grave{W}_m$ (Table 8.3).

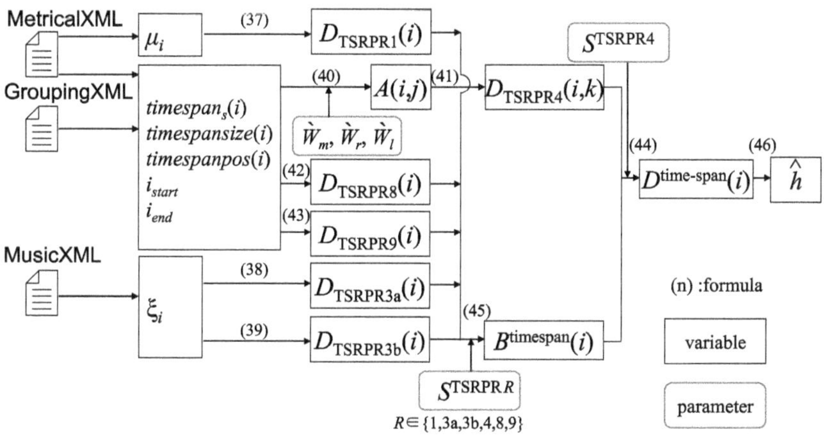

Fig. 8.17 Parameters in TSRPRs

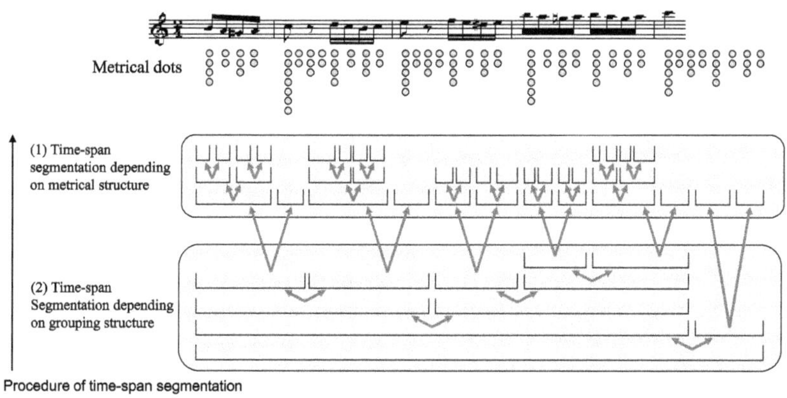

Fig. 8.18 Time-span segmentation

Time-Span Segmentation

In the procedure of time-span reduction, we divide the entire piece into hierarchical time-spans. The division procedure, shown in Fig. 8.18, is as follows:

1. Regard all of the resultant groups of grouping analysis as time-spans.
2. When a time-span in the lowest level includes more than one note, divide it into two at the strongest beat.
3. Repeat 2 recursively.

In GTTM ([15], pp. 156–157), there are two rules for time-span segmentation, called segmentation rule 1 and segmentation rule 2. Segmentation rule 1 corresponds to the first item and segmentation rule 2 corresponds to the second item.

As a result, a music piece is formed into a binary tree, i.e., a time-span tree, at each node of which the more important branch extends upward as a head note. The selection of a head at each node is hierarchically computed from the lower level. Therefore, heads are selected from leaves to root branches. For each level in the hierarchy, we provide the following basic parameters and rule application principles.

Calculation of Basic Parameters

We calculate four basic parameters:

μ_i Number of dots
ϕ_i Offset-to-onset Interval (OOI)
ψ_i Interonset interval (IOI)
ξ_i Difference in pitch

In the first three parameters, i represents the i-th gap of heads, that is, the gap between the i-th and the $(i+1)$-th head, while dot_i is the number of dots of the i-th head. i indicates the order of heads at the current level of time-span. The basic parameters are renewed at every hierarchy of time-span because the number of heads changes as a result of selecting heads at every hierarchy of time-span.

Application of TSRPR1 (Metrical Position)

TSRPR1 prefers a head with a stronger beat. We normalize the strength between 0 and 1 and define the likelihood of being a head by the number of dots divided by the maximum number of dots.

$$D_{\mathrm{TSRPR1}}(i) = \mu_i / \max_j \mu_j \tag{8.39}$$

Application of TSRPR3 (Registral Extremes)

TSRPR3 concerns the pitch of a head. TSRPR3a selects a higher pitch note as a head while TSRPR3b prefers a lower one. Thus, $D_{\mathrm{TSRPR3a}}(i)$ returns a higher value if ξ_i is higher.

$$D_{\mathrm{TSRPR3a}}(i) = \xi_i / \max_j \xi_j \tag{8.40}$$

On the contrary, $D_{\mathrm{TSRPR3b}}(i)$ returns a higher value if ξ_i is lower.

$$D_{\mathrm{TSRPR3b}}(i) = 1 - \xi_i / \max_j \xi_j \tag{8.41}$$

Application of TSRPR4 (Parallelism)

TSRPR4 concerns the parallelism and prefers a head in a parallel position in parallel time-spans. The parallelism here is different from the melodic similarity: Even though two phrases are not similar, they may be regarded as parallel due to the time-span reduction. The parallelism is evaluated among heads in the time-spans of the current hierarchy, and the evaluation method is the same as that in the grouping and metrical analysis. The similarity of head i in $[m, m+r)$ and j in $[m, m+s)$ is shown by

$$A(i, j) = G(\text{timespan}_s(i), \text{timespan}_s(j), \text{timespansize}(i)), \tag{8.42}$$

where $timespan_s(i)$ is the first beat of the time-span including i, and $timespansize(i)$ is the length (the number of beats) of the time-span including i. We define $D_{\text{TSRPR4}}(i, j)$, normalizing $A(i, j)$:

$$D_{\text{TSRPR4}}(i, j) = \begin{cases} A(i, j)/A_{\max} & \text{timespanpos}(i) = \text{timespanpos}(j) \\ 0 & \text{otherwise}, \end{cases} \tag{8.43}$$

where $A_{\max} = \max(A(i, 1), A(i, 2), \ldots, a(i, L))$ and timespanpos(i) is the interval from the inception of the time-span to i. Note that i indicates the order of heads at the current time-span level, and then $D_{\text{TSRPR4}}(i, j)$ renews at each level of time-span.

Application of TSRPR8 (Structural Beginning)

TSRPR8 prefers that a head i appear at the beginning of the time-span. $D_{\text{TSRPR8}}(i)$ returns 1 if the head is at the beginning position, and 0 otherwise.

$$D_{\text{TSRPR8}}(i) = \begin{cases} 1 & i = i_{\text{start}} \\ 0 & \text{otherwise}, \end{cases} \tag{8.44}$$

where i_{start} is the head of the beginning of the time-span.

Application of TSRPR9 (Structural Ending)

TSRPR9 prefers that a head i appear at the tail of the time-span. $D_{\text{TSRPR9}}(i)$ returns 1 if the head is at the tail position, and 0 otherwise.

$$D_{\text{TSRPR9}}(i) = \begin{cases} 1 & i = i_{\text{end}} \\ 0 & \text{otherwise}, \end{cases} \tag{8.45}$$

where i_{end} is the head of the tail of the time-span.

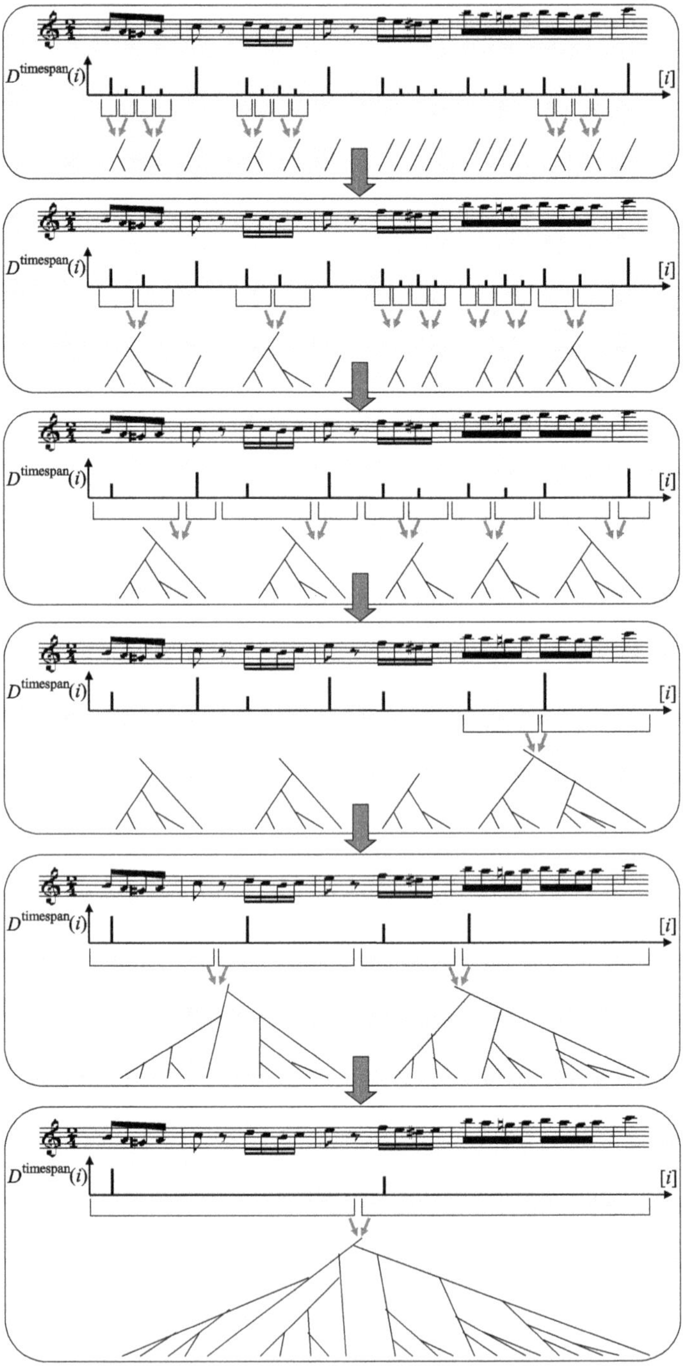

Fig. 8.19 Selecting the next-level heads

8.6.2 *Generation of Time-Span Tree*

We calculate the plausibility of the head $D^{\text{timespan}}(i)$ by $D_{\text{TSRPR1}}(i)$, $D_{\text{TSRPR3a}}(i)$, $D_{\text{TSRPR3b}}(i)$, $D_{\text{TSRPR4}}(i, j)$, $D_{\text{TSRPR8}}(i)$, and $D_{\text{TSRPR9}}(i)$.

$$D^{\text{timespan}}(i) = B^{\text{timespan}}(i) + \sum_k \begin{cases} B^{\text{timespan}}(k) \times S_{\text{TSRPR4}} \\ \quad \text{if} D_{\text{TSRPR4}}(i, k) = 1 \\ 0 \\ \quad \text{if} D_{\text{TSRPR4}}(i, k) = 0, \end{cases} \tag{8.46}$$

where

$$B^{\text{timespan}}(i) = \sum_R D_{\text{TSRPR}_R}(i) \times S_{\text{TSRPR}_R} \tag{8.47}$$

and $R \in \{1, 3a, 3b, 8, \text{and } 9\}$. $B^{\text{timespan}}(i)$ represents weighted summation of S_{TSRPR_R} and $D_{\text{TSRPR}_R}(i)$, ($R \in$ 1, 3a, 3b, 8, and 9), and $D^{\text{timespan}}(i)$ represents the sum of $B^{\text{timespan}}(i)$ and summation of $B^{\text{timespan}}(k)$, where the i-th head and k-th head are parallel and consequently $D_{\text{TSRPR4}}(i, k) = 1$.

A hierarchical time-span tree is constructed by iterating the calculation of the plausibility of the head $D^{\text{timespan}}(i)$ for the current heads, and choosing the next-level heads (Fig. 8.19).

If there are two candidate heads in the current hierarchy, we choose the next-level one $\hat{h}$ as 8.48.

$$\hat{h} = \begin{cases} i & D^{\text{timespan}}(i) \leq D^{\text{timespan}}(j) \\ j & \text{otherwise}, \end{cases} \tag{8.48}$$

The order of choosing the next-level head is the reverse order of constructing time-spans in the time-span segmentation, as described in Sect. 8.6.1. $D_{\text{TSRPR}_R}(i)$ and $D^{\text{timespan}}(i)$ are renewed at each level of hierarchy, since i indicates the order of heads in the current hierarchy and changes at each hierarchy of time-spans.

8.7 Automatic Time-Span Tree Analyzer (ATTA)

We have implemented exGTTM on a computer called ATTA: *Automatic Time-span Tree Analyzer*. ATTA has three distinctive features: an XML-based data structure, implementation in Perl, and a Java-based GUI.

8.7.1 *XML-Based Data Structure*

We use an XML format for all of ATTA's input and output data structures. Each analyzer in ATTA works independently but is integrated with the other through the

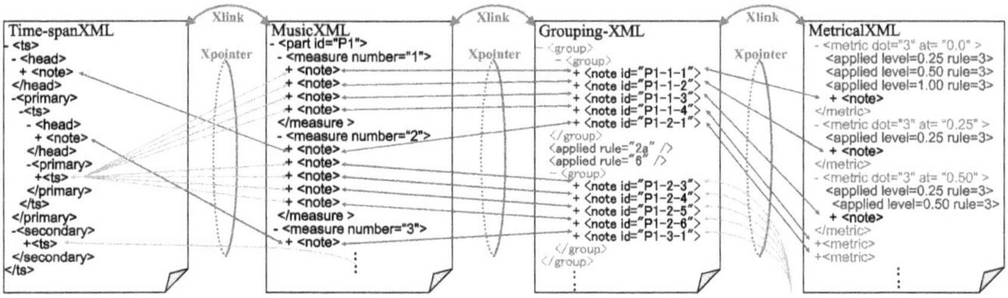

Fig. 8.20 GroupingXML, MetricalXML, Time-spanXML, and MusicXML

XML-based data structure. As a primary input format, we chose MusicXML [21] because it provides a common 'interlingua' for music notation, analysis, retrieval, and other applications. We designed GroupingXML, MetricalXML, and TimespanXML as the export formats for our analyzer (Fig. 8.20). The XML format is very capable of expressing the hierarchical grouping structures, metrical structures, and time-span trees. Note elements in GroupingXML, MetricalXML, and Time-spanXML are connected to note elements in MusicXML by using Xpointer [29] and Xlink [30]. We assume that the distribution of a MusicXML or a standard MIDI file, together with a grouping structure, metrical structure, and time-span tree, would be useful for various musical tasks such as searching and arranging.

8.7.2 Implementation in Perl

We implemented ATTA in Perl, so using CGI allows it to function through the internet (available at http://staff.aist.go.jp/m.hamanaka/atta/). We believe that the availability of this kind of resource is very important for the music-researching community. ATTA is the first application for automatically acquiring a time-span tree. We hope to benchmark ATTA against other systems to be constructed in the future.

Figure 8.21 shows screen snapshots of the grouping-structure analyzer, metrical-structure analyzer, and time-span tree analyzer. The left side of each has scrolling bars for controlling adjustable parameters, and the right side shows the analysis results.

8.7.3 Java-Based GUI

Although our analyzer implemented in Perl has a simple user interface, we also developed a graphical user interface in Java called GTTM editor (Fig. 8.22). GTTM editor has two modes, the automatic-analysis and manual-edit modes. The automatic-analysis mode performs analysis using our analyzer and displays the results. The

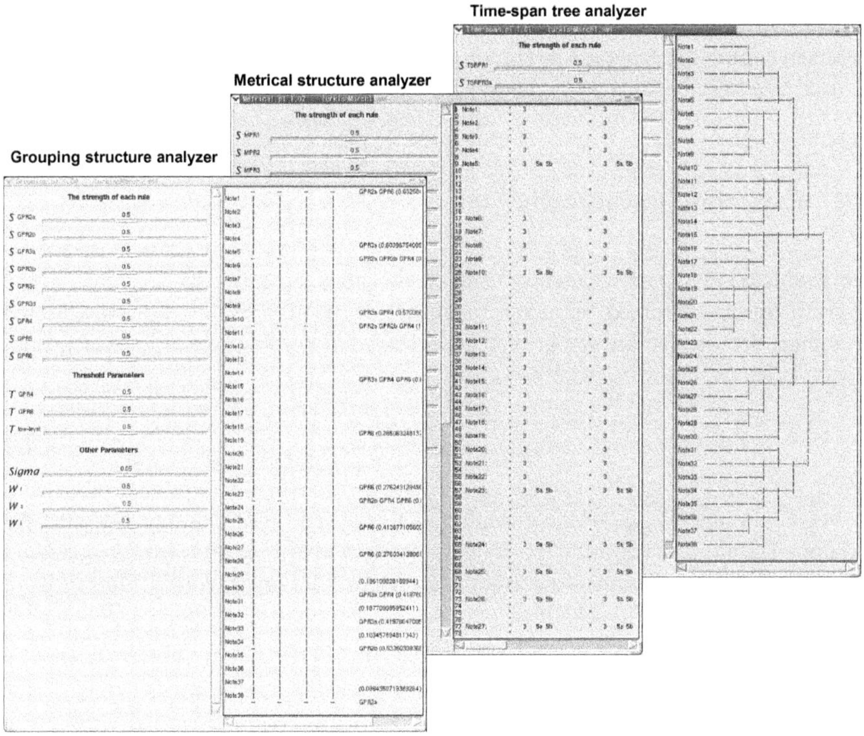

Fig. 8.21 Screen snapshots of analyzers

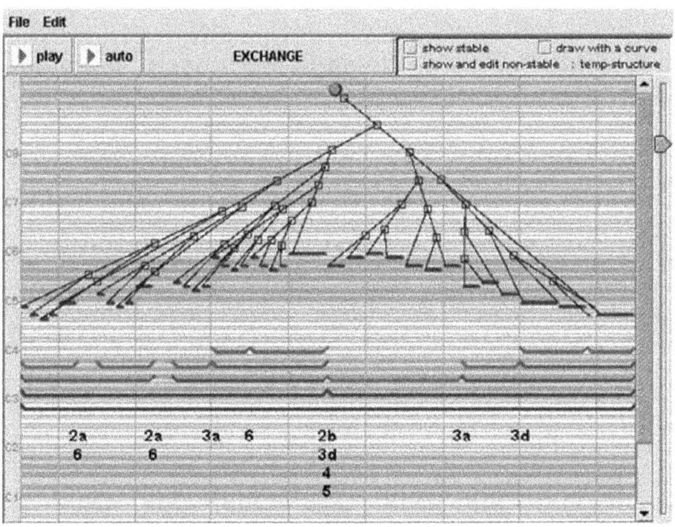

Fig. 8.22 Screen snapshot of Java-based GUI

structures change depending on the configured parameters. The manual-edit mode assists in editing the grouping structure, metrical structure, and time-span tree. It can be used to edit the results of the automatic-analysis mode.

8.8 Experimental Results

We evaluated the performance of the music analyzer using an F_{measure}, which is given by the weighted harmonic mean of Precision P (proportion of selected groupings/dots/heads that are correct) and Recall R (proportion of correct groupings/dots/heads that were identified).

$$F_{\text{measure}} = 2 \times \frac{P \times R}{P + R} \tag{8.49}$$

In calculating F_{measure} of the grouping analyzer and time-span tree analyzer, we did not take into consideration the possibility that a low-level error is propagated up to a higher level; we counted incorrect answers without regard to the differences in grouping levels and time-span levels.

8.8.1 Evaluation Data

The evaluation by F_{measure} required us to prepare correct data for the grouping structure, metrical structure, and time-span tree. Because there is no database containing the analysis results by GTTM, we prepared a novel type of evaluation data. The evaluation data consists of score data and correct data.

Score Data

We collected one hundred 8-bar-long, monophonic, classical music pieces that include notes, rests, slurs, accents, and articulations entered manually with music notation software called *Finale* [19]. In addition, we exported MusicXML by using a plugin called *Dolet* [20].

The basic parameters calculated in Sects. 8.4, 8.5, and 8.6 include parameters that cannot be acquired from MusicXML directly. For example, we could not acquire ρ_i from MusicXML directly, because its calculation requires real offset times $\hat{\varepsilon}$, but MusicXML only describes the formal offset time ε.

In the experiment, we defined $\hat{\varepsilon}$ so that the duration rate of the formal length of a note and the real length of a note would be 1.0 where the note has a slur, and otherwise it would be 0.8. We also defined the value of velocity υ so that it would be 1.0 where the note has an accent, and otherwise it would be 0.8.

Table 8.4 F_{measure} for our method and baseline

Melodies	Grouping structure		Metrical structure		Time-span tree	
	Baseline	Our method	Baseline	Our method	Baseline	Our method
1. Moments musicaux	0.18	0.56	0.95	1.00	0.71	0.84
2. Wiegenlied	0.76	1.00	0.83	0.85	0.54	0.69
3. Träumerei	0.60	0.87	0.76	1.00	0.50	0.63
4. An die Freude	0.12	0.73	0.95	1.00	0.22	0.48
5. Barcarolle	0.04	0.54	0.72	0.79	0.24	0.60
	:	:	:	:	:	:
	:	:	:	:	:	:
Total (100 melodies)	0.46	0.77	0.84	0.90	0.44	0.60

Correct Data

We asked a musicology expert to manually analyze the score data faithfully with regard to GTTM [15], using the manual-edit mode of GTTM editor to assist in editing the grouping structure, metrical structure, and time-span tree. Three other experts crosschecked these manually produced results.

8.8.2 Parameter Tuning

The grouping, metrical, and time-span tree structures will change depending on the adjustable parameters. To evaluate the baseline performance of our system, we used the following default parameters: $S_{\text{rules}} = 0.5$, $T_{\text{rules}} = 0.5$, $W_s, = 0.5$, $W_r = 0.5$, $W_l = 0.5$, and $\sigma = 0.05$. The range of parameters of T_{rules}, W_s, W_r, W_l is 0–1.0 and resolution is 0.1. The range of a parameter of σ is 0–0.1 and resolution is 0.01.

In the current stage, the parameters are configured by humans because the optimal values of the parameters depend on the piece of music. The experimenter used GTTM editor and a GUI to configure the parameters. When a user changes the parameters, the hierarchical grouping/metrical/time-span tree structures change as a result of the new analysis, and the new results are displayed on GTTM editor. It took us an average of approximately 10 minutes per piece to find the plausible tuning for the set of parameters (Tables 8.1, 8.2 and 8.3). As a result of configuring the parameters, each F_{measure} of our analyzer outperformed the baseline (Table 8.4).

8.8.3 Acquisition of Low-Level Grouping Boundary

Here, we discuss whether the low-level grouping boundary was acquired properly. GTTM [15] presents an analysis of the Mozart Sonata K. 331 as an example that can be interpreted in two ways: as a grouping structure that has a boundary between note 4 and note 5 (Fig. 8.23a) and as a grouping structure that has a boundary between note

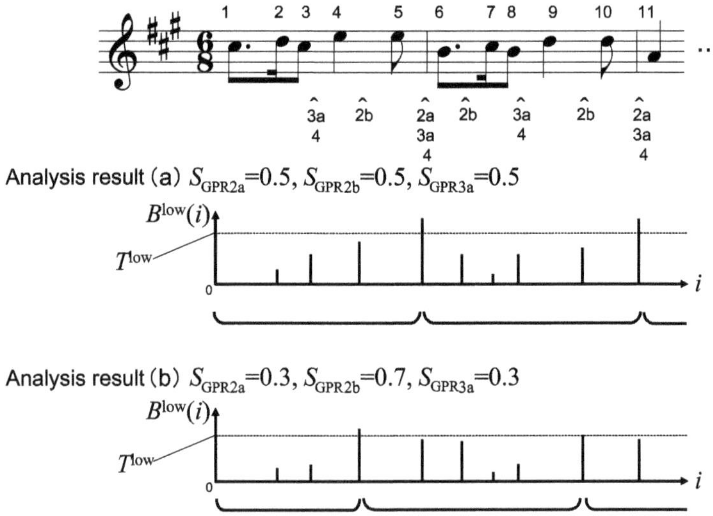

Fig. 8.23 Analysis of Mozart Sonata K. 331

5 and note 6 (Fig. 8.23b). The system can output both grouping structures properly as a result of using exGTTM for analysis by configuring S_{GPR2a}, S_{GPR2b}, and S_{GPR3a}. Figure 8.24 shows the analysis results of Chopin, Ballade op. 23, which provides an example of wrong results. The distinctive feature of this musical piece is that a characteristic of the melody changes in the middle of the piece. Figure 8.24a shows the analysis results in which the parameters are configured so that the $F_{measure}$ of the entire piece will be maximized. Although the second half of the results coincides with the correct data, there are many non-coincident structures in the first half of the piece. At the same time, when we configure the parameters so that the $F_{measure}$ of the first half of the piece will be maximized, there are many non-coincident structures in the second half of the piece (Fig. 8.24b). This is the only melody investigated in which a characteristic of the melody changes in the middle of the piece. It is necessary to further investigate how to analyze such a piece.

Figure 8.25 shows the analysis results for Bizet, *L'Arlesienne*, *Farandole* as another example of incorrect results. In the correct data, there is a group that only has a single event at the end of the piece. However, we implemented exGTTM so that it necessarily holds GPR1, which prefers to avoid a single event. It is necessary to further investigate the differences between a piece that has a group containing only a single event and a piece that does not have such a group (Figs. 8.26 and 8.27).

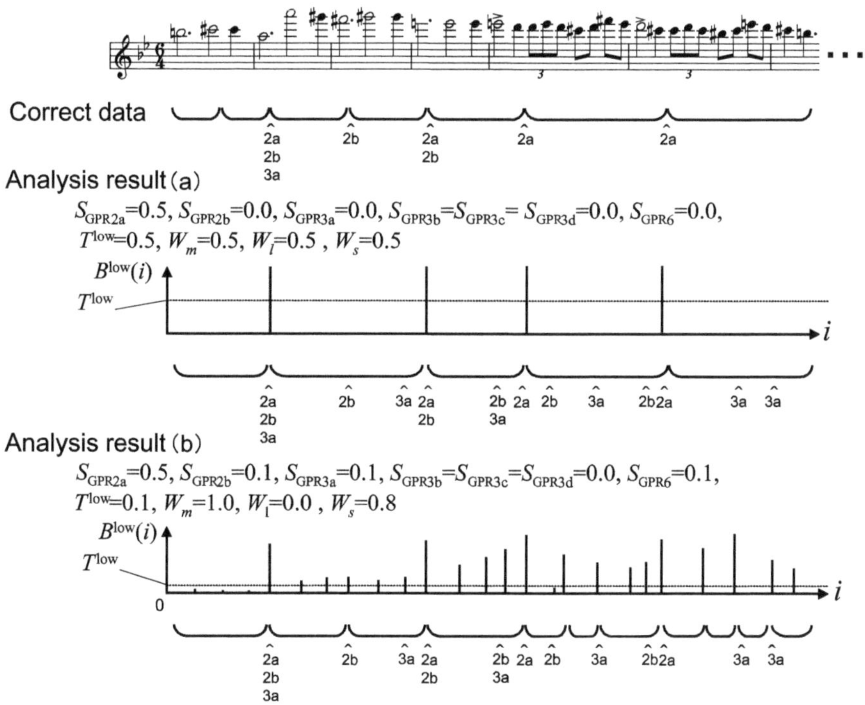

Fig. 8.24 Analysis of Chopin, Ballade op. 23

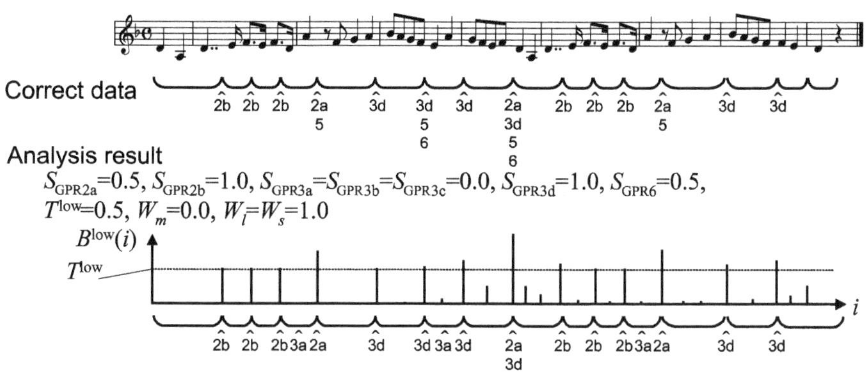

Fig. 8.25 Analysis of Bizet, *L'Arlesienne*, *Farandole*

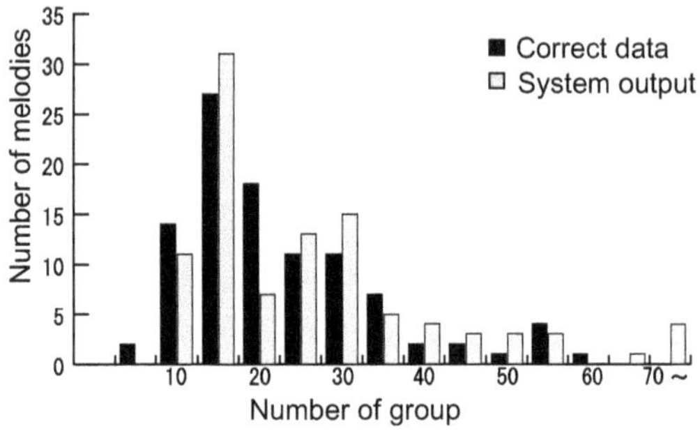

Fig. 8.26 Numbers of groups in correct data and system output

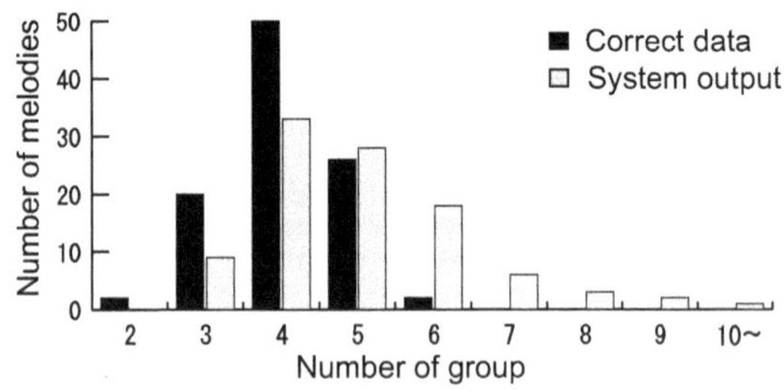

Fig. 8.27 Numbers of grouping hierarchies in correct data and system output

8.8.4 Acquisition of Hierarchical Grouping Structure

Here, we discuss whether the hierarchical grouping structure was acquired properly. Figures 8.28 and 8.29 are the histograms for comparing the correct data and system output by numbers of groups and numbers of grouping hierarchies. The system output tends to have larger numbers of both groups and hierarchies than the correct data, since we implemented exGTTM so that it must hold GPR5, which subdivides groups into two parts. For example, the correct data of Tchaikovsky, *Album pour enfants*, Waltz (Fig. 8.28) contain the three lowest-level groups (notes 1–3, notes 4–6, and notes 7–9) and combine a group at the next grouping level. However, in the system output, notes 1–3 and notes 4–6 are first combined and then notes 1–6 and notes 7–9 are combined. Therefore, the analysis result tends to have larger numbers of both groups and hierarchies than the correct data. In the evaluation data, there are 58 pieces that contain a group consisting of three low-level groups, and the average F_{measure} of these 58 pieces is 0.75, while the average F_{measure} of the other 42 pieces is 0.81. It is necessary to further investigate the algorithm for generating a group that has three low-level groups.

8.8.5 Acquisition of Metrical Structure

Although the average F_{measure} of the metrical-structure analyzer is 0.90, the F_{measures} of some pieces are very low. For example, Bach,Toccata, and Fugue in D minor

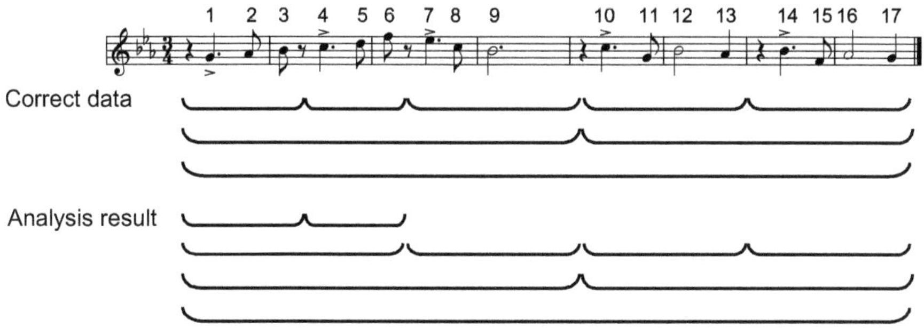

Fig. 8.28 Analysis of Tchaikovsky, *Album pour enfants*, Waltz

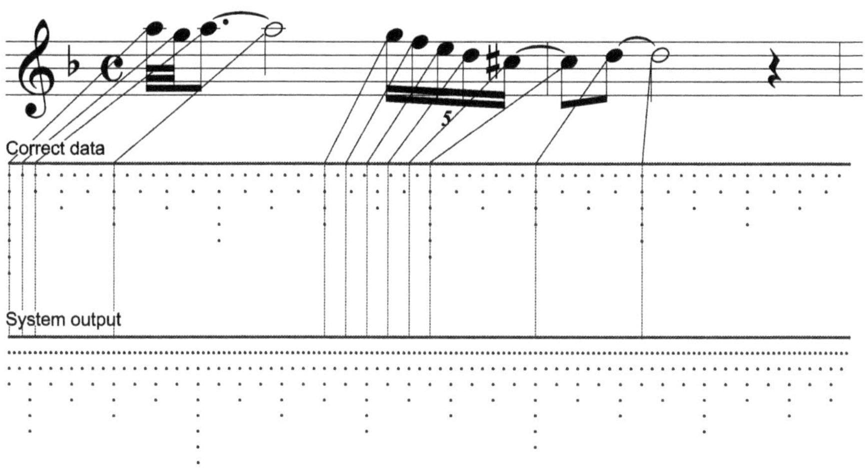

Fig. 8.29 Analysis of Bach, Toccata and Fugue in D minor

(Fig. 8.29) contains a quintuplet, which is not aligned in simple duple/triple time, cannot be analyzed properly in the current exGTTM. In the evaluation data, there are two pieces that contain a quintuplet and one piece that contains septuplets, and the average F_{measure} of these three pieces is 0.25, while the average F_{measure} of the other 97 pieces is 0.92. We plan to extend the system to allow quintuplets and septuplets.

8.8.6 Acquisition of Time-Span Tree

The average F_{measure} of the time-span tree analyzer is 0.60, which is lower than those of the grouping-structure analyzer and the metrical-structure analyzer. Figure 8.30 shows the analysis results of Beethoven, Sonata Op. 13, which is an example of a piece having a low F_{measure}. According to the correct data of the time-span tree, we can separate the entire melody into four time-spans, which are notes 1–3, notes 4–9,

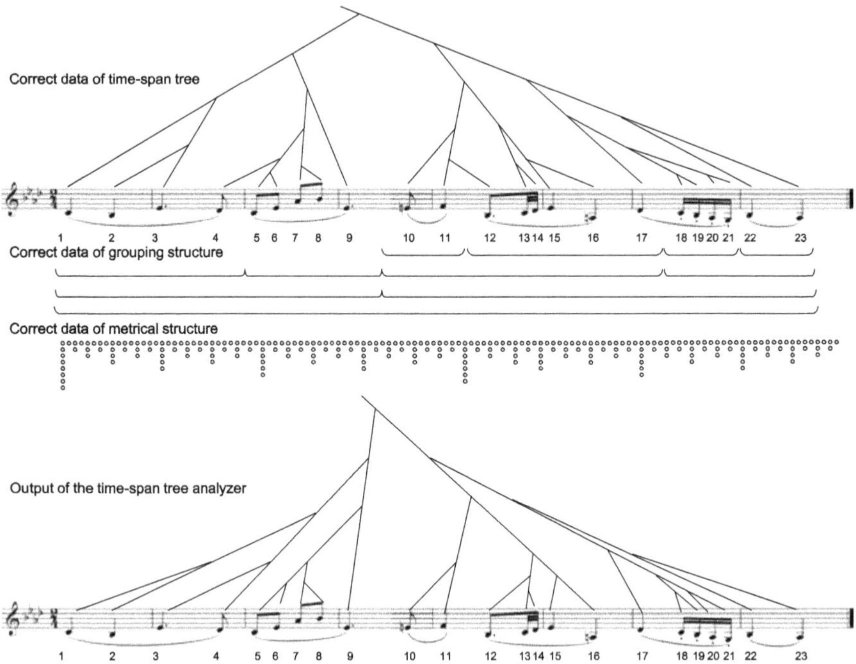

Fig. 8.30 Analysis of Beethoven, Sonata, Op. 13

notes 10–16, and notes 17–23. However, the correct data of the grouping structure also separates the entire melody into four groups, which are notes 1–4, notes 5–9, notes 10–17, and notes 18–23. Therefore, these correct data violate time-span segmentation rule 1 ([15], p. 146), which defines that "Every group in a piece is a time-span in the time-span segmentation of the piece." In the current system, we have implemented the time-span segmentation so that time-span segmentation rule 1 will always hold. It is necessary to further investigate the difference between a piece in which time-span segmentation rule 1 holds and a piece in which this rule does not hold.

In the experiment, we cannot acquire the tendency of the parameter set. In other words, we cannot acquire an efficient parameter set for every piece. This result indicates that the parameter set depends on the character of each piece and that we can classify pieces by using the parameter set after tuning. Figure 8.31 shows the analysis results of two pieces, which are tuned with the same parameters, i.e., Beethoven, Turkish March, and English Traditional, Green Sleeves. The numbers at the separations of the tree in Fig. 8.31 indicate the rules that hold. As a result of comparing two pieces, the same rules hold, i.e., TSRPR1 and TSRPR3b. We plan to investigate the classifications of genre and composer by using the parameter sets.

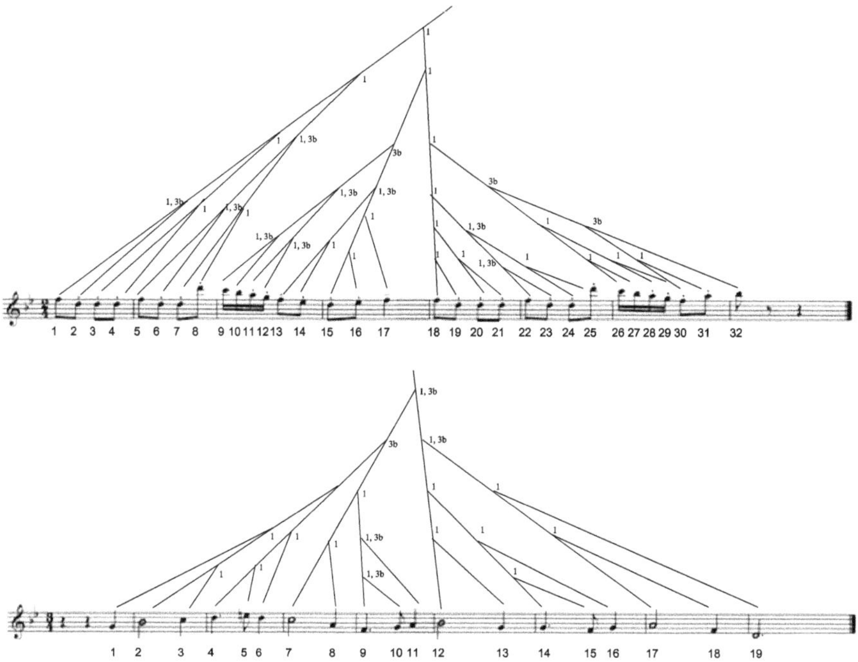

Fig. 8.31 Analysis of two pieces having the same parameter sets. **a** Beethoven, Turkish March. **b** English traditional, Green Sleeves

8.9 Concluding Remarks

We developed a music analyzing system called ATTA that derives the time-span tree of GTTM. The following three points are the main results of this study.

- **Extended GTTM proposed and implemented**
  We proposed an extended GTTM for computer implementation. The difficulty with the computer implementation of GTTM has been clarified [10], but no radical solution has been proposed. We reformalized the rules using a numerical expression with adjustable parameters so that it can separate the definition and ambiguity from the analyzed material.
  We implemented an actual working system to acquire the hierarchical grouping structure, metrical structure, and time-span tree of music, based on GTTM. This system, called ATTA, automatically acquires the time-span tree by configuring the parameters without manual analysis by experts in musicology. ATTA is the first application for automatically acquiring a time-span tree. We can benchmark ATTA against other systems, since ATTA can be used through the internet by using a CGI application, as described in Sect. 8.7.2.

- **Full externalization and parameterization**
  As we discussed in Sect. 8.3.2, we have distinguished three kinds of parameters. Among them, we have fully externalized the parameters of the first and the second categories, i.e., those which are explicitly or implicitly mentioned in GTTM [15]. Also, we could supplement those of the third category sufficiently to reify the preference rules. We would like to justify this claim as follows.
  Our working hypothesis is that we should apply all of the rules to the applicable parts. Because some rules refer to local structures and others to global ones, the process necessarily becomes from both the top-down and bottom-up directions, and it becomes entangled in a complex web of dependency as shown in Figs. 8.6, 8.14, and 8.19. Thus, our objective becomes unraveling all of these messy relations, to make the procedure deterministic. Toward this goal, we first gave a threshold (the first category) to each rule to judge whether the rule is applicable. Then, we gave a weight (the second category) to each rule to fix the order of rule application. Lastly, the global constraints represented by these parameters were recalculated every time the processing for generating a hierarchical structure moved onto an adjacent layer. As far as the process was made to be deterministic, we contend that those explicit/implicit parameters were fully externalized.
  The parameters of the third category mainly concern practical implementation and are rather independent of GTTM; thus, the parameters are insignificant from the musicological point of view. Since there remains no ambiguous step in the analyzing process, we consider that they are sufficiently elucidated.
- **A set of correct data constructed and evaluated**
  We assembled a set of one hundred correct data items, which is the greatest database of analyzed results from GTTM to date. We plan to make this database publicly available in the near future.
  Our experimental results show that, as a result of configuring the parameters, our music analyzer outperforms the baseline F_{measure}. The set of parameters tuned for a certain family of music pieces would likely reflect the common features of that family. Thus, the idealized parameter set for a music family, if any, would presumably analyze a new piece correctly, prior to human analysis.

Among the four sub-theories of GTTM, i.e., grouping-structure analysis, metrical-structure analysis, time-span reduction, and prolongational reduction, we have implemented the first three sub-theories in this study. Since the prolongational reduction involves harmonic stability, it requires the analysis of tonal structure, including chord and/or key recognition and its cadential progression. Because our objective in this study is to clarify and exemplify the computability of GTTM by externalization and parameterization, we have avoided the complication of tonal analysis; that is, we have postponed the mechanization of the fourth theory and decided to stop at the analysis of monophonic music, for the present. As a result, in reductions heads are restricted to the ordinary ones, and *fusion*, *transformation*, and *cadential retention* ([15], pp. 152–158) have been disregarded. Naturally, we are aware that the result of prolongational reduction would be fed back to the time-span tree. Therefore, the implementation of the fourth theory is an urgent and emergent goal of our future research.

We plan to develop further systems, using time-span trees and the results of the music analyzer, for other musical tasks, such as searching, harmonizing, voicing, and ad-libbing. Such systems will help to evaluate the effectiveness of implementing GTTM as a way to provide musical knowledge.

References

1. E. Cambouropoulos, The local boundary detection model (LBDM) and its application in the study of expressive timing, in *Proceedings of ICMC2001* (2001), pp. 290–293
2. G. Cooper, L.B. Meyer, *The Rhythmic Structure of Music* (The University of Chicago Press, Chicago, 1960)
3. D. Cope, *Experiments in Musical Intelligence* (A-R Editions Inc., 1995)
4. M. Ferrand, P. Nelson, G. Wiggins, Memory and melodic density: a model for melody segmentation. *Proceedings of XIV CIM* (2003), pp. 95–98
5. M. Goto, An audio-based real-time beat tracking system for music with or without drum-sounds. J. New Music Res. **30**(2), 159–171 (2001)
6. M. Hamanaka, K. Hirata, Applying voronoi diagrams in the automatic grouping of polyphony. Inform. Technol. Lett. **1**(1), 101–102 (2002)
7. M. Hamanaka, K. Hirata, S. Tojo, Automatic generation of grouping structure based on the GTTM, in *Proceedings of ICMC* (2004), pp. 141–144
8. M. Hamanaka, K. Hirata, S. Tojo, Automatic generation of metrical structure based on the GTTM, in *Proceedings of ICMC2005* (2005), pp. 53–56
9. M. Hamanaka, K. Hirata, S. Tojo, ATTA: automatic time-span tree analyzer based on extended GTTM, in *Proceedings of ISMIR2005* (2005), pp. 358–365
10. V. Heikki, *Lerdahl and Jackendoff Revisited* (2000). http://www.cc.jyu.fi/heivalko/articles/lehr_jack.htm
11. W.B. Hewlett (ed.), Melodic similarity: concepts, procedures, and application, in *Computing in Musicology*, vol. 11 (The MIT Press, Cambridge, 1998)
12. K. Hirata, T. Aoyagi, Computational music representation on the generative theory of Tonal music and the deductive object-oriented database. Comput. Music J. **27**(3), 73–89 (2003)
13. K. Hirata, R. Hiraga, Ha-Hi-Hun plays Chopin's Etude, in *Working Notes of IJCAI-03 Workshop on Methods for Automatic Music Performance and their Applications in a Public Rendering Contest* (2003), pp. 72–73
14. K. Hirata, S. Matsuda, Interactive music summarization based on generative theory of Tonal music. J. New Music Res. **32**(2), 165–177 (2003)
15. F. Lerdahl, R. Jackendoff, *A Generative Theory of Tonal Music* (The MIT Press, Cambridge, 1983)
16. A. Marsden, Generative structural representation of Tonal music. J. New Music Res. **34**(4), 409–428 (2005)
17. E. Narmour, *The Analysis and Cognition of Basic Melodic Structure* (The University of Chicago Press, Chicago, 1990)
18. T. Nord, *Toward Theoretical Verification: Developing a Computer Model of Lerdahl and Jackendoff's Generative Theory of Tonal Music*, Ph.D. Thesis (The University of Wisconsin, Madison, 1992)
19. PG Music Inc., *Finale* (2007). http://www.pgmusic.com/finale.htm
20. Recordare LLC., *MusicXML 1.1 Tutorial* (2007). http://www.recordare.com/xml~/musicxml-tutorial.pdf
21. Recordare LLC., *Dolet 3 for Finale* (2007). http://www.recordare.com/finale/index.html
22. D. Rosenthal, Emulation of human rhythm perception. Comput. Music J. **16**(1), 64–76 (1992)
23. S. Russell, P. Novig, *Artificial Intelligence: A Modern Approach* (Prentice Hall, 2002)

24. H. Schenker, *Free Composition (Der freie Satz), translated and edited by Ernst Oster* (Longman Inc, New York, 1979)
25. E. Selfridge-Field, Conceptual and representational issues in melodic comparison, in *Computing in Musicology*, vol. 11 (The MIT Press, 1998), pp. 3–64
26. D.R. Stammen, B. Pennycook, Real-time segmentation of music using an adaptation of Lerdahl and Jackendoff's grouping principles, in *Proceedings of ICMPC1994* (1994), pp. 269–270
27. D. Temperley, *The Cognition of Basic Musical Structures* (The MIT Press, Cambridge, 2001)
28. N. Todd, A model of expressive timing in Tonal music. Music. Percept. **3**(1), 33–58 (1985)
29. W3C, *XML Pointer Language (XPointer)* (2002). http://www.w3.org/TR/xptr/
30. W3C, *XML Linking Language (XLink) Version 1.0* (2001). http://www.w3.org/~TR/xlink/
31. G. Widmer, Understanding and learning musical expression, in *Proceedings of ICMC1993* (1993), pp. 268–275

Chapter 9
Application of GTTM

We propose a new methodology of melodic morphing as a tenable and trustworthy form of music manipulation. The manner of composition is very different between artistic composers, and commercial arrangers who need to modify existing melodies for movies and games. Here, we aim at satisfying the needs of the latter by developing a composition process that is transparent and understandable and of which the outcome is always predictable.

Suppose a composer intends to give a different feeling to a given melody *A* and that he/she is aware that another melody *B* possesses such a feeling. In such a situation, melodic morphing can reflect this user's intention; that is, the composer can use melodic morphing to convey the nuance of melody *B* to melody *A* [1, 2].

To formalize the melodic morphing concept, we employ an algebraic method that is mathematically and cognitively well-grounded. First, we define the maximum time-span as the longest temporal interval for each pitch event to become most salient, on the basis of time-span analysis using the generative theory of tonal music (GTTM) [3–5]. Then, we define the idea of reducible branches in a tree and the distance between trees by using the maximum time-span. Since the set of time-span trees is a lattice because of the subsumption relations among them, we can define three algebraic operations: *reduction*, *meet*, and *join*. The melodic morphing method is composed of these operations [6].

As an application of the method, we demonstrate composition of new variations from two existing variations, combining the two time-span trees of the variations in an algebraic manner with *join* and *meet* operations. Here, the *meet* operation simply reduces uncommon pitch events and can be more simply defined as the intersection of two music pieces. Thus, if we restrict our interest to the calculation of distance, *meet* may serve as an edit distance such as the earth mover's distance (EMD) or Rizo-Valero's edit distance [7]. In contrast, the *join* operation is problematic; since it may add pitch events of one melody to another, there could be incompatible pitch

K. Hirata et al., *Music, Mathematics and Language*,
https://doi.org/10.1007/978-981-19-5166-4_9

events in the two scores. Here, we propose the notion of a virtual set of time-span trees apart from the music scores in the real world, where we regard that the rendering from a tree to a score is another independent process.

9.1 Basic Algorithm of Melodic Morphing

The initial melody A, target nuance melody B, resulting morphed melody C, and the morphing method must meet the following conditions. Conditions 1 and 2 are for melody C, and 3 and 4 are for the method.

1. The distance between A and C is shorter than that of A and B, and the distance between B and C is shorter than that of A and B.
2. When B is the same as A, C is the same as A.
3. The output of multiple melodies C depends on the parameters that represent influential features of melodies A and B.
4. C is a monophony if A and B are monophonies.

9.1.1 Ideas of Melodic Morphing

The meaning of morphing is to change something, such as an image, into another through a seamless transition. For example, a method of morphing one face picture into another creates intermediate pictures through the following operations.

1. Link characteristic points such as eyes, nose, etc., in the two pictures (Fig. 9.1a).
2. Rate the intensities of the shape (position), color, etc. in each picture.
3. Combine the pictures.

Similarly, our melodic morphing method creates intermediate melodies with the following operations.

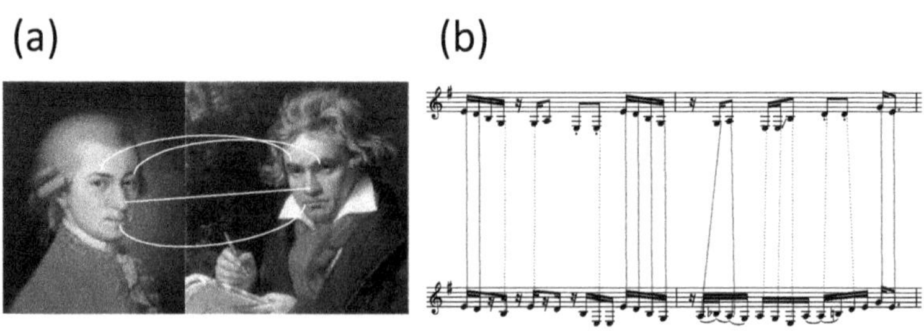

Fig. 9.1 Examples of linking two pictures/melodies

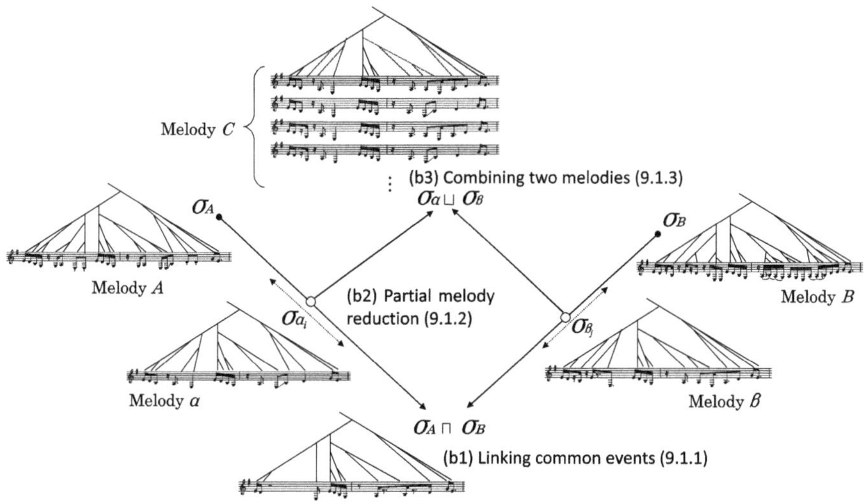

Fig. 9.2 Overview of melodic morphing method

1. Link the common pitch events of the time-span trees of two melodies (Fig. 9.1b).
2. Remove those notes which do not reside in the common part by using the partial melody reduction, explained below.
3. Combine both melodies.

By using the time-span trees σ_A and σ_B from melodies A and B, we can calculate the common events of $\sigma_A \sqcap \sigma_B$, which includes not only the essential parts of melody A but also those of melody B [Fig. 9.2(b1)]. The *meet* operation $\sigma_A \sqcap \sigma_B$ is abstracted from σ_A and σ_B, and those abstracted notes which are not included in $\sigma_A \sqcap \sigma_B$ are regarded to be the difference between σ_A and σ_B.

9.1.2 Partial Melody Reduction

Music features contained in σ_A and σ_B should exist even in what is not included in the common part. In order to retrieve these characteristics, we need a method to smoothly increase or decrease the number of features. The partial melody reduction abstracts the notes of a melody by using the reduction method described in Sect. 6.1.4.

With the method, we can first acquire melodies α_i $(i = 1, 2, \ldots, n)$ from σ_A and $\sigma_A \sqcap \sigma_B$ with the following algorithm. The subscript m of α_m indicates the number of notes that are included in σ_A but not in $\sigma_A \sqcap \sigma_B$.

Step 1: Decide the level of abstraction The user decides the parameter L that determines the level of abstraction of a melody. L is from 1 to the number of notes that are included in σ_A but not included in $\sigma_A \sqcap \sigma_B$.

Step 2: Abstraction of notes This step selects and abstracts a note that has the fewest dots, obtained by the metrical analysis (Sect. 6.1.2), in the difference of σ_A and σ_B. The numbers of dots can be acquired from the results of the analysis. If two or more notes have the fewest dots, we select the first one.

Step 3: Iteration Iterate step 2 L times.

Subsumption relations hold as follows for the time-span trees σ_{α_m} constructed with the above algorithm.

$$\sigma_A \sqcap \sigma_B \sqsubseteq \sigma_{\alpha_n} \sqsubseteq \sigma_{\alpha_{n-1}} \sqsubseteq \cdots \sqsubseteq \sigma_{\alpha_2} \sqsubseteq \sigma_{\alpha_1} \sqsubseteq \sigma_A \tag{9.1}$$

In Fig. 9.2(b2), there are nine notes included in σ_A but not included in $\sigma_A \sqcap \sigma_B$. Therefore, the value of n is 8, and we can acquire eight kinds of melody α_i ($i = 1, 2, \ldots, n$) between σ_A and $\sigma_A \sqcap \sigma_B$. Hence, melody α_i attenuates features that exist only in melody A.

In the same way, we can acquire melody β from σ_B and $\sigma_A \sqcap \sigma_B$ as follows.

$$\sigma_A \sqcap \sigma_B \sqsubseteq \sigma_{\beta_j} \sqsubseteq \sigma_B \tag{9.2}$$

9.1.3 *Combining Two Melodies*

We use the *join* operator $\sqcup$ to combine melodies σ_{α_i} and σ_{β_j}, which are the results of the partial reduction carried out using the time-span tree of melodies σ_A and σ_B [Fig. 9.2(b3)].

The simple *join* operator is not sufficient for combining σ_{α_i} and σ_{β_j}, because $\sigma_{\alpha_i} \sqcup \sigma_{\beta_j}$ is not always a monophony. Nevertheless, σ_{α_i} and σ_{β_j} are monophonies. In other words, the result of the operation may become polyphony (chords) when the time-span structures overlap each other and the pitches of the notes are different; therefore, the result violates condition 4 in Sect. 9.1.

To solve this problem, we introduce a special notation, $[n_1, n_2]$, which indicates note n_1 or note n_2, as a result of $n_1 \sqcup n_2$. Accordingly, the result of $\sigma_\alpha \sqcup \sigma_\beta$ is all possible combinations of monophony.

9.2 Implementation of Melodic Morphing Algorithm

Although we have given a priority to automate the morphing process, the melodic morphing algorithm described in Sect. 9.1 has the following two problems.

Problem 1: No order of abstract notes. The first problem has to do with the order of abstract notes in melody partial reduction. In Step 2 of Sect. 9.1.2, it was said that an abstraction is made from the notes with the fewest dots, but this is not always the case, for example, in a time-span tree where there is a structurally salient note on a weak beat. In addition, we have to consider whether it is appropriate to uniquely determine the partial reduction path, as in Eq. 9.1 in Step 3. If there are multiple paths for partial reduction, there is a possibility that more diverse melodies can be output.

Problem 2: Notes with overlapping times occur. The second problem is that two notes overlapped temporally may occur in the join of two time span trees. In such cases, it is necessary to manually select one melody from among multiple generated melodies, and it is difficult to completely automate the morphing method. Furthermore, the user remains in the dark as to the morphing process. In particular, it is difficult for the user to understand that the number of melodies output as a result of a number of melodic morphing changes. Even if the user understands the outline of the morphing method in Sect. 9.1, the outputs of multiple melodies may not match his or her expectations.

9.2.1 Two Solutions to the Two Problems

We tackle the two aforementioned problems with two approaches. The first approach (Sects. 9.2.2, 9.3.1 and Appendix 1) is to provide logically consistent melodic morphing. The definitions of $join$ and $meet$ are only applicable to unifiable pairs of trees in the sense of the branch configuration. In Sect. 9.2.2, we amend their definitions and achieve logically consistent melodic morphing based on ternary-branching representation (described in Appendix 1). In Sect. 9.3.1, we generate a morphed melody based on the ternary-branching tree and evaluate it through a subject experiment.

The second approach (Appendix 2, Sects. 9.2.3 and 9.3.2) is to define the order of notes abstracted by partial reduction and the order of notes selected by $join$. That is, when the time-span trees σ_A and σ_B of melodies A and B and the number of notes to be abstracted for each are determined, a unique melody, C, is obtained. In the experiment reported in Appendix 2, a musicologist who was familiar with GTTM and the melodic morphing method manually generated morphing melodies. The musicologist selected the notes to be abstracted by partial reduction, and notes with overlapping times, with the join operation. The first approach was different from the musicologist's expectations in that the two input melodies were monophonic but the output was homophonic. Section 9.2.3 describes automated morphing that defines the priority of branches, and Sect. 9.3.2 shows the experimental results obtained using automated morphing.

9.2.2 Melodic Morphing Based on Ternary-Branching Tree

So far, we have proposed a framework in which a time-span tree is distinguished from a written score. Here, disregarding the $join$ of two melodies in a score, we introduce

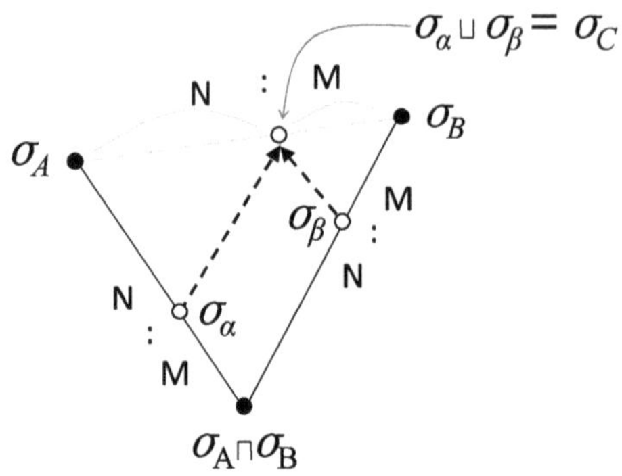

Fig. 9.3 Morphing algorithm

a ternary-branching tree that represents the superimposition of left-branching and right-branching binary trees. Appendix 1 details the introduction of the ternary-branching representation into the time-span tree.

Let σ_A and σ_B be two pieces of music and σ_C be the expected result of morphing; we require that σ_C should reside at an internal dividing point of σ_A and σ_B identified on the basis of $N{:}M$. The ratio $M{:}N$ means the ratio in terms of the total sum of maximum time-spans (denoted as $tmts$ in Sect. 7.4). Notice that there are infinitely many σ_C's, such that the ratio of the distance between σ_A and σ_C to that between σ_C and σ_B is $M{:}N$ because σ_C resides on the so-called Apollonian circles. Thus, we should restrict σ_C to the one that resides at the shortest distance from σ_A and from σ_B.

Our morphing algorithm is shown in Fig. 9.3. It consists of the following steps:

1. Find a reduction σ_α of σ_A that divides σ_A and $meet(\sigma_A, \sigma_B)$ with the ratio of $N{:}M$ in terms of the given distance.
2. Find a reduction σ_β of σ_B that divides σ_B and $meet(\sigma_A, \sigma_B)$ with the ratio of $M{:}N$.
3. $join$ σ_α and σ_β.

We see that four time-span trees σ_α, σ_β, $meet(\sigma_A, \sigma_B)$, and $join(\sigma_\alpha, \sigma_\beta)$ also form a parallelogram as in Fig. 9.3. As well, in terms of the distance between σ_A and σ_B, we have $d(\sigma_A, \sigma_B) = d(\sigma_A, join(\sigma_\alpha, \sigma_\beta)) + d(join(\sigma_\alpha, \sigma_\beta), \sigma_B)$. Moreover, $tmts(\sigma_A) \le tmts(join(\sigma_A, \sigma_B)) \le tmts(\sigma_B)$ holds if $tmts(\sigma_A) \le tmts(\sigma_B)$.

In the current implementation, a fully instantiated node is simply rendered as a chord of two notes, that is, both sounding at the same time. Otherwise, for instance, it could be rendered as a transformation of the superimposed time-spans.[1]

[1] It is like a transformation head ([3]: p. 155).

9.2.3 *Automating Melodic Morphing by Prioritization of Branches*

As shown in the previous subsection, the morphing algorithm designed through theoretical considerations has several desirable features. The distance between time-span trees satisfies the four distance axioms. Given the intrapolating ratio M to N, the algorithm can precisely generate the intended time-span tree from the input time-span trees. On the other hand, a ternary-branching time-span tree may occur if we calculate the join of differently branching nodes of two time-span trees. In this case, we regard that the ternary-branching time-span tree is a superimposition of the left-branching and right-branching time-span trees.

In this subsection, to cope with the problem of ternary-branching time-span trees, we reconstruct the morphing algorithm to make it more practical. The reconstruction involves abstracting the reduction distance, relaxing the requirement on a morphed melody having to stay at the shortest from both input melodies, and selecting arguments of the join operation. The reconstructed algorithm no longer generates a chord of two notes raised by a ternary-branching node, and it enhances musical expressibility.

The morphing process described in Sect. 9.1 is difficult to automate because a musicologist may arbitrarily determine the order of reduction. Therefore, we attempted to automate the process by defining the order in which branches are reduced. The priority of the branches of the time-span tree is determined by a breadth-first search with the maximum time-span. Since the height of the branching points in a time-span tree is sometimes arbitrary [32], we need to assign another, more rigorous order of priority.

The priority of each branch of the time-span tree is determined with a time-span tree drawn with the maximum time-span used in the time-span segmentation performed as the first step of the analysis of the time-span reduction. The branch priority is determined in accordance with the following rules.

- Priorities are assigned to each level from the top of the time-span tree drawn with the duration of the time-span .
- At the top level, the main branches take precedence.
- At the second and subsequent levels, the higher the priority of a branch X is, the higher the priority of the branch off of X becomes.

Figure 9.4 shows a time-span tree drawn with the duration of the time-span. The branch priority is determined in order from the top in accordance with the first rule. Then, in accordance with the second rule, branch 1 in Fig. 9.4 has the highest priority in this time-span tree, and branch 2 has the second-highest priority. In this time-span tree, the second level is the double-note level. In accordance with the second rule, the branch off from 1 becomes 3, and that from 2 becomes 4. In the same way, the priority is determined up to the 16th note level.

For automatic partial reduction, we decide how much each melody is to be reduced and reduce the branches of the non-common part of the two melodies. If the

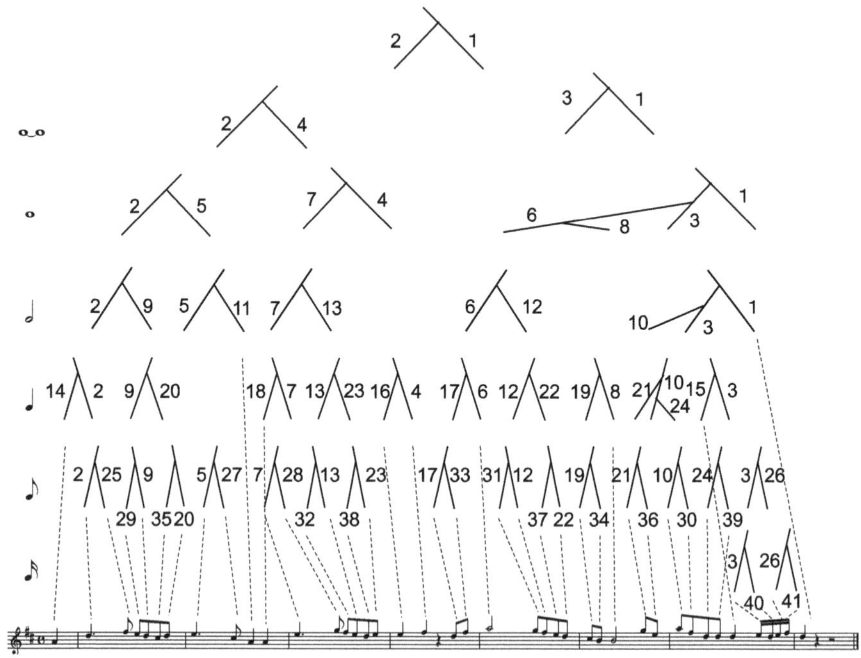

Fig. 9.4 Time-span tree leveled by the duration of time-span leveled by the duration of time-span

non-common part of the melody of A is reduced by 30%, the reduction ratio of melody B is determined to be 70%, so that the total is 100%. Then, in the non-common part of each melody, the branches are reduced in order from the branch with the lowest priority. The number of notes is finite, so reducing them in accordance with a set reduction ratio is often impossible. In such cases, the branches are reduced so as to be closest to the reduction ratio.

As described in Sect. 9.1.3, when a melody is synthesized by a *join* operation, the branches of the time-span tree may overlap at the same time. For example, if the branches and notes overlap at the same time due to the *join* operation of melody A and B, the note with the lower reduction ratio is left. If both reduction ratios are 50%, the note of A is left.

9.3 Experimental Results

Section 9.3.1 describes the variations generated by the method described in Sect. 9.2.2 and evaluates the pieces from a psychological viewpoint. Section 9.3.2 describes the results of morphing with the method described in Sect. 9.2.3.

Fig. 9.5 Variations No. 1, No. 2, and No. 5, and melodies generated by morphing

9.3.1 Subject Evaluation with Melodic Morphing Based on Ternary-Branching Tree

We implemented this morphing algorithm with SWI-Prolog [11]. The piece used in the experiment is the same as that used in Sect. 7.4: Mozart's *Twelve Variations on 'Ah vous dirai-je, Maman'* K.265/300e. In this experiment, we use the opening eight bars of variations No. 1, No. 2 and No. 5 as the original melodies and generate the intermediate melodies of those originals, by morphing (Fig. 9.5).

The reason we chose these three variations is that join can be calculated for any combination of the variations. That is to say, in all of the included join calculations the maximum time-spans are connectable. In Fig. 9.5, between the scores of the variations

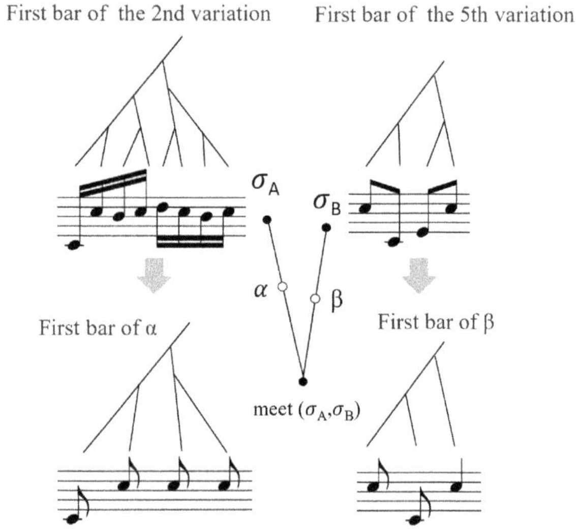

Fig. 9.6 Generation of 1:1 morphing melody from variations No. 2 and No. 5

we present the corresponding morphing melodies. For example, 'No. 2 & No. 5, 1:1' is a melody that is the exact midpoint of variations No. 2 and No. 5 Ratio '1:3' expresses distance ratio. For example, 'No. 2 & No. 5, 1:3' is a melody that corresponds to a distance of 1 from variation No. 2 and a distance of 3 from variation No. 5.

In Fig. 9.5, from variation No. 2–No. 5 there are three morphing melodies in order. You can see that the texture of the melody alters little by little in accordance with the distance ratio. Taking 'No. 2 & No. 5, 1:1' as an example, we will give a detailed explanation of the morphing process (Fig. 9.6). For the convenience of explanation, we present only the opening bar of variations No. 2 and No. 5 and α and β [2] which are generated partway through.

To obtain α by dividing σ_A (variation No. 2) and $meet(\sigma_A, \sigma_B)$ by a ratio of 1:1, from σ_A we eliminate reducible branches one at a time, stopping when we reach exactly $tmts(\alpha) = (tmts(\sigma_A) + tmts(meet(\sigma_A, \sigma_B)))/2$. This condition means that $tmts(\alpha)$ is exactly in the middle of $tmts(\sigma_A)$ and $tmts(meet(\sigma_A, \sigma_B))$. In the same way, we eliminate reducible branches one by one from σ_B and obtain β. Finally, we *join* α and β and obtain the first bar of 'No. 2 & No. 5, 1:1' (Fig. 9.5).

We confirmed the degree of similarity between the original variations and the morphing melodies through a subject experiment with six university students (of which four had over five years of musical instrument playing experience). Adopting the same experiment procedure described in Sect. 7.4, we have subjects listen to two melodies, $\langle m_i, m_j \rangle$, from among the original variations and morphing melodies consecutively and in a random order, then have subjects rate how similar the melodies are. In the same way, we used MDS to visualize the experiment results obtained as a distance matrix (Fig. 9.7).

---

[2] α, β are time-span trees, but are here regarded as the same as the melodies obtained by rendering those time-span trees.

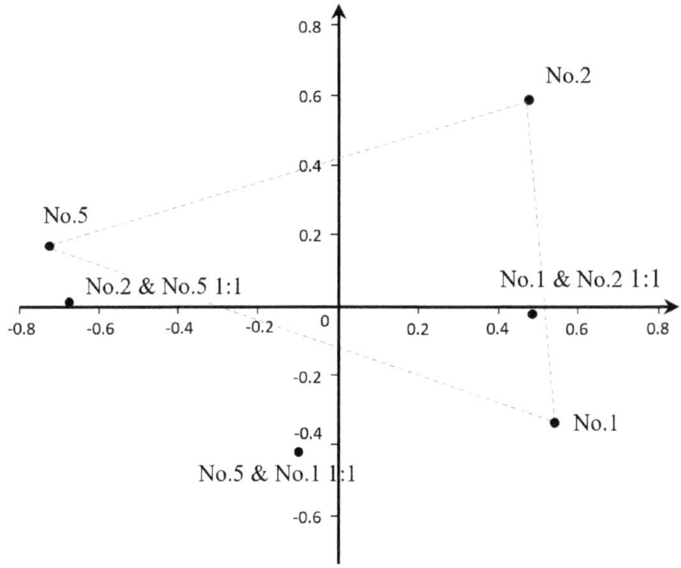

Fig. 9.7 Relative distance of variations and morphing melodies obtained from subject experiment

As expected, the 1:1 morphing of variations No. 1 and No. 2 and the 1:1 morphing of variations No. 5 and No. 1 are positioned around the midway point between the original variations. In contrast, the 1:1 morphing of variations No. 2 and No. 5 is positioned far to the left of the midpoint between the original variations. Let us consider the reason for this. If we look at the scores in Fig. 9.5, the number of notes in the morphing melody of variations No. 2 and No. 5 appears to be in the middle of the original variations, yet the morphing melody includes two eighth notes that occur at the same time, especially in the first half. We think that, as a result of this, the melody was recognized as being close to original variation No. 5.

9.3.2 Automating Melodic Morphing by Prioritization of Branches

We conducted an experiment to see if the two melodies used in Appendix 2 could be morphed. The results showed that after acquiring the time-span tree, there was no arbitrariness in the prioritization of the branches, partial reduction, and combination of melodies. Therefore, when the reduction ratio was determined, the morphed melody could be deterministically obtained. In Fig. 9.8, the notes included in melody *A* are displayed with stems up, and the notes included in melody *B* are displayed with stems down.

Fig. 9.8 Results of automatic morphing

In the manual morphing performed in Appendix 2, the melody gained a rich variation of notes because passing notes, appoggiatura notes, and auxiliary notes were used, but the note selection had arbitrariness. In contrast, in the automatic morphing, the melody gradually changed while the notes used were restricted.

9.4 Concluding Remarks

We proposed a new method of melodic morphing, based upon tree structures of music. Our method is summarized as follows.

Time-span tree GTTM analysis results in a hierarchical structure of music, where the most salient pitch event in each local time interval is externalized. We first obtain the trees from given music pieces.

Reduction A time-span tree possesses *reducible* leaves when they do not have further branches. Then, we can obtain multiple reduced trees, removing such reducible branches one by one from the original tree to barer trees, and such trees form a *reduction path*.

Meet and Join We can calculate the *meet* tree, from two arbitrarily given trees, to find a common structure, which resides on the two reduction paths of the given trees. Our target morphed tree becomes the *join* of a certain two reduced trees.

Interpolation The ratio of morphing could be given arbitrarily. Two original melodies can be mixed together by $N{:}M$, for example, when the reduction rates are N versus M from the originals to the meet tree. Then, the morphed tree resides as an interpolation with this ratio.

Algebraic domain We faced the difficulty of *join*, since we could not always find the corresponding pitch events in two trees in a strict way. Therefore, we brought the calculation process to the algebraic domain of abstract feature-structures that were equivalent to trees, independent of concrete music scores. With this, we could avoid the annoyance of locating the exact *join* points, and instead, we have employed the virtual *join* nodes with ternary junctions, superimposed from the ambiguity of left-/ right-branching.

Rendering Our methodology, however, requires an independent rendering process, that is, the assigning of concrete music notes to leaves of an abstract tree structure, to which end we need to fix a strategy for the choice of branches.

We have applied our method to the variations of K.265/300e '*Ah! Vous dirais-je, maman*' by Wolfgang Amadeus Mozart. We have placed newly composed artificial variations on the multidimensional scaling (MDS) and compared the psychological distance with the computational distance among trees.

Our method includes obvious disadvantages; one is that this method is only applicable to short pieces, short enough to identify the tree structures. However, our experimentation was done on eight-bar pieces and showed enough practicality for our purpose. The other issue is the subjectivity or arbitrariness of choice of branches in the rendering process. We need to somehow assign priority in branches, and for this we would need a future customization.

Our morphing method has appeared in the two smart-phone applications *Shake Guitar* [36] and *Melody Slot Machine* [37], which have been downloaded by a phenomenal number of people.

Appendix 1: Ternary-Branching Representation

A new representation for a time-span tree is introduced, shown in BNF as follows.

$$\langle n \rangle ::= p | c(\langle n \rangle , \langle t \rangle , \langle t \rangle) \tag{9.3}$$

$$\langle t \rangle ::= \bot \, | p | c(\langle n \rangle , \langle t \rangle , \langle t \rangle) \tag{9.4}$$

The symbol p means a pitch event as a terminal symbol, and $\bot$ on the bottom means the identify element for the *join* operation. p contains information on pitch, maximum time-span, and the corresponding note in a score. $\langle n \rangle$ and $\langle t \rangle$ stand for a time-span tree; $\langle t \rangle$ can be $\bot$, while $\langle n \rangle$ cannot. $\bot$ may occur only at the second or third place of the representation, not the first. Term $c(\langle n \rangle , \langle t \rangle , \langle t \rangle)$ represents a node of a time-span tree; the first place of the term $\langle n \rangle$ represents a primary branch, the second place (first $\langle t \rangle$) a secondary left branch, and the third place (second $\langle t \rangle$) a secondary right branch (Fig. 9.9).

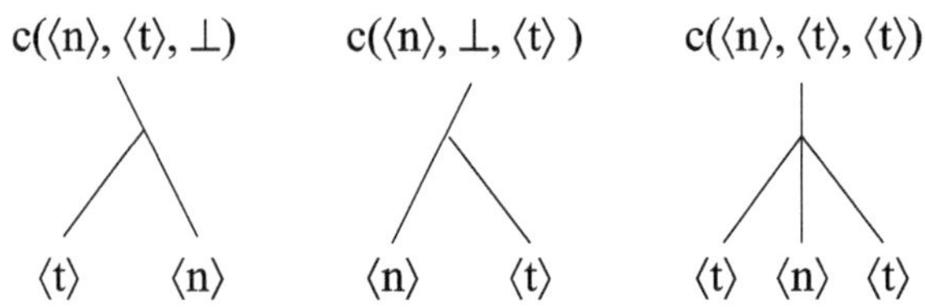

Fig. 9.9 Three node forms in novel representation of time-span tree

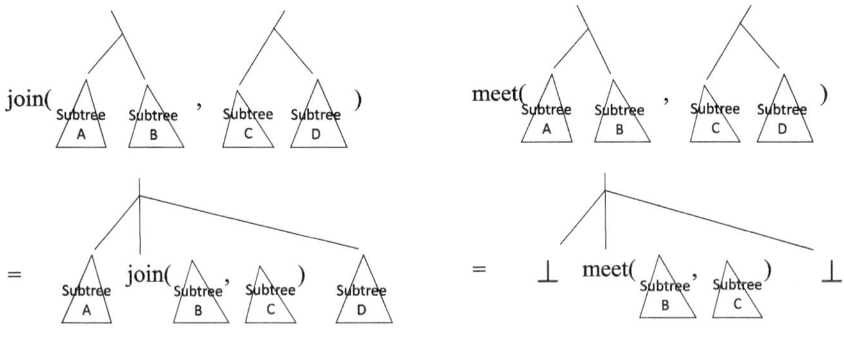

Fig. 9.10 *Join* and *meet* of unmatched-branching trees

The idea here is that node $c(\langle n\rangle, \langle t\rangle, \langle t\rangle)$ may be synthesized by joining unmatched-branching trees and joining to a fully instantiated tree $c(\langle n\rangle, \langle t\rangle, \langle t\rangle)$. The new tree representation enables the *join* operation to yield a proper result for those cases that have thus far not been unifiable. Here, joining unmatched-branching trees comprises cases such as $join(c(\langle n\rangle, \langle t\rangle, \bot), c(\langle n\rangle, \bot, \langle t\rangle))$ (upper part of Fig. 9.10) and $join(c(\langle n\rangle, \langle t\rangle, \langle t\rangle), c(\langle n\rangle, \bot, \bot))$; joining to a fully instantiated tree $c(\langle n\rangle, \langle t\rangle, \langle t\rangle)$ comprises cases such as $join(c(\langle n\rangle, \langle t\rangle, \langle t\rangle), c(\langle n\rangle, \langle t\rangle, \langle t\rangle))$ and $join(c(\langle n\rangle, \langle t\rangle, \langle t\rangle), c(\langle n\rangle, \bot, \langle t\rangle))$. Simply put, the *join* operation recursively computes an argument-wise *join*. The ternary-branching representation can be regarded as a superposition, abstracting the distinction of left-/right-branching of a binary tree , not as a node having three branches.

Moreover, the lower part of Fig. 9.10 shows the calculation of *meet* in one of the formerly non-viable cases. Similarly, the *meet* operation recursively computes the argument-wise *meet*. Thus, in this case, the *meet* operation takes into account only the primary branches, ignoring secondary branches, which is equivalent to the treatment in the previous research [33].

Note that the ternary-branching tree representation introduced here is distinguished from a ternary branching time-span tree that may occur in ternary meter.[3] The ternary-branching appears only when we tentatively calculate the *join* operation. There is still a necessary condition that calculate the *join* operation, that is, in

[3] Since GTTM restricts a time-span tree to a binary tree, a ternary-branching time-span tree is not allowed [3], pp. 326–330.

the case of a joined maximum time-span being concatenated; otherwise, the result is undefined. Let $[b, e]$ be a time-span beginning at b and ending at e; we may assume that the *join* of $[1, 3]$ and $[2, 4]$ is the connected interval of $[1, 4]$, while that of $[1, 2]$ and $[3, 4]$ remain as two separated intervals. Incidentally, the *meet* of $[1, 3]$ and $[2, 4]$ is $[2, 3]$, and that of $[1, 2]$ and $[3, 4]$ is undefined, not as $\bot$.

To introduce a proper *join*, we impose the following useful rules on the time-span tree.

Structural equivalence: Given a node c in a time-span tree representation,

$$c(p, \bot, \bot) \equiv p, \tag{9.5}$$

where p is atomic, either a pitch event or $\bot$

It follows that $\bot$ is equivalent to $c(\bot, \bot, \bot)$, $c(c(\bot, \bot, \bot), \bot, \bot)$, $c(\bot, c(\bot, \bot, \bot), \bot)$, and so on. As a result, there is an infinite number of such trees equivalent to $\bot$. For example, in the lower part of Fig. 9.10, let t be a tree; then, $c(t, \bot, \bot)$ cannot be rewritten to t if t is not atomic. Suppose p_i means a pitch event; then, $c(c(p_1, \bot, \bot), \bot, p_2)$ can be rewritten as $c(p_1, \bot, p_2)$.

As we have proposed the new representation of the time-span tree with a ternary-branching node c and structural equivalence rule, we can similarly extend all definitions of the reduction path, reduction distance, total maximum time-span, and the lemma on the uniqueness of the reduction distance that we developed in Sects. 7.3, and 7.4. Finally, we can prove the theorem on the triangle inequality of distance with the new representation of the time-span tree, although we will omit the details of the definitions, and the proofs of the lemma and the theorem.

Appendix 2: Manual Morphing by Musicologist

A musicologist created morphed melodies by manually performing time-span analysis and partial reduction from two original melodies (Fig. 9.11). The two melodies were Mozart's *Horn Concerto* No. 1 and Ponchielli's *Dance of the Hours* from *La Gioconda*. In manual morphing, first, the common and non-common parts of the melodies were obtained from the two time-span trees, and the number of nodes in each time-span tree was also acquired. The number of nodes was obtained by counting the nodes passing from a note to a root of the time-span tree.

Next, partial reduction was performed in order from the branch with the largest number of nodes in the non-common part. Although a morphed melody could be generated with this process, it became unnatural where the number of notes decreased rapidly. In those places, the musicologist adjusted the unnatural parts so that they would form a natural melody.

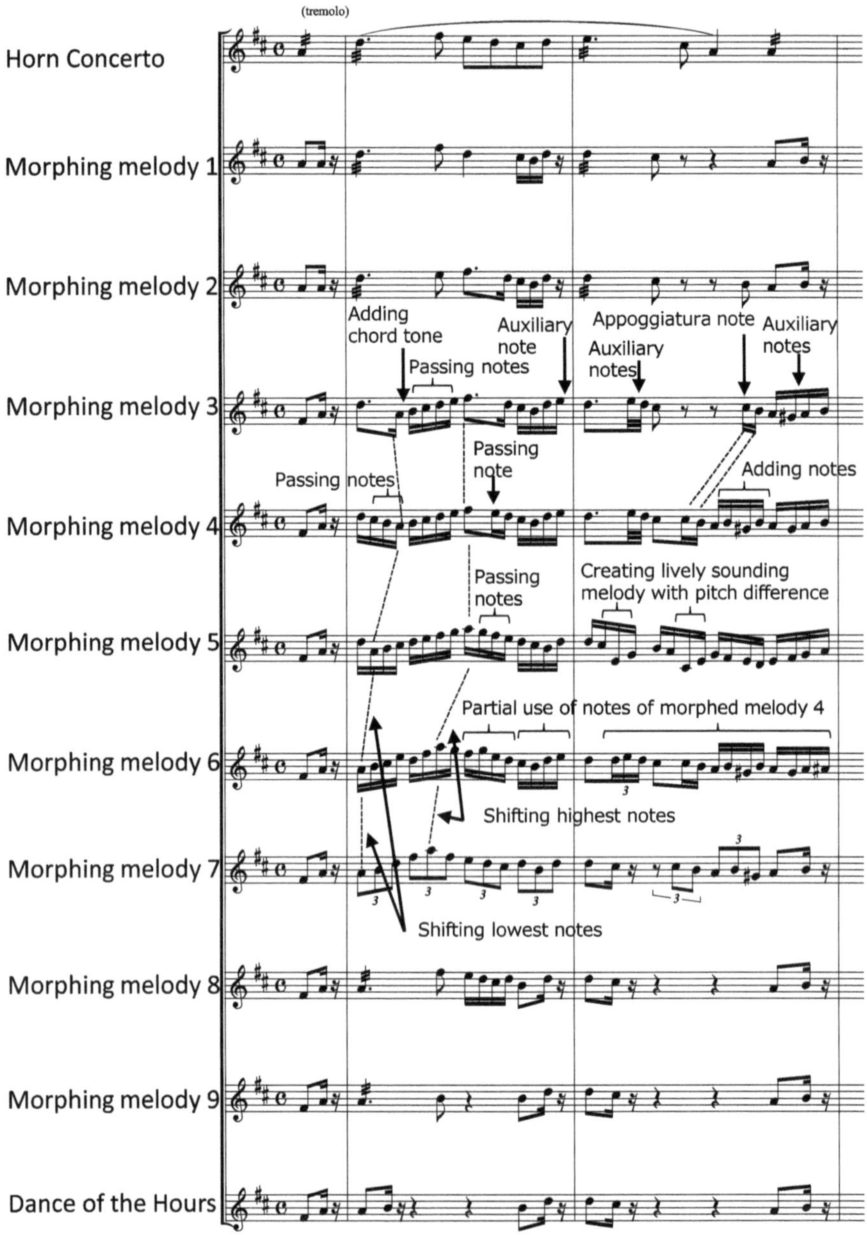

Fig. 9.11 Morphed melody generated manually

References

1. M. Hamanaka, K. Hirata, S. Tojo, Melody morphing method based on GTTM, in *Proceedings of the 2008 International Computer Music Conference, ICMC2008* (Michigan Publishing, Belfast, 2008), pp. 155–158
2. M. Hamanaka, K. Hirata, S. Tojo, Melody extrapolation in GTTM approach, in *Proceedings of the 2009 International Computer Music Conference, ICMC2009* (Michigan Publishing, Montreal, 2009), pp. 89–92
3. F. Lerdahl, R. Jackendoff, *A Generative Theory of Tonal Music* (The MIT Press, Cambridge, 1983)
4. F. Lerdahl, *Tonal Pitch Space* (Oxford University Press, Oxford, 2001)
5. F. Lerdahl, *Composition and Cognition: Reflections on Contemporary Music and the Musical Mind* (University of California Press, Berkeley, 2019)
6. K. Hirata, T. Aoyagi, Computational music representation based on the generative theory of Tonal music and the deductive object-oriented database. Comput. Music J. **27**(3), 73–89 (2003)
7. D. Rizo-Valero, *Symbolic Music Comparison with Tree Data Structure*. Ph.D. Thesis, Universitat d' Alacant (2010)
8. G. Hadjeres, F. Pachet, F. Nielsen, DeepBach: a steerable model for Bach Chorales generation, in *Proceedings of the 34th International Conference on Machine Learning, PMLR* (2017), vol. 70, pp. 1362–1371
9. S. Hochreiter, J. Schmidhuber, Long short-term memory. Neur. Comput. **9**(8), 1735–1780 (2017)
10. K. Ji-Sung, *DeepJazz* (2016). https://github.com/jisungk/deepjazz
11. M. Dinculescu, J. Engel, A. Roberts, MidiMe: personalizing a MusicVAE model with user data, in *Proceedings of Workshop on Machine Learning for Creativity and Design, NeurIPS2019* (2019), 3p
12. D.P. Kingma, M. Welling, Auto-encoding variational bayes, in *Proceedings of the International Conference of Learning Representations, ICLR2019* (2014), 14 p
13. A. Pati, A. Lerch, G. Hadjeres, Learning to traverse latent spaces for musical score inpainting, in *Proceedings of the International Society for Music Information Retrieval Conference, ISMIR2019* (2019), pp. 343–351
14. F. Pachet, P. Roy, Imitative leadsheet generation with user constraints, in *Proceedings of the 21st European Conference on Artificial Intelligence, ECAI2014*, pp. 1077–1078 (2014)
15. A. Papadopoulos, P. Roy, F. Pachet, Assisted lead sheet composition using flow composer, in *Proceedings of the 22nd International Conference on Principles and Practice of Constraint Programming*, pp. 769–785 (2016)
16. P. Langston, Six techniques for algorithmic composition, in *Proceedings of the International Computer Music Conference, ICMC1989* (1989), pp. 153–156
17. F. Drewes, J. Hogberg, An algebra for tree-based music generation, in *Algebraic Informatics, Second International Conference, CAI2007* (2007), pp. 172–188
18. J. Hogberg, Wind in the Willows—generating music by means of tree transducers, in *Proceedings of the 10th International Conference of Implementation and Application of Automata, CIAA2005*, LNCS (2005), vol. 3845, pp. 153–162
19. M. Hamanaka, K. Hirata, S. Tojo, Implementing 'a generative theory of Tonal music'. J. New Music Res. **35**(4), 249–277 (2007)
20. M. Hamanaka, K. Hirata, S. Tojo, Fatta: full automatic time-span tree analyzer, in *Proceedings of the 2007 International Computer Music Conference, ICMC2007* (Michigan Publishing, Copenhagen, 2007), pp. 153–156
21. E. Nakamura, M. Hamanaka, K. Hirata, K. Yoshii, Tree-structured probabilistic model of monophonic written music based on the generative theory of Tonal music, in *Proceedings of the 41st IEEE International Conference on Acoustics, Speech and Signal Processing, ICASSP2016*, Shanghai (2016), pp. 153–156

22. M. Hamanaka, K. Hirata, S. Tojo, Sigma GTTM III: learning based time-span tree generator based on PCFG, in *Proceedings of the 11th International Symposium on Computer Music Multidisciplinary Research, CMMR2015* (2015), pp. 303–317
23. M. Hamanaka, K. Hirata, S. Tojo, deepGTTM-III: multi-task learning with grouping and metrical structures, in *Proceedings of the 13th International Symposium on Computer Music Multidisciplinary Research, CMMR2017* (2017), pp. 238–251
24. W.B. Hewlett, E. Selfridge-Field, *Melodic similarity, in Computing in Musicology*, vol. 11 (The MIT Press, Cambridge, 1998)
25. J.S. Downie, D. Byrd, T. Crawford, Ten years of ISMIR: reflections of challenges and opportunities, in *Proceedings of the International Society for Music Information Retrieval Conference, ISMIR2009* (2009), pp. 13–18
26. E. Pampalk, *Computational Models of Music Similarity and Their Application in Music Information Retrieval*. Ph.D. Thesis, Vienna University of Technology (2006)
27. M. Grachten, J.-L. Arcos, R.L. de Mantaras, Melody Retrieval using the implication/realization model, in *Proceedings of MIREX2005* (2005). http://www.music-ir.org/evaluation/mirex-results/sym-melody/index.html
28. M. Schedl, P. Knees, S. Bock, Investigating the similarity space of music artists on the micro-blogosphere, in *Proceedings of the International Society for Music Information Retrieval Conference, ISMIR2011*, pp. 323–328 (2011)
29. ESCOM, Discussion forum 4A: similarity perception in listening to music. MusicæScientiæ (2005)
30. ESCOM, Discussion forum 4B: musical similarity. MusicæScientiæ (2005)
31. B. Carpenter, *The Logic of Typed Feature Structures* (Cambridge University Press, Cambridge, 1992)
32. A. Marsden, S. Tojo, K. Hirata, No longer 'somewhat arbitrary': calculating salience in GTTM-style reduction, in *Proceedings of the 5th International Conference on Digital Libraries for Musicology, DLfM'18*, pp. 26–33 (2018)
33. K. Hirata, S. Tojo, M. Hamanaka, Cognitive similarity grounded by tree distance from the analysis of K.265/300e, in *Proceedings of the 9th International Symposium on Computer Music Multidisciplinary Research, CMMR2013* (2013), pp. 415–430
34. SWI-Prolog (2020). http://www.swi-prolog.org/. Accessed on 1 July 2020
35. R. Groves, Automatic melodic reduction using a supervised probabilistic context-free grammar, in *Proceedings of the International Society for Music Information Retrieval Conference, ISMIR2016* (2016), pp. 775–781
36. M. Hamanaka, M. Yoshiya, S. Yoshida, Constructing music applications for smartphones. in *Proceedings of the 2011 International Computer Music Conference, ICMC2011* (Michigan Publishing, Huddersfield, 2011), pp. 308–311
37. M. Hamanaka, Melody slot machine: a controllable holographic virtual performer, in *Proceedings of the 27th ACM International Conference on Multimedia, ACM MM19*, pp. 2468–2477 (Nice/Springer, Berlin, 2019)

Epilogue

Amadeus, a blockbuster movie in 1984 directed by Milŏs Forman, based on a stage play adapted by Peter Shaffer, has contributed to advertise the supreme talent of Wolfgang Amadeus Mozart. Actually, he has been regarded as one of the most gifted among many ingenious composers. This motion picture, having humorously appealed his eccentric and indecent behaviors, rather impressed us with his idiosyncrasy as a genius. Indeed, his bright and light-hearted music has always fascinated us, however, is Mozart always pleasant for you? Of course, as liking or disliking is a subjective matter the answer to this kind of question depends on each person's gusto. But, I dare say, aren't there those who feel bored of his music? The answer could be yes, because our contemporary popular music is, in a sense, simplified arrangements of Vienna classicist music, and among those composers Mozart was a true representative. We know we are rather overstating but modern listeners have long been exposed to pseudo-Mozart under the name of popular music. As a result, common listeners may not find any novelty in Mozart. We can never degrade Mozart; on the contrary, we need more to admit that he is so influential to this day.

The development of tonal music has once completed at the end of the eighteenth century or the beginning of the nineteenth century. The established style at that time was an emotional melody accompanied by harmonic chords, that is exactly the current style of popular music. This style in due course had been developed and complicated along the progress of years by early romanticists as Schubert or Schumann and by late romanticists as Brahms or Mahler, however, without recording technique the playing time for a piece had prolonged, and an orchestra had been enlarged to exhibit *dynamique* and to show emotions sometimes rather excessively. Nowadays, few composers compose music in such a large-scale style.

In twentieth century, many composers tried to break the tradition and to escape from the classicist/romanticist style, adopting different scales, incorporating micro-tones and electric tones, and discarding melody and harmony. However, regretfully, those experimental music seem unsuccessful to acquire sufficient popularity. On the contrary, the invention of recording method and the combination with visual media have boosted the recurrence rather to the tradition. That is, the inertia of the estab-

K. Hirata et al., *Music, Mathematics and Language*,
https://doi.org/10.1007/978-981-19-5166-4

lished style is larger than we thought and the modern technology has unexpectedly shown it.

Here, we would like to get back to our original motivation of this book. We have obtained a new methodology of *computation*. Now we should consider what music would be in future from the viewpoint of computation. In order to rouse the interest of readers, we put on airs of Hilbert (1862–1943) who posed 10 unsolved mathematical problems in a conference in Paris in 1900 to show a future direction of mathematics.[1]

1. Can a new temperament replace the 12-tone equal temperament?
   12-tone equal temperament divides an octave, the frequency ratio of 1:2, into 12 semitones. We know that many people can discern *microtones* that is a more minute ratio than the semitone, however, considering our biological ear size, with the diameter of 10mm or less of our eardrum and with the depth of 3mm of cochlear canal, we also know such a subtle change of microtone is practically useless in playing music. In addition, if we divide tones into more minute steps, instruments would become harder to play with regard to our finger length or body height.
   As was discussed, the current equal temperament is a product of optimal compromises after many trials and errors as was shown in Chap. 2. If we require a new style of music, one idea is to incorporate microtones, and thus, we would be able to express subtle difference of ethnic scales or to describe *portamento* more precisely. Surely, computers can easily change pitches on demand, and then such microtones are easy to play. However, can we find pleasure in such a minute description of microtones with subtle changes of pitches?
2. When will the five-line staves be abandoned?
   The stave is a standard method to write down and to visualize music; pitches have been arranged in horizontal lines, that directly reflect pitch heights, and each line represents the progress of music according to time from left to right. However, even after the establishment of equal temperament, the pitch height of each line remained unchanged, and therefore, the pitch intervals between E and F, and B and C were left narrower though the graphical intervals are the same as others.
   Nowadays, every instrument players learn to play on this stave so that we have had no chance to change it. However, computers or electric instruments can reproduce music without relying on staves. In addition, the population of acoustic instrument players may decrease in future, as we will discuss later. If so, the importance of five-line staves will be relatively lowered. Someday, a written format of music may be replaced with MusicXML for example, however, on which occasion this critical change happens?
3. Will the black and white key arrangements of keyboard instruments survive?
   On the keyboard instruments, the same uneven arrangement remained between

[1] Later he added other problems, and the number became 23. He told his first question after 500 hears' sleep would be if Riemann conjecture had been solved. The conjecture states that the real part of non-obvious zero point of Riemann-zeta function is always 1/2 or not; thus far, ten trillion solutions have found and all these real parts are 1/2.

F and G, and B and C, as was shown as 'ebony and ivory' keys in Chap. 2. The piano-role may look to us an easy substitution for the five-line staves, but the piano-role is useless in the same reason because we still retain the problem of the uneven intervals. The key arrangement of the piano is a typical example of an aftermath of permeation. The same thing happened on computer keyboard. Its keyboard was inherited from a typewriter; its 'QWERTY' key arrangement was to avoid entangling of arms, to make the typing speed slow. But, once it was standardized and permeated, it's too late for us to amend it.

Being different from other instruments whose pitches we can adjust directly, the piano are made of keys, that are switches to produce fixed pitches. If we need microtones, such keyboard instruments are quite clumsy. Thus far, the piano has contributed to us as a convenient tool to play and to compose music, however, will the relative importance of keyboard instruments also be reduced?

4. Can any new elements in music, other than melody, rhythm, and harmony, be prevalent?

   As was mentioned before, the current music style, which consists of a melody with accompanying harmonic chords, was established 250 years ago or so. From this style, we learn a textbook knowledge that music consists of melody, rhythm, and harmony. If the music style changes, we naturally expect that then these elements also will be changed.

   In 1950s and 60s, challenging composers tried to incorporate sounds which are not originated from music instruments, and the genre was established by Varèse, Boulez, Xenakis, Stockhausen, and so on, as *musique concrète*. Later, even in popular music, the Beatles or Pink Floyd composed pieces with real-world sounds. Such sounds cannot be represented as notes on the stave and are beyond melody, rhythm, and harmony.

   When music was abstracted from lyrics, that is, when instrumental music without chanting appeared, words and language were not counted as a fundamental factor to construct music. But, current prevalence of *rap* makes us again pay attention to the combination of words and rhythm; in rap, verbal pronunciation interferes rhythm and vice versa so that these two elements cannot be independent. Will someone claim that the language or lyric is the factor of music?

   Also, we often argue what is the meaning of music. Koelsch[2] discussed that the meaning of music was often captured by external references. Music is nowadays more and more strongly connected to drama, musical, movie, and so on, and we can regard that a scene or a story in a drama can be a meaning of music. So that, such a reference, or a context in general, cannot be an element? Or, music may not possess a context, but rather be embedded in, or a part of context. Or, when music is composed and played by computers, does a new element appear? Such notions as computational complexity or algorithm are intrinsically independent of music, however, they may affect our listening and may be counted as an element of music.

[2] Stefan Koelsch. *Brain and Music*, Wiley-Blackwell (2013).

We think the exploration of the essential factors and/or elements that make the culture of 'music' possible is an important foundational topic of computational musicology.

5. Does music survive without visual media?
   This question directly succeeds the preceding one. Is the visual factor not a part of musical element? In this question, we would like to consider which kinds of equipment we require in future music. Only fifty years ago, we had a special interest in *hi-fi* (hi-fidelity) audio system. Many music lovers have stuck to listen to music with high quality sounds with expensive speakers and amplifiers. The recent hi-resolution audio systems may already exceed our biological sensitivity. Nowadays, such a culture seems lost since all the audio system came to possess decent quality, and also, listeners tend to pay more attention to convenience, e.g., head phones with no entangling electric cords.
   Instead, we wonder if music can survive without visual media. Nowadays, movie music or TV drama opening themes often acquire popularity. Dancing popular singers tend to be visual beauty. Or, a new piece of music is advertised with promotion videos. Historically, Richard Wagner built Beyreuth *Operhaus* to make the most of the visual effect, hiding the orchestra in a deep pit; however, if he were to see the current movie theater equipped with 3D vision plus surrounding speakers he would have more devoted to these advantages. Music may not be able to survive as an independent fine art, but may always be paired with, or often be subordinate to vision, that is the stronger input bias for human.
6. Will we still make efforts to learn playing instrument?
   Before there appeared a recording system, we needed human players to listen to music. If we were not aristocrats to afford to hire professional music players, we needed to play for ourselves. After then, Thomas Edison (1847–1931) invented a recording system, and the media has changed from EP record, LP record, cassette tapes, CD, and so on, to that which are downloaded to our own computers, and then to the cloud on the Internet. Nowadays, we can hear streaming music anywhere, anytime from the Internet.
   The chances we play musical instruments have relatively reduced, but can we completely abandon playing music? We play sports even though we are so clumsy amateurs compared with professional sports players, because the playing itself is fun. Even though we never can win over Federer or Djokovic in tennis, we can still enjoy physically pleasant sensation when we hit the ball at the sweet spot of a racket. Or, we feel satisfied when we realize our technique have improved. In the similar way, we play instruments because it is fun.
7. What will be the role of professional instrument players?
   As opposed to amateurs, do we need further professional players? Digital recording began in 1970's and since then almost all known classical pieces were re-recorded in CD; nowadays, we possess an accumulation of superb performances by many famous conductors with highly technical orchestras, as well as by talented pianists and violinists. It is useless now for us to argue which one is the best.

It looks to us that the current younger generations are well trained and their performance techniques are no worse than sepia-colored old *virtuosos*. In addition, there seems no more room for musicologists to find a new interpretation in old scores. We are all satisfied with existing recordings and we can choose any favorite performance as we like. Do we need a further number of recordings?
In AI era, we may be able to mix the flavor of various players automatically after learning the taste of each listener; an emotional part is like Martha Argerich, other constructive parts are like Alfred Brendel, and so on. Furthermore, once we have sampled the timbre of the best instruments like Steinway or Stradivari, computers may produce great artificial performances with them. In such an age, many young talents cannot find positions in the job market, and would be less motivated to train themselves. Thus, the *raison d'être* of professional conductor, pianist, violinist, cellist is endangered.
If we would like to listen to a technically more accurate performance, robot-playing is better. But, we claim that performance is not to compete the speed in Olympic games nor acrobatics in a circus; we want more human-like savor. Yes, we may claim we would like to see real 'human' performances. The market of concerts is the next question.

8. Will a concert still be held?
Again, let us consider the aristocrat age when they needed to hire professional musicians to hear music, where music must have been *live*. After we obtained the recording method, we can enjoy music in home freely with wine and can pause it anytime to go to toilet; even though many people still go to concerts. Why? Storr[3] argued that

> a primary function of music is collective and communal, to bring and bind people together.

If so, to go to concerts is intrinsic for music lovers. We would like to share the common emotions with others. We would like to feel relieved by sharing such sympathy, to confirm our sense of humanity in one and the same society.
But, as we have discussed, we cannot enjoy music by robot players because they only exist outside of our human emotions. Then, we need to find and raise young talents, and to provide professional players for concert halls. However, in order to pay sufficient tuition fee to train them, we need a enough size of market. It seems to us the situation is not optimistic; the market may shrink in future, as was discussed in the preceding question.

9. Which music is still heard after 100 years from now?
There is a study field relating to the evolution of music, in which the various researches are ongoing such as information retrieval of the past music popularity

[3] Anthony Storr. *Music and the Mind* (In Oliver Sacks *Musicophilia*, Vintage books (2007), p. 266).

chart[4] computer analysis of historical development of song forms,[5] and probabilistic modeling of diversity, dissemination, and disparity in terms of style and genre.[6] Then, we have obtained interesting findings which disprove established theories that were more anecdotal than scientific. In general, the accumulation of such scientific findings has allowed us to explain past events successfully based on some evidence, but predicting the future remains far more difficult.

One of the best emotional music, *St. Matthew Passion* by Johan Sebastian Bach, had once been forgotten and was discovered by Felix Mendelssohn in 1829. Even such a masterpiece was forgotten! Schoenberg (1874–1951) complacently said that people in the twenty-first century would be whistling music in *dodecaphony*, but it never occurred. When Charlie Parker Jr. (1920–1955) and Dizzy Gillespie (1917–1993) had invented *be-bop*, they thought they had invented such revolutionary and challenging new music. However, on the contrary, be-bop became commonplace, as heard as background music in restaurants and in shops. Even if the technology of musical evolution had been available at that time as it is now, could we have predicted the resurgence of Bach's pieces, the failure of Schoenberg's prophecy, and the bebop reaching a plateau in the hype cycle?

Paul McCartney said that The Beatles would be a future classical. Then, the notion of 'classical' may be replaced with well-made popular music. Perhaps, jazz music in 1940s and rock'n roll in 1960s are going to be classified as 'classical' when a new kind of 'contemporary' music is prevalent, or they may already become classical. How could Paul McCartney have obtained that projection?

Furthermore, music and humans co-evolve, or are always in interactive transition. We doubt if we human could keep the same sense of values in music masterpieces through ages. Even though we admit masterpieces are masterpieces, we may lose interest in them. Human valuation is capricious and haphazard. On the other hand, there are certainly some pieces that we discover something new every time we listen to them. It may be that there is some undiscovered charm hidden in the music, or it may be that the person listening to the music is growing up in a musical sense.

Will computational musicology someday be able to include the evolution of music in its scope? Anyway, we simply hope that the current masterpieces would be well preserved in digital format and they always have chances to be rediscovered.

10. Does computer acquire creativity?

In 2014 in Japan, a case was revealed that there was a ghost-writer for a known famed composer, who had been highly praised for his *masterpieces*. The sub-

---

[4] Matthias Mauch, Robert M. MacCallum, Mark Levy, Arnold M. Leroi, The evolution of popular music: USA 1960-2010, *Royal Society Open Science*, 2:150081 (2015). http://dx.doi.org/10.1098/rsos.150081.

[5] Ralf von Appen and Markus Frei-Hauenschild, AABA, Refrain, Chorus, Bridge, Prechorus: Song Forms and Their Historical Development, *Samples: Online Publication of the German Society for Popular Music Studies*, 13:1–83 (2015).

[6] Eita Nakamura, Dynamic cluster structure and predictive modelling of music creation style distributions, arXiv:2205.13923v1 (27 May 2022).

stitute composer had been an unknown but skillful, learned musicologist. We human are easy to be deceived by fake brand. If a piece of Schumann is said to be played by Maurizio Pollini, we easily jump to a high reputation. But, how do you react if it is revealed that the piano was actually played by an unknown but highly educated and trained student of a music school?

The Turing test[7] is a criteria for AI; if a human cannot distinguish a response of conversation made by a computer from that by a real human, we may say the computer has acquired an intelligence. If we cannot tell an *artificial* Mozart from his real composition, can we regard that the computer has composed as Mozart? David Cope had decomposed and reconfigured pieces of famous classical composers by the help of computers and had shown *new* pieces of the composers.[8] Although many of them were well composed, many critics blamed or disregarded his *masterpieces* when the true composer was known to be a computer. It was also what was expected, as we are always biased by fame.
Dreyfus[9] claimed that what computers can do was to combine various existing information and thus could not possess *creativity*. However, even though computers do not own palate sensors, they may concoct a novel but tasty cocktail that matches human savor, after a result of machine learning. In the very similar way, computers do not own emotions and auditory sensors, but they may be able to simulate our feelings and ear recognition, and compose satisfying music pieces.[10] If a computer-made piece gives us a feeling of novelty, we may say the computer has acquired creativity.
We expect that computational musicology will also bring new insights into creativity, since it can adopt a constructive approach with cognitive reality, unlike the methods for observing, analyzing, and describing phenomena and problems, or engineering imitation, described above.

Some of the above questions may be easy to answer, but others may not. An excuse is that the authors are computer scientists and are not musicologists. From the viewpoint of computers, AI may overturn our common sense which is directly rooted to our human sense; music is such an example. If our humble future prospect could trigger the same interest among readers, it's our pleasure.

---

[7] Alan Turing (1912–1954). *Computing Machinery and Intelligence* (1950).

[8] David Cope. *Computer Models of Musical Creativity*, The MIT Press (2005).

[9] Hubert Dreyfus. *What computers still can't do* (1972, 1979, 1992).

[10] It reminds us of the controversy about philosophical zombie.

Appendix

This chapter compactly summarizes the basic knowledge of computational musicology and music notation necessary to understand the contents of this book. The definitions are presented beginning with the basics and moving onto more advanced concepts, with as little ambiguity as possible.

1 Pitch, Note Name and Interval

Pitch

The notes that form a piece of music are specified by pitch heights, which are associated with typical frequencies that are physically defined. This is called **pitch**. The primary note (la) was determined to be 440 Hz, but recently is often set higher to make performance effect more splendid. The way in which the relative frequency ratio for a certain note is determined and what kind of arrangement of notes makes up a scale is as discussed in Chap. 2.

A single chunk of sound, within a piece of music, that brings about a sense of a peculiar pitch is called a **pitch event**, which also includes chords in which multiple notes sound simultaneously. As such, we can consider music as something composed of pitch events lined up in the direction of time, while a score is the instructions for what pitch event to generate, and when, set out on a two-dimensional plane consisting of time and pitch.

Note Name

First of all, 'do re mi fa so la si do' are currently the most widely used names for notes. In France and Italy, as these names are used to signify absolute pitches, B minor corresponds to the 'si' of do re mi . . . and is called si mineur. This notation system is called **fixed do**. In contrast, changing the note named do according to key is called **movable do**. In other words, whether the key is C major or G major, the start (keynote) is always 'do'. Accordingly, the 'do' of G major, the 'do' of D major and the 'do' of

K. Hirata et al., *Music, Mathematics and Language*,
https://doi.org/10.1007/978-981-19-5166-4

E♭ major are all different notes. This method is adopted in Japan, German-speaking countries and English-speaking countries. The alternative absolute note names given are 'i ro ha ni ho he to' in Japan, and A B C D E ... of the alphabet in Germany, Britain and America. Confusingly, what is called *B*/bee/in German is B♭ in English, while B/bi:/in English becomes *H*/haa/In German.[11] Here we distinguish by having the Anglo-American style in ordinary letters and the German style in italics. Below is a table showing the correspondence between note names. Even within Japan,

Japan	ha	ni	ho	he	to	i	ro
Britain, America	C	D	E	F	G	A	B
Germany	*C*	*D*	*E*	*F*	*G*	*A*	*H*
Italy	Do	Re	Mi	Fa	Sol	La	Si
France	Ut	Ré	Mi	Fa	Sol	La	Si

those who have received specialized musical education use the German movable do method, whereas generally the Anglo-American style note names (A B C ...) are used, with the Japanese system (i ro ha) being used only for the names of keys; besides which most people also use the fixed do method. In this book, we have primarily adopted the movable do method (movable do solfège) and Anglo-American style note names A B C. ...

Interval

Interval refers to the difference in pitch between two notes.[12] In twelve-tone equal temperament, since it is decided that semitones are all equal and a whole tone is worth two semitones, interval can be defined by number of semitones. A fifth spanning seven semitones is called the **perfect fifth**, and a fourth spanning five semitones is called the **perfect** fourth. In the case, in a certain scale, of a fifth spanning eight semitones, it is called the **augmented fifth**, while in the case of six semitones it is called the **diminished fifth**. A third spanning four semitones is particularly called the **major third**, while a third spanning three semitones is called the **minor third**. The remaining second, sixth and seventh are all treated in the same way as a third. In other words, the **major second** and **minor second** correspond to two semitones and one semitone, while the major sixth and minor sixth correspond to nine semitones and eight semitones, and the **major seventh** and **minor seventh** correspond to eleven semitones and ten semitones, respectively.[13]

---

[11] J. S. Bach's famous 'B minor mass' is known as Messe in *H*-moll in German, Messa en si mineur in French and Ro-tanchou misakyoku in Japanese. The same note is referred to as B[bi:], *H*[ha:], si[si] and Ro.

[12] Although cases of the term *interval* being mistakenly used to refer to pitch are often observed, a statement such as 'the interval is high' would be incorrect.

[13] Regarding the reason the fifth and fourth are described as perfect, there are several theories, such as that it is because they have no major or minor, or because the frequency ratios of the two tones that make up each interval are 2:3 and 3:4 respectively, which are the simplest ratios.

2 Scale and Mode

Scale

Among the groups of notes that are used to construct music, a scale is a set of notes lined up in order of pitch, with the interval from the lowest note to the highest note being limited to one octave (Fig. 1). A **diatonic scale** is a seven-tone scale comprising intervals of five whole tones and two semitones, unlike the whole-tone scale used by Debussy, in which all intervals are of one whole tone. In contrast, a chromatic scale is constructed from twelve tones and is a scale in which the interval between every two adjacent notes is a semitone. More precisely, a group of notes that construct a certain scale is called a diatonic collection.

Mode

In a seven-tone scale, the order in which the whole tones and semitones are arranged decides the **mode**. The Gregorian modes used prior to the Baroque era were revived in the 1960s, in the world of jazz music. The modes currently used in jazz are the **Ionian**, **Dorian**, **Phrygian**, **Lydian**, **Mixolydian**, **Aeolian** and **Locrian** modes. All these modes use only the white keys of the piano, and can be regarded as scales of which the starting points have been altered. Among the modes, Ionian corresponds to the major key, and Aeolian to the minor key. For example, the arrangement of intervals in the major key 'whole-whole-semi-whole-whole-whole-semi' is the Ionian in Gregorian modes, and if the order is 'whole-semi-whole-whole-whole-semi-whole', it becomes the Dorian mode.

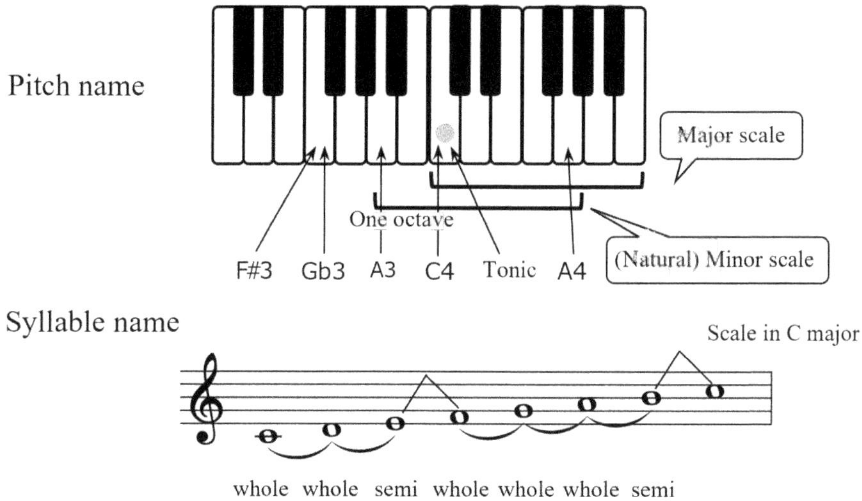

Fig. 1 Note name, name in movable do, scale

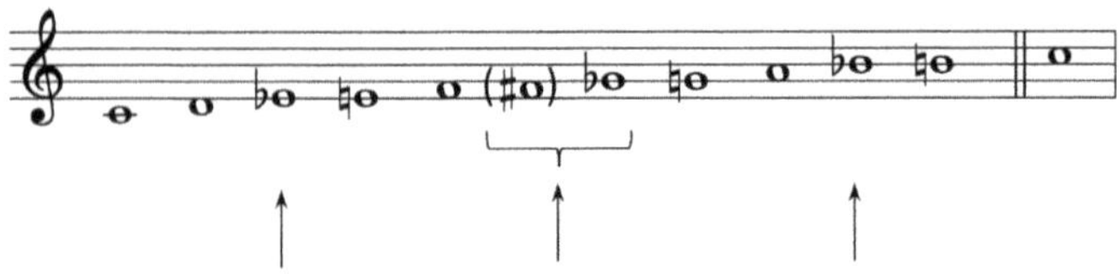

Fig. 2 Blue note scale

Blue Note Scale

Among the scales used in recent popular music, there is the blue note scale (Fig. 2). Firstly, by lowering the third, fifth, or seventh from the original notes in a major scale by a semitone, we have what are called **blue notes**, and a blue note scale is the original major scale with these blue notes added. For the blue notes that are actually used in performance, there are cases in which the original notes are lowered by less than a semitone, depending on the musician or genre. Although this is a deviation from twelve-tone equal temperament, and thus has components that conflict with western tonal music theory, in certain musical conditions blue notes are recognized as legitimate notes that endow a sense of blues or jazz.

Degree

The first note in a scale, that is, the note from which the mode begins, is called the **keynote** or **tonic**, and the central note is called the **tonal center**. The notes in a scale are counted up from the keynote, as first, second, third etc.; these may also be expressed in Roman numerals as I, II, III, IV, V, VI, VII, or in Arabic numerals as $\hat{1}$, $\hat{2}$, $\hat{3}$, $\hat{4}$, $\hat{5}$, $\hat{6}$, $\hat{7}$. These are called the **degrees** of a scale.

3 Key

We say that music constructed from major scales and minor scales has **tonality** (Fig. 3). Major scales form the **major key**, while minor scales form the **minor key**. In both types of scale, the fifth note (V) counted from the keynote (I) forms the perfect fifth and **tonal music** is the system of adding the major third or minor third to the harmony of these two notes to construct a major triad or minor triad.

In music that has tonality, **key** refers to the pitch that is central to a piece of music. Key may additionally include the distinction between whether the governing scale is major or minor. For example, if a piece of music has C as its tonal center and is based on a major scale, we say it is in the key of C major. If the tonal center is A and the scale is minor, we say it is in the key of A minor.

Key signature refers to the group of sharps (♯) and flats (♭) written directly to the right of clefs on a stave, which indicates key. **Relative key** refers to major and minor keys that have the same key signature, while **parallel key** refers to major and

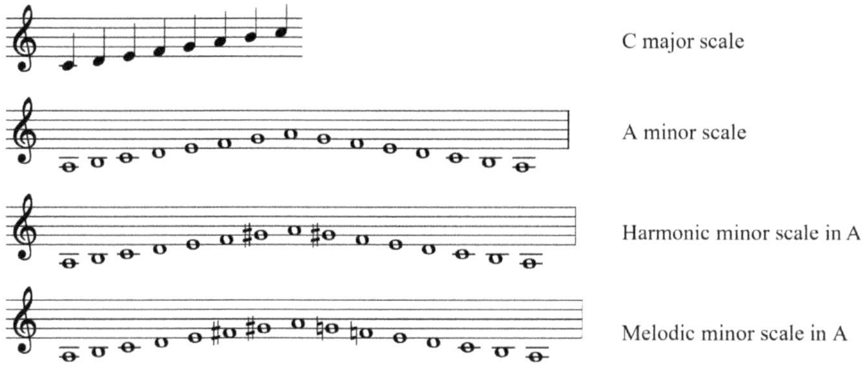

Fig. 3 Major and minor scales

Fig. 4 Circle of fifths

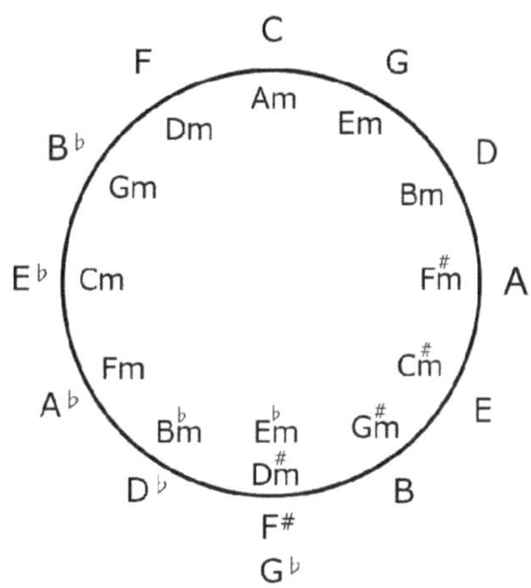

minor keys that have the same tonic. **Dominant key** refers to the key that is a perfect fifth above a certain key, while **subdominant key** refers to the key that is a perfect fourth above a certain key (both are preserved in major and minor keys). **Related key** includes relative keys, parallel keys, dominant keys, and subdominant keys, and the keys that are a combination of these.

The **circle of fifths** presents each key with its dominant key (up a perfect fifth) and subdominant key (down a perfect fourth) placed to its left and right respectively, arranged so that the twelve major keys and twelve minor keys form a circle (Fig. 4). Moving up or down in increments of a fifth from a certain tone or key cycles through all twelve tones, taking into account the equivalence of F♯ with G♭ and D♯ with E♭. Various aspects of music can be intuitively comprehended from the circle of fifths, such as the meaning of 'dominant to tonic motion',[14] the interrelationship of related

[14] Please see the section of Cadence p. 244.

keys, the distance between chords, and the keys that are easy to modulate (keys of which the scales share many of the same notes).

4 Melody and Counterpoint

When people listen to a series of individual notes, gestalt occurs in the time and pitch directions. Melody is recognized from the gestalt of both these directions. There are various names for melodies because the rules that govern cognition of melody based on gestalt differ depending on the length of a melody. First of all, in music, **figure** refers to a note series pattern that is repeated many times and is rhythmically or melodically coherent in music. A figure used ornamentally is called an **ornament figure**, while a figure used as accompaniment is called an **accompaniment figure**. **Motif** is the smallest unit that makes up a melody and ranges in length from one note to a few measures. **Phrase** and **period** refer to short parts of a piece of music that are of approximately four bars and have a certain degree of coherence. However, the definitions of these terms vary among different composers, theorists, eras, and so on, and thus there are no agreed-upon definitions.

We call a composition comprising one melody (voice) **monophony**, and a composition comprising several melodies **polyphony**. The case in which there is only one melody recognized although multiple notes and/or voices sound simultaneously, or the case of a composition made of one melody and its accompaniment, is called **homophony**. When a single melody is performed on different instruments or by different voices, this is called **heterophony**. There is no definite division between polyphony and homophony, and whether or not an accompaniment melody is viewed as independent from other voices is influenced by the form of the composition and the interpretation of the listener. Accordingly, even in polyphony, there is the case in which harmonic stability is required between the main melody and sub-melody to some extent; such a system of composition is **counterpoint**.

5 Chords and Functional Harmony

Chords

A chord is a pitch event in which two or more notes sound simultaneously. Various acoustics are produced depending on the relationships between the notes that form a chord. The notes that form a chord are called **harmonic tones**, while the other notes are called **non-harmonic tones**. **Consonance** refers to the state in which multiple notes that sound simultaneously are in harmony. Physically, it means that the two notes are in a simple frequency ratio. **Dissonance** refers to the opposite state to consonance. A **triad** is a chord of three notes stacked in intervals of thirds, and a **tetrad** is a chord of four notes stacked in intervals of thirds. The lowest note is called the **root**. The triads of the diatonic scale of C major are presented in Fig. 5, with the

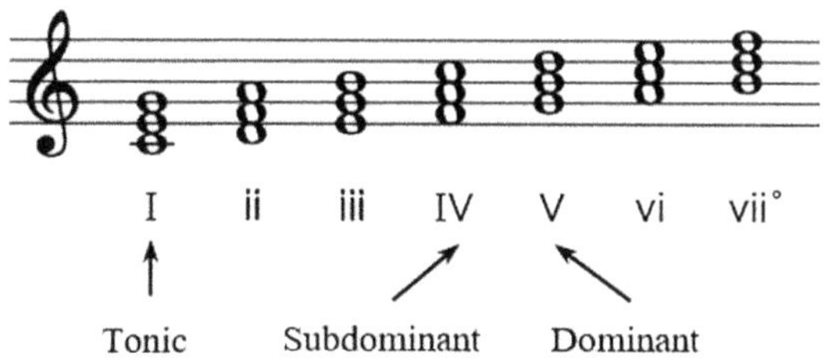

Fig. 5 Chords by name in movable do

chord names in the movable do system appended below. Among the triads, a triad of which the interval between the lower two notes, including the root, is a major third and the interval between the root and the highest note (the third note) is a perfect fifth is called a **major triad**, while a triad of which the interval between the lower two notes is a minor third and the interval between the root and the third note is a perfect fifth is called a **minor triad**. The names in the movable do solfège are expressed in upper and lower-case roman numerals, for major and minor triads respectively. Specifically, a triad of the tonic on a scale is called a **tonic chord**, a triad of which the root is a perfect fourth above the tonic is called a **subdominant chord**, and a triad of which the root is a perfect fifth above is called a **dominant chord**. Also, a tetrad of which the root is the fifth of a major scale is called a **dominant seventh chord**. Regarding tetrad seventh chords, there are two types: major seventh chord and minor seventh chord. The harmonic tones of the major seventh chord are I, III, V, VII, those of the minor seventh chord are I, III♭, V, VII♭, and those of the seventh chord are I, III, V, VII♭. In Fig. 5, a degree in lower case and 'o', for instance vii° stand for the **diminished triad** at seventh.

Inversion

A chord of the kind is called an **inversion** if the harmonic tones are of the same degrees but the arrangement of the tones differs. Let us take a chord of which the harmonic tones are in the order of first, third, fifth, from the bottom up, as the basic form. A chord of which the first, at the bottom in the basic form, has been raised an octave is called the **first inversion**. A chord which is the result of the third, which is the lowest note, from this first inversion having been raised an octave is called the **second inversion**. The lowest note of those that make up a chord is called the **bass**, but in inversion the bass is not always consistent with the root.

Regarding the notation of chord names, in the case of the basic form, only the note name, or name in movable do solfège, of the lowest tone is written. This is because the interval from the lowest note to the second is a third, and is thus omitted, and the interval from the lowest note to the highest is a fifth, so is also omitted. As the first inversion is arranged in the order of third, fifth, first, from the bottom up, the interval between the lowest note and the second note is a third (omitted) and the interval between the lowest note and the highest note is a sixth (not omitted). Accordingly, it is written V^6, as shown in Fig. 6. In the same manner, in the case of the second inversion, the interval between the lowest note and the second note is a fourth and

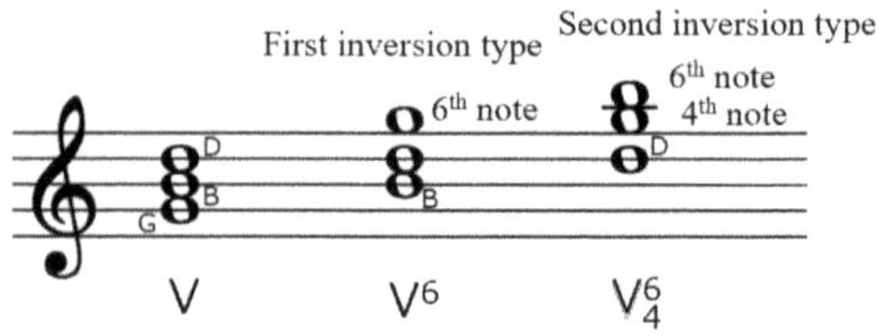

Fig. 6 Basic form and inversions of dominant chord

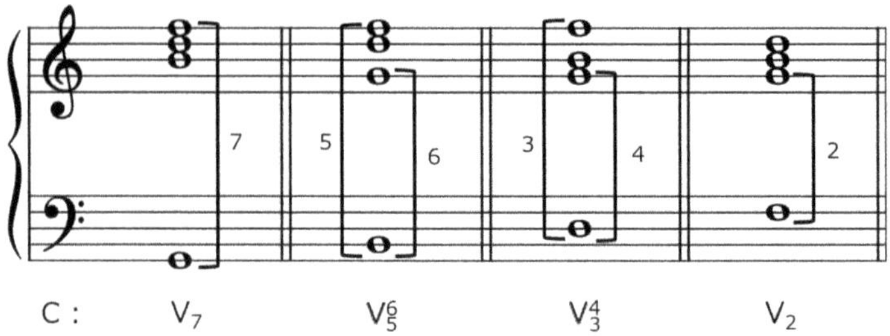

Fig. 7 Basic form and inversions of dominant seventh chords

Fig. 8 Open and close positions

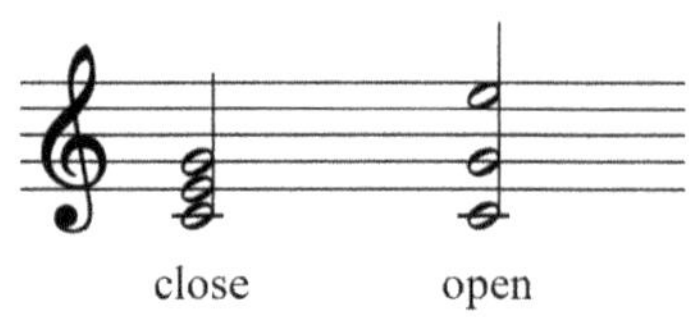

the interval between the lowest note and the highest note is a sixth, both of which are not omitted, so it is written V^6_4.

Dominant seventh chords also have a basic form, first inversion, second inversion, and third inversion (Fig. 7).

For the inversions of the seventh chord, we also have the basic form, 6/5 chord, 4/3 chord and 2 chord. In the same way as the aforementioned notation of triad inversions, omitting the third and the fifth, the intervals from the lowest note in order are expressed written as V_7, V^6_5, V^4_3, V_2 in the figure, respectively.

Given the set of notes to form a chord, a chord is in **close position** if the notes are arranged by raising or lowering some of the chord tones an octave so that the difference between the highest and lowest notes is as small as possible. When the arrangement is not close, the chord is described as being in **open position**. Alternatively, in some cases a chord is in **close position** if the difference between the highest and lowest notes is within one octave; otherwise a chord is in open position (Fig. 8).

Cadence

When listening to a succession of chords, people feel a sense of termination, suspension, progression, tension/relaxation, stability/instability, and so on. In general, a succession of chords is called a chord progression. In particular, the sequence pattern

Fig. 9 Basic chord progressions

of chords is called a **cadence** or **Kadenz** if the sequence pattern induces a sense that the piece is about to be completed, approaching the end of a piece of music. The musical progression produced by a chord sequence and/or the horizontal connections of harmonic tones in the temporal direction is called **harmony**.

In most cases, melodies in tonal music start from the tonic (or else, a harmonic tone of the tonic chord) and end on the tonic (or a harmonic tone of the tonic chord). Similarly, a chord progression governed by a certain scale is said to have tonality and usually starts from the tonic chord of the major or minor key and ends on that tonic chord. As forms of cadence, there are **authentic cadence**, **deceptive cadence**, **plagal cadence** and **half cadence**. In Fig. 9, let us suppose that T means tonic chord, S subdominant chord and D dominant chord; an authentic cadence refers to a chord progression from D to T. A deceptive cadence (or suspended cadence) is the one in which D does not progress to T, instead progressing to a different chord (VI etc.). A plagal cadence, also known as the Amen cadence, is the one from not D but S (or one of its substitute chords (explained hereafter)) to T. A half cadence is the one that does not go to T from D, but remains on D and ends partway through a piece of music. The **leading tone** is the seventh note of a major or minor scale. It is a semitone below the tonic and is the note that leads the tonic. The movement from this leading tone to the tonic is commonly explained as being one of the factors that induce a sense of termination. The chord progression of a typical piece of music takes the structure of beginning in a stable state, becoming tense and reaching an unstable state, then relaxing and returning to a state of stability. This corresponds to a chord progression starting from a tonic chord and returning to a tonic chord. The following three sequences are the basic progressions of this type: T→D→T, T→S→T, T→S→D→T. Note that these do not include the cadence of blues progression, which is T→D→S→T.

When chord progression moves from a chord other than T to T, which induces the sense of a transition from tension to relaxation, instability to stability, this is called **resolution**. A chord that is the dominant of a dominant is called a **double dominant** or **Doppeldominante** in German. Generalizing further, a chord that is configured as the dominant of an arbitrary chord is called a **secondary dominant**. To give these a general term, a chain of chords moving down a perfect fifth (up a perfect fourth) is referred to as a **dominant to tonic motion** or **dominant to tonic resolution**.

Chords that include the same harmonic tones tend to have a similar sound. Utilizing this property of chords, a certain chord may be replaced with another chord that includes the same harmonic tones. Accordingly, the terms dominant and tonic do not refer to specific chords of a scale, but rather the role those chords play in a cadence, that is to say, their functions. This kind of thinking is called **functional harmony**.

A chord that has replaced an original chord, according to the concept of functional harmony, is called the **substitution chord** of an original chord. For example, the first chord is composed of the harmonic tones $\hat{1}$, $\hat{3}$, $\hat{5}$, and the sixth chord is composed of the harmonic tones $\hat{6}$, $\hat{1}$, $\hat{3}$. Since chord I and chord VI have $\hat{1}$ and $\hat{3}$ in common, it seems that they can be used as substitution chords for each other. In reality, however, chord VI can be used as a substitution for chord I, but not vice versa. This is because the function of chord I is more important than that of chord VI. For the same reason, the second and sixth chords can be used as substitutes for the fourth chord, and the third and seventh chords can be used as substitutes for the fifth chord. If a substitution chord is used to replace some chords that appear in a cadence, the sense of termination may be diminished.

Non-chord Tones

The tones that, while sounding at the same time as a chord, are not included in its chord tones are called non-chord tones, non-harmonic tones, or embellishing tones, among other names. An **appoggiatura** is one type of non-chord tone and is introduced unreservedly on a strong beat, as a neighbor tone directly preceding a harmonic tone (Fig. 10). It is a tone that temporarily creates a state of dissonance. The figure shows a typical and famous example of an appoggiatura (marked as '$*$'), occurring at the very beginning of one of The Beatles songs: 'Yesterday'. A **suspension**, another type of non-chord tone, is a note of the preceding chord that is temporarily suspended to create a state of dissonance possibly at a strong beat through the delayed progression to the note that should originally have been progressed to. Such suspension eventually brings about resolution. In Fig. 10, the top note B, actually a leading note, is suspended until the second beat of the second bar, going beyond the first beat which is a strong beat, and is finally resolved to C, the tonic note.

6 Beat and Rhythm

Among the attributes held by an individual pitch event, there is **duration** as well as pitch. This means the different time lengths of a musical note, which correspond to one bar divided into halves, quarters, eighths, and so on. A **beat** is an event or a series of pulses that occurs successively at fixed time intervals. **Tactus** is a flexible time measurement that occurs approximately 60–70 times a minute[15]; the frequency of 60–70 times a minute corresponds to the pace of repeating the movement sequence

[15] The unit 'n times per minute' is notated as M.M. (Malzel's Metronome) or BPM (beats per minute).

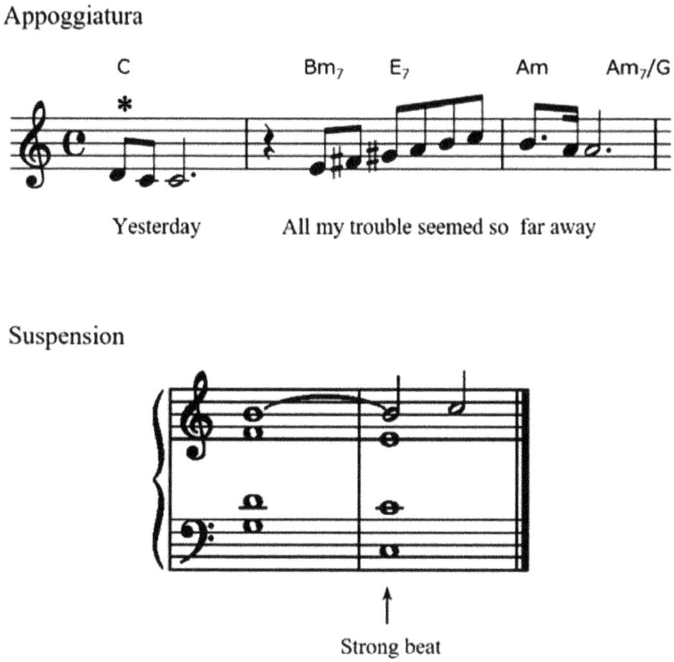

Fig. 10 Appoggiatura and suspension

of lowering and raising the hands (downbeat, upbeat) when conducting musicians, or of human breathing. In the fifteenth to sixteenth century, the word tactus was used to mean almost exactly the same as beat.

There are accented beats and unaccented beats. An accented beat is called a **strong beat**, while an unaccented beat is called a **weak beat**. **Meter**, or **time**, is the periodic pattern of a number of successive beats including strong beats and weak beats. In western tonal music, the section from a strong beat to another strong beat is designated as one **bar** (one **measure**). For example, if a quarter note is taken as one beat and a periodic pattern of the duration of three beats is recognized, it is called three-four time or triple time. Time is indicated by the **time signature** written on a stave. Rhythm means a repeated pattern that is characterized by its combination of strong and weak beats. **Downbeat** means the strong beat at the beginning of a bar, while **upbeat** means a beat that precedes a downbeat and causes a listener to anticipate that the downbeat will follow (Fig. 11). In most cases, the upbeat refers to the last beat of the preceding bar. The first beat and third beat of four-four time are called **on-beats**, while the second beat and fourth beat are called **off-beats**.

Crusis is a phrase that starts on a downbeat and completes at the end of a bar. **Anacrusis** (or, auftakt) is a phrase that begins and ends midway through a bar. **Syncopation** is the accentuation of a beat that would not typically be accented, or vice versa. It can also refer to the temporary alteration of a regular rhythmic

Fig. 11 Upbeat and downbeat

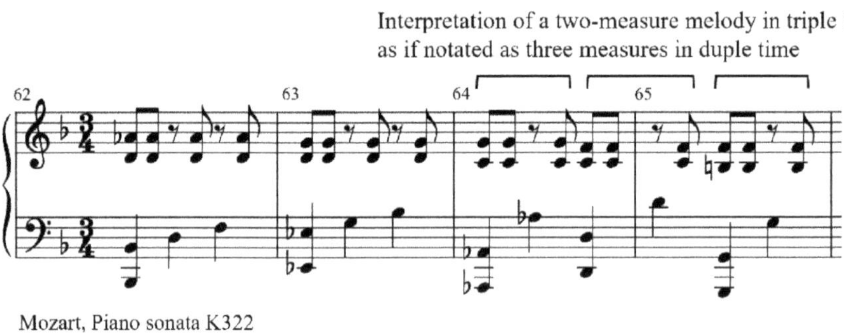

Fig. 12 Hemiola

pattern. **Hemiola** is the dividing, in a piece of music in triple time, of the six beats from two bars into three parts. In other words, the interpretation of a two-measure melody in triple time as though it were notated as three measures in duple time. The term originally means one and a half (= 3/2) (Fig. 12). **Backbeat** is a kind of syncopation that accentuates all of the second and fourth off-beats in four-four time. In this chain of beats and measures, as notations for adding expressions by further making only specified notes strong or weak, there are **forte** (*f*)/**fortissimo** (*ff*), **piano** (*p*)/**pianissimo** (*pp*), and so on.

Index

K. Hirata et al., *Music, Mathematics and Language*,
https://doi.org/10.1007/978-981-19-5166-4

N

O

Milton Keynes UK
Ingram Content Group UK Ltd.
UKHW020629081123
432193UK00010B/469

9 789811 951671